Bloom's Shakespeare Through the Ages

Bloom's Shakespeare Through the Ages

RICHARD III

Edited and with an introduction by
Harold Bloom
Sterling Professor of the Humanities
Yale University

Volume Editor
Janyce Marson

BLOOM'S
LITERARY CRITICISM
An imprint of Infobase Publishing

Bloom's Shakespeare Through the Ages: Richard III

Copyright © 2010 by Infobase Publishing
Introduction © 2010 by Harold Bloom

Bloom's Literary Criticism
An imprint of Infobase Publishing
132 West 31st Street
New York NY 10001

Library of Congress Cataloging-in-Publication Data
Richard III / edited and with an introduction by Harold Bloom ; volume editor, Janyce Marson.
     p. cm. — (Bloom's Shakespeare through the ages)
Includes bibliographical references and index.
ISBN 978-1-60413-719-4
1. Shakespeare, William, 1564–1616. King Richard III. I. Bloom, Harold.
II. Marson, Janyce.
PR2821.R53 2010
822.3'3—dc22
                         2009052218

You can find Bloom's Literary Criticism on the World Wide Web at
http://www.chelseahouse.com

Text design by Erika A. Arroyo
Cover design by Ben Peterson
Composition by IBT Global, Inc., Troy NY
Cover printed by IBT Global, Inc., Troy NY
Book printed and bound by IBT Global, Inc., Troy NY
Date printed: March 2010
Printed in the United States of America

10 9 8 7 6 5 4 3 2 1

This book is printed on acid-free paper.

CONTENTS

❧

SERIES INTRODUCTION

Shakespeare Through the Ages presents not the most current of Shakespeare criticism, but the best of Shakespeare criticism, from the seventeenth century to today. In the process, each volume also charts the flow over time of critical discussion of a particular play. Other useful and fascinating collections of historical Shakespearean criticism exist, but no collection that we know of contains such a range of commentary on each of Shakespeare's greatest plays and at the same time emphasizes the greatest critics in our literary tradition: from John Dryden in the seventeenth century, to Samuel Johnson in the eighteenth century, to William Hazlitt and Samuel Coleridge in the nineteenth century, to A. C. Bradley and William Empson in the twentieth century, to the most perceptive critics of our own day. This canon of Shakespearean criticism emphasizes aesthetic rather than political or social analysis.

Some of the pieces included here are full-length essays; others are excerpts designed to present a key point. Much (but not all) of the earliest criticism consists only of brief mentions of specific plays. In addition to the classics of criticism, some pieces of mainly historical importance have been included, often to provide background for important reactions from future critics.

These volumes are intended for students, particularly those just beginning their explorations of Shakespeare. We have therefore also included basic materials designed to provide a solid grounding in each play: a biography of Shakespeare, a synopsis of the play, a list of characters, and an explication of key passages. In addition, each selection of the criticism of a particular century begins with an introductory essay discussing the general nature of that century's commentary and the particular issues and controversies addressed by critics presented in the volume.

Shakespeare was "not of an age, but for all time," but much Shakespeare criticism is decidedly for its own age, of lasting importance only to the scholar who wrote it. Students today read the criticism most readily available to them, which means essays printed in recent books and journals, especially those journals made available on the Internet. Older criticism is too often buried in out-of-print books on forgotten shelves of libraries or in defunct periodicals. Therefore, many students, particularly younger students, have no way of knowing that some of the most profound criticism of Shakespeare's plays was written decades or centuries ago. We hope this series remedies that problem, and more importantly, we hope it infuses students with the enthusiasm of the critics in these volumes for the beauty and power of Shakespeare's plays.

INTRODUCTION BY
HAROLD BLOOM

Why, I, in this weak piping time of peace,
Have no delight to pass away the time,
Unless to spy my shadow in the sun,
And descant on my own deformity.
And therefore since I cannot prove a lover
To entertain this fair well-spoken days,
I am determine'd to prove a villain,
And hate the idle pleasure of these days.

    (1.1.24–31)

The opening ferocity of Richard, still duke of Gloucester, in *The Tragedy of Richard the Third* is hardly more than a fresh starting point for the development of the Elizabethan and Jacobean hero-villain after Marlowe, and yet it seems to transform Tamburlaine and Barabas utterly. Richard's peculiarly self-conscious pleasure in his own audacity is crossed by the sense of what it means to see one's own deformed shadow in the sun. We are closer already not only to Edmund and Iago than to Barabas but especially closer to Webster's Lodovico who so sublimely says: "I limn'd this nightpiece and it was my best." Except for Iago, nothing seems further advanced in this desperate mode than Webster's Bosola:

    O direful misprision!
I will not imitate things glorious
No more than base; I'll be mine own example.—
On, on, and look thou represent, for silence,
The thing thou bear'st.

    (5.4.87–91)

Iago is beyond even this denial of representation, because he does will silence:

Demand me nothing; what you know, you know:
From this time forth I never will speak word.

  (5.2.303–04)

Iago is no hero-villain, and no shift in perspective will make him into one. Pragmatically, the authentic hero-villain in Shakespeare might be judged to be Hamlet, but no audience would agree. Macbeth could justify the description, except that the cosmos of his drama is too estranged from any normative representation for the term hero-villain to have its oxymoronic coherence. Richard and Edmund would appear to be the models, beyond Marlowe, that could have inspired Webster and his fellows, but Edmund is too uncanny and superb a representation to provoke emulation. That returns us to Richard:

Was ever woman in this humor woo'd?
Was ever woman in this humor won?
I'll have her, but I will not keep her long.
What? I, that kill'd her husband and his father,
To take her in her heart's extremest hate,
With curses in her mouth, tears in her eyes,
The bleeding witness of my hatred by,
Having God, her conscience, and these bars against me,
And I no friends to back my suit at all
But the plain devil and dissembling looks?
And yet to win her! All the world to nothing!
Hah!
Hath she forgot already that brave prince,
Edward, her lord, whom I, some three months since,
Stabb'd in my angry mood at Tewksbury?
A sweeter and a lovelier gentleman,
Fram'd in the prodigality of nature—
Young, valiant, wise, and (no doubt) right royal—
The spacious world cannot again afford.
And will she yet abase her eyes on me,
That cropp'd the golden prime of this sweet prince
And made her widow to a woeful bed?
On me, whose all not equals Edward's moi'ty?
On me, that halts and am misshapen thus?
My dukedom to a beggarly denier,
I do mistake my person all this while!
Upon my life, she finds (although I cannot)
Myself to be a marv'llous proper man.
I'll be at charges for a looking-glass,

And entertain a score or two of tailors
To study fashions to adorn my body:
Since I am crept in favor with myself,
I will maintain it with some little cost.
But first I'll turn yon fellow in his grave,
And then return lamenting to my love.
Shine out, fair sun, till I have bought a glass,
That I may see my shadow as I pass.

   (1.2.227–63)

Richard's only earlier delight was "to see my shadow in the sun / And descant on mine own deformity." His savage delight in the success of his own manipulative rhetoric now transforms his earlier trope into the exultant command: "Shine out, fair sun, till I have bought a glass, / That I may see my shadow as I pass." That transformation is the formula for interpreting the Jacobean hero-villain and his varied progeny: Milton's Satan, the Poet in Shelley's *Alastor*, Wordsworth's Oswald in *The Borderers*, Byron's Manfred and Cain, Browning's Childe Roland, Tennyson's Ulysses, Melville's Captain Ahab, Hawthorne's Chillingworth, down to Nathanael West's Shrike in *Miss Lonelyhearts*, who perhaps ends the tradition. The manipulative, highly self-conscious, obsessed hero-villain, whether Machiavellian plotter or later, idealistic quester, ruined or not, moves himself from being the passive sufferer of his own moral and/or physical deformity to becoming a highly active melodramatist. Instead of standing in the light of nature to observe his own shadow, and then have to take his own deformity as subject, he rather commands nature to throw its light upon his own glass of representation, so that his own shadow will be visible only for an instant as he passes on to the triumph of his will over others.

BIOGRAPHY OF
WILLIAM SHAKESPEARE
❧

William Shakespeare was born in Stratford-on-Avon in April 1564 into a family of some prominence. His father, John Shakespeare, was a glover and merchant of leather goods, who earned enough to marry the daughter of his father's landlord, Mary Arden, in 1557. John Shakespeare was a prominent citizen in Stratford, and at one point, he served as an alderman and bailiff.

Shakespeare presumably attended the Stratford grammar school, where he would have received an education in Latin, but he did not go on to either Oxford or Cambridge universities. Little is recorded about Shakespeare's early life; indeed, the first record of his life after his christening is of his marriage to Anne Hathaway in 1582 in the church at Temple Grafton, near Stratford. He would have been required to obtain a special license from the bishop as security that there was no impediment to the marriage. Peter Alexander states in his book *Shakespeare's Life and Art* that marriage at this time in England required neither a church nor a priest or, for that matter, even a document— only a declaration of the contracting parties in the presence of witnesses. Thus, it was customary, though not mandatory, to follow the marriage with a church ceremony.

Little is known about William and Anne Shakespeare's marriage. Their first child, Susanna, was born in May 1583, and twins, Hamnet and Judith Shakespeare, in 1585. Later on, Susanna married Dr. John Hall, but the younger daughter, Judith, remained unmarried. When Hamnet died in Stratford in 1596, the boy was only eleven years old.

We have no record of Shakespeare's activities for the seven years after the birth of his twins, but by 1592 he was in London working as an actor. He was also apparently well known as a playwright, for reference is made of him by his contemporary, Robert Greene, in *A Groatsworth of Wit*, as "an upstart crow."

Several companies of actors were in London at this time. Shakespeare may have had connection with one or more of them before 1592, but we have no record that tells us definitely. However, we do know of his long association with the most famous and successful troupe, the Lord Chamberlain's Men. (When James I came to the throne in 1603, after Elizabeth's death, the troupe's name changed to the King's Men.) In 1599, the Lord Chamberlain's Men provided the financial backing for the construction of their own theater, the Globe.

The Globe was begun by a carpenter named James Burbage and finished by his two sons, Cuthbert and Robert. To escape the jurisdiction of the Corporation of London, which was composed of conservative Puritans who opposed the theater's "licentiousness," James Burbage built the Globe just outside London, in the Liberty of Holywell, beside Finsbury Fields. This also meant that the Globe was safer from the threats that lurked in London's crowded streets, like plague and other diseases, as well as rioting mobs. When James Burbage died in 1597, his sons completed the Globe's construction. Shakespeare played a vital role, financially and otherwise, in the construction of the theater, which was finally occupied some time before May 16, 1599.

Shakespeare not only acted with the Globe's company of actors, he was also a shareholder and eventually became the troupe's most important playwright. The company included London's most famous actors, who inspired the creation of some of Shakespeare's best-known characters, such as Hamlet and Lear, as well as his clowns and fools.

In his early years, however, Shakespeare did not confine himself to the theater. He also composed some mythological-erotic poetry, such as *Venus and Adonis* and *The Rape of Lucrece*, both of which were dedicated to the earl of Southampton. Shakespeare was successful enough that in 1597 he was able to purchase his own home in Stratford, which he called New Place. He could even call himself a gentleman, for his father had been granted a coat of arms.

By 1598, Shakespeare had written some of his most famous works, *Romeo and Juliet*, *The Comedy of Errors*, *A Midsummer Night's Dream*, *The Merchant of Venice*, *Two Gentleman of Verona*, and *Love's Labour's Lost*, as well as his historical plays *Richard II*, *Richard III*, *Henry IV*, and *King John*. Somewhere around the turn of the century, Shakespeare wrote his romantic comedies, *As You Like It*, *Twelfth Night*, and *Much Ado about Nothing*, as well as *Henry V*, the last of his history plays in the Prince Hal series. During the next ten years he wrote his great tragedies, *Hamlet*, *Macbeth*, *Othello*, *King Lear*, and *Antony and Cleopatra*.

At this time, the theater was burgeoning in London; the public took an avid interest in drama, the audiences were large, the plays demonstrated an enormous range of subjects, and playwrights competed for approval. By 1613, however, the rising tide of Puritanism had changed the theater. With the desertion of the theaters by the middle classes, the acting companies were compelled to depend more on the aristocracy, which also meant that they now had to cater to a more sophisticated audience.

Perhaps this change in London's artistic atmosphere contributed to Shakespeare's reasons for leaving London after 1612. His retirement from the theater is sometimes thought to be evidence that his artistic skills were waning. During this time, however, he wrote *The Tempest* and *Henry VIII*. He also wrote the "tragicomedies," *Pericles, Cymbeline,* and *The Winter's Tale.* These were thought to be inspired by Shakespeare's personal problems and have sometimes been considered proof of his greatly diminished abilities.

However, so far as biographical facts indicate, the circumstances of his life at this time do not imply any personal problems. He was in good health, financially secure, and enjoyed an excellent reputation. Indeed, although he was settled in Stratford at this time, he made frequent visits to London, enjoying and participating in events at the royal court, directing rehearsals, and attending to other business matters.

In addition to his brilliant and enormous contributions to the theater, Shakespeare remained a poetic genius throughout the years, publishing a renowned and critically acclaimed sonnet cycle in 1609 (most of the sonnets were written many years earlier). Shakespeare's contribution to this popular poetic genre are all the more amazing in his break with contemporary notions of subject matter. Shakespeare idealized the beauty of man as an object of praise and devotion (rather than the Petrarchan tradition of the idealized, unattainable woman). In the same spirit of breaking with tradition, Shakespeare also treated themes that hitherto had been considered off limits—the dark, sexual side of a woman as opposed to the Petrarchan ideal of a chaste and remote love object. He also expanded the sonnet's emotional range, including such emotions as delight, pride, shame, disgust, sadness, and fear.

When Shakespeare died in 1616, no collected edition of his works had ever been published, although some of his plays had been printed in separate unauthorized editions. (Some of these were taken from his manuscripts, some from the actors' prompt books, and others were reconstructed from memory by actors or spectators.) In 1623, two members of the King's Men, John Hemings and Henry Condell, published a collection of all the plays they considered to be authentic, the First Folio.

Included in the First Folio is a poem by Shakespeare's contemporary Ben Jonson, an outstanding playwright and critic in his own right. Jonson paid tribute to Shakespeare's genius, proclaiming his superiority to what previously had been held as the models for literary excellence—the Greek and Latin writers. "Triumph, my Britain, thou hast one to show / To whom all scenes of Europe homage owe. / He was not of an age, but for all time!"

Jonson was the first to state what has been said so many times since. Having captured what is permanent and universal to all human beings at all times, Shakespeare's genius continues to inspire us—and the critical debate about his works never ceases.

SUMMARY OF
RICHARD III
❧

Act 1

Act 1, scene 1: When the play opens, Richard is the duke of Gloucester and delivers a soliloquy that reveals his rage against humanity, his displeasure with English society and its peacetime entertainments, and anger toward the circumstances of an unnatural birth that brought him into the world a deformed child destined to be an outcast. This opening monologue sets forth for the audience many of the conflicts and tensions that will be presented in the work as well as his absolute determination to pursue an evil agenda as his only option for establishing a place for himself in the world. Most particularly, those tensions concern his hideous appearance, a stigma that precludes him from any hope of a romantic relationship with a woman. " . . . [s]ince I cannot prove a lover / . . . I am determined to prove a villain / And hate the idle pleasures of these days." The political situation at the beginning of the play, with its strong sexual implications from Richard's perspective, is that after a lengthy civil war, peace has been restored in England. For Richard, however, this is a reality he laments for he thrives on war and violence. Moreover, Richard is jealous of his older brother, King Edward IV, for his political power and attractiveness to women. While everyone else is celebrating, Richard is busy plotting and scheming. His goal is to make others as miserable as he is, and he plots to seize the throne. A power-hungry man with no concern for anyone but himself, Richard vows to assume control of the entire court. His plan is to generate various schemes, "with inductions dangerous, / By drunken prophecies, libels and dreams" that create strife and suspicion among the other noblemen at court. His first victim is none other that his own brother George, the duke of Clarence. Richard concocts a rumor that effectively convinces Edward IV his brother Clarence is a serious threat to him. Richard concocts a scenario in which Clarence is thought to be "closely . . . mewed up / About a prophecy which says that 'G' / Of Edward's heirs the murderer shall be." Edward IV is quite ill, equally as gullible and thus easy prey to Richard's malicious lies. Richard has no trouble planting a rumor that will ultimately have fatal consequences for both his brothers.

5

Clarence enters, under armed guard, being lead to the tower, as he tells Richard, simply and inexplicably because his name is George. The wily Richard knows that his rumor-mongering has worked, but plays the innocent, first protesting that both he and Clarence are in grave danger and, more audaciously, persuading Clarence that the cause of the problem is the group of libelous women surrounding the king, namely Edward's wife and his lover, Mistress Shore. To add credence to this malicious lie, Richard makes reference to Shore's influence at court in securing the release of Lord Hastings from prison. Richard tells Clarence that he will attempt to gain his release, but his promise is couched in ominous terms, even if Clarence does not interpret it so. "Well, your imprisonment shall not be long. / I will deliver you or else lie for you." After Clarence is lead offstage to the tower, Richard happily announces that Clarence will never return.

Lord Hastings, the lord Chamberlain of the court, then enters having been set free. Feigning ignorance of the latest news and concern for Hastings welfare during his imprisonment, Richard asks about Edward IV's current condition. Hastings replies that the king is "sickly, weak and melancholy." Though Richard appears distressed in his response to Hastings, once left alone onstage he gloats over this welcome news, for Edward's death will bring him one step closer to the throne. First, Clarence must be removed and the king must succumb to his illness. "He cannot live, I hope, and must not die / Till George be packed with post-horse up to heaven." Richard, ever looking to the future he is attempting to construct, speaks as though both his brothers are dead and the world now exists to serve his needs, "[a]nd leave the world for me to bustle in." Richard is already planning on marrying Warwick's youngest daughter, the noblewoman named Lady Neville, an alliance that will redress the wrongs done by his family in killing her husband, Edward, and father-in law, Henry VI, of the house of Lancaster. Richard reveals that it will be a totally advantageous arrangement, devoid of love and good faith.

Act 1, scene 2: Lady Anne, the widow of King Henry VI's son, enters anguished as a group of attendants carry the coffin of Henry VI. She immediately begins to curse Richard (who for the first 32 lines is offstage), for his family having killed both Henry VI and Edward. Anne gives vent to her deep-seated anger while revisiting the circumstances of Richard's monstrous birth. Ironically, however, and unbeknownst to her at the moment, this curse will turn out to be prophetic for her own life. "If ever he have child, abortive be it, / Prodigious, and untimely brought to light, / Whose ugly and unnatural aspect / May fright the hopeful mother at the view." Not only does she wish that Richard's child be deformed like him, but that any woman he marries be made to feel as wretched as she is at that moment.

When Richard suddenly enters, Anne's initial response is one of horror as she proceeds to hurl invectives at him. "Foul devil, for God's sake hence, and trouble us not, / For thou hast made the happy earth thy hell, / Filled it with cursing cries and deep exclaims." Notwithstanding Anne's moral outrage, and true to Richard's remorseless character, he begins to manipulate events in order to advance his own agenda. He orders the pallbearers to stop the procession so that he can speak with her. Though he approaches Anne in a gentle manner, her initial response is full of rage as she points to the bloody wounds on the corpse of the dead Henry VI, stating that they have begun to bleed in the presence of the murderer. "Blush, blush, thou lump of foul deformity, / For 'tis thy presence that exhales this blood." Completely ignoring her fury, Richard proceeds to flirt with Anne, praising her gentleness and beauty though at first she remains steadfast in her outrage. Richard's ironic response is that Anne should forgive him as an act of Christian charity, "[w]hich renders good for bad, blessings for curses." Though Richard has still not vindicated himself as a murderer in Anne's eyes, he then makes a most audacious attempt to justify his actions in explaining that "'twas thy heavenly face that set me on." Anne gradually allows herself to be persuaded by both Richard's eloquent and chivalrous, though wholly insincere, gesture as he kneels before her, handing her his sword and asks that she kill him if she will not forgive him, for he cannot live without her. Anne cannot bring herself to stab him as Richard continues with his protestations of love, which he claims are genuine and well intentioned. Richard then slips his ring onto Anne's finger, begging her to accept his marriage proposal. Incredibly, he succeeds in convincing her that he is truly contrite and worthy to become her husband. "With all my heart, and much it joys me, too, / To see you are become so penitent." Anne agrees to marry him.

As soon as Richard is left alone onstage, however, he joyfully celebrates his duplicitous conquest of Anne and reveals his true intentions toward his yet-to-be queen. "I'll have her, but I will not keep her long, / What, I that killed her husband and his father, / To take her in her heart's extremest hate / . . . And I no friends to back my suit withal." Richard reveals the depth of his depravity as the scene ends with his plans to adorn his body with the finest fashions and admire his reflection in a mirror.

Act 1, scene 3: A fearful Queen Elizabeth, wife of the ailing King Edward IV, enters with her brother, Lord Rivers, and her two sons from a prior marriage, Lord Grey and the Marquis of Dorset. They try to lighten her spirits and offer encouragement about the king's recovery. Elizabeth, nonetheless, remains anxious as Edward seems unlikely to survive, putting the fate of her family in Gloucester's hands, for she knows that he may become the realm's protector and most certainly bears no love for her. To complicate matters, though the king and queen have two sons, the princes are still too young to rule. Thus, if Edward IV dies, the throne will go to Richard until the oldest son comes of age.

The duke of Buckingham, and Stanley, the earl of Derby, then enter bearing news that King Edward is feeling better and "speaks cheerfully." They also report that he desires to make peace at court between Richard and Elizabeth's kinsmen, divided by a longstanding hostility. For her part, Elizabeth thinks it utterly impossible. "Would all were well, but that will never be."

Richard suddenly enters with Lord Hastings, vehemently decrying those that would have the king believe that Richard loves him not. "By holy Paul, they love his grace but lightly / That fill his ears with such dissentious rumours." Richard responds to their "false reports" by proclaiming that, because he is so honest and forthright in his speaking, the people at court slander him by spreading lies that he is hostile to Elizabeth and her family. "Cannot a plain man live and think no harm, / But thus his simple truth must be abused." To counteract this "false" report, Richard decides to accuse Elizabeth and her kinsmen of hastening Edward's demise. "A plague upon you all / . . . But you must trouble him with lewd complaints," he states, to which Elizabeth responds by explaining that Edward simply wants to make peace among all of them. Not to be outdone, Richard counterattacks, blaming her for Clarence's arrest and imprisonment, repeating a lie he had previously told Clarence. "Our brother is imprisoned by your means, / My self disgraced, and the nobility / Held in contempt."

As hostilities between Elizabeth and Richard escalate, Old Queen Margaret, Richard's avenging spirit, enters unobserved. As she listens to Richard, Margaret bitterly reflects on her own history, blaming Richard for his part in the death of her husband, Henry VI, and the king's son, Prince Edward. When Margaret finally makes her presence known, Richard calls her a "foul wrinkled witch." Addressing Richard, she admits that though her previous banishment was painful, her current state of affairs is far worse. She accuses both Richard and Elizabeth of having caused her downfall and tells them that they do not know what sorrow is. "But I do find more pain in banishment / Than death can yield me here by my abode. / A husband and a son thou ow'st to me / And thou a kingdom—all of you allegiance." She adds that Elizabeth wrongfully occupies the position of queen, as the throne, and all the honors that come with it, properly belongs to her. "Poor painted queen, vain flourish of my fortune." Margaret's use of the word *flourish* is important in that it serves as an organic metaphor indicating her belief that she remained the lawful queen despite her husband's death, that she is the natural and rightful extension of her husband and is therefore due royal status, despite her exile in *3 Henry VI*. She tells Elizabeth the day will come when she will wish the old queen was there to help her with this "poisonous bunch-backed toad." Her worst curse is, of course, reserved for Richard: "Stay, dog, for thou shalt hear me . . . / On thee, the troubler of the poor world's peace. / The worm of conscience still begnaw thy soul." Other members of the royal retinue are present—Rivers, Dorset, and Buckingham—and are equally surprised at Margaret's appearance. They, too, join in the heated exchange, hurling abuses at her, Hastings calling her "a false boding woman" and Dorset declaring her a "lunatic." Margaret is aware of what they have been up to all along, "snarling all before I came," and in her fury responds to all in turn for the terrible loss she has endured and her status as a pariah to which she believes she has been unjustly consigned. Her response to Dorset and Hastings is that they are shameless and impudent, while she sternly warns Buckingham to beware the man he serves. "Look when he fawns, he bites; and when he bites, / His venom tooth will rankle to the death."

Once Margaret has left the stage, Richard professes false remorse for the besieged old woman, "I repent / My part thereof that I have done to her," while Elizabeth proclaims she bears no responsibility in bringing about Margaret's present state. Catesby then enters to summon everyone to Edward IV's chamber and, while the others leave, Richard remains behind to reveal his schemes, confessing that he is deceiving everybody into thinking that he has only the most benign intentions with respect to Clarence's cruel treatment. "I lay unto the grievous charge of others. Clarence, who I have cast in darkness, / I do beweep to many simple gulls, / . . . And seem a saint when most I play the devil." Richard also reveals that once he is done with Clarence, the others—Rivers, Dorset, and Grey—will suffer a similar fate. Appropriately, the soliloquy ends with the entrance of the two murderers he has commissioned to kill his Clarence. Richard compliments them on their anticipated ability and duplicity in carrying out his plan and clearly identifies with them. "Your eyes drop millstones when fools' eyes fall tears. / I like you lads."

Act 1, scene 4 opens with Clarence, incarcerated in the Tower of London, speaking with the Keeper, who asks why Clarence looks so aggrieved. He begins to describe a strange dream about escaping his imprisonment in a voyage fraught with peril, accompanied by Richard, the two of them young men sailing across the channel to France. In the dream, Richard induces Clarence to walk along the deck with him, while thinking about all the tribulations suffered by the houses of York and Lancaster during the War of the Roses, when a terrible accident occurs on deck. According to Clarence's dream, Richard stumbles on some loose boards and knocks Clarence overboard in the process. Clarence then recounts the horrifying experience of a man drowning in slow motion, unable to draw his terrible fate to conclusion. "O Lord, methought what pain it was to drown / What dreadful noise of water in mine ears, / What sights of ugly death within mine eyes." Instead, Clarence is treated to the fearsome sight of sunken treasure and skeletal remains. The dream proves so fantastical that the Keeper even questions him: "Had you such leisure in the time of death / To gaze upon these secrets of the deep?" Clarence's response is that he simply could not die and, ironically, could not awaken from this nightmare. Instead, Clarence is made to endure his judgment day when he is forced to confront the souls of those he has wronged. The first is his father-in-law, Warwick, who accuses him of perjury, followed by a shadowy figure, "with bright hair / Dabbled in blood" who again reminds him of his treachery, "false, fleeting, perjured Clarence, / That stabbed me in the field by Tewkesbury." Having experienced visions of Hell, Clarence confesses to the Keeper that he is guilty as charged for committing perjury in the recent overthrow of Henry VI's monarchy. In particular, Clarence has dreamed that he saw the ghost of Edward—the prince of Wales and the son of Queen Margaret and Henry VI (and in *Richard III*, Anne's now deceased husband)—whom Clarence had helped to kill. In the dream, Prince Edward cries out, cursing Clarence, while the Furies seize Clarence and drag him down to Hell. Clarence then reports that he awoke from the dream, trembling and terrified. He ends his conversation with the Keeper by pleading for mercy for his family, all who are innocent of his crimes. Brackenbury, the lieutenant of the tower, then enters and also hears of Clarence's strange dream.

In the brief scene in which Brakenbury and Clarence are alone together, the former commiserates with a deeply agitated Clarence, observing that the powerful and mighty, though seemingly cloaked in glory, nevertheless pay a heavy price for their status. "They often feel a world of restless cares; / So that between their titles and low name / There's nothing differs but the outward fame." Brakenbury's philosophizing abruptly ends when Richard's hired assassins arrive unannounced. They burst in, demanding to speak with Clarence, who has fallen asleep in Brakenbury's reassuring presence. Though Brakenbury tries to intercede on Clarence's behalf, they hand him a warrant, and Brakenbury promptly leaves Clarence, unwittingly, in the care of his murderers. "I'll to the king and signify to him / That thus I have resigned to you my charge."

Left alone with the sleeping Clarence, a debate ensues in which the two murderers deliberate how best to accomplish their foul deed. During their grisly discussion on the most expedient method of carrying out the execution, they nonetheless exhibit some evidence of misgiving, most especially the Second Murderer who states that "[t]he urging of that word judgment hath bred a / kind of remorse in me" for he will be condemned by divine justice no matter that he had a supposed legal writ to kill Clarence. The First Murderer responds to these pangs of self-doubt by accusing the other of being a coward. Nevertheless, the promise of payment is the decisive factor in enabling them to fulfill their mission as the First Murder predicts that "[w]hen he opens his purse to give us our reward, thy / conscience flies out." For a brief ironic moment, the Second Murderer has to persuade the First. In they end, however, they resolve to stab Clarence with their swords and then drown him in a vat of malmsey, a kind of wine, in an adjoining room. Unexpectedly, though, Clarence awakens and pleads with them for his life and, once again, there is a brief moment of deliberation in which the murderers seem to waver in their determination, admitting that Clarence has done them no personal harm. Clarence argues eloquently, forcing them to consider their humanity: "Are you drawn forth among a world of men / To slay the innocent?" He even questions the legitimacy of their mission. Richard has conjured the entire plot, though Clarence has been duped into thinking Richard is his supporter and advocate. When Clarence finally states that he will direct Richard to reward them for sparing his life, he is confronted with the undeniable truth that Richard has betrayed him. Clarence, however, refuses to believe this. "Oh no, he loves me, and he holds me dear." Though the Second Murderer hesitates for a moment, the First Murderer stabs Clarence and places him in the vat of wine and then deposits the body in a hole to await Richard's burial instructions. The murderers then flee.

Act 2

Act 2, scene 1: Scene 1 begins with a flourish of trumpets as the royal family and advisors, Elizabeth, Doreset, Rivers, Hastings, Catesby and Buckingham, enter King Edward IV's room. With the group gathered before him, Edward congratulates himself for a mission accomplished. Recognizing that he will soon die, the king wants to set things right and restore peace to his kingdom. He says that there has been too much dissension at court and insists that they all make peace with one another or face the consequences of their final judgment day. "Take heed you dally not before your king, / Lest he that is the supreme King of kings / Confound your hidden falsehood and award." Everyone cooperates by apologizing and swearing love and loyalty toward one another and immediately thereafter Richard and Ratcliffe appear on the scene. Edward even expresses his determination to make peace with Richard and offers seemingly sincere, heartfelt protestations of love to his sovereign lord and his family. "I do not know that Englishman alive / With whom my soul is any jot at odds / More than the infant that is born tonight. / I thank my God for my humility." However, unbeknownst to Edward IV, who tells all assembled that he has forgiven Clarence and sent a letter to the Tower of London ordering his release, Richard delivers the disastrous news that Clarence has been executed, assigning blame to Edward who originally condemned Clarence to death. Richard further states that the king's pardon has unfortunately come too late. "Some tardy cripple bare the countermand, / That came too lag to see him buried." With this devastating news and believing himself the author of Clarence's execution, Edward IV is filled with remorse. When Derby enters seeking pardon for his "riotous servant's life," Edward has no choice but to grant his request in light of Clarence's tragic execution. Edward delivers a lengthy discourse in which he grieves for his deceased brother and takes responsibility for his execution, while reminding the others that they, too, are culpable for none of them pleaded on Clarence's behalf. "Sinfully plucked, and not a man of you / Had so much grace to put it in my mind." The ailing king has now grown more feeble, suffering from inconsolable grief and remorse as he is helped to his bed.

Act 2, scene 2 opens in another room in the palace where the duchess of York—the mother of Richard, Clarence, and King Edward—is attempting to console her two grandchildren, Clarence's young son and daughter. At first, in response to their question whether their father is really dead, the duchess tries to deny it and thus spare them the painful truth, stating that it is sickly King Edward for whom she cries. The boy nonetheless knows the truth. "Then you conclude, my grandam, he is dead. / The king mine uncle is to blame for it." The duchess has no choice but to tell them he is dead and that their uncle Richard is responsible, for she knows how evil her son really is and regrets that she ever gave birth to him. Nevertheless, the children still believe what Richard told them, namely that Queen Elizabeth was behind the murder. "[F]or my good uncle Gloucester / Told me the king, provoked to it by the queen, / Devised impeachments to imprison him." The Duchess can only repeat the sentiment that she rues the day she brought Richard into this world. "He is my son, ay, and therein my shame."

Suddenly, Elizabeth enters, wailing inconsolably, her hair disheveled, to deliver the news that King Edward has died. In her grief, she cannot comprehend how life can go on without its foundation.

> Why grow the branches when the root is gone? / Why wither not the leaves that want their sap?" The duchess and children join her in mourning. The Duchess seems the most pained and grieved, not only has she lost a husband, she has unwittingly, through an accident of nature, unleashed a monster on the world who bears responsibility in the death of her other two sons. "I have bewept a worthy's husband's death / . . . But now two mirrors are of his princely semblance / Are cracked in pieces by malignant death, / And I for comfort have but one false glass.

Rivers and Dorset, who are also present, remind Elizabeth that she must now look after and care for her eldest son, the young Prince Edward, named after his father, for he is heir to the throne and must fulfill his royal obligation. Rivers advises her that the prince must go to London to be crowned and that she must find consolation in this responsibility for, through this royal inheritance, Edward's immortality is assured. "And plant you joys in living Edward's throne." Suddenly, Richard enters, along with Buckingham, Hastings, Derby, and Ratcliffe. He gives voice to false feelings of encouragement in the face of so great a loss. "All of us have cause / To wail the dimming of our shining star, / But none can help our harms by wailing them." Richard and Buckingham then urge that the young prince be brought to London, also advising that only a few people should be in attendance and that they will be the designated guardians. Buckingham declares it best in the interest of the prince's safety, lest "[t]he new-healed wound of malice should break out." The others depart to discuss who will fetch the prince, with Richard and Buckingham staying behind. Buckingham suggests they go together to fetch the prince and that they will find another way to separate the prince from Elizabeth and her family. Richard gleefully accepts and addresses Buckingham as his friend and advisor. "My other self, my counsel's consistory, / My oracle, my prophet, my dear cousin."

Act 2, scene 3: This scene opens with three ordinary London citizens, none of whom is named, conferring on the sad state of political affairs in the kingdom, as they have just heard news of King Edward IV's death. The Second Citizen expresses fear and anxiety, seeing the king's death as an omen of troubled times to come. The Third Citizen concurs, stating that it forebodes a world of calamity. The First Citizen naively reads the situation as optimistic, pinning his great hope on Edward's young son who will assume the throne. The other two citizens, most specially the third, are nonetheless apprehensive given that young Prince Edward, who is still too young to rule, is surrounded by internal strife and jealousy. They point out that the two sides of his family at set against each other, while the prospect of Richard is the most fearful scenario of all, as the Third Citizen, the most pessimistic of the group, states: "Oh, full of danger is the Duke of Gloucester, / And the queen's sons and brothers haughty and proud." They believe it would be far better if the prince had no uncle than one such as Gloucester. In a telling contradiction of Richard's opening soliloquy, where he lamented the passing of a warrior culture transformed into a peace-time world, the Third Citizen remarks that winter is at hand as the hope for peace is dying with the setting sun. "When great leaves fall, then winter is at hand; / When the sun sets, who doth not look for night?"

Act 2, scene 4: The scene switches back to the palace, where the archbishop of York, an ally of Elizabeth's family, informs Elizabeth, the duchess of York, and Elizabeth's youngest son (the duke of York) that young Prince Edward is well on his way to London and is expected to arrive there within a day or two. The three family members present are looking forward to his arrival when a most interesting subject is raised, namely the benefits and drawbacks of growing up too quickly, which echoes the subject matter of a previous conversation between the young Duke of York and his treacherous uncle Richard. The young boy then relates a discussion in which his uncle advised that a child growing too quickly is highly undesirable and an ill omen. "'Small herbs have grace; great grace; great weeds do grow apace.'" As a result of these words, the young boy desires to grow slowly, like "a sweet flower." The irony suggested here is in the chronicles and reports that contend Richard has grown up the quickest of all, born with teeth so that "he could gnaw a crust at two hours old." His grand-mother, however, does not give this any credence, stating that the person who reported that detail was an imposter, not Richard's nurse who was dead before he was born. This comment may indicate that Shakespeare likewise did not attach any credence to this legendary account.

The scene then shifts when the Marquess of Dorset arrives with the news that Elizabeth's kinsmen, Rivers and Gray, have been arrested along with their ally, Sir Thomas Vaughan. They have been sent to Pontefract Castle in Yorkshire, a place notorious, like the Tower of London, for executing its prisoners. The order to arrest the men came from Richard and his equally despised ally, Buckingham. Elizabeth and the duchess immediately realize that this news bodes ill for their family, as Richard intends to harm the young prince who is about to assume the kingship. "The tiger now hath seized the gentle hind; / Insulting tyranny begins to jut / Upon the innocent and aweless throne." The duchess likewise echoes these fears as she rues the fate of her sons who "[m]ake war upon themselves, brother to brother." Apprehending Richard's evil intentions, Elizabeth takes her youngest son and flees to the sanctuary of Westminster Abbey where she hopes to find protection from Richard's designs. The cardinal, for his part, gives Elizabeth the Great Seal of England, to which she legally has no right since she is not the monarch.

Act 3

Act 3, scene 1: With a flourish of trumpets, the young Prince Edward, the heir to the throne, arrives in London with his retinue, where Richard, Buckingham, and Catesby are there to greet him. Richard greets the prince, proclaiming his young nephew to be "my thoughts' sovereign." This is a clever manipulation of words on Richard's part because, indeed, his thoughts are really about installing himself as sovereign and ridding the kingdom of young Prince Edward. Prince Edward, though, sees through Richard's deceptive wit, for he is suspicious of his uncle and proves himself a worthy opponent in countering Richard's flattering language with rhetoric as dexterous as his uncle's. When the prince responds that he wishes more of his uncles were in attendance, meaning the uncles on his mother's side, Richard quickly denounces them as dangerous to the prince's well-being and accuses them of using the sweetness of their words to conceal their evil ways. "Your grace attended to their sugared words / But looked not on the poison of their hearts." Prince Edward recognizes Richard's deception for what it is and implies that he knows Richard to be the real culprit and betrayer. "God keep me from false friends, but they were none."

Lord Hastings then enters, announcing that Elizabeth and her younger son, the duke of York, have taken sanctuary. Buckingham's response is derisive, referring to Hasting as "the sweating lord." Disconcerted by the news that Elizabeth has sought sanctuary, Buckingham appeals to the Lord Cardinal (Bourchier), who is also onstage, to either persuade Elizabeth to give up the young duke of York or, if she refuses, to take him by force. As assurance that the mission will be accomplished, Buckingham orders Hastings to accompany the cardinal. He at first refuses on the grounds that he cannot violate the sacred privilege of sanctuary that God has granted Elizabeth, but the cardinal proves to be weak willed and acquiesces to Buckingham's argument that a young child, who does not have the legal right to claim sanctuary, cannot be protected by this benefit. "This prince hath neither claimed it nor deserved it, / And therefore, in mine opinion, cannot have it. . . . You break no privilege nor charter there." So the cardinal and Lord Hastings set out to fetch young York, while Prince Edward is left alone with Richard and Buckingham. While Edward looks forward to being reunited with his brother, Richard informs him that the two of them will be staying in the Tower of London until the young prince's coronation, on the pretense that it will be best for their "health and recreation." Prince Edward protests this move and prophetically comments that for a man of honor death cannot claim victory. In an aside, Richard reveals that Prince Edward will not live much longer.

Hastings and the cardinal then return with the young duke of York. When Edward sees his young brother, they lament the death of their father. When Richard asks how his young nephew has been, the boy reminds him of the ominous comment he once made about the preternatural growth of children. "You said that idle weeds are fast in growth; / The prince my brother hath outgrown me far." Richard and York then engage in a rhetorical contest when the prince asks for Richard's sword as a "gift." Buckingham responds that young York has a biting wit and is as adroit with words as his uncle Richard. "He prettily and aptly taunts himself. / So cunning and so young is wonderful." The two young princes are then immediately sent to the tower, with Richard promising to send for their mother. Young York remarks that the ghost of his uncle Clarence will haunt him there.

With the children gone, Richard holds a private conference with Buckingham and Catesby. Buckingham is fearful of young York, whom he refers to as a "prating" boy, and Richard readily agrees that the child is dangerous, just like his mother, Elizabeth. Buckingham and Catesby then discuss how to bring about Richard's master plan and whether Hasting and Lord Stanley will be amenable to enabling Richard to seize the throne through his murderous schemes. Catesby responds that, though Hastings bears no love for Elizabeth, he loves the young princes and remains loyal to the deceased King Edward IV. Hastings will not be a party to Richard's treachery, and Lord Stanley, likewise, will follow Hastings's lead. Nevertheless, Buckingham means to test Hastings and instructs Catesby to summon the lord to the tower on the pretext of observing the supposed coronation of Edward. "If thou dost find him tractable to us, / Encourage him, and tell him our reasons. / If he be leaden, icy, cold, unwilling, / Be thou too, and so break off the talk." Richard suggests that a more ambiguous message be delivered to Hastings, namely that his enemies will be killed on the following day and that he can dally with Mistress Shore. When Catesby exits, Buckingham questions Richard on how to proceed should Lord Hastings prove unyielding to their schemes. Richard, without a moment's hesitation, commands execution by beheading, while promising Buckingham he will give him the earldom of Hereford once Richard becomes king.

Act 3, scene 2 begins early in the morning, with a messenger knocking at Lord Hasting's door, stating that he has been sent by Lord Stanley. The messenger tells Hastings that Stanley has learned about Richard's plan to hold "divided counsels" in order to test their loyalties. Richard's plan is to hold two meetings: one at Crosby Place, at which he will be offered the crown, and the other at the tower on the pretext of Edward's coronation, which will never come to pass. The messenger further relates a nightmare Stanley had the previous night, in which a boar "razed off his helm," implying that Richard will kill both Hastings and himself. The boar was Richard's heraldic symbol. Stanley's servant thus urges Hastings to leave immediately on horseback and flee with Stanley to safety. "And with all speed post with him toward the north, / To shun the danger that his soul divines." However, the foolish and naive Hastings dismisses Stanley's fears and instructs the servant instead to send assurances that all is well, especially since Catesby is a man to be trusted. The messenger departs to tell Stanley of Hasting's response, as Catesby arrives at Hastings's house to test his true loyalties. When Catesby presents his "worldview" to Hastings, that things have gone awry in the kingdom and only Richard can restore order by seizing the crown from Prince Edward, Hastings recoils in horror, stating that he would sooner lose his own head than give assent to such treason. "I'll have this crown of mine cut from my shoulders / Before I'll see the crown so foul misplaced." Hastings is not enticed by learning that Richard will eliminate Hastings's adversaries, "[t]he kindred of the Queen" who are to be executed at Pomfret Castle. Though Hastings bears no love for his relations, he will not turn on the young princes, and thus refuses to the death to participate in Richard's diabolical plan. Seeing that Hastings will not change his mind, Catesby commends his courage and loyalty, and Hastings remains deluded, thinking he is still safe from Richard: "As thou and I, who, as thou know'st, are dear / To princely Richard and to Buckingham."

Lord Stanley then arrives, fearful that his nightmare is a sign of bad things to come, but Hastings remains confident of their safety and will not be persuaded otherwise. A pursuivant (a state messenger authorized to execute warrants) arrives at Hastings's house while Catesby and Stanley depart. Hastings reassserts his confidence in his own safety and well-being. The pursuivant leaves, and a priest then enters whom Hastings promises to pay the next Sunday in recompense for his failure to make an offering. Buckingham arrives, noting that the condemned men at Pomfret Castle are in greater need of a priest than Hastings, and the two depart for the council meeting. Hastings remains hopeful that Elizabeth's kinsmen will be executed, while believing Stanley and he having nothing to fear from Richard and Buckingham. Buckingham's final aside, however, reveals that Hastings's trust in Richard with be his undoing.

Act 3, scene 3 opens with the armed Sir Richard Ratcliffe leading Rivers and Grey, and their friend Sir Thomas Vaughan, to Pomfret Castle. Rivers laments their imminent death by declaring to Ratcliffe that they are being executed for their loyalty and faithfulness, while Grey prays for the young princes. When Ratcliffe declares their time is up, Rivers is reminded of Richard II's slaughter, Grey observing that Margaret's curse has finally come to pass. "Now Margaret's curse is fall'n upon our heads, / . . . For standing by when Richard stabbed her son."

Act 3, scene 4: At Richard's council session in the Tower of London, Hastings, unaware that the meeting is a ruse intended to trap him, asks when the coronation is to take place, while Buckingham deceitfully plays along inquiring of Stanley whether all the necessary preparations have been made. Stanley responds in the affirmative, noting that the only element missing is the actual nomination. The bishop of Ely declares that the coronation will take place the next day. The foolish Hastings once again proclaims his confidence in Richard's benevolence: "I know he loves me well." Richard then enters the council room, cheerfully wishing everyone "good morrow" and, after hearing Buckingham's information, pronounces Hastings a courageous man for whom he bears great affection. "Than my Lord Hastings no man might be bolder. / His lordship knows me well and loves me well." Richard then asks the bishop to send for a bowl of strawberries from his garden which, among other things, further convinces Hastings of Richard's high regard for him. "There's some conceit or other likes him well / When that he bids good morrow with such spirit." The suspicious Lord Stanley, for his part, is uncomfortable with the rapid timing of the coronation. Buckingham draws Richard aside to inform him of what Catesby has learned in regard to Hastings's true sentiments and loyalty to the princes.

When Richard and Buckingham return to the meeting, there is a marked and ominous change in Richard's demeanor, as he accuses Hastings of conspiring against him. "I pray you all, tell me what they deserve / That do conspire my death with devilish plots." Displaying his arm for all to see, Richard states that Queen Elizabeth, in league with Hastings's mistress Shore, has cast a spell on him to cause the arm to shrink: "Then be your eyes the witness of their evil. / Look how I am bewitched. Behold, mine arm / Is like a blasted sapling, withered up." Richard accuses Hastings of betrayal and immediately orders his execution. Left alone with his executioners, Hastings is shocked and finally understands that Stanley was right in his assessment of Richard's evil plans. "Woe, woe for England, not a whit for me, / For I, too fond, might have prevented this." In his apprehension that the kingdom is doomed with Richard at the helm, Hastings is forced to confront the reality that Margaret's curse has now descended on him as well. "O Margaret, Margaret, now thy heavy curse / Is light on poor Hastings' wretched head."

Act 3, scene 5 opens with Richard questioning Buckingham's loyalty, as Richard detects fear and misgiving on Buckingham's part about committing murder. "Come, cousin, canst thou quake and change thy colour, / Murder thy breath in middle of a word, . . . As if thou were distraught and mad with terror." Buckingham assures Richard that he is up to the task, that he is able to lie, cheat, and kill, and, moreover, is willing to use any of those talents to further Richard's cause. "Intending deep suspicion, ghastly looks / Are at my service like enforcèd smiles." Citizens of London then enter, followed by Catesby who is carrying Hastings's head. Richard and Buckingham tell the Mayor of Hastings's treachery, stating that he got what he deserved. The Mayor is convinced and completely won over to Richard's cause, while Buckingham observes that, for his part, he was never deceived by Hastings. "I never looked for better at his hands / After he once fell in with Mistress Shore." In response, the Mayor tells them he will be their advocate and announce to the people that Hastings's execution was justified for he was a dangerous traitor. "But I'll acquaint our duteous citizens / With all your just proceedings in this case." With this, the Mayor exits.

Richard then instructs Buckingham to go before the people at Guildhall and slander the dead King Edward IV. He wants Buckingham to proclaim Edward's children to be bastards, the result of Edward's sexual appetites and indiscretions and, therefore, illegitimate heirs to the throne. Richard further adds that Buckingham should play on the crowd's emotions by revealing that Edward had a citizen wrongfully executed. "Moreover, urge his hateful luxury / And bestial appetite in change of lust, / Which stretched unto their servants, daughters, wives." Finally, Richard wants Buckingham to inform the citizens that King Edward IV was himself illegitimate owing to the "fact" that the duchess of York conceived him while her husband was away at war. "My princely father, then had wars in France, / And by true computation of the time / Found that the issue was not his begot." The ultimate goal is to turn the people against the princes and in favor of Richard being crowned. Buckingham promises to deliver. "Doubt not, my lord, I'll play the orator." While Buckingham leaves on his mission, Richard sends Lovell to summon Doctor Shaw and Friar Penker, both of whom are his supporters, to meet with him at Baynard's Castle. After everyone else has left the stage, Richard lingers to reveal that he will now give some secret order to guarantee that no one may visit the young princes in the tower.

Act 3, scene 6 takes place on the streets of London where a scrivener, a professional scribe authorized to write letters and legal documents, states that he has just finished his last assignment, commissioned by Catesby, for the defamation of Hastings's character. The document is to be read aloud to all of London later that day. "Here is the indictment of the good Lord Hastings," and, as the scrivener recognizes, is nothing more than a malicious lie meant to justify Richard's killing of his rival. The scrivener decries its hypocrisy: "Here's a good world the while. / Who is so gross that cannot see this palpable device?"

Act 3, scene 7: Buckingham, much to Richard's disappointment, reports that his speech to the London crowd was received in silence. Richard questions whether Buckingham attempted to agitate the people, to which Buckingham responds by enumerating the "facts" he relayed concerning Edward's greed and sexual indiscretions, "his enforcement of the city wives," and his own illegitimate entrance into this world, "his resemblance being not like the duke." Instead of applause, however, Buckingham's oration was met with terrified silence. Revealing his contempt for the common man, Buckingham says they remained stupefied. "But like dumb statues or breathing stones / Stared each on other and looked deadly pale." However, Buckingham had planted a few supporters among the assembly so that it would appear that Richard had some advocates among the populace. "When we had done, some followers of mine own / . . . hurled up their caps, / And some ten voices cried 'God save King Richard.'" Richard is furious to hear that the people do not favor him; he and Buckingham decide to go forward nonetheless, as Buckingham suggests that they play on the gullible Mayor's emotions by promoting Richard's piety. "The Mayor is here at hand; intend some fear. / Be not you spoke with but by mighty suit. / And look you get a prayer book in your hand." Richard's intention is to appear completely disinterested in becoming king and, instead, to have only the good of the people as his sole concern. To this end, Catesby, who follows the Mayor and citizens, attempts to advance Richard's cause by portraying him as a true spiritual being whose absence from the scene is proof of his obedience to God. "He is within, with two right reverend fathers, / Divinely bent to meditation, / And in no world suits could he be moved." When Richard finally enters the stage, flanked by two bishops, Buckingham flatters Richard as "a Christian prince" devoid of all vanity. Richard, of course, feigns ignorance as to why he has been called away from his religious devotions to appear before the crowd. In a beautifully crafted and eloquently delivered speech, Buckingham makes a great pretense of pleading with Richard to accept his royal responsibility despite his unwillingness to do so. "Know, then, it is your fault that you resign / The supreme seat, the throne majestical, / The sceptred office of your ancestors." Buckingham lends credibility not only to Richard's pious disinterestedness in political power but to his rightful and legal claim to the throne by lawful inheritance. Buckingham adds that, should Richard decline, the people will install someone other than Edward's children as their sovereign. "To the disgrace and downfall of your house / And in this resolution here we leave you." The ruse works, and Richard finally accepts, though protesting that it goes against all he holds sacred. "But penetrable to your kind entreaties, / Albeit against my conscience and my soul."

Act 4

Act 4, scene 1: Assembled outside the Tower of London, Elizabeth, her elder son Dorset by Sir John Grey, and the duchess of York meet with Lady Anne (who is now Richard's wife) and Clarence's young daughter, all of whom have come to visit the young princes. Their hopes are soon dashed when Brakenbury tells them that, though the princes are doing well, Richard forbids anyone from seeing them and he cannot disobey these orders. "The king hath strictly charged the contrary." They are baffled to learn that Richard is now lord protector. Stanley, earl of Derby, suddenly arrives with the news that Richard is about to be crowned king and that Anne has no other choice than to attend the coronation and become his queen. Elizabeth exclaims that the news is suffocating. "Ah, cut my lace asunder, / That my pent heart may have some scope to beat" and further advises Dorset to flee for his life and join forces with Richmond, far "from the reach of hell." Stanley agrees with this advice, encouraging her son to leave immediately and "[t]ake all the swift advantage of the hours." The duchess laments ever giving birth to such a son: "O my accursed womb, the bed of death. A cockatrice hast thou hatched to the world." For her part, Anne is completely repulsed with these "despiteful tidings" and wishes for death rather than having to go through with the ceremony. "Anointed let me be with deadly venom / And die ere men can say 'God save the queen.'" Anne further reflects on how she should have resisted Richard's seductive words and marriage proposal, remembering how she at first cursed him while attending Henry's corpse. The scene concludes with the duchess of York likewise advising Dorset to quickly join up with Richmond, while she wishes for the final peace of her grave.

Act 4, scene 2: Back at the palace, Richard, having been crowned king of England, makes a dramatic and victorious entrance, followed by his heretofore trusted advisors, Buckingham and Catesby. Despite his great achievement, though, Richard reveals his insecurity to Buckingham that while the two young princes are alive his power is not assured and, so, calls for their murder. "I wish the bastards dead, / And I would have it suddenly performed. / What say'st thou now? Speak suddenly, be brief." Buckingham has misgivings about committing such a crime and his initial response is to request some time to think, for "some little breath, some pause, dear lord," and leaves the stage. Catesby notes Richard's anger at this reluctance. Richard now distrusts Buckingham as one who deliberates and will not blindly obey him. Richard prefers unscrupulous fools who will act swiftly and decisively at his bidding. "I will converse with iron-witted fools / And unrespective boys. None are for me / That look into me with considerate eyes." A page suggests that, instead of Buckingham, Richard find someone without conscience who will do it happily for pay and indeed he knows of such a one, "whose humble means match not his haughty spirit. / Gold were as good as twenty orators." The man's name is Tyrrel, a name Richard seems somewhat familiar with, so the king tells the page to summon him. Alone again onstage, Richard reveals that Buckingham has now fallen out of his favor. Stanley then arrives to inform Richard that Dorset has fled to join forces with Richmond. Without a moment's hesitation, Richard instructs Catesby to spread a rumor that Queen Anne is sick and likely to die, while he ensures that no one has access to her. Here, Richard all but states his plan to murder Queen Anne. "[I]t stand me much upon / To stop all hopes whose growth may damage me." In the same moment, Richard declares his intention to murder his nephews and marry his niece Elizabeth of York, King Edward IV's daughter. To do otherwise would be the end of his illegitimate monarchy. "Or else my kingdom stands on brittle glass." James Tyrrel then enters and introduces himself to Richard. When asked if he is ready to commit murder, Tyrrel responds that he would prefer to kill adversaries. Richard quickly responds that that is exactly the situation, for the two young princes are his "deep enemies, / Foes to my rest and my sweet sleep's disorders." Tyrrel sets off to perform the deed. Buckingham returns to claim the reward Richard promised him, the earldom of Hereford, but Richard ignores his request, summarily dismissing Buckingham before promptly leaving. "Thou troublest me; I am not in the vein." Buckingham is aware, for the first time, that Richard has turned on him and that he must flee to his family's home. "Oh, let me think on Hastings and be gone / To Brecknock, while my fearful head is on."

Act 4, scene 3: Tyrrell returns to the palace to inform Richard that the act is done, though he admits to being deeply troubled by it for it is the most horrible crime imaginable. "The most arch deed of piteous massacre / That ever yet this land was guilty of." Tyrrel further relates that the two men he procured to murder the young princes, Dighton and Forrest, were similarly disturbed and filled with deep regret after smothering the two children to death in their sleep. "Albeit they were fleshed villains, bloody dogs / . . . Melted with tenderness and mild compassion, / Wept like to children in their deaths' sad story." Richard has no time or patience for such misgivings and is delighted to hear the news, instead asking for confirmation that Tyrrel witnessed their death and burial. Tyrrel tells Richard that the chaplain of the tower took care of matters. Richard then invites Tyrrel to come back later to tell him more about the murders and promises to reward his efforts. Once Tyrrel leaves, Richard reveals his various plots to get rid of everyone who might threaten his grasp on power. With the two young princes disposed of, Clarence's daughter married to an inconsequential man, Clarence's son confined, and Queen Anne now deceased, Richard is intent on simultaneously securing his power and undermining Richmond by marrying his niece Elizabeth, who is also the object of Richmond's affections. Ratfcliffe then enters to deliver the news that some of Richard's noblemen have defected to Richmond's side in France and that Buckingham has returned to Wales where he has taken charge of a large army against Richard. Though Richard is alarmed, he decides to gather his own army to meet the challenge: "Go muster men. My counsel is my shield. / We must be brief when traitors brave the field."

Act 4, scene 4 begins with Old Queen Margaret's entrance. Hidden from view from the others behind a wall, she remarks that the tide has turned against Richmond, as she surreptitiously watches and waits on the sidelines. Elizabeth and the duchess of York enter next, lamenting the deaths of the two young princes while Margaret, in a further series of asides, provides her own commentary on the scene of mourning, essentially maintaining that justice has been served and that of the three women, she has suffered the most. Margaret then begins to speak with the others directly, telling the duchess that she has unleashed a monster on the world, from "the kennel" of her womb, that a "hell-hound" has ushered forth who hunts and kills them. Margaret predicts that Richard will not stop the carnage until they are all dead and rejoices in knowing that her curses against the York and Woodeville families have come to pass. She says that the York deaths are fair payment for the deaths of her husband, Henry VI, and her son, Prince Edward.

The mood then shifts when the aggrieved Elizabeth beseeches Margaret's sympathy as she has mourned for the old queen's losses. Elizabeth asks Margaret to tutor her in the art of cursing, but Margaret is resistant, maintaining her hostile stance in reminding Elizabeth that she has usurped Margaret's royal position and thus remains a false representative of the monarchy. "I called thee then vain flourish of my fortune; / . . . A sign of dignity, a breath, a bubble, / A queen in jest, only to fill the scene." Despite the older woman's deep-seated bitterness, Elizabeth persuades Margaret to give her instruction in issuing curses. "O thou well skilled in curses, stay awhile, / And teach me how to curse mine enemies." Margaret advises Elizabeth to nurture and enhance her outrage by comparing her former joys to her present afflictions, always remembering Richard as the author of their collective misery. After Margaret leaves, Elizabeth and the duchess become allies, agreeing that Richard must be destroyed. When Richard enters with his noblemen and the commanders of his army, his mother, the duchess, begins to hurl insults at him, wishing he had never been born, while both she and Elizabeth condemn him for the bloody murder of the young princes and the rest of his extended family. Richard grows furious at their display of temerity and false accusations, while representing himself as sanctimonious. "Let not the heavens hear these telltale women / Rail on the Lord's anointed. Strike, I say!" He orders his men to strike up loud music to try to drown out their curses, but to no avail as the duchess continues to recount the strange history of his childhood—"tetchy and wayward was thy infancy"—and the treacherous and cunning man he has become.

Richard speaks with Elizabeth in private, having the audacity to ask for her young daughter's hand in marriage, though Elizabeth has previously vowed that her daughters will become "praying nuns, not weeping queens." The former queen is aghast at such an unthinkable suggestion and promises to scandalize herself and her family before giving consent to such an unimaginable scenario. "And I'll corrupt her manners, stain her beauty, / Slander myself as false to Edward's bed." Despite Elizabeth's resistance, Richard is shameless and unrelenting in convincing the former queen that she can make restitution to her remaining family members by allowing her daughter to marry Richard and bear him children. "Even all I have, ay, and myself and all, / Will I withal endow a child of thine." To this last argument, Elizabeth responds with fury, stating that Richard should send her daughter the bleeding hearts of the young princes he has slain. Refusing to be deterred, Richard persists, contending that this proposed marriage would be for the good of the kingdom as it is the only way to prevent the otherwise unavoidable civil war being fomented by such men as her son Dorset for whom he promises a safe and rewarding return. "Dorset, your son, that with a fearful soul, / Leads discontented in foreign soil, / This fair alliance quickly will call home / To high promotions and great dignity."

Elizabeth finally assents and says she will speak with her daughter about it, though her true feelings are highly ambiguous, as she reminds Richard of his murderous actions. She possibly only appears to be agreeing with him, since she knows he will destroy anyone who resists his desires or stands in his way. She exits, saying that she will write to Richard and inform him of her daughter's feelings. As soon as she is gone, Richard disparages her as a weak-willed woman. "Relenting fool and shallow, changing woman."

Ratcliffe and Catesby enter and report on Richmond's impending invasion, his formidable navy headed toward Richard. Lord Stanley brings further bad news. Richard begins to panic for the first time, exhibiting signs of increasing insecurity as he appears to be losing control of his own allies. He even chastises Stanley for speaking in riddles as to the gravity of the news he has come to deliver. Stanley reports that Richmond has set sail for England with Dorset, Buckingham, and Morton, all of whom are resolute in their determination to defeat Richard. Richard grows suspicious even of Stanley's loyalties as he predicts that "[t]hou wilt revolt and fly to him, I fear." Nothing Stanley says, however, can convince Richard otherwise. Throughout the realm, the nobility are prepared to fight with Richmond. While a steady stream of messengers comes before Richard to report on various aspects of the imminent invasion, one shred of good news is delivered. By accident and the forces of nature, Buckingham's army has been dispersed and Buckingham captured, as Catesby has come to report. The scene, however, ends on a direful note, as Richard learns that Richmond has at last landed with an overwhelming force. Richard wastes no time as he sets off to lead his army to engage Richmond in battle.

Act 4, scene 5: Stanley, as Richard correctly surmised, is conspiring against the tyrant and holds a secret audience with Sir Christopher, a nobleman from Richmond's forces. As an assurance, however, against Stanley's act of betrayal, Richard has insisted that Stanley leave behind his young son, George. As his father realizes all too well, "If I revolt, off goes young George's head." Nevertheless, Stanley manages to convey his good wishes to Richmond and to let him know that Richard plans to marry the young Elizabeth. Sir Christopher tells Stanley Richmond's location and names many of the English noblemen who are allied with him. Stanley leaves after handing Sir Christopher a letter he has written to Richmond declaring his true allegiance.

Act 5

Act 5, scene 1: As Buckingham is being led to his execution by an armed sheriff, he asks to speak with King Richard, but the request is denied. Instead, the sheriff advises him to be patient while waiting to be beheaded. In his last few moments, Buckingham reflects on all of Richard's victims, whom he imagines are watching over this next execution, and cries out for their divine intervention. "If that your moody, discontented souls / Do through the clouds behold this present hour, / Even for revenge mock my destruction." Notably, it is All Souls' Day (November 2), a day on the Christian calendar for remembering the dead. For Buckingham, it is his doomsday, and in his last few remaining moments, he remembers his life with deep regret for all the sins he has committed, including his faithless promise to protect King Edward IV's children and Elizabeth's kinsmen. "False to his children and his wife's allies." Buckingham is also reminded of his own foolishness, much like that of Hastings, in placing his trust in Richard, who "[h]ath turned my feigned prayer on my head / And given in earnest what I begged in jest." In his final moments, Buckingham acknowledges that he is now receiving justice for his own crimes. Finally, he remembers Margaret's prophecy that Richard would one day tear his heart asunder and thus Buckingham is forced to confront the truth of her prediction. A willing accomplice and advisor to a bloodthirsty man who is loyal to no one, Buckingham tells the officers to bring him to "the block of shame" and so is led to his death.

Act 5, scene 2 takes place at the camp of Richmond's army, which is advancing steadily and unchallenged toward Richard. Richmond informs his men that he has just received a letter from his relative, Stanley, informing him that Richard's army is closing in but still a day's march away. Richmond's men need no further encouragement, all of them aligned against Richard and sworn to defeat "this guilty homicide." Recounting the multitude of crimes Richard has perpetrated, they are determined to restore peace and are certain of victory for Richard has no few remaining supporters. While some of his so-called allies have deserted, others remain only out of fear.

Act 5, scene 3 takes place in Richard's camp as he orders his men to pitch their tents in Bosworth Field for the night, asserting that he has only the greatest optimism that he will be victorious. "My heart is ten times lighter than my looks." In his boasting, Richard is as bold and intrepid as ever, as he proclaims the power of his political status, which he likens to an impenetrable fortress. "Besides, the king's name is a tower of strength." Richard summons his men and bids them all to be disciplined in their preparations. In the meantime, there is a brief parallel scene, which takes place the same evening, in which Richmond appears with some of his noblemen and likewise predicts victory for the following morning. Richmond asks Blunt to find an excuse to see Richard and deliver a note to him, though it is not revealed what message it contains.

The action then returns to Richard's camp where he directs Ratcliffe to engage the services of a pursuivant and bring Stanley to him, while threatening him if he is resistant. "Bid him bring his power / Before sunrising, lest his son George fall / Into the blind cave of eternal night." Ratcliffe exits the stage with Richard's final instructions to return in the middle of night and help him with his armor.

The scene then shifts again to Richmond's camp with Stanley promising victory the next day and offering his prayers that the ensuing battle will be Richard's final judgment. However, since his son is still held captive, Stanley is mindful that he must proceed with great caution. He bids Richmond farewell, saying that he looks forward to their being reunited. "God give us leisure for these rites of love. / Once more adieu. Be valiant, and speed well." Stanley then receives safe conduct back to Richard's camp while Richmond, alone, prays for God's intercession on his behalf before falling asleep.

As the scene reverts back to Richard's tent, a parade of ghosts appears to haunt his slumber. They are the spirits of those he has mercilessly killed. The first to appear is the ghost of Prince Edward, son to Henry VI, who has come with a disturbing reminder of how Richard stabbed him, in the prime of life, at Tewkesbury. The ghost of the prince's father, Henry VI, is close behind and taunts Richard for killing his "anointed body" in the tower, departing from the nightmare wishing Richard dead and Richmond the best of luck. When the ghost of Clarence appears, Richard is reminded of how his brother was drowned in a barrel of wine. "Tomorrow in the battle think on me, / And fall thy edgeless sword, despair, and die." Clarence, too, concludes with a prayer of good wishes for Richmond. The ghosts of Rivers, Grey, Vaughan, and Hastings follow in rapid succession and echo the same sentiments, while the twin ghosts of the young princes tell Richard to think of them during the battle so that he may be "weigh[ed] down to ruin, shame, and death." As for his murdered wife, Anne, her ghost returns to disturb his sleep. Buckingham, the last spectre to appear, reminds Richard of the trust he violated. "Oh, in the battle think on Buckingham, / And die in terror of thy guiltiness."

Richard wakes from his troubling dreams and begs for another horse, crying out for help for he imagines he has been seriously wounded. He has been awakened, instead, by the workings of his guilty conscience. In an impassioned soliloquy, Richard questions himself and the cause for the nightmare. "What? Do I fear myself? There's none else by. / Richard loves Richard, that is, I am I." Richard concludes that he has no cause to love himself, recognizing that the many voices of the deceased have come to air their grievances and judge him for his tyrannical pursuit of power. "My conscience hath a thousand several tongues, / And every tongue brings in a several tale, / And every tale condemns me for a villain." Hopeless and devoid of his vainglorious optimism, Richard finally fears for his soul. Acknowledging that no one will mourn him, he knows he is about to be defeated and that justice will be served.

Following this terrifying realization, Ratcliffe enters Richard's tent to let him know that the rooster has crowed and that the battle is near at hand. The visibly shaken Richard tells Ratcliffe of his nightmare, but Ratcliffe tells him he need not fear these shadows. Richard, however, is not convinced and continues to insist that he is more terrified of his dream than the opposing forces he is about to face. Nevertheless, some of his former spirit returns as Richard bids Ratcliffe to join him in some eavesdropping on his men to see if any are planning to desert him.

Back at Richmond's camp, Richmond tells his advisers of his auspicious dream of victory in which the many ghosts of Richard's victims have wished him well. "I promise you, my heart is very jocund / In the remembrance of so fair a dream." Richmond then delivers a stirring prebattle oration to his soldiers, reminding them that they are defending their native country from a fearsome tyrant and murderer and that God is on their side. "The prayers of holy saints and wronged souls, / Like high-reared bulwarks, stand before our faces. / Richard except, those whom we fight against / Had rather have us win than him they follow." Richmond's men head off to battle.

Back in the other camp, Richard asks Ratcliffe about Richmond's army, which Ratcliffe characterizes as a group of untrained men. Richard readily accepts this description as accurate. As he notes that the sun has not yet appeared, Richard dismisses his self-doubt by suggesting that this ill omen could apply to Richmond as much as to him. "For the self-same heaven / That frowns on me looks sadly upon him." Richard then proceeds to deliver his own battle speech, which not only lacks the eloquence of Richmond's oration but, more importantly, evidences a severely diminished Richard who has lost the rhetorical authority he has consistently used to get his own way, especially in regard to his most preposterous arguments. Richard's battle speech is instead focused on the ragtag nature of Richmond's forces, comprised of men of ill repute who in their ignorance were easily recruited. "A sort of vagabonds, rascals, and runaways, / A scum of Bretons and base lackey peasants, / Whom their o'ercloyed country vomits forth / To desperate adventures and assured destruction." A messenger then brings the bad news that Stanley has deserted and refuses to bring his army. Though Richard orders that Stanley's son be beheaded, there is not enough time to execute the young man for the enemy is already upon them. Richard and his forces make their way to the battle.

Act 5, scene 4: Catesby appears onstage and calls out to Richard's ally, Norfolk, asking that he help Richard. The king's horse has been killed, while Richard continues to fight like a madman on foot in his crazed pursuit of Richmond. "Seeking for Richmond in the throat of death. / Rescue, fair lord, or else the day is lost." Richard then appears, calling out for a horse. "A horse, a horse, my kingdom for a horse!" Despite his increasingly desperate situation, he refuses Catesby's offer of assistance, stating that he will stay the course no matter what befalls him. He even thinks that Richmond has filled the field with decoys for he claims to have killed five of them already. "I think there be six Richmond in the field; / Five have I slain today instead of him." Once again, Richard repeats his need for a horse.

Act 5, scene 5: Richard and Richmond enter, and Richmond kills his enemy with his sword. Richmond proclaims victory. Stanley locates Richard's crown and turns it over to Richmond. "From the dead temples of this bloody wretch / Have I plucked off to grace thy brows withal." Richmond accepts the crown, orders the dead to be buried and the defectors pardoned. Moreover, George Stanley is still alive. Richmond, now King Henry VII, declares the old rivalries concluded stating that "[w]e will unite the white rose and the red," as the insanity and violence of Richard's reign have been brought to an end. The scene closes with Richmond announcing his intention to marry young Elizabeth, as the two of them are the "true succeeders of each royal house" and asking for God's blessing.

LIST OF CHARACTERS IN
RICHARD III

🙞🙜

Richard, Duke of Gloucester, later King Richard III, the eleventh child of Richard, duke of York, was born in 1452. In Shakespeare's play, Richard is a dangerous and unethical villain. Shakespeare's Tudor sources, most especially that of Thomas More, portrayed Richard as a monster, a model of iniquity. Though Shakespeare would utilize many aspects of Richard's ignoble character and misshapen physique, he nevertheless created a highly imaginative and unique character, the product of his poetic genius. Shakespeare was interested in exploring the workings of his brilliant-minded tyrant far more than representing onstage the heinous crimes attributed to him. As a historic figure, civil war was fomenting at the time of Richard's birth, due to his father's intention to gain the crown. Thus, both he and his brother George were sent to France for safety and were later brought back to England by their brother Edward IV, who became king in 1461 and made Richard the duke of Gloucester. Following the death of Edward IV, for which Shakespeare holds Richard indirectly culpable, Richard became the protector of Edward's children, including the young Edward V, the rightful heir to the throne. Following the murder of young Edward and his brother at the tower, for which Shakespeare makes Richard directly complicit, Richard seizes power and is crowned on July 6, 1483, at Westminster. Richard's reign ends with his fatal battle with Richmond at Bosworth Field on August 22, 1485, Richmond becoming King Henry VII.

George, Duke of Clarence, the younger brother of Edward IV and older brother of Richard III. In *Richard III*, this gentle and trusting man becomes the victim of Richard's malicious lies. Richard III convinces Edward IV to send his own brother Clarence to jail because his name starts with a *G* (George, duke of Clarence). Richard creates suspicion by convincing Edward IV that certain prophecies have predicted that someone whose name starts with the letter *G* will disinherit his children. Edward IV has Clarence sent to the tower and, although he issues an order to release him, Richard makes sure that Clarence is executed there and has the murderers drown him in a butt of malmsey (like a cask of wine) to ensure the task has been completed. For Clarence's part, up to the moment of his execution, he believes Richard loves him and will intercede on his behalf until he is told by the executioners that they have come as a result of Richard's orders.

Sir Robert Brakenbury is lieutenant of the tower by appointment of Richard III. A minor and rather weak-willed character, Brakenbury reluctantly leaves the young princes to the supervision of Sir James Tyrrel, who has come to execute the children.

Lord William Hastings, who was made chamberlain in the household of Edward IV, remains faithful to Edward's son after the king's death. Hastings refuses to be associated with Richard's illegal seizure of the throne and, as a result, Richard has him beheaded.

Lady Anne, Anne Neville, is the younger daughter of the powerful earl of Warwick and is married to Edward, the son of Henry VI. Following Edward's death at Tewkesbury, Richard, while Duke of Gloucester, makes an audacious proposal to marry her; in the face of his disarming flattery, she acquiesces. To her great misfortune, she later becomes his queen in 1483 and dies two years later, according to Shakespeare almost certainly by Richard's doing.

Sir William Tressel and **Berkeley** are noble attendants to Lady Anne at the funeral of Henry VI. They speak no lines and exit the stage with her in act 1, scene 2.

Queen Elizabeth, wife of King Edward IV and daughter of Sir Richard Woodville, she was formerly married to Sir John Grey, who was killed on the Lancastrian side in the War of the Roses. She was then secretly married to Edward IV in 1464 and became his queen in 1465. Following the death of Edward IV and Richard III's usurpation of the throne, Elizabeth takes sanctuary at Westminster Abbey, though she later appears to acquiesce to Richard's request for her daughter's hand in marriage. The marriage to Richard, however, never takes place. Elizabeth's daughter eventually marries Henry VII after his defeat of Richard III.

Earl Rivers, Anthony Woodville, brother to Queen Elizabeth. Rivers previously aided King Henry VI in his war against the Lancastrians. Richard III is suspicious of Rivers and, in the play, has him executed without trial at Pomfret Castle.

Lord Grey, Richard, is the younger son of Queen Elizabeth by her first husband, Sir John Grey, and brother of the marquess of Dorset. Both he and his uncle, Lord Rivers, are responsible for Edward IV's son (Edward V) following the king's death. However, while accompanying the young Edward to London for his coronation ceremony, Richard has Grey and Rivers arrested on the pretext that they alienated the young prince from Richard's affections. Grey is executed at Pomfret Castle.

Marquess of Dorset, Thomas Dorset, is the elder son of Queen Elizabeth and Sir John Grey. He allegedly took part in the battle at Teweskbury, fighting on the side of Edward IV. Dorset supported the duke of Buckingham in his revolt against Richard III in 1484 and joined Richmond in Brittany, though he was not in attendance at Richmond's invasion in 1485.

Duke of Buckingham, is Richard's co-conspirator and supports his usurpation of the throne in order to secure his own advancement and reward. Buckingham held the position of lord high steward of England under Edward IV and was married to Catherine Woodville, sister of Queen Elizabeth. Buckingham is treacherous and complicit in arresting Rivers, Vaught, and Grey. However, he eventually turns on Richard and is captured and beheaded as a result.

Lord Stanley, Thomas, earl of Derby, is married to Richmond's mother, Margaret Beaufort, but serves during the reigns of both Edward IV and Richard III until Richmond's invasion in 1485. Though he does not enter the battle at Bosworth Field, he supports Richmond and allegedly finds Richard's fallen crown, which he presents to Richmond. He is rewarded by Richmond and made first earl of Derby.

Queen Margaret, Margaret of Anjou, is the widow of King Henry VI and Richard's nemesis throughout the play. She fought furiously to restore Henry VI to the throne until he was defeated by Edward IV at the battle of Tewkesbury in 1471. In 1476, Margaret fled England and went into exile in France, where she died in poverty in 1482. Shakespeare resurrects her character to function as Richard III's avenging spirit.

Sir William Catesby was named chancellor of the exchequer by Richard III in 1483 after having assisted in the removal of his predecessor, Lord Hastings. Catesby is ultimately captured at Bosworth and executed.

Two Murderers are sent to take the lives of the young princes in the tower. Their deliberation before committing the crime creates an interesting pause in an otherwise rapid succession of violent acts to remove all of Richard's perceived enemies. Their hesitation, likewise, serves to underscore the especially heinous nature of infanticide, and several other unscrupulous characters in the play will echo this same resistance to killing children.

King Edward IV is the son of Richard, duke of York, and his duchess, Cicely Neville. Having defeated Henry VI at Northampton, he became king in 1461. He also appoints his brothers, George and Richard, as dukes of Clarence and Gloucester, respectively. He married Elizabeth Grey in 1461. Though he was attacked by the earl of Warsick, Clarence, and Queen Margaret in 1470, he is reconciled with Clarence, kills Warwick, and captures the irascible Margaret at Tewkesbury after murdering her son, Edward. Though he orders his brother Clarence's execution as a result of Richard's scheming and dissembling, the historical reason for the killing is not verifiable.

Sir Richard Ratcliffe, chief advisor to Richard III, was previously knighted by Edward IV at Tewkesbury. A willing accomplice to Richard's murderous schemes, he was a participant in the council held in the tower in 1483, the same day he was carrying out the executions of Rivers, Grey, and Vaughan at Pomfret Castle. Ratcliffe is eventually killed fighting for Richard on Bosworth Field.

Duchess of York, Cecily Neville, was married to Richard, duke of York. She is also the mother of King Edward IV and Clarence, both of whom die in the play through the malicious scheming of her other son, Richard. Her regret for having given birth to the monstrous Richard is profound, and she wishes her son dead.

The **Children of Clarence** are Edward and Margaret Plantagenet. When Clarence is executed in 1485, they are left orphans. Richard III has the young Edward imprisoned where he remained until Henry VII had him executed in 1499. His daughter, Margaret, is married to Sir Richard Pole by Henry VII, not by Richard III as is portrayed in the play.

Three Citizens act as a chorus commenting on the state of unstable political situation in England following the death of Edward IV.

Archbishop of York, Thomas Rotherham, is imprisoned by Richard III though later released, living out the rest of his life far from the political arena.

Duke of York, Richard, is the younger son of Edward IV and Queen Elizabeth and married in 1478, at the age of six, to Anne of Norfolk, a child of the same age. Following the death of Edward IV, Elizabeth takes him with her into sanctuary at Westminster Abbey but regrettably turns him over to Cardinal Bourchier. Richard's fate is to die with his older brother in the tower.

Prince Edward is the older son of Edward IV and Queen Elizabeth. He proves himself a precocious child in his debate with Richard and Buckingham while imprisoned at the tower. Though too young to assume the throne at the time of his father's death, many are hopeful that he will become England's future ruler. However, he poses a great threat to Richard and is executed along with his younger brother.

Lord Cardinal, Thomas Bourchier, archbishop of Canterbury, is lord chancellor to Henry VI. Having been an ally to both of the warring factions during the War of the Roses, Bourchier also served Edward IV and is responsible for convincing Elizabeth to surrender her young son to Richard of Gloucester after her husband's death. Bourchier would go on to officiate at the coronations of both Richard III and Henry VII.

Lord Mayor of London is a gullible and weak individual who Richard and Buckingham use as a pawn. In their ploy to make Richard king, they enlist the mayor as their apologist for Hastings's execution. Richard manipulatively evokes the mayor's sympathy when he protests how he loved Hastings and was blind to his betrayal. Richard even invokes Christian teachings to prove the extent that he was deceived by Hastings, and the mayor is thus completely won over to Richard's cause, so much so that he becomes Richard's willing advocate and plans to justify Hastings's murder to the people.

A Pursuivant is a state messenger authorized to execute warrants.

Sir Thomas Vaughan is a supporter of Edward IV and later his young son Edward V. Vaughan is taken prisoner along with Earl Rivers and Lord Grey and executed.

John Morton, bishop of Ely, participates in Richard's council session in the Tower of London in act 3, scene 4. Ely declares that Richard's coronation should take place the next day and is sent to fetch a bowl of strawberries from his garden as a way of deceiving Lord Hastings into believing Richard's intentions are benign.

Duke of Norfolk, John Howard, an ally of Richard III, he fights alongside him at Bosworth Field.

Lord Lovell, Sir Francis Lovell, is also a supporter of Richard III. Lovell carries out the execution of Hastings in act 3 and returns with the victim's head, as ordered by Richard.

A Scrivener is a professional scribe authorized to write letters and legal documents. He appears in act 3, scene 6, when he has been commissioned to defame

Hastings's character and reads the proclamation to all of London. However, the scrivener recognizes the document for what it is, a malicious lie to justify Richard's murdering a rival.

Two Bishops accompany Richard as he appears before a crowd of Londoners misrepresenting himself as a pious man who is heavily committed to spiritual concerns and has no interest in becoming England's next king.

Sir James Tyrrel is a murderer for hire who Buckingham knows and whom Richard commissions to kill the young princes in the tower. Though he at first expresses reluctance at killing two young innocents, Tyrrel eventually agrees and is dispatched to carry out the deeds. Nevertheless, the task is repugnant to Tyrrel so he, in turn, procures two other hired killers, Dighton and Forrest, to complete the task. When Tyrrel reports back to Richard, he relates how the two hired assassins were themselves deeply disturbed and filled with remorse for smothering the two children in their sleep.

Earl of Richmond, Henry Tudor, was exiled to France during the reign of Edward IV. He does not enter the play until act 5, when in 1485 he returns to England and defeats Richard at Bosworth Field and is crowned King Henry VII.

Earl of Oxford, John de Vere is a Lancastrian in exile. He appears briefly in act 5, scene 2. Oxford joins Richmond's forces in 1483.

Sir James Blunt is the third son of Sir Walter Blunt. He joins forces with Richmond.

Earl of Surrey, Thomas Howard, is a supporter of Richard III. He makes a brief appearance in act 5, scene 3.

Sir William Brandon serves as a standard bearer for the earl of Richmond at Bosworth. He is killed by Richard III.

KEY PASSAGES IN
RICHARD III
❧

Act 1, 1, 1–40

Enter Richard Duke of Gloucester, solus
Now is the winter of our discontent
Made glorious summer by this sun of York,
And all the clouds that loured upon our house
In the deep bosom of the ocean buried.
Now are our brows bound with victorious wreaths,
Our bruisèd arms hung up for monuments,
Our stern alarums changed to merry meetings,
Our dreadful marches to delightful measures.
Grim-visaged war hath smoothed his wrinkled front,
And now, instead of mounting bardèd steeds
To fright the souls of fearful adversaries,
He capers nimbly in a lady's chamber
To the lascivious pleasing of a lute.
But I, that am not shaped for sportive tricks,
Nor made to court an amorous looking-glass,
I that am rudely stamped, and want love's majesty
To strut before a wanton ambling nymph,
I that am curtailed of this fair proportion,
Cheated of feature by dissembling nature,
Deformed, unfinished, sent before my time
Into this breathing world, scarce half made up,
And that so lamely and unfashionable,
That dogs bark at me as I halt by them,
Why, I, in this weak piping time of peace,
Have no delight to pass away the time,
Unless to spy my shadow in the sun
And descant on mine own deformity.
And therefore, since I cannot prove a lover
To entertain these fair well-spoken days,

I am determinèd to prove a villain
And hate the idle pleasures of these days.
Plots have I laid, inductions dangerous,
By drunken prophecies, libels and dreams
To set my brother Clarence and the king
In deadly hate the one against the other.
And if King Edward be as true and just
As I am subtle, false and treacherous,
This day should Clarence closely be mewed up
About a prophecy, which says that 'G'
Of Edward's heirs the murderer shall be.
Dive, thoughts, down to my soul, here Clarence comes.

Richard's well-known and grandiloquent soliloquy establishes many of the dynamics of the entire play. Richard's opening speech can be analyzed in three parts. The first thirteen lines provide a summary of his perspective on the status of political events, a situation to which he takes great exception and for which he sees himself an outsider. The second part, in lines 14 to 27, reveals his negative feelings about his appearance and his great anger about a birth that has left him deformed and the subject of society's scorn and mockery. In the third part, extending from lines 28 to 40, Richard discloses his diabolical plan to take revenge on the world and thereby seize all that has previously been denied to him. What is perhaps most noteworthy about this brilliantly crafted soliloquy are the many tensions and multifaceted meanings behind the words he chooses to describe both his dilemma and his plan for seizing control.

The first part of Richard's soliloquy can be characterized as a lament for the masculine pursuits of war and conflict, which have now been replaced by the objectionable femininity of peacetime and leisurely activities. Richard begins with disparaging remarks in his allusion to the present king, Edward IV, by calling him this "sun of York," a reference to both his desire to restore calm to the realm and the fact that he is a son, like Richard, of the former Richard Plantagenet, the third duke of York. Richard sees himself as thriving only in times of strife and civil war and, further, claims to want nothing to do with women and leisurely pursuits. Still, the following two sections of his soliloquy reveal an ambivalence on his part and, indeed, through a careful consideration of his words, an intent to actually become an active participant in the very same pleasure and pursuits that he at first so vociferously rejects. The reference to a lute, a popular musical instrument during the Renaissance, bears a secondary meaning, as the word was also used during Shakespeare's time to refer to a type of clay or substance used to close and seal a space between two pipes. Thus, by extension, there is a possibility that the lute is a defense mechanism for Richard, an indication of his wish to surround himself with an impenetrable barrier, as he seeks to establish his legacy.

In the second section of the soliloquy, Richard turns to his monstrous appearance and pariahlike status in the world at large. Physically revolting to everyone, including dogs that bark at him, Richard sees himself as utterly repugnant to women and therefore precluded from any possibility of an intimate relationship. Richard lists the ways in which he has been denied the opportunities that other men enjoy due to his deformity, implying an anger at both nature and women, including his mother, for having brought him into the world prematurely. Nevertheless, he betrays a desire to be a part of the world from which he has been so cruelly "exiled." In his vehement protest, Richard states that one of the only satisfactions left to him is to "descant on mine own deformity," and in his use of the rhetorical expression, *to descant*, reveals some hidden meanings to the infinitive. As applied in his soliloquy, by descanting on his physicality, Richard is stating that he is left with nothing else to do but observe and comment on his problems. However, *to descant* also means "to play or sing in harmony with a fixed theme," and while Richard is certainly obsessed with his appearance, he is also expressing a desire to participate in the same pleasurable, social activities he professes to despise. Though he lives in a "weak piping time of peace," he is divulging a wish to fashion a unique "song" for himself and mark time to his own particular beat.

In the final part of Richard's soliloquy, he makes clear his intention is to seize control of his own destiny and manipulate the fate of all others by means of as many unscrupulous schemes and maneuvers he can possibly conjure in his fertile imagination. Richard has every intention of deriving satisfaction from the world he is forced to inhabit and revels in his devilish designs. Richard is determined to overturn the "idle pleasures" he sees pursued around him and transform them into his own vision of a chaos. Given that his first crime will be fratricide, Richard reveals that he will manipulate Edward's gullibility by planting a false prophecy regarding the potential threat posed by a man whose name is George (Clarence's first name). At the same time, he pledges to reduce Clarence to a whimper, sealing him in the tower where eventually he will beg for his life. Richard even implies that Clarence will die from drowning, a reference to his later immersion in the vat of wine. By the end of this opening soliloquy, Richard has established himself as the dominant personality who will define, control, and rule over all others. At the same time, by revealing his innermost thoughts and plans, Richard has already established an intimate relationship with the audience or reader. He has presented himself as one completely self-absorbed, whose only concern is to eliminate all sources of competition to his plans for acquiring absolute authority. While the soliloquy offers an initial glimpse of Richard's corrupted moral state, Shakespeare, at the same time, presents a charismatic and flawed villain, worthy of being the protagonist of his tragedy.

———⟨⟩——— ———⟨⟩——— ———⟨⟩———

Act 1, 2, 1–11, 17–28

Anne: Set down, set down your honourable load,
If honour may be shrouded in a hearse,
Whilst I a while obsequiously lament
The untimely fall of virtuous Lancaster.
Poor key-cold figure of a holy king!
Pale ashes of the house of Lancaster!
Thou bloodless remnant of that royal blood!
Be it lawful that I invocate thy ghost,
To hear the lamentations of poor Anne,
Wife to thy Edward, to thy slaughtered son,
Stabbed by the self-same hand that made these wounds.

* * *

More direful hap betide that hated wretch,
That makes us wretched by the death of thee,
Than I can wish to adders, spiders, toads,
Or any creeping venom'd thing that lives!
If ever he have child, abortive be it,
Prodigious, and untimely brought to light,
Whose ugly and unnatural aspect
May fright the hopeful mother at the view;
And that be heir to his unhappiness!
If ever he have wife, let her be made
More miserable by the death of him
Than I am made by my young lord and thee!

This scene helps to demonstrate Anne's sincere mourning for the loss of her beloved father-in-law, Henry VI, as well as her faithful adherence to seeing that the proper burial rites are carried out. The passage also points to the ways her character stands in stark contrast to Richard's villainous nature. When Richard makes his presence known to Anne, following her opening soliloquy, he reveals his complete emotional detachment from and invalidation of the funeral procession that stands before him. At the same time, in comparing these two selections, an important temporal distinction becomes apparent, namely that Anne is able to stay in the present moment with a complete lack of concern for herself, while Richard, utterly incapable of living in the present, must always project himself into the future, as if his grand intentions had already come to fruition. In the following passage, Anne actually addresses Henry's corpse, a seeming attempt to invoke his spirit, and in so doing obeys an ethical obligation to remember the dead. It is important to note that inasmuch as this is a play set in medieval England where the culture of the times was dominated by the church, the dead occupied a sacred place.

In Peter Marshall's discussion of this recognized obligation to the dead in late medieval England, in his *Beliefs and the Dead in Reformation England*, he points out that, in pre-Reformation times, it was expected that survivors of the deceased would speak for their departed loved ones. The afterlife of the dead in a world far removed from the living was of great concern to both the church and its faithful adherents. In addition to her honoring Henry's memory, two other aspects of Anne's opening soliloquy are important. First, in her vivid recollection of Henry's regal and sacred status, Anne revives and highlights the historical events that Richard seeks to obliterate. Secondly, though Richard has not yet made his presence known to her, he so dominates the play that he is always latently present, as evidenced in Anne's initial imprecations against him. Tragically, however, the curse she casts on Richard, that his future wife experience more agony than Anne is presently feeling, is a wish that will be fulfilled when she becomes Richard's queen.

⚜ ⚜ ⚜

Act 1, 2, 33–37, 89–136

Gloucester: Stay, you that bear the corpse, and set it down.
Anne: What black magician conjures up this fiend
To stop devoted charitable deeds?
Gloucester: Villains! set down the corpse, or by Saint Paul,
I'll make a corpse of him that disobeys.

* * *

Gloucester: Say that I slew them not.
Anne: Then say they were not slain.
But dead they are, and, devilish slave, by thee.
Gloucester: I did not kill your husband.
Anne: Why, then he is alive.
Gloucester: Nay, he is dead, and slain by Edward's hand.
Anne: In thy foul throat thou liest. Queen Margaret saw
Thy murd'rous falchion smoking in his blood,
The which thou once didst bend against her breast,
But that thy brothers beat aside the point.
Gloucester: I was provoked by her sland'rous tongue,
That laid their guilt upon my guiltless shoulders.
Anne: Thou wast provoked by thy bloody mind,
That never dream'st on aught but butcheries.
Didst thou not kill this king?

Gloucester: I grant ye.
Anne: Dost grant me, hedgehog? Then, God grant me too
Thou mayst be damned for that wicked deed.
Oh, he was gentle, mild, and virtuous.
Gloucester: The fitter for the King of heaven that hath him.
Anne: He is in heaven, where thou shalt never come.
Gloucester: Let him thank me, that helped to send him thither,
For he was fitter for that place than earth.
Anne: And thou unfit for any place but hell.
Gloucester: Yes, one place else, if you will hear me name it.
Anne: Some dungeon.
Gloucester: Your bedchamber.
Anne: Ill rest betide the chamber where thou liest.
Gloucester: So will it, madam, till I lie with you.
Anne: I hope so.
Gloucester: I know so. But, gentle Lady Anne,
To leave this keen encounter of our wits
And fall somewhat into a slower method,
Is not the causer of the timeless deaths
Of these Plantagenets, Henry and Edward,
As blameful as the executioner?
Anne: Thou wast the cause, and most accursed effect.
Gloucester: Your beauty was the cause of that effect:
Your beauty, that did haunt me in my sleep
To undertake the death of all the world,
So might I live one hour in your sweet bosom.
Anne: If I thought that, I tell thee, homicide,
These nails should rend that beauty from my cheeks.
Gloucester: These eyes could not endure that beauty's wrack;
You should not blemish it if I stood by.
As all the world is cheered by the sun,
So I by that. It is my day, my life.

Distinguished from this sympathetic portrait of an aggrieved wife and daughter-in-law is Richard's temerity in approaching Lady Anne, whose attendants are carrying the coffin of Henry VI. Richard transforms a lamentable situation to his own advantage and, most shockingly, turns the scene of mourning into an occasion for a marriage proposal. In complete disregard to her invectives against him, Richard abusively orders the pallbearers to stop in their tracks, branding them villains, so that he may speak to Anne. In approaching Anne, Richard is at the height of his powers of trickery and self-aggrandizement. Richard's approach is gentle and his manner that of the courtly lover, a potential reference to the medieval literary convention in which the male suitor adopted various emotional responses to an unattainable and idealized woman. A complex conceit, the court-ly love tradition included certain ritual proclamations on the part of the male suitor, including a highly refined diction, a declaration to the lady that he will be her devoted servant, a spiritual idealization of the woman, a readiness to endure all tests of faithfulness, and a professed lament for unrequited love. The courtly love tradition was an attempt to create a fictive ideal, but in Richard's hand it becomes a parody of the rhetoric of courtship and self-representation. Though Richard professes great love and admiration, claiming to be smitten by Anne's beauty, such assertions are offered only to assuage her rage against him. Once he runs out of rhetorical maneuvers to openly deny his part in killing Edward and Henry VI, Richard exhibits a reckless impropriety in stating that Anne's beauty was the cause of his murderous acts for Edward, who stood in his way. Incredibly, Richard succeeds in persuading Anne of his penitence, and she agrees to marry him. Nevertheless, as soon as Anne exits the stage, Richard exults in his ability to delude and convince her and vows that she will not live long as his queen. Richard is so hopelessly unrepentant that he mocks Anne for being so easily duped by his duplicitous ways and tells the audience that he has no intention of keeping her. "And yet to win her, all the world to nothing! / Ha!" Always with an eye to his own future gain, Richard can never live in the present nor dwell on his past evil deeds, for they would only serve to distract him from his goals. One way of encapsulating Richard's character is to describe it as proleptic in nature, a term for a rhetorical device in which the speaker projects himself into the future and then refers to those events as if they have already taken place.

Act 1, 4, 1–75

Enter Clarence and Keeper
Keeper: Why looks your Grace so heavily to-day?
Clarence: Oh, I have passed a miserable night,
So full of fearful dreams, of ugly sights,
That, as I am a Christian faithful man,
I would not spend another such a night
Though 'twere to buy a world of happy days-
So full of dismal terror was the time.
Keeper: What was your dream, my lord? I pray you tell me.
Clarence: Methoughts that I had broken from the Tower
And was embarked to cross to Burgundy;
And in my company my brother Gloucester,
Who from my cabin tempted me to walk
Upon the hatches. There we looked toward England,
And cited up a thousand heavy times

During the wars of York and Lancaster
That had befall'n us. As we paced along
Upon the giddy footing of the hatches,
Methought that Gloucester stumbled, and in falling
Struck me, that thought to stay him, overboard
Into the tumbling billows of the main.
O Lord, methought what pain it was to drown,
What dreadful noise of waters in my ears,
What sights of ugly death within my eyes
Methoughts I saw a thousand fearful wracks,
A thousand men that fishes gnawed upon,
Wedges of gold, great anchors, heaps of pearl,
Inestimable stones, unvalued jewels,
All scattered in the bottom of the sea.
Some lay in dead men's skulls, and in the holes
Where eyes did once inhabit there were crept,
As 'twere in scorn of eyes, reflecting gems,
That wooed the slimy bottom of the deep
And mocked the dead bones that lay scattered by.
Keeper: Had you such leisure in the time of death
To gaze upon these secrets of the deep?
Clarence: Methought I had; and often did I strive
To yield the ghost, but still the envious flood
Stopped in my soul and would not let it forth
To find the empty, vast, and wandering air;
But smothered it within my panting bulk,
Who almost burst to belch it in the sea.
Keeper: Awaked you not in this sore agony?
Clarence: No, no, my dream was lengthened after life.
Oh, then began the tempest to my soul
I passed, methought, the melancholy flood,
With that sour ferryman which poets write of,
Unto the kingdom of perpetual night.
The first that there did greet my stranger-soul
Was my great father-in-law, renowned Warwick,
Who spake aloud 'What scourge for perjury
Can this dark monarchy afford false Clarence?'
And so he vanished. Then came wandering by
A shadow like an angel, with bright hair
Dabbled in blood, and he shrieked out aloud,
'Clarence is come-false, fleeting, perjur'd Clarence,
That stabbed me in the field by Tewksbury.

Seize on him, Furies, take him unto torment.'
With that, methoughts, a legion of foul fiends
Environed me, and howled in mine ears
Such hideous cries that with the very noise,
I trembling waked, and for a season after
Could not believe but that I was in hell,
Such terrible impression made my dream.
Keeper: No marvel, lord, though it affrighted you.
I am afraid, methinks, to hear you tell it.
Clarence: Ah, keeper, keeper, I have done these things
That now give evidence against my soul
For Edward's sake, and see how he requites me.
O God, if my deep prayers cannot appease thee,
But thou wilt be avenged on my misdeeds,
Yet execute thy wrath in me alone.
Oh, spare my guiltless wife and my poor children.
Keeper, I prithee sit by me awhile;
My soul is heavy, and I fain would sleep.
Keeper: I will, my lord. God give your Grace good rest.
[Clarence sleeps]

Clarence's dream is significant for it provides one of the few instances, besides Margaret's apparent skill at heaping invective against Richard, in which another character demonstrates a position of rhetorical strength. The dream, which relies on prophecy and classical literary conventions in its depiction of the underworld, also succeeds in evoking sympathy for Clarence, for though he is guilty of treason, he is also truly penitent. Unlike Richard's monologues in which he reveals his crimes to the audience only, Clarence confesses his guilt to his jailer, and though he has been tricked into imprisonment in the tower by his evil brother, Clarence nevertheless accepts the punishment he faces for his prior treasonous behavior in the *Henry VI* plays, while expressing concern for the safety of his wife and children. Thus, Clarence's dream has a psychological dimension to the extent that he recognizes his guilty conscience. This is made clear in his introductory remarks to his keeper, as he professes himself "a Christian faithful man" burdened by a terrifying vision of what lies ahead (ll. 1–7) which he begins to recount in vivid and frightful detail.

In lines 9–63, the dream can be analyzed according to four distinct parts: the circumstances surrounding Clarence's falling overboard, his vision of a classical/medieval conception of the underworld, his inability to complete the drowning and thereby end his suffering, and the recognition of his guilty conscience. In the first section, which relates to the "accident" that caused him to fall into the ocean (ll. 9–20), Clarence recalls a childhood voyage he and Richard took to France and reflects on the strife caused by the War of the Roses. In his description of the accident, Clarence attributes it first to faulty construction of the ship and "the giddy footing of the hatches." The use of the word *giddy* applied to an object is both curious and evocative of events to come. In its literal sense, giddiness is an attribute most commonly applied to human beings and portrays the person in question as insane, foolish, or full of rage. This meaning would more aptly describe Richard rather than the wooden planks on which the two men walked. Clarence also seems foolishly deceived into thinking that Richard accidentally sent him overboard. Until his murderers arrive shortly thereafter and convince him that Richard has ordered his execution, Clarence has been pathetically misguided in trusting his brother. Secondly, to be in a state of giddiness can also mean to be confused, possibly dizzy, or about to fall down. Thus, in this second sense, the "giddy hatches" presage or anticipate the mishap that is about to befall Clarence. Instead of escaping civil war, Clarence is headed toward a far worse experience

The second part of the dream (ll. 21–33) offers a terrifying vision of the underworld. Heavily informed by both classical and medieval literary traditions, it introduces notions of conscience, judgment, and the transience of human life. One medieval literary convention consisted of the presentation of images known as *memento mori* or reminders of death (in its Latin translation, "remember to die"). The memento mori were meant to serve as warnings of the inevitability of death and reminders of the meaninglessness of earthly possessions and achievements, while directing the individual's thoughts on the afterlife of the soul. The objects that Clarence finds at the bottom of the ocean serve as a catalog of the types of objects that are consistent with references to memento mori: the empty skulls whose eye sockets are filled by brilliant gems and "wedges of gold," riches of a former lifetime that are now devoid of all value. At the same time, the physical body, without regard to an individual's social or political status, has fully disintegrated and is now mere food for the fish. This underwater vision of hell serves as a derisive statement of the vanity of earthly desires and aspirations.

In response to his keeper's amazement at the amount of time Clarence had to view these visions of hell (ll. 34–41), Clarence presents a scene far more terrifying than the remembrances of death that he has been forced to reflect on. This part of the dream represents a horrifying but unsuccessful attempt to finally complete his drowning and thereby end his suffering. These lines describe a "death-in-life" experience as Clarence, immersed in water, cannot "yield the ghost" and is, instead, kept alive by a malicious force, an "envious flood" that is intent only on providing endless agony. Unable to breathe, the ocean is portrayed as determined to prolong his gradual suffocation, so that his soul will be forced to confront the crimes for which he is about to die.

In the final section of Clarence's dream (ll. 42–75), he is implicitly transported across one of the rivers of the underworld described in classical mythology. Clarence's reference to "that sour ferryman which poets write of" in classical epic poetry implies that Charon, the ill-humored figure from Greek mythology who conveys the souls of the deceased, is transferring Clarence to Hades. Though not stated explicitly, Clarence is referring to traveling across the River Styx. Furthermore, according to mythology, since Clarence is not really dead, he would be doomed to wander along the banks of that river. Most importantly, in this last part of the dream, Clarence is forced to encounter the souls of those he has wronged, his murder of Prince Edward on the field by Tewkesbury and the treason he committed against his father-in-law, Warwick, during the War of the Roses. The avenging Furies of classical mythology, the goddesses of retribution who mercilessly punish all wrongdoers, parade before him with horrifying shrieks.

Act 2, 3, 1–49

[London. A street.]
[*Enter two Citizens meeting*]
First Citizen: Good morrow, neighbour. Whither away so fast?
Second Citizen: I promise you, I scarcely know myself:
Hear you the news abroad?
First Citizen: Ay, that the king is dead.
Second Citizen: Ill news, by'r Lady; seldom comes the better.
I fear, I fear 'twill prove a giddy world.
[*Enter another* [third] *Citizen*]
Third Citizen: Neighbours, God speed.
First Citizen: Give you good morrow, sir.
Third Citizen: Doth this news hold of good King Edward's death?
Second Citizen: Ay, sir, it is too true; God help the while.
Third Citizen: Then, masters, look to see a troublous world.
First Citizen: No, no, by God's good grace his son shall reign.
Third Citizen: Woe to the land that's governed by a child.
Second Citizen: In him there is a hope of government,
That in his nonage, council under him,
And in his full and ripened years, himself,
No doubt shall then, and till then, govern well.
First Citizen: So stood the state when Henry the Sixth
Was crowned in Paris but at nine months old.
Third Citizen: Stood the state so? No, no, good friends, God wot;
For then this land was famously enriched
With politic grave counsel. Then the king
Had virtuous uncles to protect his grace.
First Citizen: Why, so hath this, both by the father and mother.

Third Citizen: Better it were they all came by his father,
Or by his father there were none at all.
For emulation who shall now be nearest,
Will touch us all too near, if God prevent not.
Oh, full of danger is the Duke of Gloucester,
And the queen's sons and brothers haught and proud:
And were they to be ruled, and not to rule,
This sickly land might solace as before.
First Citizen: Come, come, we fear the worst; all shall be well.
Third Citizen: When clouds are see, wise men put on their cloaks;
When great leaves fall, the winter is at hand;
When the sun sets, who doth not look for night?
Untimely storms make men expect a dearth.
All may be well, but if God sort it so,
'Tis more than we deserve or I expect.
Second Citizen: Truly, the souls of men are full of fear.
You cannot reason almost with a man
That looks not heavily and full of dread.
Third Citizen: Before the days of change, still is it so.
By a divine instinct, men's minds mistrust
Ensuing danger; as by proof, we see
The water swell before a boisterous storm.
But leave it all to God. Whither away?
Second Citizen: Marry, we were sent for to the justices.
Third Citizen: And so was I: I'll bear you company.

Act 2, scene 3 is a unique choral scene within the context of *Richard III*, the presentation of the unified "voice," a feature derived from Greek drama and characteristic of Elizabethan drama as well in which the chorus functioned as a commentator on events in the play. In Shakespeare's time, the chorus was comprised of ordinary people, not professional actors. While on the surface it may appear to be a distraction from the main plot, introducing flat character types that are distinguished by numbers rather than names, this scene realizes several objectives. In a play almost wholly consumed by affairs at court and the infighting among aristocratic factions, this scene allows ordinary citizens to express, from a distance, their opinions concerning current political events and debate among themselves as to the possible outcome. In fashioning this scene, Shakespeare also creates an opportunity for expressing aspects of the Elizabethan worldview, referred to by scholars as "the Great Chain of Being." This notion rested on the existence of a hierarchical universe, structured according to divine plan and that governed human nature and all of creation. Within this enormous interconnected network, each link, animal, plant, or human, was endowed with specific intellectual and physical capabilities and ranked above or below the other link based on these criteria. Humans, of course, were at the apex of God's earthly creation and thus granted ultimate authority to rule over lesser creatures and forms of life, while spiritual beings, such as angels, ranked higher. Ultimately, this notion of a chain of being sought to impose order on the world with God's love as its ultimate source. At the same time, this conception of a rational world served as a moral imperative for humans to understand their responsibility in maintaining the harmonious functioning of God's plan. These beliefs form the background of the discussion amongst the three citizens.

The First and Second Citizens, trusting in God's plan, are hopeful that young Prince Edward will assume the throne and peace will be restored to the realm. Recognizing that the prince is too young to rule, the Second Citizen prays that good counselors will be in control until Edward comes of age. However, the Third Citizen does not share in their optimism and, instead, given that Richard is at the helm, sees only a grim outcome for the current instability. The most eloquent of the three interlocutors, the Third Citizen renders a bleak portrait of a general malaise infecting the kingdom, referring to England as "this sickly land." He states that the dire consequences of Richard's power will be like the "onset of winter." This prediction then serves as a reflection on and counterstatement to Richard's opening soliloquy in which the tyrant laments the transformation of civil war into a summer of peacetime entertainment and happiness. Thus, this scene serves as a reminder that many more people, well beyond Richard's immediate circle, are adversely affected by his tyrannical quest for power.

Finally, a close reading of the three Citizens' various descriptions of the political situation demonstrates how closely connected the scene is to the events that have taken place in *Richard III*, especially in the way their choice of words mirrors Clarence's dream and eventual execution. While the First Citizen comments on the "giddy world" in which they live, reminiscent of the "giddy hatches" that caused Clarence to fall overboard, the Third Citizen refers to their perilous political situation as one in which waters "swell before a boisterous storm." Once again, we are reminded of Clarence's horrific nightmare of drowning and Richard's bloodthirsty, "giddy" madness in pursuit of absolute power.

Act 3, 1, 60–94

Prince Edward: Good lords, make all the speedy haste you may
Say, uncle Gloucester, if our brother come,
Where shall we sojourn till our coronation?
Richard: Where it seems best unto your royal self.
If I may counsel you, some day or two
Your highness shall repose you at the Tower:

Then where you please, and shall be thought most fit
For your best health and recreation.
Prince Edward: I do not like the Tower, of any place.
Did Julius Caesar build that place, my lord?
Buckingham: He did, my gracious lord, begin that place;
Which, since, succeeding ages have re-edified.
Prince Edward: Is it upon record, or else reported
Successively from age to age, he built it?
Buckingham: Upon record, my gracious lord.
Prince Edward: But say, my lord, it were not registered,
Methinks the truth should live from age to age,
As 'twere retailed to all posterity,
Even to the general all-ending day.
Richard: [Aside]
So wise so young, they say, do never live long.
Prince Edward: What say you, uncle?
Richard: I say, without characters, fame lives long.
[Aside] Thus, like the formal vice, Iniquity,
I moralize two meanings in one word.
Prince Edward: That Julius Caesar was a famous man;
With what his valour did enrich his wit,
His wit set down to make his valour live.
Death makes no conquest of this conqueror;
For now he lives in fame, though not in life.
I'll tell you what, my cousin Buckingham.
Buckingham: What, my gracious lord?
Prince Edward: And if I live until I be a man,
I'll win our ancient right in France again,
Or die a soldier, as I lived a king.
Gloucester: [Aside]
Short summers lightly have a forward spring.

The dialogue that begins between the duplicitous Richard and his young
nephew, Prince Edward, the rightful heir to the throne, is highly ironic and,
at the same time, highlights some important themes and conventions that
Shakespeare was referencing and transforming in his work. The conversation
also provides a convenient interval of time in which Hastings and the cardinal,
at Richard's direction, set out to seize the prince's brother, the young duke of
York, from his lawful sanctuary. When Richard announces to Prince Edward
his intention to keep him and his brother in the tower for their own well-being
until the coronation, Edward demonstrates a precocious insight not only into
the history of the Tower but the foundations of historical reputation. The young

prince proves himself a worthy opponent to both Richard and his henchman, Buckingham, by questioning whether Julius Caesar was the tower's architect. By raising this doubt, Edward displays an impressive knowledge of the way in which fiction can be transformed into historical reality through time and the repetition of distorted facts. Buckingham quickly responds to Edward by explaining that Caesar, indeed, built the tower and that succeeding centuries "re-edified" this impressive structure. The use of the word *re-edify* serves as a pun, for while it denotes the construction of a building, it also refers to the process by which something is imaginatively invented. Furthermore, the word can also signify something that serves to inform, instruct, or even provide moral improvement. With respect to Richard and Buckingham's unscrupulous natures, the multiple ironies are obvious. Finally, in stating that later ages have "re-edified" the tower, Buckingham is implicitly stating that both he and Richard invent and propogate myths and specious lies in order to manipulate and deceive others. Shakespeare, along with his vainglorious Buckingham, would have been well aware of the myth that had accrued in regard to Julius Caesar as architect of the tower.

The construction of the tower dates to 1078 during the reign of William the Conqueror, and it was originally intended to be an awe-inspiring demonstration of his power to the people of London. The structure had been strategically placed between the Thames River and the ancient Roman wall that then surrounded the city. During the reigns of Elizabeth I and James I, the majesty of the tower was promoted by associating it with Julius Caesar. By making that link, the English monarchy was attempting to capitalize on Caesar's reputation as a powerful political leader. As Kristin Deiter points out in *The Tower of London in English Renaissance Drama*, an increasingly elaborate myth evolved regarding Caesar as the tower's architect, and this myth, in turn, became an important feature in English history plays of the 1590s. Thus, Prince Edward's insistence on debating the point with Buckingham and questioning the existence of documentary proof not only calls into question the myth of the tower but also transforms the issue at hand into a debate on the nature of posthumous fame. The young prince utters one of the play's most ironic observations in noting that, while Caesar's courageous deeds will ensure his exalted place in history, "With what his valour did enrich his wit, / His wit set down to make his valour live / Death makes no conquest of this conqueror," Richard's strivings will seal forever his monstrous reputation.

Act 4, 4, 1–135

[*Enter* old Queen Margaret]
Queen Margaret: So now prosperity begins to mellow
And drop into the rotten mouth of death.
Here in these confines slyly have I lurked,

To watch the waning of mine enemies.
A dire induction am I witness to,
And will to France, hoping the consequence
Will prove as bitter, black, and tragical.
Withdraw thee, wretched Margaret: who comes here?
[*Enter* Queen Elizabeth and the Duchess of York]
Queen Elizabeth: Ah, my young princes! Ah, my tender babes!
My unblown flowers, new-appearing sweets!
If yet your gentle souls fly in the air
And be not fixed in doom perpetual,
Hover about me with your airy wings
And hear your mother's lamentation!
Queen Margaret: [*Aside.*] Hover about her; say, that right for right
Hath dimmed your infant morn to agèd night.
Duchess of York: So many miseries have crazed my voice
That my woe-wearied tongue is still and mute.
Edward Plantagenet, why art thou dead?
Queen Margaret: [*Aside.*] Plantagenet doth quit Plantagenet;
Edward for Edward pays a dying debt.
Queen Elizabeth: Wilt thou, O God, fly from such gentle lambs
And throw them in the entrails of the wolf?
When didst thou sleep when such a deed was done?
Queen Margaret: [*Aside.*] When holy Harry died, and my sweet son.
Duchess of York: Dead life, blind sight, poor mortal living ghost;
Woe's scene, world's shame, grave's due by life usurped;
Brief abstract and recòrd of tedious days,
Rest thy unrest on England's lawful earth,
Unlawfully made drunk with innocent blood.
Queen Elizabeth: Ah, that thou wouldst as soon afford a grave
As thou canst yield a melancholy seat.
Then would I hide my bones, not rest them here.
Ah, who hath any cause to mourn but I?
Queen Margaret: If ancient sorrow be most reverend,
Give mine the benefit of seniory,
And let my griefs frown on the upper hand,
If sorrow can admit society.
I had an Edward, till a Richard killed him;
I had a husbabd, till a Richard killed him.
Thou hadst an Edward, till a Richard killed him;
Thou hadst a Richard, till a Richard killed him.
Duchess of York: I had a Richard too, and thou didst kill him;
I had a Rutland too, thou holp'st to kill him.

Queen Margaret: Thou hadst a Clarence too,
And Richard killed him.
From forth the kennel of thy womb hath crept
A hell-hound that doth hunt us all to death:
That dog, that had his teeth before his eyes,
To worry lambs and lap their gentle blood,
That foul defacer of God's handiwork
That reigns in gallèd eyes of weeping souls,
That excellent grand tyrant of the earth
Thy womb let loose to chase us to our graves.
O upright, just, and true-disposing God,
How do I thank thee, that this carnal cur
Preys on the issue of his mother's body
And makes her pew-fellow with others' moan.
Duchess of York: O Harry's wife, triumph not in my woes.
God witness with me, I have wept for thine.
Queen Margaret: Bear with me. I am hungry for revenge,
And now I cloy me with beholding it.
Thy Edward he is dead, that killed my Edward;
Thy other Edward dead to quit my Edward;
Young York he is but boot, because both they
Matched not the high perfection of my loss.
Thy Clarence he is dead that stabbed my Edward,
And the beholders of this tragic play,
Th'adulterate Hastings, Rivers, Vaughan, Grey,
Untimely smothered in their dusky graves.
Richard yet lives, hell's black intelligencer,
Only reserved their factor, to buy souls
And send them thither. But at hand, at hand
Ensues his piteous and unpitied end.
Earth gapes, hell burns, fiends roar, saints pray.
To have him suddenly conveyed from hence.
Cancel his bond of life, dear God, I pray,
That I may live to say the dog is dead.
Queen Elizabeth: Oh, thou didst prophesy the time would come
That I should wish for thee to help me curse
That bottled spider, that foul bunch-backed toad!
Queen Margaret: I called thee then vain flourish of my fortune;
I called thee then poor shadow, painted queen,
The presentation of but what I was,
The flattering index of a direful pageant,
One heaved a-high, to be hurled down below,

A mother only mocked with two fair babes,
A dream of what thou wast, a garish flag
To be the aim of every dangerous shot,
A sign of dignity, a breath, a bubble,
A queen in jest, only to fill the scene.
Where is thy husband now? Where be thy brothers?
Where are thy two sons? Wherein dost thou joy?
Who sues to thee and kneels and says 'God save the queen'?
Where be the bending peers that flattered thee?
Where be the thronging troops that followed thee?
Decline all this, and see what now thou art:
For happy wife, a most distressèd widow;
For joyful mother, one that wails the name;
For one being sued to, one that humbly sues;
For queen, a very caitiff crowned with care;
For she that scorned at me, now scorned of me;
For she being feared of all, now fearing one;
For she commanding all, obeyed of none.
Thus hath the course of justice whirled about
And left thee but a very prey to time,
Having no more but thought of what thou wast,
To torture thee the more, being what thou art.
Thou didst usurp my place, and dost thou not
Usurp the just proportion of my sorrow?
Now thy proud neck bears half my burdened yoke,
From which even here I slip my wearied head
And leave the burden of it all on thee.
Farewell, York's wife, and queen of sad mischance.
These English woes will make me smile in France.
Queen Elizabeth: O thou well skilled in curses, stay awhile,
And teach me how to curse mine enemies.
Queen Margaret: Forbear to sleep the nights, and fast the day;
Compare dead happiness with living woe;
Think that thy babes were sweeter than they were,
And he that slew them fouler than he is.
Bett'ring thy loss makes the bad causer worse:
Revolving this will teach thee how to curse.
Queen Elizabeth: My words are dull; O, quicken them with thine.
Queen Margaret: Thy woes will make them sharp, and pierce like mine.

This lengthy scene marks the avenging Margaret's return to the action since
act 1, scene 3. Her reappearance in act 4 begins with a soliloquy delivered

while she lurks in the background, unbeknownst to Queen Elizabeth and the duchess of York who enter after Margaret's initial eight lines. This scene is significant in that Margaret serves a twofold purpose. She not only fulfills her mission or function as Richard's nemesis, she is also able to bond with the other aggrieved women as they become unified in their purpose and intent. In her opening soliloquy, old Queen Margaret already announces that her task is beginning to wind down, as her "prosperity begins to mellow," for she has witnessed the elimination of so many former adversaries except for Ricard, the most wicked one of all. Having watched the fulfillment of the retribution that she has set in motion, Margaret is already planning her departure from the stage. She will return to France and back into the pages of history from which Shakespeare plucked her, praying for the final destruction of Richard.

After listening to the lamentations of the duchess of York and Queen Elizabeth (ll. 9–35), Margaret makes her presence known to them by protesting that, of the three women, she has been the one most afflicted. She adds that, if her losses are unconvincing, she will claim precedence over their grievances by virtue of her venerable old age. "If ancient sorrow be most reverend, / Give mine the benefit of seniory." Nevertheless, the contest of victimization continues at length among the three women, with Margaret hurling accusations at the duchess for having given birth to a "hell-hound." She taunts Queen Elizabeth with the prospect that she will lose her royal status, "the flattering index of a direful pageant," as well as other horrible misfortunes. Elizabeth is made to bear the brunt of Margaret's jealousy and hatred for the loss of her own regal stature. Margaret implies that she is numb and exhausted from the many bloody prophesies that have come to fruition. "I am hungry for revenge, / And now I cloy me with beholding it." Her last wish is to live long enough to see Richard dead.

Her mission all but complete, Margaret is finally open to reconciliation with Queen Elizabeth and the duchess of York. When Elizabeth asks for her instruction in the art of putting a curse on another, Margaret readily prescribes a regimen of physical deprivation and obsessive contemplation of the wrongs she has suffered by Richard's hand, counseling that revenge is achieved through exaggeration or extremity: "Bett'ring thy loss makes the bad causer worse: / Revolving this will teach thee how to curse." Promising Elizabeth success, Margaret makes her final exit. As some critics have pointed out, this final bonding of the women affords them a degree of equality with Richard who has, up until this point in the play, denigrated and disempowered them. Thus, this scene signals a crucial turning point in Richard's fortunes in that it serves as a prelude to his final downfall and presages the peace and harmony that will be reestablished with the crowning of Henry VII at the end of act 5.

Act 5, 3, 180–223

King Richard III: Give me another horse! Bind up my wounds!
Have mercy, Jesu! Soft, I did but dream.
O coward conscience, how dost thou afflict me?
The lights burn blue. It is now dead midnight.
Cold, fearful drops stand on my trembling flesh.
What? Do I fear myself? There's none else by.
Richard loves Richard, that is, I am I.
Is there a murderer here? No. Yes, I am.
Then fly. What, from myself? Great reason why:
Lest I revenge. What, myself upon myself?
Alack, I love myself. Wherefore? For any good
That I myself have done unto myself?
Oh, no. Alas, I rather hate myself
For hateful deeds committed by myself.
I am a villain. Yet I lie, I am not.
Fool, of thyself speak well. Fool, do not flatter.
My conscience hath a thousand several tongues,
And every tongue brings in a several tale,
And every tale condemns me for a villain.
Perjury in the highest degree,
Murder, stern murder, in the direst degree,
All several sins, all used in each degree,
Throng all to th'bar, crying all, 'Guilty! guilty!'
I shall despair. There is no creature loves me,
And if I die no soul shall pity me.
Nay, wherefore should they, since that I myself
Find in myself no pity to myself?
Methought the souls of all that I had murdered
Came to my tent, and every one did threat
Tomorrow's vengeance on the head of Richard.
[*Enter* Ratcliff]
Ratcliff: My lord.
King Richard III: Who's there?
Ratcliff: Ratcliff, my lord, 'tis I. The early village-cock
Hath twice done salutation to the morn.
Your friends are up and buckle on their armour.
King Richard III: O Ratcliff, I fear, I fear.
Ratcliff: Nay, good my lord, be not afraid of shadows.

King Richard III: By the apostle Paul, shadows tonight
Have struck more terror to the soul of Richard
Than can the substance of ten thousand soldiers
Armèd in proof and led by shallow Richmond.
'Tis not yet near day. Come, go with me.
Under our tents I'll play the eaves-dropper,
To hear if any mean to shrink from me.

Act 5, scene 3 is the climax of *Richard III*. Given that the scene opens with Richard's camp on Bosworth Field the night before the final battle, it is important to keep in mind what precedes the preceding passage, namely that Richard initially exhibits the same bravura and defiance that has defined his character from the start. Likening himself to the Tower of London, that impenetrable fortress to which he has consigned so many of his victims, Richard exhorts his men to make preparations for war. However, Richard's defiance comes to an abrupt halt with the terrifying nightmare to which he is subjected the evening before his final battle, when the ghosts of his victims return to recount the details of their execution, bidding him to remember them as he faces his final defeat the next morning. As a result of these tortuous visions, Richard awakens trembling and afraid.

Another significant aspect of the passage is that, rather than taking violent action against a perceived adversary, Richard is here left to hold court with himself, weighing the incriminating evidence of his bloody deeds and treasonous acts. For the first time and so close to the end, Richard manifests an ability to reflect and look within himself. Though he attempts to resist self-condemnation by stating that he loves himself, his efforts at exculpation are doomed to failure as he is ultimately forced to confront his guilty conscience. In asking whether he fears himself since there is no one else present to threaten him, Richard arrives at an answer that he has not previously offered with respect to his own being. Though he states that "Richard loves Richard, that is, I am I," he nevertheless contradicts himself in the next line. "Is there a murderer here? No. Yes, I am." Thus, Shakespeare presents a schism or split in Richard's personality, as his former skills at fashioning "ironclad" arguments no longer work when applied to himself alone. He has now become his own victim and is compelled to finally admit the possibility that he hates himself, as he openly declares that he must stop indulging in self-praise and stands instead self-accused. Furthermore, Richard recognizes what his existence has been from his opening soliloquy up until now, namely that of a man isolated from all others, a pariah who has chosen to live outside the boundaries of humanity while desperately trying to maintain his control over his world. As a result of this debate within himself, Richard must finally accept his terrible fate, for no one will mourn his death and he will leave behind a regrettable chronicle of his reign. The justice and retribution that Margaret and his victims have devoutly wished for all along are about to be realized. Though Richard will rally his courage one more time before the battle as he speaks to Ratcliffe of his unvanquished courage, his former arrogance has nevertheless been permanently altered if not replaced. No longer the presumptuous and usurping ruler of his former days, Richard's final defeat on Bosworth Field is imminent.

CRITICISM THROUGH THE AGES

RICHARD III IN THE SEVENTEENTH CENTURY
❧

Shakespeare's *Richard III* was written sometime between 1593 and 1594 and builds on events related in the play that serves as its prequel, *Henry VI, Part 3,* which is believed to have been written around 1592. *Richard III* is the conclusion of Shakespeare's tetralogy on the civil strife known as the War of the Roses, a thirty-two-year conflict that began in 1455 when Richard III's father—Richard, duke of York—challenged Henry VI's sovereignty. In 1461, Richard's son, Edward IV, became king and ruled for nine years until Henry VI, who had previously fled, returned and briefly regained the throne in 1470. Edward IV soon prevailed, however, and when he died, Richard, duke of Gloucester (later Richard III), became regent until the young Edward V was old enough to assume the throne. While Richard presided over this protectorate government, both of Edward IV's sons mysteriously disappeared, an event that enabled Richard III to declare himself king. As to the name War of the Roses, Renaissance writers linked the House of York (Richard III's sphere) with a white rose and the opposing House of Lancaster with a red rose.

Unlike some of Shakespeare's great tragedies, such as *Macbeth*, there are no eyewitness accounts of *Richard III*'s earliest performances. It is possible that Shakespeare wrote and acted for a theater company known as the Lord Strange's Men and that *Richard III* may have been among the plays performed prior to 1594. However, based on the 1597 title page of the first Quarto, *Richard III* was presented by the Lord Chamberlain's Men, one of the two leading London theater companies at the time. *Richard III* is reported to have been popular with Elizabethan audiences, based on the fact that it was reprinted in 1597, 1598, and 1602, in addition to the many brief references to the play by various contemporary commentators. As early as 1595, John Weever, an English poet, wrote of the "honie-ton'g Shakespeare," believed to be an allusion to the character of Richard III, while Francis Meres's 1598 volume, *Palladis Tamia*, considered to be an important primary document, praised *Richard III* as one of several Shakespearean tragedies written in the Senecan tradition.

In writing *Richard III*, Shakespeare used a variety of historical sources. Chief among them are Sir Thomas More's 1513 historical account, titled the *History of King Richard the Thirde*, a work that influenced Edward Hall's 1550 work, *The Union of the two noble and illustre families of Lancastre and Yorke* and, in turn, influenced Holinshed's *Chronicles of England, Scotland and Ireland*, written in 1587. Thus, Thomas More's *History* is recognized as the essential historical authority for Shakespeare, a work that has set into motion a contentious critical debate from the earliest Shakespearean commentators onward as to whether Richard III was actually the horribly deformed monster and arch villain that More presented. Though today it is widely believed that the vilification of Richard III, as to both his character and his competence as a ruler, were deliberate misrepresentations intended to augment the reputation of his successor, Henry VII, Shakespeare's *Richard III* has had its defenders from the seventeenth century onward. Sir William Cornwallis takes great exception to the libelous misrepresentation of Richard's character and leadership abilities in both Shakespeare and the chroniclers, accusing them of a malice. William Winstanley echoes those same sentiments in attributing jealousy to Richard's detractors.

Finally, as discussed in detail by the critics contained in this volume, Shakespeare drew on a wide range of literary conventions, both classical and medieval, as well as absorbed influences from other playwrights of his day. Thus, although Shakespeare wrote what is classified as a history play, he was not a historian but a brilliant and uniquely imaginative artist who experimented with a multitude of sources to create a work far advanced for his time. In his representation of the superhuman intellect of his arch villain, Shakespeare created a complex human character who fascinates us with his audacious wit and disarming sense of humor while, at the same time, plotting and carrying out heinous acts and, perhaps in some small measure, even succeeding in eliciting a sympathetic understanding for his pathological behavior. The quotation, in this section, from Christopher Brooke's poem pays tribute to the enduring charm and enchantment of Shakespeare's artistry in *Richard III*.

Colley Cibber's *Tragical History of King Richard III*, written in 1699, emerged as one of the most noteworthy responses to Shakespeare's play at the close of the seventeenth century. In that same year, Cibber, a noted theater manager, actor, and playwright, made a disastrous attempt to stage the play at Drury Lane. Apparently, the master of revels, a position that required the overseeing of royal festivities and controlling the content of plays, censored the entire first act, which Cibber had completely revised. As stated in John Jowett's introduction to Shakespeare's *Richard III*, the master of revels was afraid that the depiction of Henry VI would somehow evoke sympathy in the audience for the deposed and now deceased James II. When his play was published in 1700, in its entirety, Cibber included a short note on this incident and highlighted with italics and quotation marks all those parts of his play that remained faithful to Shakespeare. Ironically, despite its inauspicious beginnings, Colley Cibber's melodramatic adaptation proved a success and formed the basis for all performances in the eighteenth century until the version was finally challenged in the nineteenth century. Cibber apparently had shrewdly observed some of the problems with Shakespeare's play such as the need to shorten the text to about half its original size. He also radically altered other parts, while utilizing fewer than 800 lines from Shakespeare. Among Cibber's revisions were the infamous first act, which focused on Richard's early evildoings (events born almost completely of Cibber's imagination); an abbreviated version of Richard's opening soliloquy; the deletion of the colorful Queen Margaret, which removed the presence of one of Richard's most virulent enemies; the removal of the scenes surrounding Clarence's murder and Hastings's arrest; and a reduction in the number of ghosts featured in Richard's nightmare. Finally, instead of the rhetorical virtuosity and superior intellect in Shakespeare's characterization of Richard III, Cibber transforms his protagonist into a far less complex villain.

1614—Christopher Brooke. From
The Ghost of Richard the Third

To him that impt my fame with Clio's quill, Whose magick rais'd me from oblivion's den; That writ my storie on the Muses hill, And with my actions dignifi'd his pen: He that from Helicon sends many a rill, Whose nectared veines, are drunke by thirstie men; Crown'd be his stile with fame, his head with bayes; And none detract, but gratulate his praise.

1617—William Cornwallis. From
Essays of Certaine Paradoxes

Sir William Cornwallis (1579–1614) was an early English essayist. He is the author of *Essayes of Certaine Paradoxes* (1617), which contains the *Encomium on Richard III* and *Discourses upon Seneca the Tragedian* (1601).

Malicious credulitie rather embraceth the partiall writings of indiscreet chroniclers, and witty Play-Makers, then his [Richard III's] lawes and actions, the most innocent and impartiall witnesses.

* * *

Yet neither can his blood redeem him [Richard III] from injurious tongues, nor the reproach offered his body be thought cruell enough, but that we must stil make him more cruelly infamous in Pamphlets and Plays.

1684—William Winstanley. "The Life of King Richard the Third," from *England's Worthies*

Winstanley (1628?–98) was considered a speculative writer who was also a pioneer of biographical and bibliographic research. He is the author of *Lives of the Most Famous English Poets* (1687) and *The Protestant Almanack for the Year from the Incarnation of Jesus Christ 1682, from Our Deliverance from Popery by Queen Elizabeth* (1682).

But as Honour is always attended on by Envy, so hath this worthy Princes fame been blasted by malicious traducers, who like *Shakespear* in his Play of him, render him dreadfully black in his actions, a monster of nature, rather than a man of admirable parts; whose slanders having been examined by wise and moderate men, they have only found malice and ignorance to have been his greatest accusers, persons who can onely lay suspition to his charge; and suspition in Law is no more guilt than imagination.

RICHARD III IN THE EIGHTEENTH CENTURY

The eighteenth century marked both the beginning and the burgeoning of Shakespeare studies and criticism. The first standard collected edition of Shakespeare's plays was produced by Nicholas Rowe (1709). This was followed by the editions of Alexander Pope (1725), Lewis Theobald (1734), Samuel Johnson (1765–58), George Steevens (1773 and 1778), and many others. Rowe's edition is significant in that it also provided a biography of Shakespeare, using the scant information available, some of dubious reliability, concerning Shakespeare's life.

The eighteenth century has also been commonly referred to as the neoclassical age, a description that is true only in the general sense that it held a reverence for and observance of the rules for dramatic writing as set forth by ancient writers, in particular Aristotle. Aristotle's so-called "unities," as interpreted by eighteenth-century critics, decreed that plays should observe the unities of time (occur within a single day), place (happen in one particular setting), and action (have one plot and no subplots). In his critique of *Richard III*, Voltaire renders an unfavorable evaluation of Shakespeare's disregard for these classical precepts. However, more specifically with respect to *Richard III* and its classical antecedents, Shakespeare's play has been consistently identified as heavily influenced by the tragedies of the Roman philosopher and dramatist Lucius Annaeus Seneca (3 B.C.–65 A.D.). Seneca has been described by recent scholars as being postclassical, employing a pattern of five-act plays that begin with an expository monologue or prologue scene. Considered to be far more pessimistic than the Greek tragedians, Seneca's tragedies are marked by a flamboyant rhetoric, a discontinuity of action with unanswered speeches and inexplicable exits, and a chorus that is either absent or merely witnesses dialogue, collective characteristics that have led scholars to believe that his plays were not meant for the stage. Most important to *Richard III* are the dark elements of Senecan tragedy, which are concerned with the dire consequences of uncontrollable passions and the resulting destruction wrought on humanity and nature. His writings are also replete with violent plots, including ghosts and supernatural incidents. Ultimately, Seneca was interested in the triumph of good over evil, and his plays were especially attractive to late sixteenth-century English dramatists.

With respect to the eighteenth century's evaluation of *Richard III*, it is worth noting that there is far less commentary at this time than exists for the later tragedies, such as *Macbeth*; still, a number of commentaries exist that compare Richard's character to Macbeth's. Likewise, the eighteenth century exhibits an equal proportion of praise and blame for what Shakespeare achieved and/or failed to accomplish in this early history play. The earliest evaluation of *Richard III* revolves around a fascination with an otherwise villainous character, as indicated by Richard Steele. Steele describes an experience one evening when, in a somewhat melancholy mood, he decided to read the play as a distraction, only to find himself steeped even further in disturbing thoughts, especially after reading Richard's nightmare scene on the eve of his fatal battle at Bosworth Field. Though praising Shakespeare's highly imaginative presentation of Richard as he is finally forced to confront all the death and destruction he has wrought, Steele expresses his appreciation for the poet in creating a character both terrifying and fascinating at the same time. Steele's emotional response to Richard's character leaves him with a mind filled with "a very agreeable horror," as he enumerates the procession of ghosts that parade before the tyrant, uttering the dire prophecies of his imminent demise. Steele seems to have captured the essence of what is both repugnant yet fascinating in Shakespeare's imaginative construction of Richard's reign of terror and, in so doing, identifies an area of critical analysis that extended to present scholarly studies. Though Steele is enamored of Richard's speech upon awaking from his nightmare, he is rendered incapable of reading any more that evening and instead indulges in a meditation on kingship.

Steele's essay is followed by Voltaire's attack on Shakespeare for his deliberate overturning of the time-honored dramatic tradition of the unities of time and place. The French author also faults the bard for certain seemingly incomprehensible characters. Voltaire attacks *Richard III* as inferior to Pierre Corneille's *Cinna* (which takes place in ancient Rome but is concerned with the age of Louis XIV and contains ideas regarding the institution of royal power over the nobility). Above all considerations, however, Voltaire takes great exception to the implausibility of Richard's wooing of Queen Anne. Rather that seeing the scene as one example among many of Richard's superb rhetorical skills, as later critics will acknowledge, Voltaire finds Anne's weakness in succumbing to Richard's false flattery to be utterly repugnant and concludes his evaluation of the play on a note of dismay. Voltaire finds it incomprehensible that a culture that could have produced an esteemed intellect such as Sir Isaac Newton, an advanced mathematician and scientist who contributed important work in the field of optics and gravitational force, could also have such high regard for such reprehensible characters.

Horace Walpole's essay is significant in that it is an early formulation of serious questions about the veracity or factual accuracy of Shakespeare's sources for *Richard III* as well as his dramatic reinterpretation of those sources. Walpole's book, *Historic Doubts on the Life and Reign of King Richard the Third*, is an early example of the perennial questioning of the historical accuracy of Shakespeare's play and the sources on which he relied. In the selection included here, Walpole's comments on the legend that developed concerning Richard's physical deformity. While it is true that one of Richard's shoulders was higher than the other, Walpole attributes his monstrosity to political interests, the passage of centuries, and the consequent fiction of physical disfigurement and ugliness that has accrued through time. Walpole bases his understanding of Richard's physiognomy on a drawing he purchased of Richard and his queen, in which the monarch reveals a "comely" face. He also cites a portrait he has seen in a book titled *Royal and Noble Authors.*

With respect to Richard III's moral character, Elizabeth Griffith's essay views the play as the ultimate triumph of good over evil. However, unlike Steele, Griffith is disturbed by the fact that Shakespeare has fashioned such a malevolent character who nevertheless can disarm us with his wit and humor. As the title of her book indicates Elizabeth Griffith's intention is to articulate Shakespeare's particular moral teaching in *Richard III*, the ultimate triumph of virtue over Richard's villainy. Focusing on select scenes, Griffith traces the way in which the audience's attention is at first captivated through a heightened tension between war and peace and a repugnance toward the malice Richard proposes in his opening soliloquy through his final self-censuring soliloquy when he is compelled to confront his tormented conscience, an indication that good will soon triumph over evil. Nevertheless, she admits that Richard succeeds in seducing us through his innate optimism and sense of humor, which she sees as an essential flaw, indeed an absurdity, in the presentation of so malevolent a being. As to some of the particular vices presented over the course of the play, Griffith notes that we are being warned against the pitfalls of relying on malicious gossip and human vulnerability in accepting the report of malingerers. The play, she suggests, also cautions about the danger of being seduced by the "vanity of ambition." In essence, Griffith states that Shakespeare's intention in *Richard III* is to advocate piety and acceptance of God's plan for our lives, noting that the exchange between the three citizens in act 2, scene 4 is an acknowledgement of God's providence. She also makes a point of noting that, since Shakespeare did not live in the distressing world of Richard III, he is writing from a philosophical, meditative standpoint rather than from direct experience of the turmoil he attempts to portray. Griffith's commentary also contains some telling remarks about Shakespeare's use of historical sources, including her observation that the representation of women as frail and vulnerable is actually the poet's "yield[ing] too easy a credence to a fictitious piece of history which rested upon no better authority than the fame that affirmed the deformity of Richard."

William Richardson's essay takes an opposing position to Griffith's, in that he can find no moral center in *Richard III*, his major complaint being the ambiguity that results from presenting a figure of evil who nevertheless captivates the audience with his superhuman intellect. His essay on *Richard III* is essentially a complaint about the work's lack of a clear moral center. In a play in which Richard's character dominates all others, Richardson argues that our attention is riveted on a figure whose deformity, which incorporates every vice that could be attached to a human being, is compensated for by a supreme intelligence. Thus, rather than presenting the audience with a dramatic composition that seeks to present a lesson in virtue, Shakespeare has fashioned a character and indeed an entire play in which the horrifying traits of the protagonist are diminished by his superior skills in language and brilliant manipulations of those around him. Richardson's chief complaint, therefore, is that Richard's heinous actions do not serve as a yardstick by which others may measure their own lives; rather, they serve to highlight the crimes he commits since the other characters themselves lack moral clarity. Moreover, Richardson argues that this lack of moral clarity is attributable to various deficiencies of representation in such characters as Clarence and Edward who are weak, while Richmond, who has the potential to provide the audience with proper moral instruction, is relatively unseen until the final act where his actions are essentially remote and reported on rather than observed. In sum, because Richard III possesses a hypnotic charm despite it being completely devoid of humanity, Richardson faults Shakespeare in having presented an ambiguous character, one who simultaneously delights and unsettles the audience, so that we are left confused, in a state of "unusual agitation, neither painful nor pleasant." For Shakespeare's imbuing a villain like Richard III with any admirable character traits, Richardson feels great indignation.

Finally, by comparing Richard to the later and more ethically complex character of Macbeth, a man of virtue who tragically succumbs to evil influences, Thomas Whately's essay provides a more in-depth analysis of Richard's character, a villain from start to finish, who merely seeks to revenge himself on a world that has greatly wronged him. In order to accentuate the opposing moral and ethical premises in the characterization of Richard III and Macbeth, Thomas Whately begins his evaluation by pointing out the similarities in their respective situations. Thus, he is able to heighten the reader's awareness of the vast gulf that exists between a fundamental villain who delights in the carnage he engineers and a man of honor who first struggles with and then succumbs to temptation, before becoming a party to violent deeds. As to Richard and Macbeth's similarities, both are soldiers, both are ambitious, and both achieve and then lose the throne through violence, deceit, and treason. While the two protagonists' circumstances are comparable, however, their motives and propensities for committing crime as well as their responses after the bloody deeds are accomplished differ greatly. While Macbeth is influenced by supernatural prophecies and a ruthless, power-hungry wife who must work hard at convincing her husband to commit murder for the throne, Richard needs no such convincing, nor does he even have the potential for such persuasion from any female intimate. Moreover, while Macbeth struggles and deliberates with his conscience, most especially in the murder of his king, Duncan, to whom he owes loyalty and hospitality, Richard rushes from one bloody act to the next in his attempts at marshaling power. Whately attributes this critical difference in character flaws to a qualitative difference in each character's ambition. While Macbeth is vulnerable to vanity and flattery, Richard is filled with pride in his relentless pursuit of power. Whately, thus, offers a form of apology for Macbeth which he cannot extend to Richard.

1709—Richard Steele. From *The Tatler*

Sir Richard Steele (1672-1729) was a British essayist, dramatist, and politician best known for his collaboration with Joseph Addison on a series of periodical essays for the *Tatler* and the *Spectator*. Both men were interested in improving the minds, morals, and manners of their readers as well as introducing them to new social ideas and influencing good taste.

I came home this evening in a very pensive mood; and to divert me, took up a volume of Shakespeare, where I chanced to cast my eye upon a part in the tragedy of Richard the Third, which filled my mind with a very agreeable horror. It was the scene in which that bold but wicked prince is represented as sleeping in his tent the night before the battle in which he fell. The poet takes the occasion to set before him in a vision a terrible assembly of apparitions, the ghosts of all those innocent persons whom he is said to have murdered. Prince Edward, Henry VI., the Duke of Clarence, Rivers, Gray, and Vaughan, Lord Hastings, the two young princes, sons to Edward IV., his own wife, and the Duke of Buckingham rise up in their blood before him, beginning their speeches with that dreadful salutation, "Let me sit heavy on thy soul to-morrow;" and concluding with that dismal sentence, "Despair and die." This inspires the tyrant with a dream of his past guilt, and of the approaching vengeance. He anticipates the fatal day of Bosworth, fancies himself dismounted, weltering in his own blood; and in the agonies of despair (before he is thoroughly awake), starts up with the following speech:

Give me another horse—Bind up my wounds!
Have mercy, Jesu—Soft, I did but dream.

O coward Conscience! How dost thou afflict me?
The lights burn blue! Is it not dead midnight?
Cold fearful drops stand on my trembling flesh;
What do I fear? Myself! &c.

A scene written with so great strength of imagination indisposed me from further reading, and threw me into a deep contemplation. I began to reflect upon
the different ends of good and bad kings: and as this was the birthday of our
late renowned monarch, I could not forbear thinking on the departure of that
excellent prince, whose life was crowned with glory, and his death with peace.
I let my mind go so far into this thought, as to imagine to myself, what might
have been the vision of his departing slumbers. He might have seen confederate
kings applauding him in different languages, slaves that had been bound in fet-
ters lifting up their hands and blessing him, and the persecuted in their several
forms of worship imploring comfort on his last moments. The reflection upon
this excellent prince's mortality had been a very melancholy entertainment to
me, had I not been relieved by the consideration of the glorious reign which
succeeds it.

1760—François Marie Arouet de Voltaire. From a letter to Marie Vichy de Chamrond, Marquise du Deffand

François Marie Arouet de Voltaire (1694–1778) was a French
Enlightenment writer, essayist, and philosopher known for his wit, philosophical ideas, his interest in science, and his defense of civil liberties,
including freedom of religion, freedom of the press, and free speech. A
prolific writer, he is the author of *Letters on the English* (1778), *Candide*
(1759), and *Philosophical Dictionary* (1764).

December 9, 1760
I am angry with the English. Not only have they taken Pondichery from me, I
believe, but they have just expressed in print that their Shakespeare is infinitely
superior to Corneille. Their Shakespeare is infinitely inferior to Gilles. Imagine
the tragedy of Richard III, which they compare to Cinna, has nine years for
unity of time, a dozen cities and battlefields for unity of place, and thirty-seven
principal events for unity of action. But that is nothing. In the first act, Richard
says that he is a hunchback and smells, and to take his revenge against nature,
he is going to be a hypocrite and a scoundrel. As he says these beautiful things,
he sees a funeral procession—King Henry VI's. He stops the bier and the widow

who is leading the procession. The widow cries out loudly; she reproaches him for killing her husband. Richard replies that he is delighted because he will be able to sleep with her more conveniently. The queen spits in his face; Richard thanks her and claims that nothing is as sweet as her spit. The queen calls him a toad, an ugly toad: "I wish my spit were poison." "Well, madam, kill me if you like; here is my sword." She takes it. "Hang it, I don't have the courage to kill you." "Well, then I am going to kill myself." "No, do not kill yourself since you found me pretty." She goes and buries her husband, and the two lovers do not speak of love any more for the remainder of the play. Isn't it true that if our water bearers wrote plays, they would make them more honest? I tell you all of this because I have had my fill. Isn't it sad that the same country that produced Newton has produced these monsters and admires them? Be well, madam. Try to have some pleasure. This is not an easy thing but not impossible.

1768—Horace Walpole. "Richard III's Physical Appearance," from *Historic Doubts on the Life and Reign of King Richard the Third*

Horace Walpole (1717–97) was a man of letters, art historian, antiquarian, and politician. He is the author of *A Catalogue of the Royal and Noble Authors of England, with Lists of Their Works* (1759), *The Castle of Otranto: A Gothic Story* (1764), and *Hieroglyphic Tales* (1785).

With regard to the person of Richard, it appears to have been as much misrepresented as his actions. Philip de Comines, who was very free spoken even on his own masters, and therefore not likely to spare a foreigner, mentions the beauty of Edward the Fourth; but says nothing of the deformity of Richard, though he saw them together. This is merely negative. The old countess of Desmond, who had danced with Richard, declared he was the handsomest man in the room except his brother Edward, and was very well made. But what shall we say to Dr. Shaw, who in his sermon appealed to the people, whether Richard was not the express image of his father's person, who was neither ugly nor deformed? Not all the protector's power could have kept the muscles of the mob in awe and prevented their laughing at so ridiculous an apostrophe, had Richard been a little, crooked, withered, hump-back'd monster, as later historians would have us believe—and very idly? Cannot a foul soul inhabit a fair body? The truth I take to have been this. Richard, who was slender and not tall, had one shoulder a little higher than the other: a defect, by the magnifying glasses of party, by distance of time, and by the amplification of tradition, easily swelled to shocking deformity; for falsehood itself generally pays so much respect to truth as to make it the basis of its superstructure.

I have two reasons for believing Richard was not well made about the shoulders. Among the drawings which I purchased at Vertue's sale was one of Richard and his queen, of which nothing is expressed but the out-lines. There is no intimation from whence the drawing was taken; but by a collateral direction for the colour of the robe, if not copied from a picture, it certainly was from some painted window; where existing I do not pretend to say: in this whole work I have not gone beyond my vouchers. Richard's face is very comely, and corresponds singularly with the portrait of him in the preface to the Royal and Noble Authors. He has a sort of tippet of ermine doubled about his neck, which seems calculated to disguise some want of symmetry thereabouts. I have given two (51) prints of this drawing, which is on large folio paper, that it may lead to a discovery of the original.

My other authority is John Rous, the antiquary of Warwickshire, who saw Richard at Warwick in the interval of his two coronations, and who describes him thus: "Parvae staturae erat, curtam habens faciem, inaequales humeros, dexter superior, sinisterque inferior." What feature in this portrait gives any idea of a monster? Or who can believe that an eye-witness, and so minute a painter, would have mentioned nothing but the inequality of the shoulders, if Richard's form had been a compound of ugliness? Could a Yorkist have drawn a less disgusting representation? And yet Rous was a vehement Lancastrian; and the moment he ceased to have truth before his eyes, gave into all the virulence and forgeries of his party, telling us in another place, "that Richard remained two years in his mother's womb, and came forth at last with teeth, and hair on his shoulders." I leave it to the learned in the profession to decide whether women can go two years with their burden, and produce a living infant; but that this long pregnancy did not prevent the duchess, his mother, from bearing afterwards, I can prove; and could we recover the register of the births of her children, I should not be surprized to find, that, as she was a very fruitful woman, there was not above a year between the birth of Richard and his preceding brother Thomas (52). However, an ancient (53) bard, who wrote after Richard was born and during the life of his father, tells us,

Richard liveth yit, but the last of all Was Ursula, to him whom God list call.

Be it as it will, this foolish tale, with the circumstances of his being born with hair and teeth, was coined to intimate how careful Providence was, when it formed a tyrant, to give due warning of what was to be expected. And yet these portents were far from prognosticating a tyrant; for this plain reason, that all other tyrants have been born without these prognostics. Does it require more time to ripen a foetus, that is, to prove a destroyer, than it takes to form an Aristides? Who was handsomer than Alexander, Augustus, or Louis the Fourteenth? And yet who ever commanded the spilling of more human blood?

Having mentioned John Rous, it is necessary I should say something more of him, as he lived in Richard's time, and even wrote his reign; and yet I have omitted him in the list of contemporary writers. The truth is he was pointed out to me after the preceding sheets were finished; and upon inspection I found him too despicable and lying an author, even amongst monkish authors, to venture to quote him, but for two facts; for the one of which as he was an eye-witness, and for the other, as it was of public notoriety, he is competent authority.

The first is his description of the person of Richard; the second, relating to the young earl of Warwick, I have recorded in its place.

This John Rous, so early as the reign of Edward the Fourth, had retired to the hermitage of Guy's Cliff, where he was a chantry priest, and where he spent the remaining part of his life in what he called studying and writing antiquities. Amongst other works, most of which are not unfortunately lost, he composed a history of the kings of England. It begins with the creation, and is compiled indiscriminately from the Bible and from monastic writers. Moses, he tells us, does not mention all the cities founded before the deluge, but Bernard of Beyedenback, dean of Mayence, does. With the same taste he acquaints us, that, though the Book of Genesis says nothing of the matter, Giraldus Cambrensis writes, that Caphera or Cefara, Noah's neice, being apprehensive of the deluge, set out for Ireland, where with three men and fifty women, she arrived safe with one ship, the rest perishing in the general destruction.

A history, so happily begun, never falls off: prophesies, omens, judgments, and religious foundations compose the bulk of the book. The lives and actions of our monarchs, and the great events of their reigns, seemed to the author to deserve little place in a history of England. The lives of Henry the Sixth and Edward the Fourth, though the author lived under both, take up but two pages in octavo, and that of Richard the Third, three. We may judge how qualified such an author was to clear up a period so obscure, or what secrets could come to his knowledge at Guy's Cliff: accordingly he retails all the vulgar reports of the times; as that Richard poisoned his wife, and put his nephews to death, though he owns few knew in what manner; but as he lays the scene of their deaths before Richard's assumption of the crown, it is plain he was the worst informed of all. To Richard he ascribes the death of Henry the Sixth; and adds, that many persons believed he executed the murder with his own hands: but he records another circumstance that alone must weaken all suspicion of Richard's guilt in that transaction. Richard not only caused the body to be removed from Chertsey, and solemnly interred at Windsor, but it was publickly exposed, and, if we will believe the monk, was found almost entire, and emitted a gracious perfume, though no care had been taken to embalm it. Is it credible that Richard, if the murderer, would have exhibited this unnecessary mummery, only to revive the memory of his own guilt? Was it not rather intended to recall the cruelty of his brother Edward, whose children he had set aside, and whom by the comparison of this act of piety, he hoped to (54) depreciate in the eyes of the people? The very example had been pointed out to him by Henry the Fifth, who bestowed a pompous funeral on Richard the Second, murdered by order of his father.

Indeed the devotion of Rous to that Lancastrian saint, Henry the Sixth, seems chiefly to engross his attention, and yet it draws him into a contradiction; for having said that the murder of Henry the Sixth had made Richard detested by all nations who heard of it, he adds, two pages afterwards, that an embassy arrived at Warwick (while Richard kept his court there) from the (55) king of Spain, to propose a marriage between their children. Of this embassy Rous is a proper witness: Guy's Cliff, I think, is but four miles from Warwick; and he is too circumstantial on what passed there not to have been on the spot. In other respects he seems inclined to be impartial, recording several good and generous acts of Richard.

But there is one circumstance, which, besides the weakness and credulity of the man, renders his testimony exceedingly suspicious. After having said, that, *if he may speak truth in Richard's favour* (56), he must own that, though small in stature and strength, Richard was a noble knight, and defended himself to the last breath with eminent valour, the monk suddenly turns, and apostrophizes Henry the Seventh, to whom he has dedicated his work, and whom he flatters to the best of his poor abilities; but, above all things, for having bestowed the name of Arthur on his eldest son, who, this injudicious and over-hasty prophet foresees, will restore the glory of his great ancestor of the same name. Had Henry christened his second son Merlin, I do not doubt but poor Rous would have had still more divine visions about Henry the Eighth, though born to shake half the pillars of credulity.

In short, no reliance can be had on an author of such a frame of mind, so removed from the scene of action, and so devoted to the Welsh intruder on the throne. Superadded to this incapacity and defects, he had prejudices or attachments of a private nature: He had singular affection for the Beauchamps, earls of Warwick, zealous Lancastrians, and had written their lives. One capital crime that he imputes to Richard is the imprisonment of his mother-in-law, Ann Beauchamp countess of Warwick, mother of his queen. It does seem that this great lady was very hardly treated; but I have shown from the Chronicle of Croyland, that it was Edward the Fourth, not Richard, that stripped her of her possessions. She was widow too of that turbulent Warwick, the king-maker; and Henry the Seventh bore witness that she was faithfully loyal the Henry the Sixth. Still it seems extraordinary that the queen did not or could not obtain the enlargement of her mother. When Henry the Seventh attained the crown, she recovered her liberty and vast estates: yet young as his majesty was both in years and avarice, for this magnificence took place in his third year, still he gave evidence of the falshood and rapacity of his nature; for though by act of parliament he cancelled the former act that had deprived her, *as against all reason, conscience, and course of nature, and* contrary *to the laws of God and man* (57) and restored her possessions to her, this was but a farce, and like his wonted hypocrisy; for the very same year he obliged her to convey the whole estate to him, leaving her nothing but the manor of Sutton for her maintenance. Richard had married her daughter; but what claim had Henry to her inheritance? This attachment of Rous to the house of Beauchamp, and the dedication of his work to Henry, would make his testimony most suspicious, even if he had guarded his work within the rules of probability, and not rendered it a contemptible legend.

Every part of Richard's story is involved in obscurity: we neither know what natural children he had, nor what became of them. Sandford says, he had a daughter called Katherine, whom William Herbert earl of Huntingdon covenanted to marry, and to make her a fair and sufficient estate of certain of his manors to the yearly value of 200 £ over and above all charges. As this lord received a confirmation of his title from Henry the Seventh, no doubt the poor young lady would have been sacrificed to that interest. But Dugdale seems to think she died before the nuptials were consummated: "whether this marriage took effect or not I cannot say; for sure it is that she died in her tender years (58)." Drake (59) affirms, that Richard knighted at York a natural son called Richard of Gloucester, and supposes it to be the same person of whom Peck has preserved so extraordinary an account (60). But never was a supposition worse grounded. The relation given the latter of himself, was, that he never saw the king till the night before the battle of Bosworth; and that the king had not then acknowledged, but intended to acknowledge him, if victorious. The deep privacy in which this person had lived, demonstrates how severely the persecution had raged against all that were connected with Richard, and how little truth was to be expected from the writers on the other side. Nor could Peck's Richard Plantagenet be the same person with Richard of Gloucester, for the former was never known till he discovered himself to Sir Thomas Moyle; and Hall says that king Richard's natural son was in the hands of Henry the Seventh. Buck says, that Richard made his son Richard of Gloucester, captain of Calais; but it appears from Rymer's Foedera, that Richard's natural son , who was captain of Calais, was called John. None of these accounts accord with Peck's; nor, for want of knowing his mother, can we guess why king Richard was more secret on the birth of this son (if Peck's Richard Plantagenet was truly so) than on those of his other natural children. Perhaps the truest remark that can be made on this whole story is, that the avidity with which our historians swallowed one gross ill-concocted legend, prevented them from desiring or daring to sift a single part of it. If crumbs of truth are mingled with it, at least they are now undistinguishable in such a mass of error and improbability.

It is evident from the conduct of Shakespeare, that the house of Tudor retained all their Lancastrian prejudices, even in the reign of queen Elizabeth. In his play of Richard the Third, he seems to deduce the woes of the house of York from the curses which queen Margaret had vented against them; and he could not give that weight to her curses, without supposing a right in her to utter them. This indeed is the authority which I do not pretend to combat. Shakespeare's immortal scenes will exist, when such poor arguments as mine are forgotten. Richard at least will be tried and executed on the stage, when his defence remains on some obscure shelf of a library. But while these pages may excite the curiosity of a day, it may not be unentertaining to observe, that there is another of Shakespeare's plays, that may be ranked among the historic, though not one of his numerous critics and commentators have discovered the drift of it; I mean *The Winter Evening's Tale,* which was certainly intended (in compliment to queen Elizabeth) as an indirect apology for her mother Anne Boleyn. The address of the poet appears no where to more advantage. The subject was too delicate to be exhibited on the stage without a veil; and it was too recent, and touched the queen too nearly, for the bard to have ventured so home an allusion on any other ground than compliment. The unreasonable jealousy of Leontes, and his violent conduct in consequence, form a true portrait of Henry the Eighth, who generally made the law the engine of his boisterous passions. Not only the general plan of the story is most applicable, but several passages are so marked, that they touch the real history nearer than the fable. Hermione on her trial says,

> ————————————for honour,
> 'Tis a derivative from me to mine,
> And only that I stand for.

This seems to be taken from the very letter of Anne Boleyn to the king before her execution, where she pleads for the infant princess his daughter. Mamillius, the young prince, an unnecessary character, dies in his infancy; but it confirms the allusion, as queen Anne, before Elizabeth, bore a still-born son. But the most striking passage, and which had nothing to do in the tragedy, but as it pictured Elizabeth, is, where Paulina, describing the new-born princess, and her likeness to her father, says, *she has the very trick of his frown.* There is one sentence indeed so applicable, both to Elizabeth and her father, that I should suspect the poet inserted it after her death. Paulina, speaking of the child, tells the king,

> ————————————'Tis yours;
> And might we lay the old proverb to your charge,
> So like you, 'tis the worse————

The Winter's Evening's Tale was therefore in reality a second part of *Henry the Eighth*.

With regard to Jane Shore, I have already shown that it was her connection with the marquis Dorset, not with lord Hastings, which drew on her the resentment of Richard. When an event is thus wrested to serve the purpose of a party, we ought to be very cautious how we trust an historian, who is capable of employing truth only as cement in a fabric of fiction. Sir Thomas More tells us, that Richard pretended Jane "was of councell with lord Hastings to destroy him; and in conclusion, when no colour could fasten upon these matters, then he layd seriously to her charge that what she could not deny," namely her adultery; "and for this cause, as a godly continent prince, cleane and faultless of himself, sent out of heaven into this vicious world for the amendment of mens manners, he caused the bishop of London to put her to open penance."

This sarcasm on Richard's morals would have had more weight, if the author had before confined himself to deliver nothing but the precise truth. He does not seem to be more exact in what relates to the penance itself. Richard, by his proclamation, taxed mistress Shore with plotting treason in confederacy with the marquis Dorset. Consequently, it was not from defect of proof of her being accomplice with lord Hastings that she was put to open penance. If Richard had any hand in that sentence, it was, because he *had* proof of her plotting with the marquis. But I doubt, and with some reason, whether her penance was inflicted by Richard. We have seen that he acknowledged at least two natural children; and Sir Thomas More hints that Richard was far from being remarkable for his charity. Is it therefore probable, that he acted so silly a farce as to make his brother's mistress do penance? Most of the charges on Richard are so idle, that instead of being an able and artful usurper, as his antagonists allow, he must have been a weaker hypocrite than ever attempted to wrest a sceptre out of the hands of a legal possessor.

It is more likely that the churchmen were the authors of Jane's penance; and that Richard, interested to manage that body, and provoked by her connection with so capital an enemy as Dorset, might give her up, and permit the clergy (who had probably burned incense to her in her prosperity) to revenge his quarrel. My reason for this opinion is grounded on a letter of Richard extant in the Museum, by which it appears that the fair, unfortunate, and amiable Jane (for her virtues far outweighed her frailty) [being] a prisoner, by Richard's order, in Ludgate, had captivated the king's solicitor, who contracted to marry her. Here follows the letter:

Harl. MSS, No. 2378
By the K I N G.
"Right reverend fadre in God, &c. Signifying unto you, that it is shewed unto us, that our servaunt and solicitor, Thomas Lynom, merveillously

blinded and abused with the late (wife) of Willm Shore, now being in
Ludgate by oure commandment, hath made contract of matrymony
with hir (as it is said) and entendith, to our full grete merveille, to
procede to th'effect of the same. We for many causes wold be sory that
hee soo shulde be disposed. Pray you therefore to send for him, and
in that ye goodly may, exhorte and sture hym to the contrarye. And if
ye finde him utterly set for to marye hur, and noen otherwise will be
advertised, then (if it may stand with the law of the churche) We be
content (the tyme of mariage deferred to our comyng next to London)
that upon sufficient suertie founde of hure good abering, ye doo send for
hure keeper, and discharge him of our said commandment by warrant of
these, committing hur to the rule and guiding of hure fadre, or any other
by your descretion in the mene season. Yeven, &c. To the right reverend
fadre in God, &c. the bishop of Lincoln, our chauncellor."

It appears from this letter, that Richard thought it indecent for his sollicitor
to marry a woman who suffered public punishment for adultery, and who was
confined by his command? But where is the tyrant to be found in this paper? Or,
what prince ever spoke of such a scandal, and what is stronger, of such contempt
of his authority, with so much lenity and temper? He enjoins his chancellor to
dissuade the sollicitor from the match? Should he persist the tyrant would have
ordered the sollicitor to prison to—but Richard? Richard, if his servant will not
be dissuaded, allows the match; and in the meantime commits Jane to whose
custody?—her own father's. I cannot help thinking that some holy person had
been her persecutor, and not so patient and gentle a king. And I believe so,
because of the salvo for the church: "Let them be married," says Richard, "if it
may stand with the lawe of the church."

From the proposed marriage, one should at first conclude that Shore, the
former husband of Jane, was dead; but by the king's query, whether the marriage
would be lawful? And by her being called in the letter *the late wife of William
Shore,* not *of the late William Shore,* I should suppose that her husband was living,
and that the penance itself was the consequence of a suit preferred by him to
the ecclesiastical court for divorce. If the injured husband ventured, on the
death of Edward the Fourth, to petition to be separated from his wife, it was
natural enough for the church to proceed farther, and enjoin her to perform
penance, especially when they fell in with the king's resentment of her. Richard's
proclamation and the letter above-recited seem to point out this account of Jane's
misfortunes; the letter implying, that Richard doubted whether her divorce was
so complete as to leave her at liberty to take another husband. As we hear no
more of the marriage, and as Jane to her death, retained the name of Shore, my
solution is corroborated; the chancellor-bishop, no doubt, going more roundly to
work than the king had done. Nor, however Sir Thomas More reviles Richard

for his cruel usage of mistress Shore, did either of the succeeding kings redress her wrongs, though she lived to the eighteenth year of Henry the Eighth. She had sown her good deeds, her good offices, her alms, her charities, in a court. Not one took root; nor did the ungrateful soil repay her a grain of relief in her penury and comfortless old age.

I have thus gone through the several accusations against Richard; and have shown that they rest on the slightest and most suspicious ground, if they rest on any at all. I have proved that they ought to be reduced to the sole authorities of Sir Thomas More and Henry the Seventh; the latter interested to blacken and misrepresent every action of Richard; and perhaps driven to father on him even his own crimes. I have proved that More's account cannot be true. I have shown that the writers, contemporary with Richard, either do not accuse him, or give their accusations as mere vague and uncertain reports: and what is as strong, the writers next in date, and who wrote the earliest after these events are said to have happened, assert little or nothing from their own information, but adopt the very words of Sir Thomas More, who was absolutely mistaken or misinformed.

For the sake of those who have a mind to canvas this subject, I will recapitulate the most material arguments that tend to disprove what has been asserted; but as I attempt not to affirm what *did* happen in a period that will still remain very obscure, I flatter myself that I shall not be thought either fantastic or paradoxical, for not blindly adopting an improbable tale, which our historians have never given themselves the trouble to examine.

What mistakes I may have made myself, I shall be willing to acknowledge; what weak reasoning, to give up: but I shall not think that a long chain of arguments, of proofs and probabilities, is confuted at once, because some single fact may be found erroneous. Much less shall I be disposed to take notice of detached or trifling cavils. The work itself is but an inquiry into a short portion of our annals. I shall be content, if I have informed or amused my readers, or thrown any light on so clouded a scene; but I cannot be of opinion that a period thus distant deserves to take up more time than I have already bestowed upon it.

It seems to me to appear, that Fabian and the authors of the Chronicle of Croyland, who were contemporaries with Richard, charge him directly with none of the crimes, since imputed to him, and disculpate him of others.

That John Rous, the third contemporary, could know the facts he alleges but by hearsay, confounds the dates of them, dedicated his works to Henry the Seventh, and is an author to whom no credit is due, from the lies and fables with which his work is stuffed.

That we have no authors, who lived near the time, but Lancastrian authors, who wrote to flatter Henry the Seventh, or who spread the tales which he invented.

That the murder of prince Edward, son of Henry the Sixth, was committed by king Edward's servants, and is imputed to Richard by no contemporary.

That Henry the Sixth was found dead in the Tower; that it was not known how he came by his death; and that it was against Richard's interest to murder him.

That the duke of Clarence was defended by Richard; that the parliament petitioned for his execution; that no author of the time is so absurd as to charge Richard with being the executioner; and that king Edward took the deed wholly on himself.

That Richard's stay at York on his brother's death had no appearance of a design to make himself king.

That the ambition of the queen, who attempted to usurp the government, contrary to the then established custom of the realm, gave the first provocation to Richard and the princes of the blood to assert their rights; and that Richard was sollicited by the duke of Buckingham to vindicate those rights.

That the preparation of an armed force under earl Rivers, the seizure of the Tower and treasure, and the equipment of a fleet, by the marquis Dorset, gave occasion to the princes to imprison the relations of the queen; and that, though they were put to death without trial (the only cruelty which is proved on Richard) it was consonant to the manners of that barbarous and turbulent age, and not till after the queen's party had taken up arms.

That the execution of lord Hastings, who had first engaged with Richard against the queen, and whom Sir Thomas More confesses Richard was lothe to lose, can be accounted for by nothing but absolute necessity, and the law of self-defence.

That Richard's assumption of the protectorate was in every respect agreeable to the laws and usage; was probably bestowed on him by the universal consent of the council and peers, and was a strong indication that he had then no thought of questioning the right of his nephew.

That the tale of Richard aspersing the chastity of his own mother is incredible; it appearing that he lived with her in perfect harmony, and lodged with her in her palace at that very time.

That it is as little credible that Richard gained the crown by a sermon of Dr. Shaw, and a speech of the duke of Buckingham, if the people only laughed at those orators.

That there had been a precontract or marriage between Edward the Fourth and lady Eleanor Talbot; and that Richard's claim to the throne was founded on the illegitimacy of Edward's children.

That a convention of the nobility, clergy, and people invited him to accept the crown on that title.

That the ensuing parliament ratified the act of the convention, and confirmed the bastardy of Edward's children.

That nothing can be more improbable than Richard's having taken no measures before he left London, to have his nephews murdered, if he had had any such intention.

That the story of Sir James Tirrel, as related by Sir Thomas More, is a notorious falsehood; Sir James Tirrel being at that time master of the horse, in which capacity he had walked at Richard's coronation.

That Tirrel's jealousy of Sir Richard Ratcliffe is another palpable falsehood; Tirrel being already preferred, and Ratcliffe being absent.

That all that relates to Sir Robert Brakenbury is no less false: Brakenbury either being too good a man to die for a tyrant or murderer, or too bad a man to have refused being his accomplice.

That Sir Thomas More and lord Bacon both confess that many doubted, whether the two princes were murdered in Richard's day or not; and it certainly never was proved that they were murdered by Richard's order.

That Sir Thomas More relied on nameless and uncertain authority; that it appears by dates and facts that his authorities were bad and false; that if sir James Tirrel and Dighton had really committed the murder and confessed it, and if Perkin Warbeck had made a voluntary, clear, and probable confession of his imposture, there could have remained no doubt of the murder.

That Green, the nameless page, and Will Slaughter, having never been questioned about the murder, there is no reason to believe what is related of them in the supposed tragedy.

That Sir James Tirrel not being attainted on the death of Richard, but having, on the contrary, been employed in great services by Henry the Seventh, it is not probable that he was one of the murderers. That lord Bacon owning that Tirrel's confession did not please the king so well as Dighton's; that Tirrel's imprisonment and execution some years afterwards for a new treason, of which we have no evidence, and which appears to have been mere suspicion, destroy all probability of his guilt in the supposed murder of the children.

That the impunity of Dighton, if really guilty, was scandalous; and can only be accounted for on the supposition of his being a false witness to serve Henry's cause against Perkin Warbeck.

That the silence of the two archbishops, and Henry's not daring to specify the murder of the princes in the act of attainder against Richard, wears all the appearance of their not having been murdered.

That Richard's tenderness and kindness to the earl of Warwick. Proceeding so far as to proclaim him his successor, betrays no symptom of that cruel nature, which would not stick at assassinating any competitor.

That it is indubitable that Richard's first idea was to keep the crown but till Edward the Fifth should attain the age of twenty-four.

That with this view he did not create his own son prince of Wales till after he had proved the bastardy of his brother's children.

That there is no proof that those children were murdered.

That Richard made, or intended to make, his nephew Edward the Fifth walk at his coronation.

That there is strong presumption form the parliament-roll and from the Chronicle of Croyland, that both princes were living some time after Sir Thomas More fixes the dates of their deaths.

That when his own son was dead, Richard was so far from intending to get rid of his wife, that he proclaimed his nephews, first the earl of Warwick, and then the earl of Lincoln, his heirs apparent.

That there is not the least probability of his having poisoned his wife, who died of a languishing distemper: that no proof was ever pretended to be given of it; that a bare supposition of such a crime, without proofs or very strong presumptions, is scarce to be credited.

That he seems to have had no intention of marrying his neice, but to have amused her with the hopes of that match, to prevent her marrying Richmond.

That Buck would not have dared to quote her letter as extant in the earl of Arundel's library, if it had not been there: that others of Buck's assertions having been corroborated by subsequent discoveries, leave no doubt of his veracity on this; and that that letter disculpates Richard from poisoning his wife; and only shews the impatience of his neice to be queen.

That it is probable that the queen-dowager knew her second son was living, and connived at the appearance of Lambert Simnel, to feel the temper of the nation.

That Henry the Seventh certainly thought that she and the earl of Lincoln were privy to the existence of Richard duke of York, and that Henry lived in terror of his appearance.

That the different conduct of Henry with regard to Lambert Simnel and Perkin Warbeck, implies how different an opinion he had of them; that, in the first case, he used the most natural and most rational methods to prove him an impostor; whereas his whole behavior in Perkin's case was mysterious, and betrayed his belief or doubt that Warbeck was the true duke of York.

That it was morally impossible for the duchess of Burgundy at the distance of twenty-seven years to instruct a Flemish lad so perfectly in all that had passed in the court of England, that he would not have been detected in few hours.

That she could not inform him, nor could he know, what had passed in the Tower, unless he was the true duke of York.

That if he was not the true duke of York, Henry had nothing to do but to confront him with Tirrel and Dighton, and the imposture must have been discovered.

That Perkin, never being confronted with the queen-dowager, and the princesses her daughters, proves that Henry did not dare to trust to their acknowledging him.

That if he was not the true duke of York, he might have been detected by not knowing the queens and princesses, if shown to him without his being told who they were.

That it is not pretended that Perkin ever failed in language, accent, or circumstances; and that his likeness to Edward the Fourth is allowed.

That there are gross and manifest blunders in his pretended confession.

That Henry was so afraid of not ascertaining a good account of the purity of his English accent, that he makes him learn English twice over.

That lord Bacon did not dare to adhere to this ridiculous account; but forges another, though in reality, not much more credible.

That a number of Henry's best friends, as the Lord Chamberlain, who placed the crown on his head, knights of the garter, and men of the fairest character, being persuaded that Perkin was the true duke of York, and dying for that belief, without recanting, makes it very rash to deny that he was not so.

That the proclamation in Rymer's Foedera against Jane Shore, for plotting with the marquis Dorset, not with lord Hastings, destroys all the credit of Sir Thomas More, as to what relates to the latter peer.

In short, that Henry's character, as we have received it from his own apologists, is so much worse and more hateful than Richard's, that we may well believe that Henry invented and propagated by far the greater part of the slanders against Richard : that Henry, not Richard, probably put to death the true duke of York, as he did the earl of Warwick : and that we are not certain whether Edward the Fifth was murdered; nor, if he was, by whose order he was murdered.

After all that has been said, it is scarce necessary to add a word on the supposed discovery that was made of the skeletons of the two young princes, in the reign of Charles the Second. Two skeletons found in that dark abyss of so many secret traditions, with no marks to ascertain the time, the age of their interment, can certainly verify nothing. We must believe that both princes died there, before we can believe that their bones were found there : and upon what that belief can be founded, or how we shall cease to doubt whether Perkin Warbeck was not one of those children, I am at a loss to guess.

As little is it requisite to argue on the grants made by Richard the Third to his supposed accomplices in that murder, because the argument will serve either way. It was very natural that they, who had tasted most of Richard's bounty, should be suspected as the instruments of his crimes. But till it can be proved that those crimes were committed, it is in vain to bring evidence to show who assisted him in perpetrating them. For my own part, I know not what to think of the death of Edward the Fifth : I can neither entirely acquit Richard of it, nor condemn him ; because there are no proofs on either side; and though a court of justice would, from that defect of evidence, absolve him; opinion may fluctuate backwards and forwards, and at last remain in suspense.

For the younger brother, the balance seems to incline greatly on the side of Perkin Warbeck, as the true duke of York; and if one was saved, one knows not how or why to believe that Richard destroyed only the elder.

We must leave this whole story dark, though not near so dark as we found it: and it is perhaps as wise to be uncertain on one portion of our history, as to believe so much as is believed in all histories, though very probably as falsely delivered to us, as the period which we have here been examining.

NOTES

51. In the prints, the single head is most exactly copied from the drawing, which is unfinished. In the double plate, the reduced likeness of the king could not be so perfectly preserved.

52. The author I am going to quote, gives us the order in which the duchess Cecily's children were born, thus; Ann duchess of Exeter, Henry, Edward the Fourth, Edmund earl of Rutland, Elizabeth duchess of Suffolk, Margaret duchess of Burgundy, William, John, George duke of Clarnce, Thomas, Richard the Third, and Ursula. Cox, in his history of Ireland, says, that Clarnce was born in 1451. Buck computed Richard the Third to have fallen at the age of thirty -four or five; but, by Cox'x account, he could not be more than thirty-two. Still this makes it probable, that their mother bore them and intervening brother Thomas as soon as she well could one after another.

53. See Vincent's Errors in Brooke's Heraldry, p.623.

54. This is not a mere random conjecture, but corroborated by another instance of like address. He disforested a large circuit, which Edward had annexed to the forest of Whichwoode, to the great annoyance of the subject. This we are told by Rous himself, p. 216

55. Drake says, that an embassador from the queen of Spain was present at Richard's coronation at York. Rous himself owns, that, amidst a great concourse of nobility that attended the king at York, was the duke of Albany, brother of the king of Scotland. Richard therefore appears not to have been abhorred by either of the courts of Spain or Scotland.

56. Attamen fi ad ejus honorem veritatem dicam, p. 218.

57. Vide Dugdale's Warwickshire in Beauchamp.

58. Baronage. P. 258

59. In his History of York

60. See his Desiderata Curiosa

1775—Elizabeth Griffith. "Richard the Third," from *The Morality of Shakespeare's Drama*

Elizabeth Griffith (1727–93) was an eighteenth-century Irish dramatist, fiction writer, essayist, and actress. She is the author of *Essays, Addressed to Young Married Women* (1782), several plays including *The Platonic Wife* (1765) and *The School for Rakes* (1769), several novels including *The Delicate Distress* (1769) and *The Gordon Knot* (1769), as well as the dramatic poem, *Amana* (1764).

Act I. Scene I.

Every representation, either of a scene or season of peace, is peculiarly soothing to the human mind. 'Tis its own most natural and pleasing state. But when it is contrasted with the opposite condition of tumult and war, the delight rises infinitely higher. There are many such descriptions as this is Shakespeare; and as the imbuing the mind with such contemplations, must certainly have a moral tendency in it, I am glad to transcribe every passage of the kind I meet with in him.

> Richard *alone*
> Now is the winter of our discontent
> Made glorious summer by this sun of York;
> And all the clouds that lour'd upon our house
> In the deep bosom of the ocean buried.
> Now are our brows bound with victorious wreaths;
> Our bruised arms hung up for monuments;
> Our stern alarums chang'd to merry meetings,
> Our dreadful marches to delightful measures.
> Grim-visag'd war hath smooth'd his wrinkled front,
> And now, instead of mounting barbed steeds
> To fright the souls of fearful adversaries,
> He capers nimbly in a lady's chamber
> To the lascivious pleasing of a lute.

In the following part of the same speech, our poet, zealous for the honour of the human character, most artfully contrives to make Richard's wickedness appear to arise from a resentment against the partiality of Nature, in having stigmatize him with so deformed a person, joined to an envious jealousy towards the rest of mankind, for being endowed with fairer forms, and more attractive graces. By this admirable address, he moves up to a sort of compassion for the misfortune, even while he is raising an abhorrence for the vice, of the criminal.

> *Richard.* But I that am not shap'd for sportive tricks,
> Nor made to court an amorous looking-glass—
> I that am rudely stamp'd, and want love's majesty
> To strut before a wanton ambling nymph—
> I that am curtail'd of this fair proportion,
> Cheated of feature by dissembling nature,
> Deform'd, unfinish'd, sent before my time
> Into this breathing world scarce half made up,
> And that so lamely and unfashionable
> That dogs bark at me as I halt by them—

Why, I, in this weak piping time of peace,
Have no delight to pass away the time,
Unless to spy my shadow in the sun
And descant on mine own deformity.
And therefore, since I cannot prove a lover
To entertain these fair well-spoken days,
I am determined to prove a villain
And hate the idle pleasures of these days.

Scene II

This long Scene, in which Richard courts Lady Anne, relict of the first Prince of Wales, son to Henry the Sixth, whom he had murdered, is so well known to every one who has ever read or seen this Play, that I need not be at the trouble of transcribing it, though I shall take the liberty of remarking on the very improbably conclusion of it.

Women are certainly most extremely ill used, in the unnatural representation of female frailty, here given. But it may, perhaps, be some palliation of his offence, to observe, that this strange fable was not any invention of the poet; though it must indeed be confessed that he yielded too easy a credence to a fictitious piece of history, which rested upon no better authority than the fame that affirmed the deformity of Richard; which fact has lately, from a concurrence of cotemporary testimonies, been rendered problematical at least, by a learned and ingenious author.

The conclusion of the Fifth Scene of Act the Fourth, in this Play, where the Queen, widow of Edward the Fourth, after the death of Lady Anne, promises her daughter to this tyrant and usurper, who had killed her sons, is founded likewise upon the same disingenuous authority with the two former passages.

Scene III.

Lord Stanley, upon the Queen's expressing a suspicious that his wife, the countess of Richmond, bears her some ill will, makes her defense, in a speech which would conduce greatly to the peace of our minds, and the preserving many of our most friendly connections unbroken, if properly attended to, and made the rule of our conduct through life.

Stanley. I do beseech you, either not believe
    The envious slanders of her false accusers;
    Or, if she be accus'd on true report,
    Bear with her weakness, which I think proceeds
    From wayward sickness and no grounded malice.

The evil report of things said to be spoken to the disadvantage of other, behind their backs, has so frequently been found to proceed either from the malice or mistake of eaves-droppers, listeners, or incendiaries, that it should warn us, upon such occasions, to suspend our resentment against the persons charged, till we find the indictment to be grounded on better evidence than those pests of society, the informers, intermeddlers, or tale-bearers. Besides which, as is above observed, every reasonable allowance ought to be made for the natural forwardness and peevishness of disorder, or other uneasiness of body or mind, which often sests us first at variance with ourselves, before it inclines us to quarrel with others

"Infirmity doth still neglect all office,
"Whereto our health is bound." *Lear.*

Scene V.

Shakespeare is here again at his frequent reflection on the vanity of ambition and the cares of greatness.

Brackenbury. Sorrow breaks seasons and reposing hours,
    Makes the night morning and the noontide night—
    Princes have but their titles for their glories,
    An outward honour for an inward toil;
    And for unfelt imaginations
    They often feel a world of restless cares—
    So that between their tides and low name
    There's nothing differs but the outward fame.

Act II. Scene II.

When the Queen is lamenting the death of Edward the Fourth, the marquis of Dorset, her son by a former husband, says to her,

Dorset. Comfort, dear mother. God is much displeas'd
    That you take with unthankfulness his doing.
    In common worldly things 'tis called ungrateful
    With dull unwillingness to repay a debt,
    Which with a bounteous hand was kindly lent;
    Much more to be thus opposite with Heaven;
    For it requires the royal debt it lent you.

Shakespeare is extremely rich in such sentiments of piety and resignation. It is a vast ease to the distressed mind, to communicate its griefs to the ear of a friend, though he can only condole, but not relieve them. How infinitely higher, then, must the comfort rise, to repose them on the bosom of our God, who can not only console, but compensate them! Christ has not taken the *sins* alone, but the *sorrows* also, of mankind upon himself, for those who place their hope and put their trust in him. He not only says, "Thy sins are forgiven thee;" but adds this comfort in affliction, "Come unto me, all ye that *labour*, and are *heavy laden*, and I will give ye *rest*."

Scene III.

There is a natural representation of a distempered state, just preceding a revolution, given in this Scene.

Three citizens, conferring together on the circumstances of the times, hold the following dialogue together.

> *First Citizen.* Come, come, we fear the worst; all will be well.
> *Second Citizen.* When clouds are seen, wise men put on their cloaks;
>   When great leaves fall, then winter is at hand;
>   When the sun sets, who doth not look for night?
>   Untimely storms make men expect a dearth.
>   *All may be well*; but, if God sort it so,
>   'Tis more than we deserve or I expect.
> *Third Citizen.* Truly, the hearts of men are fun of fear;
>   You cannot reason almost with a man,
>   That looks not heavily and fun of dread.
> *Second Citizen.* Before the days of change, still is it so—
>   By a divine instinct men's minds mistrust
>   Ensuing danger; as by proof we see
>   The water swell before a boist'rous storm—
> *But leave it all to God.*

Now nothing can demonstrate the investigating faculties of Shakespeare, more than this passage does. He never lived in any times of commotion himself, therefore the particular knowledge he here shows, in the general nature of such a crisis, must be owing more to philosophy than experience; rather to his own reflection, than any knowledge of history. I speak with regard to the English writers only, on such subjects; who were all, before his time, most barren of observation and maxim. And as to the Greek and Roman historiographers, who were rich in both, the invidious Commentators of our Poet have denied him any manner of acquaintance with such *outlandish literari*; and I also, though from a very different principle, have *joined issue* with them before, in this particular. For learning gives no talents, but only supplies the faculty of showing them; and this he could do, without any foreign assistance.

Act III. Scene I.

The poor unhappy Prince of Wales, successor to Edward the Fourth, makes a reflection here, so becoming the natural spirit of a noble mind, that it must raise a regret in the Reader, that he was not permitted to live and reign over a brave and a free people.

When his wicked uncle Richard appoints the Prince's residence at the *Tower*, till his coronation, he asks who built that fortress? And being told it was Julius Caesar, he says,

> That Julius Caesar was a famous man;
> With what his valour did enrich his wit,
> His wit set down to make his valour live.
> Death makes no conquest of this conqueror;
> For now he lives in fame, though not in life.

Scene V.

Richard. My lord of Ely, when I was last in Holborn
    I saw good strawberries in your garden there;
    I do beseech you send for some of them.
Ely. Marry, and will, my lord, with all my heart. [*Exit Ely.*

Could any writer but Shakespeare have ever thought of such a circumstance, in the midst of a deep tragedy, as the sending an old grave Bishop on an errand for a *leaf of strawberries*? And this, in the most formal scene of the Play too, where the lords are met in council, to settle about the day for the coronation?

But could any writer but himself have attempted such a whim, without setting the audience a-laughing at the ridiculousness and absurdity of such an incident? And yet he contrives, some-how or other, to hold us in awe, all the while; though he must be a very ingenious critic, indeed, who can supply any sort of reason for the introduction of such a familiar and comic stroke, upon so serious an occasion. And what renders the solution of this passage still more difficult, is, that the request is made by a person, too, whose mind was deeply intent on murder and usurpation, at the very time.

None of the editors have taken the least notice of this article; and the first notion that occurred to me upon it, was, that perhaps Richard wanted to get rid of old Ely, after any manner, however indecent or abrupt, in order to be at liberty to plot with Buckingham in private; for the moment the Bishop goes out on his errand, he says,

Cousin of Buckinham, a word with you.

But as he did not send the rest of the Council-Board a-packing after him, and adjourn them from *the bed of justice* to the *strawberry bed*, but retires immediately himself with his complotter Buckingham, we cannot suppose this idea to have been the purpose intended by so extraordinary a motion.

There is, then, no other way left us to resolve this text, than to impute it solely to the peculiar character that Shakespeare has given us all along of this extraordinary personage; whom he has represented throughout, as preserving a facetious humour, and exerting a sort of careless ease, in the midst of his crimes.

I am sorry not to be able to give a better account of this particular, than what I have here offered; because, if it is to rest upon such a comment, out author must, in this instance, be thought to have betraed a manifest ignorance in human nature, or the nature of guilt at least; as no vicious person, I do not mean those of profligate manners merely, but no designing or determined villain was ever cheerful, yet, or could possibly be able to assume even the semblance of carelessness of ease, upon any occasion whatsoever.

In the latter part of the Scene, poor Hastings, just before he mounts the scaffold, makes a reflection, which too frequently occurs to those *who put their trust in princes*; or, indeed, in general, to all who rest their hope on any other stay but their own uprightness and virtue.

Hastings. O momentary grace of mortal men,
    Which we more hunt for than the grace of God!
    Who builds his hope in air of your good looks
    Lives like a drunken sailor on a mast,
    Ready with every nod to tumble down
    Into the fatal bowels of the deep.

Act IV. Scene III.

Among the various crimes of man, murder stands in a different class above them all; except, perhaps, suicide, as being of the same species, may be allowed to rank with, or even to exceed, it. The latter part of this position, tho', has been disputed by some moral casuists; but I shall enter no further into the argument here, than just to observe, that one of these acts does not shock the human mind so much as the other. We are sensible of a tenderness and compassion for the unhappy self-devoted victim, but are impressed both with an horror and detestation against the homicide.

But the circumstance which most eminently distinguishes both of these crimes from every other species of guilt, is their being so wholly repugnant to nature. In other vices, we must suffer a temptation, and have only a moral struggle to conquer; but one must be trained, be *educated* to these, must stifle sympathy, and overcome our *first*, by a *second* nature.

And of all murders, from the days of *Herod* to these, the killing a child must surely raise a stronger war in the most hardened villain's breast, than the slaughter of an adult. Its innocence, its engaging manners, even its very helplessness, must plead so movingly in its defence, as to render the deed, one should think, impossible! Might not the idea of a child's coming so recently out of the hands of its Creator, serve also to impress an additional awe on the mind of the malefactor, at such a time? If superstition can ever be excused for its weakness, it must surely be in such an instance as this.

Shakepeare has wrought up an horrid and affecting picture, in this scene, upon the latter part of this subject, where he makes one of the murderers give an accound of the massacre of Edward's two children.

> *Tirrel.* The tyrannous and bloody act is done!
>   The most arch deed of piteous massacre
>   That ever yet this land was guilty of!
>   Dighton and Forrest, who I did suborn
>   To do this piece of ruthless butchery,
>   (Albeit they were flesh'd villains, bloody dogs),
>   Melted with tenderness and mild compassion,
>   Wept like two children in their deaths' sad story.
>   O, thus quoth Dighton lay the gentle babes—
>   Thus, thus, quoth Forrest girdling one another
>   Within their alabaster innocent arms.
>   Their lips were four red roses on a stalk,
>   And in their summer beauty kiss'd each other.
>   A book of prayers on their pillow lay;
>   Which once, quoth Forrest almost chang'd my mind—
>   But, O, the devil—there the villain stopp'd;
>   When Dighton thus told on: We smothered
>   The most replenished sweet work of nature
>   That from the prime creation e'er she framed—
>   Hence both are gone with conscience and remorse
>   They could not speak.

In the latter part of the same Scene is expressed a just and spirited maxim, which, I believe, will be sufficiently vouched by experience, That in difficult matters, quick resolves and brisk actions generally succeed better than slow counsels and circumspect conduct.

Richard, on hearing of the defection of his forces:

> Come, I have learn'd that fearful commenting
> Is leaden servitor to dull delay.
> Delay leads impotent and snail-pac'd beggary—
> Then fiery expedition be my wing,
> Jove's Mercury, and herald for a king.
> Go, muster men. My counsel is my shield.
> We must be brief when traitors brave the field.

Scene IV.

The temporary relief which an opportunity of expressing its sorrows affords to the mind of a person in affliction, is poetically described in a passage here.

Duchess. Why should calamity be fun of words?
Queen. Windy attorneys to their client woes,
    Airy succeeders of *intestate joys*,
    Poor breathing orators of miseries,
    Let them have scope; though what they will impart
    Help nothing else, yet do they case the heart.

Act V. Scene V.

In this Scene, the adverse camps are supposed to be pitched near each other at night, ready to join battle in the morning; and in the space between, the spirits of all the persons murdered by *Richard* arise, threatening destruction to him, and promising success to *Richmond*. But the ghosts here are not to be taken literally; they are to be understood only as an allegorical representation of those images or ideas which naturally occur to the minds of men during their sleep, referring to the actions of their lives, whether good or bad.

"Sweet are the slumbers of the virtuous man,"

says Addison, in his Cato; and a modern writer, in a poem on the subject of dreams, most emphatically expresses himself thus:
    "Nor are the oppressor's crimes in sleep forgot;
    "He starts appalled, *for conscience slumbers not.*"
That this is the sense in which our Poet meant this scene to be accepted, is fully evident from his representing both *Richard* and *Richmond* to have been asleep during the appariting, and therefore capable of receiving those notices in *the mind's eye* only, as Hamlet says; which intirely removes the seeming absurdity of such an exhibition.

The soliloquy of self-accusation, which Richard enters upon alone, immediately after the spectral vision is closed, though so strongly marked, is nothing more than might be supposed natural, in the circumstances and situation of the speaker, as there described.

                    Richard, *starting from his couch*
    Give me another horse—bind up my wounds—
    Have mercy, Jesu—Soft! I did but dream.
    O coward conscience, how dost thou afflict me!
    The lights burn blue. It is now dead midnight.

Cold fearful drops stand on my trembling flesh—
What do I fear? Myself? There's none else by. . . .
My conscience hath a thousand several tongues,
And every tongue brings in a several tale,
And every tale condemns me for a villain. . . .
All several sins, all us'd in each degree,
Throng to the bar, crying all *Guilty! guilty!*
I shall despair. There is no creature loves me;
And if I die no soul will pity me:
And wherefore should they, since that I myself
Find in myself no pity to myself?
Methought the souls of all that I had murder'd
Came to my tent, and every one did threat
To-morrow's vengeance on the head of Richard.
>   *Enter* Ratcliff.

Richard. Who's there?
Ratcliff. My lord, the early village-cock
Hath twice done salutation to the morn;
Your friends are up and buckle on their armour.
Richard. Ratcliff, I fear, I fear.
Ratcliff. Nay, good my lord, be not afraid of shadows.
Richard. By the apostle Paul, shadows, to-night,
Have stuck more terror to the soul of *Richard*
Than can the substance of ten thousand soldiers
Armed in proof and led by shallow *Richmond*.

* * *

I shall here close my observation on this Play with a reflection upon the last paragraph above.

Such is the nature of man, that the slightest alarm, arising from within, discomfits him more than the greatest dangers presenting themselves from without. Body may be overcome by body, but the mind only can conquer itself. Notions of religion are natural to all men, in some sort or other. The good are inspired by devotion, the bad terrified by superstition. The admonitions of conscience are taken for supernatural emotions, and this awes us more than any difficulty in the common course of things. Man has been severally defined a *risible*, a *rational*, a *religious*, and a *bashful* animal. May I take the liberty of adding the farther criterion of his being a *conscientious* one? And this distinction, I shall venture to say, is less equivocal than any of the others.

1784—William Richardson. "On the Dramatic Character of King Richard the Third," from *Essays on Shakespeare's Dramatic Characters of "Richard III," "King Lear," and "Timon of Athens"*

William Richardson (1743–1814) was a Scottish university professor and scholar. With a talent for learning languages, he traveled to Russia with Lord Cathcart, who was appointed ambassador to Russia in 1768. Six years later, Richardson published *Anecdotes of the Russian Empire*. Following his return to England, Richardson became a professor of humanities at the University of Glasgow in 1773 and published several works criticizing Shakespeare, such as "On Shakespeare's Imitation of Female Characters" (1788).

The "Life and Death of King Richard the Third" is a popular tragedy: yet the poet, in his principal character, has connected deformity of body with every vice that can pollute human nature. Nor are those vices disguised or softened. The hues and lineaments are as dark and as deeply impressed as we are capable of conceiving. Neither do they receive any confiderable mitigation from the virtues of any other persons represented in the poem. The vices of Richard are not to serve as a foil or a test to *their* virtues; for the virtues and innocence of others serve no other purpose than to aggravate his hideous guilt. In reality, we are not much attached by affection, admiration, or esteem, to any character in the tragedy. The merit of Edward, Clarence, and some others, is so undecided, and has such a mixture of weakness, as hinders us from entering deeply into their interests. Richmond is so little seen, his goodness is so general or unfeatured, and the difficulties he has to encounter are so remote from view, are thrown, if I may use the expression, so far into the back ground, and are so much lessened by concurring events, that he cannot, with any propriety, be deemed the hero of the performance. Neither does the pleasure we receive proceed entirely from the gratification of our resentment, or the due display of poetical justice. To be pleased with such a display, it is necessary that we enter deeply into the interests of those that suffer. But so strange is the structure of this tragedy, that we are less interested in the miseries of those that are oppressed, than we are moved with indignation against the oppressor. The sufferers, no doubt, excite some degree of compassion; but, as we have now observed, they have so little claim to esteem, are so numerous and disunited, that no particular interest of this sort takes hold of us during the whole exhibition. Thus were the pleasure we receive to depend solely on the fulfilment of poetical justice, that half of it would be lost which arises from great regard for the sufferers, and esteem for the hero who performed the exploit. We may also add, that if the punishment of Richard were to constitute our chief enjoyment, that event is put off for too long a period. The poet might have exhibited his cruelties in shorter space, sufficient, however, to excite our resentment; and so might have brought us sooner to the catastrophe, if that alone was to have yielded us pleasure. In truth, the catastrophe of a good tragedy is only the completion of our pleasure, and not the chief cause of it. The fable, and the view which the poet exhibits of human nature, conducted through a whole performance, must produce our enjoyment. But in the work now before us there is scarcely any fable; and there is no character of eminent importance, but that of Richard. He is the principal agent: and the whole tragedy is an exhibition of guilt, where abhorrence for the criminal is much stronger than our interest in the sufferers, or esteem for those, who, by accident rather than great exertion, promote his downfall. We are pleased, no doubt, with his punishment; but the display of his enormities, and their progress to this completion, are the chief objects of our attention. Thus Shakespeare, in order to render the shocking vices of Richard an amusing spectacle, must have recourse to other expedients than those usually practised in similar situations. Here, then, we are led to enquire into the nature of these resources and expedients: for why do we not turn from the Richard of Shakespear, as we turn from his Titus Andronicus ? Has he inverted him with any charm, or secured him by some secret talisman from disgust and aversion? The subject is curious, and deserves our attention.

We may observe in general, that the interest is produced, not by veiling or contrasting offensive features and colours, but by so connecting them with agreeable qualities residing in the character itself, that the disagreeable effect is either entirely suppressed, or by its union with coalescing qualities, is converted into a pleasurable feeling. In particular, though Richard has no sense of justice, nor indeed of any moral obligation, he has an abundant mare of those qualities which are termed intellectual. Destitute of virtue, he professes ability. He shows discernment of character; artful contrivance in forming projects; great address in the management of mankind; fertility of resource; a prudent command of temper; much versatility of deportment; and lingular dexterity in concealing his intentions. He possesses along with these, such perfect consciousness of the superior powers of his own understanding above those of other men, as leads him not ostentatiously to treat them with contempt, but to employ them, while he really contemns their weakness, as engines of his ambition. Now, though these properties are not the objects of moral approbation, and may be employed as the instruments of fraud no less than of justice, yet the native and unmingled effect which *most* of them produce on the spectator, independent of the principle that employs them, is an emotion of pleasure. The person possessing them is regarded with deference, with reflect, and with admiration. Thus, then, the satisfaction we receive in contemplating the character of Richard, in the various situations in which the poet has shown him, arises from a mixed feeling: a feeling, compounded of horror, on account of his guilt; and of admiration, on account of his talents. By the concurrence of these two emotions the mind is thrown into a state of unusual agitation; neither painful nor pleasant, in the extremes of pain or of pleasure, but strangely delightful. Surprise and amazement, excited by the striking conjunctures which he himself very often occasions, and which give exercise to his talents, together with astonishment at the determined boldness and success of his guilt, give uncommon force to the general impression.

It may be apprehended, that the mixed feelings now mentioned may be termed indignation; nor have I any objection to the use of the term. Indignation seems to arise from a comparative view of two objects: the one worthy, and the other unworthy; which are, nevertheless, united; but which, on account of the wrong or impropriety occasioned by this incongruous union, we conceive mould be disunited and independent. The man of merit suffering neglect or contempt, and the unworthy man raised to distinction, provoke indignation. In like manner, indignation may be provoked, by feeing illustrious talents perverted to inhuman and perfidious purposes. Nor is the feeling, for it arises from elevation of foul and consciousness of virtue, by any means disagreeable. Indeed, the pleasure it yields us is different from that arising from other emotions of a more placid and softer character; different, for example, in a very remarkable manner, from our sympathy with successful merit. We may also observe, that suspence, wonder, and surprise, occasioned by the actual exertion of great abilities, under the guidance of uncontrolled inhumanity, by their awful effects, and the postures they assume, together with solicitude to fee an union so unworthy dissolved, give poignancy to our indignation, and annex to it, if I may use the expression, a certain wild and alarming delight.

But, by what term soever we recognise the feeling, I proceed to illustrate, by a particular analysis of some striking scenes in the tragedy, "that the pleasure we receive from the Character of Richard, is produced by those emotions which arise in the mind, on beholding great intellectual ability employed for inhuman and perfidious purposes."

I. In the first scene of the tragedy we have the loathsome deformity of Richard displayed, with such indications of mind as altogether suppress our aversion. Indeed the poet, in the beginning of Richard's soliloquy, keeps that deformity to which he would reconcile us, out of view; nor mentions it till he throws discredit upon its opposite: this he does indirectly. He possesses the imagination with dislike at those employments which are the usual concomitants of grace and beauty. The means used for this purpose are suited to the artifice of the design. Richard does not inveigh with grave and with solemn declamation against the sports and pastime of a peaceful Court: they are unworthy of such serious assault. He treats them with irony: he scoffs at them; does not blame, but despises them.

> Now are our brows bound with victorious wreaths;
> Our bruised arms hung up for monuments;
> Our stern alarums chang'd to merry meetings;
> Our dreadful marches to delightful measures.
> Grim-visaged war hath smooth'd his wrinkled front:
> And now, instead of mounting barbed steeds,
> To fright the fouls of fearful adversaries,
> He capers nimbly in a lady's chamber,
> To the lascivious pleasing of a lute.

By thus throwing discredit on the usual attendants of grace and beauty, he lessens our esteem for those qualities; and proceeds with less reluctance to mention his own hideous appearance. Here, too, with great judgment on the part of the poet, the speech is ironical. To have justified or apologized for deformity with serious argument, would have been no less ineffectual than a serious charge against beauty. The intention of Shakespeare is not to make us admire the monstrous deformity of Richard, but to make us endure it.

> But I, that am not shap'd for sportive tricks,
> Nor made to court an am'rous looking-glass;
> I that am rudely stampt, and want Love's majesty
> To strut before a wanton ambling nymph;
> I that am curtail'd of this fair proportion,
> Cheated of feature by dissembling nature,
> Deform'd, unfinish'd, sent before my time
> Into this breathing world, scarce half made up,
> And that so lamely and unfashionably,
> That dogs bark at me as I halt by them:
> Why I (in this weak piping time of peace)
> Have no delight to pass away the time,
> Unless to spy my shadow in the fun,
> And descant on mine own deformity:
> And, therefore, since I cannot prove a lover,
> To entertain these fair well-spoken days,
> I am determined to prove a villain,
> And hate the idle pleasures of these days.

His contempt of external appearance, and the easy manner in which he considers his own defects, impress us strongly with the apprehension of his superior understanding. His resolution, too, of not acquiescing tamely in the misfortune of his form, but of making it a motive for him to exert his other abilities, gives us an idea of his possessing great vigour and strength of mind.

Not dispirited with his deformity, it moves him to high exertion. Add to this, that our wonder and astonishment are excited at the declaration he makes of an atrocious character; of his total insensibility; and resolution to perpetrate the blackest crimes.

> Plots have I laid, inductions dangerous,
> By drunken prophecies, libels and dreams,
> To set my brother Clarence and the king
> In deadly hate, the one against the other:
> And if King Edward be as true and just,
> As I am subtle, false, and treacherous,
> This day mould Clarence closely be mew'd up.

It may be said, perhaps, that the colouring here is by far too strong, and that we cannot suppose characters to exist so full of deliberate guilt, as thus to contemplate a criminal conduct without subterfuge, and without imposing upon themselves. It may be thought, that even the Neros and the Domitians who disgraced human nature, did not confider themselves so atrociously wicked as they really were: but, transported by lawless passions, deceived themselves, and were barbarous without perceiving their guilt. It is difficult to ascertain what the real state of such perverted characters may be; nor is it a pleasing task to analyse their conceptions. Yet the view which Shakespeare has given us of Richard's sedate and deliberate guilt, knowing that his conduct was really guilty, is not inconsistent. He only gives a deeper shade to the darkness of his character. With his other enormities and defects, he represents him incapable of feeling, though he may perceive the difference between virtue and vice. Moved by unbounded ambition; vain of his intellectual and political talents; conceiving himself, by reason of his deformity, as of a different species from the rest of mankind; and inured from his infancy to the barbarities perpetrated during a desperate civil war; surely it is not incompatible with his character, to represent him incapable of feeling those pleasant or unpleasant sensations that usually, in other men, accompany the discernment of right and of wrong. I will indeed allow, that the effect would have been as powerful, and the representation would have been better suited to our ideas of human nature, had Richard, both here and in other scenes, given indication of his guilt rather by obscure hints and surmises, than by an open declaration.

II. In the scene between Richard and Lady Anne, the attempt seems as bold, and the situation as difficult, as any in the tragedy.

It seems, indeed, altogether wild and unnatural; that Richard, deformed and hideous as the poet represents him, would offer himself as suitor to the widow of an excellent young prince whom he had slain, at the very time she is attending the funeral of her husband, and while she is expressing the most bitter hatred against the author of her misfortune. But, in attending to the progress of the dialogue, we shall find ourselves more interested in the event, and more astonished at the boldness and ability of Richard, than moved with abhorrence at his shameless effrontery, or offended with the improbability of the situation.

In considering this scene, it is necessary that we keep in view the character of Lady Anne. The outlines of this character are given us in her own conversation; but we see it more completely finished and filled up, indirectly indeed, but not less distinctly, in the conduct of Richard. She is represented by the poet, of a mind altogether frivolous; incapable of deep affection; guided by no steady principles of virtue, produced of strengthened by reason and reflection; the prey of vanity, which is her ruling passion; susceptible of every feeling and emotion; sincere in their expression while they last; but hardly capable of distinguishing the propriety of one more than another; and so exposed alike to the influence of good and of bad impressions. There are such characters: persons of great sensibility, of great sincerity, of no rational or steady virtue, and consequently of no consistency of conduct. They now amaze us with, their amiable virtues; and now confound us with apparent vices.

Richard, in his management of Lady Anne, having in view the accomplishment of his ambitious designs, addresses her with the most perfect knowledge of her constitution. He knows that her feelings are violent; that they have no foundation in steady determined principles of conduct; that violent feelings are soon exhausted; and that the undecided mind, without choice or sense of propriety, is equally accessible to the next that occur. All that he has to do, then, is to suffer the violence of one emotion to pass away, and then, as skillfully as possible, to bring another, more suited to his designs, into its place. Thus he not only discovers much discernment of human nature, but also great command of temper, and great dexterity of conduct.

In order, as soon as possible, to exhaust her temporary grief and resentment, it is necessary that they be swollen and exasperated to their utmost measure. In truth, it is resentment, rather than grief, which he expresses in her lamentation for Henry. Accordingly Richard, inflaming her disorder to its fiercest extreme, breaks in abruptly upon the funeral procession. This stimulates her resentment; it becomes more violent, by his appearing altogether cool and unconcerned at her abuse; and thus she vents her emotion in fierce invectives and imprecations:

> O God, which this blood mad'ft, revenge his death!
> O earth, which this blood drink'ft, revenge his death!
> Or heav'n, with lightning strike the murderer dead!
> Or earth, gape open wide, and eat him quick!

This invective is general. But before the vehemence of this angry mood can be entirely abated, She must bring home to her fancy every aggravating circum-

stance, and must ascertain every particular wrong she has suffered. When she
has done this, and expressed the consequent feelings, she has no longer any
topics or food for anger, and the passion will of course subside. Richard, for
this purpose, pretends to justify or to extenuate his seeming offences; and thus,
instead of concealing his crimes, he overcomes the resentment of Lady Anne, by
bringing his cruelties into view. This has also the effect of impressing her with
the belief of his candour.

> Vouchsafe, divine perfection of a woman,
> Of these supposed crimes, to give me leave,
> By circumstance but to acquit myself, &c.
> *Anne.* Didst thou not kill this king ?
> *Glo.* I grant ye.
> *Anne.* Dost grant me? then God grant me, too
> Thou may'st be damned for that wicked deed.

Here also we may observe the application of those flatteries and apparent
obsequiousness, which, if they cannot take effect: at present, otherwise than to
give higher provocation; yet, when her wrath subsides, will operate in a different
direction, and tend to excite that vanity which is the predominant disposition of
her mind, and by means of which he will accomplish his purpose.

It was not alone sufficient to provoke her anger and her resentment to the
utmost, in order that they might immediately subside; but by alledging apparent
reasons for change of sentiment, to assist them in their decline. Though Lady Anne
possesses no decided, determined virtue, yet her moral nature, uncultivated as it
appears, would discern impropriety in her conduct; would suggest scruples, and so
produce hesitation. Now, in order to prevent the effect of these, it was necessary
to aid the mind in finding subterfuge or excuse, and thus assist her in the pleasing
business of imposing upon herself. Her seducer accordingly endeavours to gloss his
conduct, and represents himself as less criminal than me at first apprehended.

> To leave this keen encounter of our wits,
> And fall somewhat into a flower method:
> Is not the causer of the timeless deaths
> Of these Plantagenets, Henry and Edward,
> As blameful as the executioner ?
> *Anne.* Thou wast the cause, and most accurst effect.
> *Glo.* Your beauty was the cause of that effect. Your beauty, which did
> haunt me in my sleep, &c.

In these lines, besides a confirmation of the foregoing remark, and an
illustration of Richard's persevering flattery, there are two circumstances that

mark great delicacy and fineness of pencil in Shakespeare's execution of this striking scene. The invective and resentment are now so mitigated and brought down, that the conversation, assuming the more patient form of dialogue, is not so much the expression of violent passion, as a contest for victory in a smart dispute, and becomes a "keen encounter of wits." The other circumstance to be observed is that Richard, instead of speaking of her husband and father-in-law, in the relation in which they stood to her, falls in with the subsiding state of her affection towards them, and using terms of great indifference, speaks, of "these Plantagenets, Henry and Edward."

Lady Anne having listened to the conversation of Richard, after the first transport of her wrath on the subject of Edward's death, showed that the real force of the passion was abating; and it seems to be perfectly subdued, by her having listened to his exculpation. In all this the art of the poet is wonderful; and the skill he ascribes to Richard, profound. Though the crafty seducer attempts to justify his conduct to Lady Anne, he does not seek to convince her reason; for she had no reason worth the pains of convincing; but to afford her the means and opportunity to vent her emotion. When this effect is produced, he proceeds to substitute some regard for himself in its place. As we have already observed, he has been taking measures for this purpose in every thing he has said; and by soothing expressions of adulation during the course of her anger, he was gradually preparing her mind for the more pleasing, but not less powerful, dominion of vanity. In the foregoing lines, and in what follows, he ventures a declaration of the passion he entertains for her. Yet he does this indirectly, as suggested by the tendency of their argument, and as a reason for those parts of his conduct that seem so heinous:

Your beauty was the cause, &c.

Richard was well aware, that a declaration of love from him would of course renew her indignation. He accordingly manages her mind in such a manner as to soften its violence, by mentioning his passion, in the part of the dialogue containing, in his language, the "keen encounter of their wits," as a matter not altogether serious; and afterwards when he announces it more seriously, by mentioning it as it were by chance, and indirectly. Yet, notwithstanding all these precautions to introduce the thought with an easy and familiar appearance, it must excite violent indignation. Here, therefore, as in the former part of the scene, he must have recourse to the fame command of temper, and to the fame means of artfully irritating her emotion, till it entirely subsides. Accordingly, he adheres without deviation to his plan; he persists in his adulation; provokes her anger to its utmost excess; and finally, by varying the attitudes of his flatteries, by assuming an humble and suppliant address, he subdues and restores her foul to the ruling passion. In the close of the dialogue, the decline of her emotion

appears distinctly traced. It follows the fame course as the passion she expresses
in the beginning of the scene. She is at first violent; becomes more violent; her
passion subsides: yet, some notions of propriety wandering across her mind, she
makes an effort to recall her resentment. The effort is feeble; it only enables
her to express contempt in her aspect; and at last she becomes the prey of her
vanity. In the concluding part of the dialogue, she does not, indeed, directly
comply with the suit of Richard, but indicates plainly that total change in her
disposition which it was his purpose to produce.

III. We shall now consider the manner in which Richard manages his
accomplices, and those from whom he derives his assistance in the fulfilment
of his designs.

We discern in his conduct towards them, as much at least as in their own
deportment, the true colour of their characters: we discern the full extent of
their faculties, and the real value of their virtues. According as they are variously
constituted, his treatment of them varies. He uses them all as the tools of his
ambition; but assumes an appearance of greater friendship and confidence
towards some than towards others. He is well acquainted with the engines
he would employ: he knows the compass of their powers, and discovers great
dexterity in his manner of moving and applying them. To the Mayor and his
followers he affects an appearance of uncommon devotion and piety; great zeal
for the public welfare; a scrupulous regard for the forms of law and of justice;
retirement from the world; aversion to the toils of state; much trust in the good
intentions of a magistrate so conspicuous; still more in his understanding; and
by means of both, perfect confidence in his power with the people.—Now, in
this manner of conducting himself, who is not more struck with the address
and ability displayed by Richard, and more moved with curiosity to know their
effects, than mocked at his hypocrisy and safe deceit? Who does not distinctly,
though indirectly, indeed, discern the character of the Mayor? The deportment
of Richard is a glass that reflects every limb, every lineament, and every colour,
with the most perfect truth and propriety.

What, think you we are Turks or Infidels,
Or that we would, against the form of law,
Proceed thus rashly in the villain's death? &c.
Alas! why would you heap those cares on me?
I am unfit for state or Majesty, &c.

The behaviour of Richard towards Buckingham is still more striking and
peculiar. The situation was more difficult, and his conduct appears more masterly.
Yet, as in former instances, the outlines and sketch of Buckingham's character
are filled up in the deportment of his seducer.

This accomplice possesses some talents, and considerable discernment of human nature: his passions are ardent; he has little zeal for the public welfare, or the interests of virtue or religion; yet, to a certain degree, he possesses humanity and a sense of duty. He is moved with the love of power and of wealth. He is susceptible, perhaps, of envy against those who arise to such pre-eminence as he thinks might have suited his own talents and condition. Possessing some political abilities, or, at least, possessing that cunning, that power of subtile contrivance, and that habit of activity, which sometimes pass for political abilities, and which, imposing upon those who possess them, make them fancy themselves endowed with the powers of distinguished statesmen; he values himself for his talents, and is desirous of displaying them. Indeed, this seems to be the most striking feature in his character; and the desire of exhibiting his skill and dexterity, appears to be the foremost of his active principles. Such a person is Buckingham; and the conduct of Richard is perfectly consonant. Having too much penetration, or too little regard to the public weal, to be blindfolded or imposed upon like the Mayor, Richard treats him with apparent confidence. Moved, perhaps, with envy against the kindred of the Queen, or the hope of pre-eminence in consequence of their ruin, he concurs in the accomplishment of their destruction, and in assisting the Usurper to attain his unlawful preferment. But above all, excessively vain of his talents, Richard borrows aid from his counsels, and not only uses him as the tool of his designs, but seems to share with him in the glory of their success. Knowing, too, that his sense of virtue is faint, or of little power, and that the secret exultation and triumph for over-reaching their adversaries, will afford him pleasure sufficient to counterbalance the pain, that may arise in his breast from the perpetration of guilt, he makes him, in, a certain degree, the confident of his crimes. It is also to be remarked, that Buckingham, stimulated with the hope of reward, and elated frill more with, vanity in the display of his talents, appears more active than the usurper himself; more inventive in the contrivance of expedients, and more alert in their execution. There are many such persons, the instruments of designing men: persons of some ability, of less virtue, who derive consequence to themselves, by fancying they are privy to the vices or designs of men whom they respect and who triumph in the fulfilment of crafty projects. Richard, however, sees the slightness of Buckingham's mind, and reveals no more of his projects and vices than he reckons expedient for the accomplishment of his purpose: for, as some men, when at variance, so restrain their resentments as to leave room for future reconciliation arid friendship; so Richard manages his seeming friendships, as to leave room, without the hazard of material injury to himself, for future hatred and animosity. A rupture of course ensues, and in a manner perfectly compatible with both of their characters. Richard wishes for the death of his brother Edward's children; and that his friend should on this, as on former occasions, partake of the shame or the glory. But here the ambition or envy of Buckingham had no particular concern; nor was there any great ability requisite for the assassination of two helpless infants. Thus his humanity and sense of duty, feeble as they were, when exposed to stronger principles, not altogether extinguished, were left to work uncontrouled; and consequently would suggest hesitation. They might be aided in their operation by the insatiate desire of reward for former services, not gratified according to promise or expectation; and, by the same invidious disposition, transferred from the ruined kindred of the Queen to the successful Usurper. Richard, somewhat aware that this project was more likely to encounter scruples than any of the former, hints his design with caution: he insinuates it with acknowledgment of obligation; and endeavours to anticipate his conscience, by suggesting to him, along with this acknowledgment, the recollection of former guilt. Not aware, however, of the force contained in the resisting principles, and apprehending that the mind of his assistant was now as depraved as he desired, he hazards too abruptly the mention of his design. The consequence, in perfect consistency with both their natures, is coldness and irreconcilable hatred.

>   *Rich.* Stand all apart.—Cousin of Buckingham—
>   *Buck.* My gracious Sovereign !
>   *Rich.* Give me thy hand. Thus high, by thy advice
>   And thy assistance, is King Richard seated:
>   But shall we wear these glories for a day ?
>   Or shall they last, and we rejoice in them ?
>   *Buck.* Still live they, and for ever let them last.
>   *Rich.* Ah, Buckingham I now do I play the touch,
>   To try if thou be current gold indeed:
>   Young Edward lives ! think now what I would speak.
>   *Buck.* Say on, my loving Lord.
>   *Rich.* Why, Buckingham, I say I would be King.
>   *Buck.* Why, so you are, my thrice renowned Liege.
>   *Rich.* Ha! am I a King ?—'Tis so—but Edward lives—
>   *Buck.* True, noble Prince.
>   *Rich.* O bitter consequence !
>   That Edward Hill should live—True, noble Prince—
>   Cousin, thou waft not wont to be so dull.
>   Shall I be plain ? I wish the bastards dead,
>   And I would have it suddenly perform'd.
>   What say'st thou now? Speak suddenly—be brief.
>   *Buck.* Your Grace may do your pleasure.
>   *Rich.* Tut, tut, thou art all ice; thy kindness
>   freezes:
>   Say, have I thy consent that they still die?

Buck. Give me some breath, some little pause,
dear Lord,
Before I positively speak in this:
I will resolve your Grace immediately.
Cates. The King is angry; see, he gnaws his lip.

The conduct of Richard to Catesby is different from his deportment towards the Mayor or Buckingham. Regarding him as totally unprincipled, servile, and inhuman, he treats him like the meanest instrument of his guilt. He treats him without respect for his character, without management of his temper, and without the least apprehension that he has any feelings that will shudder at his commands.

IV. We shall now confider the decline of Richard's prosperity, and the effect of his conduct on the fall of his fortunes.

By dissimulation, perfidy, and bloodshed, he paves his way to the throne: by the same inhuman means he endeavours to secure his pre-eminence; and has added to the lift of his crimes, the assassination of his wife and his nephews. Meanwhile he is laying a snare for himself. Not Richmond, but his own enormous vices, proved the cause of his ruin. The cruelties he perpetrates, excite in the minds of men hatred, indignation, and the desire of revenge. But such is the deluding nature of vice, that of this consequence he is little aware. Men who lose the sense of virtue, transfer their own depravity to the rest of mankind, and believe that others are as little mocked with their crimes as they are themselves. Richard having trampled upon every sentiment of justice, had no conception of the general abhorrence that had arisen against him. He thought resentment might belong to the sufferers, and their immediate adherents; but, having no faith in the existence of a disinterested sense of virtue, he appears to have felt no apprehension left other persons mould be offended with his injustice, or inclined to punish his inhuman guilt. Add to this, that success administers to his boldness; and that he is daily more and more inured to the practice of violent outrage. Before he obtained the diadem, he proceeded with caution; he endeavoured to impose upon mankind the belief of his sanctified manners; he treated his associates with suitable deference; and seemed as dexterous in his conduct, as he was barbarous in disposition. But caution and dissimulation required an effort; the exertion was laborious; and naturally ceased when imagined to be no longer needful. Thus rendered familiar with perfidious cruelty; flushed with success; more elate with confidence in his own ability, than attentive to the suggestions of his suspicion; and from his incapacity of feeling moral obligation, more ignorant of the general abhorrence he had incurred, than averse to revenge; as he becomes, if possible, more inhuman, he certainly becomes more incautious. This appears in the wanton display of his real character, and of those vices which drew upon him even the curses of a parent.

Dutch. Either thou'lt die by God's suft ordinance,
Ere from this war thou turn a conqueror;
Or I with grief and extreme age shall perish,
And never look upon thy face again :
Therefore, take with thee my molt heavy curse,
Which in the day of battle tire thee more
Than all the complete armour that thou wear'ft.

His incautious behaviour after he has arisen to supreme authority, appears very striking in his conduct to his accomplices. Those whom he formerly seduced, or deceived, or flattered, he treats with indifference or disrespect. He conceives himself no longer in need of their aid: he has no occasion, as he apprehends, to assume disguise. Men of high rank, who still seem to give him advice or assistance, and so by their influence with the multitude, reconcile them to his crimes, or bear a part of his infamy, cease to be reckoned necessary; and he has employment for none, but the desperate assassin, or implicit menial. All this is illustrated in his treatment of Buckingham. Blinded by his own barbarity, he requires his assistance in the death of his nephews. Buckingham, having less incitement than formerly to participate in his guilt, hesitates, and seems to refuse. Richard is offended; does not govern his temper as on former occasions; expresses his displeasure; refuses to ratify the promises he had given him; behaves to him, in the refusal, with supercilious insult, and so provokes his resentment.

Buck. My Lord, I claim the gift, my due by promise,
For which your honour and your faith are pawn'd;
Th' Earldom of Hereford, and the moveables,
Which you have promised I shall possess, &c.
Rich. Thou trouble!! me : I am not in the vein.
                                                                 [Exit.

Buck. Is it even so?—Repays he my deep service
With such contempt ?—Made I him king for this?
O, let me think on Hastings, and be gone
To Brecknock, while my fearful head is on.

Thus the conduct of Richard involves him in danger. The minds of men are alienated from his interests. Those of his former associates, who were in public esteem, are dismissed with indignity, and incensed to resentment. Even such of his adherents as are interested in his fortunes, on their own account, regard him with utter aversion. A stroke aimed at him in his perilous situation, must prove effectual. He arrives at the brink of ruin, and the slightest impulse will push him down. He resembles the misshapen rock described in a fairy tale. "This astonishing rock," says the whimsical novelist, "was endowed, by infernal sorcery, with the power of impetuous motion. It rolled through a flourishing kingdom; it crushed down its opponents; it laid the land desolate; and was followed by a stream of blood. It arrived unwittingly at an awful precipice; it had no power of returning; for the bloody stream that pursued it was so strong, that it never rolled back. It was pushed from the precipice; was slivered into fragments; and the roar of its downfall arose unto heaven."

The pleasure we receive from the ruin of Richard, though intimately connected with that arising from the various displays of his character, is, nevertheless, different. We are not amazed, as formerly, with his talents and his address, but shocked at his cruelty; our abhorrence is softened, or converted into an agreeable feeling, by the satisfaction we receive from his punishment. Besides, it is a punishment inflicted, not by the agency of an external cause, but incurred by the natural progress of his vices. We are more gratified in feeing him racked with suspicion before the battle of Bosworth; listening from tent to tent, left his soldiers should meditate treason; overwhelmed on the eve of the battle with presages of calamity, arising from inauspicious remembrance; and driven, by the dread of danger, to contemplate and be shocked at his own heinous transgressions. We are more affected, and more gratified with these, than with the death he so deservedly suffers. Richard and his conscience had long been strangers. That importunate monitor had been dismissed, at a very early period, from his service; nor had given him the least interruption in the career of his vices. Yet they were not entirely parted. Conscience was to visit him before he died, and chose for the hour of her visitation, the eve of his death. She comes introduced by Danger; spreads before him, in hues of infernal impression, the picture of his enormities; shakes him with deep dismay; pierces his foul with a poisoned arrow; unnerves and forsakes him.

O coward Conscience, how dost thou afflict me!
The light burns blue—is it not dead midnight ?
Cold, fearful drops, stand on my trembling flesh.
What do I fear? myself ? There's none else by.—
Is there a murth'rer here ? No:—Yes—I am.—
My conscience hath a thousand several tongues,
And ev'ry tongue brings in a several tale,
And ev'ry tale condemns me for a villain.

Upon the whole, certain objects, whether they actually operate on our senses, or be presented to the mind by imitation, are disagreeable. Yet many disagreeable objects may be so imitated, by having their deformities veiled, or by having any agreeable qualities they may possess, improved or judiciously brought forward, that so far from continuing offensive, they afford us pleasure. Many actions of mankind are in their own nature horrible and disgusting. Mere deceit, mere grovelling appetite, cruelty and meanness, both in the imita-

tion and the original, occasion pain and aversion. Yet these vices may be so
represented by the skill of an ingenious artist, as to afford us pleasure. The
most usual method of rendering their representation agreeable is, by setting
the characters in whom they predominate, in opposition to such characters
as are eminent for their opposite virtues. The dissimulation, ingratitude, and
inhumanity of Goneril, set in opposition to the native simplicity, the filial
affection, and sensibility of Cordelia, though in themselves hateful, become
an interesting spectacle. The pleasure we receive is, by having the agreeable
feelings and sentiments that virtue excites, improved and rendered exquisite
by contrast, by alternate hopes and fears, and even by our subdued and coin-
ciding abhorrence of vice. For the painful feeling, overcome by delightful
emotions, loses its direction and peculiar character; but retaining its force,
communicates additional energy to the prevailing sensation, and so augments
its efficacy. Another more difficult, though no less interesting method of producing the same effect is when with scarce any attention to opposite virtues
in other persons, very aggravated and heinous vices are blended and united in
the same person, with agreeable intellectual qualities. Boldness, command of
temper, a spirit of enterprise, united with the intellectual endowments of discernment, penetration, dexterity, and address, give us pleasure. Yet these may
be employed as instruments of cruelty and oppression, no less than of justice
and humanity. When the representation is such, that the pleasure arising from
these qualities is stronger than the painful aversion and abhorrence excited by
concomitant vices, the general effect; is agreeable. Even the painful emotion,
as in the former cafe, losing its character, but retaining its vigour, imparts
additional force to our agreeable feelings. Thus, though there is no approbation of the vicious character, we are, nevertheless, pleased with the representation. The foul is overshadowed with an agreeable gloom, and her powers
are suspended with delightful horror. The pleasure is varied and increased,
when the criminal propensities, gaining strength by indulgence, occasion the
neglect of intellectual endowments, and disregard of their assistance; so that
by natural coneequence, and without the interposition of uncommon agency
from without, the vicious person, becoming as incautious as he is wicked, is
rendered the prey of his own corruptions: fosters those makes in his bosom
that shall devour his vitals; and suffers the most condign of all punishment,
the miseries intailed by guilt.

Shakespeare, in his Richard the Third, has chosen that his principal
character should be constructed according to the last of these methods; and this
I have endeavoured to illustrate, by considering the manner in which Richard is
affected by the consciousness of his own deformity; by considering the dexterity
of his conduct in seducing the Lady Anne; by observing his various deportment
towards his seeming friends or accomplices; and finally, by tracing the progress
of his vices to his downfall and utter ruin.

The other excellencies of this tragedy besides the character of Richard, are, indeed, of an inferior nature, but not unworthy of Shakespeare. The characters of Buckingham, Anne, Hastings, and Queen Margaret, are executed with lively colouring and striking features; but, excepting Margaret, they are exhibited indirectly; and are more fully known by the conduct of Richard towards them, than by their own demeanour. They give the sketch and outlines in their own actions; but the picture appears finished in the deportment of Richard. This, however, of itself, is a proof of very singular skill. The conduct of the story is not inferior to that in Shakespeare's other historical tragedies. It exhibits a natural progress of events, terminated by one interesting and complete catastrophe. Many of the episodes have uncommon excellence. Of this kind are, in general, all the speeches of Margaret. Their effect is awful; they coincide with the style of the tragedy; and by wearing the fame gloomy complexion, her prophecies and imprecations suit and increase its horror. There was never in any poem a dream superior to that of Clarence. It pleases, like the prophecies of Margaret, by a solemn anticipation of future events, and by its consonance with the general tone of the tragedy. It pleases, by being so ample, so natural, and so pathetic, that every reader seems to have felt the same or similar horrors; and is inclined to say with Brakenbury,

> No wonder, Lord, that it affrighted you;
> I am afraid, methinks, to hear you tell it.

This tragedy, however, like every work of Shakespeare, has many faults; and, in particular, it seems to have been too hastily written. Some incidents are introduced without any apparent reason, or without apparent necessity. We are not, for instance, sufficiently informed of the motive that prompted Richard to marry the widow of Prince Edward. In other respects, as was observed, this scene possesses very singular merit. The scene towards the close of the tragedy, between the Queen and Richard, when he solicits her consent to marry her daughter Elizabeth, seems no other than a copy of that now mentioned. As such, it is faulty; and still more so, by being executed with less ability. Yet this incident is not liable to the objection made to the former. We fee a good, prudential reason, for the marriage of Richard with Elizabeth; but none for his marriage with Lady Anne. We almost wish that the first courtship had been omitted, and that the dialogue between Richard and Anne had been suited and appropriated to Richard and the Queen. Neither are we sufficiently informed of the motives, that, on some occasions, influenced the conduct of Buckingham. We are not enough prepared for his animosity against the Queen and her kindred; nor can we pronounce, without hazarding conjecture, that it proceeded from envy of their sudden greatness, or from having his vanity flattered by the seeming deference of Richard. Yet these motives seem highly probable. The young-Princes bear too great a share in the drama. It would seem the poet intended to interest us very much in their misfortunes. The representation, however, is not agreeable. The Princes have more smartness than simplicity; and we are more affected with Tyrrel's description of their death, than pleased with any thing in their own conversation. Nor does the scene of the ghosts, in the last act, seem equal in execution to the design of Shakespeare. There is more delightful horror in the speech of Richard awakening from his dream, than in any of the predictions denounced against him. There seems, indeed, some impropriety in representing those spectres as actually appearing, which were only seen in a vision. Besides, Richard might have described them in the succeeding scene, to Ratcliff, so as to have produced, at least in the perusal of the work, a much stronger effect. The representation of ghosts in this passage, is by no means so affecting, nor so awful, as the dream related by Clarence. Lastly, there is in this performance too much deviation in the dialogue from the dignity of the buskin; and deviations still more blameable, from the language of decent manners. Yet, with these imperfections, this tragedy is a striking monument of human genius; and the success of the poet, in delineating the character of Richard, has been as great as the singular boldness of the design.

1785—Thomas Whately. From *Remarks on Some of the Characters of Shakespere*

Thomas Whately (1726–72) was a Member of Parliament from 1761 until his death, in addition to holding various other political posts. He was best known during his lifetime as the author of *Observations on Modern Gardening* (1770). In his book *Remarks on Some of the Characters of Shakespeare* (1785), Whately had intended to present eight or ten of Shakespeare's characters, but he could not complete the project and the book was published posthumously. Whately's book attracted the attention of Charles Knight in 1811, which led to his edition of Shakespeare. Whately also won the acclaim of Horace Walpole who, in 1786, declared Whately to have provided the best commentary on Shakespeare's genius.

Every play of Shakespere abounds with instances of his excellence in distinguishing characters. It would be difficult to determine which is the most striking of all that he drew; but his merit will appear most conspicuously by comparing two opposite characters, who happen to be placed in similar circumstances:—not that on such occasions he marks them more strongly than on others, but because the contrast makes the distinction more apparent; and of these none seem to agree so much in situation, and to differ so much in disposition, as RICHARD THE THIRD and MACBETH. Both are soldiers, both usurpers; both attain the throne by the same means, by treason and murder; and both lose it too in the same manner, in battle against the person claiming it as lawful heir. Perfidy, violence and tyranny are common to both; and those only, their obvious qualities, would have been attributed indiscriminately to both by an ordinary dramatic writer. But Shakespere, in conformity to the truth of history, as far as it led him, and by improving upon the fables which have been blended with it, has ascribed opposite principles and motives to the same designs and actions, and various effects to the operation of the same events upon different tempers. Richard and Macbeth, as represented by him, agree in nothing but their fortunes.

The periods of history, from which the subjects are taken, are such as at the best can be depended on only for some principal facts; but not for the minute detail, by which characters are unravelled. That of Macbeth is too distant to be particular; that of Richard, too full of discord and animosity to be true: and antiquity has not feigned more circumstances of horror in the one, than party violence has given credit to in the other. Fiction has even gone so far as to introduce supernatural fables into both stories: the usurpation of Macbeth is said to have been foretold by some witches; and the tyranny of Richard by omens attending his birth. From these fables, Shakespere, unrestrained and indeed uninformed by history, seems to have taken the hint of their several characters; and he has adapted their dispositions so as to give to such fictions, in the days he wrote, a show of probability. The first thought of acceding to the throne is suggested, and success in the attempt is promised, to Macbeth by the witches: he is therefore represented as a man, whose natural temper would have deterred him from such a design, if he had not been immediately tempted, and strongly impelled to it. Richard, on the other hand, brought with him into the world the signs of ambition and cruelty: his disposition, therefore, is suited to those symptoms; and he is not discouraged from indulging it by the improbability of succeeding, or by any difficulties and dangers which obstruct his way.

Agreeable to these ideas, Macbeth appears to be a man not destitute of the feelings of humanity. His lady gives him that character.

> —I fear thy nature;
> It is too full o' the milk of human kindness,
> To catch the nearest way[1].—

Which apprehension was well founded; for his reluctance to commit the murder is owing in a great measure to reflections which arise from sensibility:

> —He's here in double trust
> First, as I am his kinsman and his subject;

Strong both against the deed; then as his host,
Who should against his murderer shut the door,
Not bear the knife myself[2].—

Immediately after he tells Lady Macbeth,—

We will proceed no further in this business;
He hath honoured me of late[3].

And thus giving way to his natural feelings of kindred, hospitality, and gratitude, he for a while lays aside his purpose. A man of such a disposition will esteem, as they ought to be esteemed, all gentle and amiable qualities in another: and therefore Macbeth is affected by the mild virtues of Duncan; and reveres them in his sovereign when he stifles them in himself. That

      —This Duncan
Hath borne his faculties so meekly; hath been
So clear in his great office,[4]—

is one of his reasons against the murder: and when he is tortured with the thought of Banquo's issue succeeding him in the throne, he aggravates his misery by observing, that,

For them the gracious Duncan have I murder'd;[5]

which epithet of *gracious* would not have occurred to one who was not struck with the particular merit it expresses.

The frequent references to the prophecy in favour of Banquo's issue, is another symptom of the same disposition: for it is not always from fear, but sometimes from envy, that he alludes to it: and being himself very susceptible of those domestic affections, which raise a desire and love of posterity, he repines at the succession assured to the family of his rival, and which in his estimation seems more valuable than his own actual possession. He therefore reproaches the sisters for their partiality, when

Upon my head they plac'd a fruitless crown,
And put a barren sceptre in my gripe,
Thence to be wrench'd with an unlineal hand,
No son of mine succeeding. If 'tis so,
For Banquo's issue have I 'fil'd my mind,
For them the gracious Duncan have I murder'd;

Put rancours in the vessel of my peace
Only for them; and mine eternal jewel
Given to the common enemy of man,
To make them kings, the seed of Banquo kings!
Rather than so, come, Fate, into the list,
And champion me to the utterance.[6]—

Thus, in a variety of instances, does the tenderness in his character shew itself; and one who has these feelings, though he may have no principles, cannot easily be induced to commit a murder. The intervention of a supernatural cause accounts for his acting so contrary to his disposition. But that alone is not sufficient to prevail entirely over his nature: the instigations of his wife are also necessary to keep him to his purpose; and she, knowing his temper, not only stimulates his courage to the deed, but, sensible that, besides a backwardness in daring, he had a degree of softness which wanted hardening, endeavours to remove all remains of humanity from his breast, by the horrid comparison she makes between him and herself:

—I have given suck, and know
How tender 'tis to love the babe that milks me
I would, while it was smiling in my face,
Have pluck'd my nipple from his boneless gums,
And dash'd the brains out, had I but so sworn
As you have done to this.[7]—

The argument is, that the strongest and most natural affections are to be stifled upon so great an occasion: and such an argument is proper to persuade one who is liable to be swayed by them; but is no incentive either to his courage or his ambition.

Richard is in all these particulars the very reverse to Macbeth. He is totally destitute of every softer feeling:

I that have neither pity, love, nor fear,[8]

is the character he gives of himself, and which he preserves throughout; insensible to his habitudes with a brother, to his connexion with a wife, to the piety of the king, and the innocence of the babes, whom he murders. The deformity of his body was supposed to indicate a similar depravity of mind; and Shakespere makes great use both of that, and of the current stories of the times concerning the circumstances of his birth, to intimate that his actions proceeded not from the occasion, but from a savageness of nature. Henry therefore tells him,

> Thy mother felt more than a mother's pain,
> And yet brought forth less than a mothers hope;
> To wit, an undigested, deform'd lump,
> Not like the fruit of such a goodly tree.
> Teeth hadst thou in thy head when thou wart born,
> To signify thou cam'st to bite the world;
> And, if the rest be true which I have heard,
> Thou cam'st into the world with thy legs forward.[9]

Which violent invective does not affect Richard as a reproach; it serves him only for a pretence to commit the murder he came resolved on and his answer while he is killing Henry is,

> I'll hear no more; die, prophet, in thy speech!
> For this, among the rest, was I ordain'd.[10]

Immediately afterwards he resumes the subject himself; and, priding himself that the signs given at his birth were verified in his conduct, he says,

> Indeed 'tis true that Henry told me of;
> For I have often heard my mother say,
> I came into the world with my legs forward.
> Had I not reason, think ye, to make haste,
> And seek their ruin that usurp'd our right?
> The midwife wonder'd; and the women cried,
> O Jesus bless us! he is born with teeth!
> And so I was; which plainly signified
> That I should snarl, and bite, and play the dog.
> Then, since the heavens have shap'd my body so,
> Let bell make crook'd my mind to answer it.[11]

Several other passages to the same effect imply that he has a natural propensity to evil; crimes are his delight: but Macbeth is always in an agony when he thinks of them. He is sensible, before he proceeds, of

> —the heat-oppressed brain.[12]

He feels

> —The present horror of the time
> Which now suits with it.[13]—

And immediately after he has committed the murder, he is

—afraid to think what he has done.[14]

He is pensive even while he is enjoying the effect of his crimes; but Richard is in spirits merely at the prospect of committing them; and what is effort in the one, is sport to the other. An extraordinary gaiety of heart shews itself upon those occasions, which to Macbeth seem most awful; and whether he forms or executes, contemplates the means, or looks back on the success, of the most wicked and desperate designs, they are at all times to him subjects of merriment. Upon parting from his brother, he bids him

> Go, tread the path that thou shalt ne'er return;
> Simple, plain Clarence! I do love thee so,
> That I will shortly send thy soul to heaven,
> If heaven will take the present at our hands.[15]

His amusement, when he is meditating the murder of his nephews, is the application of some proverbs to their discourse and situation:

> So wise, so young, they say, do ne'er live long.[16]

And,

> Short summer lightly has a forward spring.[17]

His ironical address to Tyrrel,

> Dar'st thou resolve to kill a friend of mine?[18]

is agreeable to the rest of his deportment: and his pleasantry does not forsake him when he considers some of his worst deeds, after he has committed them; for the terms in which he mentions them are, that,

> The sons of Edward sleep in Abraham's bosom;
> And Ann my wife hath bid the world good night.[19]

But he gives a still greater loose to his humour, when his deformity, and the omens attending his birth, are alluded to, either by himself or by others, as symptoms of the wickedness of his nature. The ludicrous turn which he gives to the reproach of Henry has been quoted already; and his joy at gaining the consent of Lady Ann to marry him, together with his determination to get rid of her, are expressed in the same wanton vein, when amongst other sallies of exultation, he says,

> Was ever woman in this humour woo'd?
> Was ever woman in this humour won?
> I'll have her, but I will not keep her long:
> What! I that kill'd her husband and her father,
> To take her in her heart's extremest hate,
> With curses in her mouth, tears in her eyes,
> The bleeding witness of her hatred by!
> With God, her conscience, and these bars against me,
> And I no friends to back my suit withal,
> But the plain Devil, and dissembling looks,
> And yet to win her,—All the world to nothing!—
> My dukedom to a beggarly denier,
> I do mistake my person all this while!
> Upon my life, she finds, although I cannot,
> Myself to be a marvellous proper man!
> I'll be at charges for a looking-glass,
> And entertain a score or two of taylors
> To study fashions to adorn my body.[20]

And yet, that nothing might be wanting to make him completely odious, Shakespere has very artfully mixed with all this ridicule, a rancorous envy of those who have greater advantages of figure.

> To shrink mine arm up like a wither'd shrub;
> To make an envious mountain on my back,
> Where sits deformity to mock my body![21]

and,

> I, that am curtail'd of this fair proportion,
> Cheated of feature by dissembling nature,
> Deform'd, unfinish'd, sent before my time
> Into this breathing world, scarce half made up,
> And that so lamely and unfashionably,
> That dogs bark at me, as I halt by them,[22]

are starts of spleen which he determines to vent on such

As are of better person than himself.[23]

There is, besides, another subject on which he sometimes exercises his wit, which is his own hypocrisy. I shall have occasion hereafter to take more notice of that part of his character; at present it is sufficient to observe, that to himself he laughs at the sanctified appearances which he assumes, and makes ridiculous applications of that very language by which he imposed upon others. His answer to his mother's blessing,

Amen! and make me die a good old man!
This is the butt-end of a mother's blessing;
I marvel that her grace should leave it out,[24]

is an example both of his hypocrisy and his humour: his application of the story of Judas to the affection he had just before expressed for Edward's family,

To say the truth, so Judas kiss'd his master;
And cried, All hail! when as he meant all harm,[25]

is another instance of the same kind; and there are many more. But still all this turn to ridicule does not proceed from levity; for Macbeth, though always serious, is not so considerate and attentive in times of action and business. But Richard, when he is indulging that wickedness and malice, which he is so prone to and fond of, expresses his enjoyment of it by such sallies of humour; on other occasions he is alert, on these only is he gay; and the delight he takes in them gives an air to his whole demeanour, which induces Hastings to observe, that as

His Grace looks cheerfully and well this morning
There's some conceit or other likes him well,
When that he bids good-morrow with such spirit;[26]

which observation is made at the moment when he was meditating, and but just before he accomplished, the destruction of the nobleman who makes it. That Macbeth, on the other hand, is constantly shocked and depressed with those circumstances which inspire Richard with extravagant mirth and spirits, is so obvious, that more quotations are unnecessary to prove it.

The total insensibility to every tender feeling, which distinguishes the character of Richard, makes him consider the mild virtues of Henry as so many weaknesses, and insult him for them, at the very moment when they would have been allowed all their merit, and have attracted some compassion from any other person.

See how my sword weeps for the poor king's death![27]

is the taunt he utters over his bloody corse: and when afterwards Lady Ann aggravates the assassination of Henry, by exclaiming,

O he was gentle, mild, and virtuous![28]

his answer is, that he was therefore

The fitter for the King of Heaven that hath him![29]

Richard despises Henry for his meekness, and turns it into a jest, when it is urged against himself as a matter of reproach. But Macbeth esteems Duncan for the same quality; and of himself, without being reminded, reflects upon it with contrition.

It would have been an inconsistency to have attributed to Richard any of those domestic affections which are proper in Macbeth: nor are they only omitted; but Shakespere has with great nicety shown, that his zeal for his family springs not from them, but from his ambition, and from that party-spirit which the contention between the Houses of York and Lancaster had inspired. His animosity therefore is inveterate against all

—who wish the downfall of our House;[30]

and he eagerly pursues their destruction, as the means of his own advancement. But his desire for the prosperity of his family goes no further: the execration he utters against his brother Edward,

Would he were wasted, marrow, bones, and all![31]

is to the full as bitter as any against the Lancastrians. The fear of children from Edward's marriage provokes him to this curse; yet not a wish for posterity from his own marriage ever crosses him: and though childless himself, he does not hesitate to destroy the heirs of his family. He would annihilate the House he had fought for all his life, rather than be disappointed of the throne he aspired to; and after he had ascended it, he forgets the interests of that House, whose accession had opened the way to his usurpation. He does not provide, he does not wish, for its continuance; the possession, not the descent, of the crown is his object: and when afterwards it is disputed with him, he considers Richmond only as a pretender. The circumstance of his being also a Lancaster does not occur to him; and he even, when he seems to contemn him more, does not hate

him so much as he did Henry, though Richmond was far the less amiable, as
well as the less despicable, of the two: all which conduct tallies with the principle he avows, when he declares,

I have no brother; I am like no brother:
And this word love, which grey-beards call divine,
Be resident in men like one another,
And not in me: I am myself alone.[32]

But the characters of Richard and Macbeth are marked not only by opposite
qualities; but even the same qualities in each differ so much in the cause, the
kind, and the degree, that the distinction in them is as evident as in the others.
Ambition is common to both; but in Macbeth it proceeds only from vanity,
which is flattered and satisfied by the splendour of a throne: in Richard it is
founded upon pride his ruling passion is the lust of power:

—this earth affords no joy to him,
But to command, to check, and to o'erbear.[33]

And so great is that joy, that he enumerates among the delights of war,

To fright the souls of fearful adversaries;[34]

which is a pleasure brave men do not very sensibly feel; they rather value

—Battles
Nobly, hardly fought.—

But, in Richard, the sentiments natural to his high courage are lost in the
greater satisfaction of trampling on mankind, and seeing even those whom
he despises crouching beneath him; at the same time, to submit himself to
any authority, is incompatible with his eager desire of ruling over all; nothing less than the first place can satiate his love of dominion: he declares that
he shall

Count himself but bad, till he is best:[35]

and,

While I live account this world but hell,
Until the misshap'd trunk that bears this head
Be round impaled with a glorious crown.[36]

Which crown he hardly ever mentions, except in swelling terms of exultation; and which, even after he has obtained it, he calls

> The high imperial type of this earth's glory.[37]

But the crown is not Macbeth's pursuit through life: he had never thought of it till it was suggested to him by the witches; he receives their promise, and the subsequent earnest of the truth of it, with calmness. But his wife, whose thoughts are always more aspiring, hears the tidings with rapture, and greets him with the most extravagant congratulations; she complains of his moderation; the utmost merit she can allow him is, that he is

> —not without ambition.[38]

But it is cold and faint, for the subject of it is that of a weak mind; it is only pre-eminence of place, not dominion. He never carries his idea beyond the honour of the situation he aims at; and therefore he considers it as a situation which Lady Macbeth will partake of equally with him: and in his letter tells her,

> This have I thought good to deliver thee, my dearest partner of greatness, that thou mightest not lose the dues of rejoicing, by being ignorant of what greatness is promised thee.[39]

But it was his rank alone, not his power, in which she could share: and that indeed is all which he afterwards seems to think he had attained by his usurpation. He styles himself,

> —high-plac'd Macbeth:[40]

but in no other light does he ever contemplate his advancement with satisfaction; and when he finds that it is not attended with that adulation and respect which he had promised himself, and which would have soothed his vanity, he sinks under the disappointment, and complains that

> —my way of life
> Is fallen into the sear, the yellow leaf;
> And that which should accompany old age,
> As honour, love, obedience, troops of friends,
> I must not look to have.[41]—

These blessings, so desirable to him, are widely different from the pursuits of Richard. He wishes not to gain the affections, but to secure the submission of his subjects, and is happy to see men shrink under his control. But Macbeth, on the contrary, reckons among the miseries of his condition

> —mouth-honour, breath,
> Which the poor heart would fain deny, but dare not:[42]

and pities the wretch who fears him.

The towering ambition of Richard, and the weakness of that passion in Macbeth, are further instances wherein Shakespere has accommodated their characters to the fabulous parts of their stories. The necessity for the most extraordinary incitements to stimulate the latter, thereby becomes apparent; and the meaning of the omens, which attended the birth of the former, is explained. Upon the same principle, a distinction still stronger is made in the article of courage, though both are possessed of it even to an eminent degree; but in Richard it is intrepidity, and in Macbeth no more than resolution: in him it proceeds from exertion, not from nature; in enterprise he betrays a degree of fear, though he is able, when occasion requires, to stifle and subdue it. When he and his wife are converting the murder, his doubt,

> —If we should fail,[43]

is a difficulty raised by apprehension; and as soon as that is removed by the contrivance of Lady Macbeth, to make the officers drunk, and lay the crime upon them, he runs with violence into the other extreme of confidence, and cries out, with a rapture unusual to him,

> —Bring forth men-children only!
> For thy undaunted metal should compose
> Nothing but males. Will it not be receiv'd,
> When we have mark'd with blood these sleepy two
> Of his own chamber, and us'd their very daggers,
> That they have done it?[44]—

NOTES

1. Macbeth, Act I. sc. 7.
2. Ibid., Act I. sc. 10.
3. Ibid., Act I. sc. 9.
4. Ibid., Act I. sc. 10.
5. Ibid., Act III. sc. 2.
6. Ibid.
7. Ibid., Act I. sc. 10.
8. 3 Henry VI, Act V. sc. 7.
9. Ibid.
10. Ibid.
11. Ibid.

12. Macbeth, Act II. sc. 2.
13. Ibid.
14. Ibid. sc. 3.
15. Richard III, Act I. sc. 1.
16. Ibid.
17. Ibid.
18. Ibid., Act IV. sc. 2.
19. Ibid., Act IV. sc. 3.
20. Ibid., Act I. sc. 2.
21. 3 Henry VI, Act III. sc. 3.
22. Richard III, Act I. sc. 1.
23. 3 Henry VI, Act III. sc. 3.
24. Richard III, Act II. sc. 3.
25. 3 Henry VI, Act V. sc. 8.
26. Richard III, Act III. sc. 3.
27. 3 Henry VI, Act V. sc. 7.
28. Richard III, Act I. sc. 2.
29. Ibid.
30. 3 Henry VI, Act V. sc. 7.
31. Ibid., Act III. sc. 3.
32. 3 Henry VI, Act V. sc. 7.
33. Ibid., Act III. sc. 3.
34. Richard III, Act I. sc. I.
35. 3 Henry VI, Act V. sc. 7.
36. Ibid.
37. Richard III, Act IV. sc. 5.
38. Macbeth, Act I. sc. 7.
39. Ibid.
40. Ibid., Act IV. sc. 2.
41. Ibid., Act V. sc. 3.
42. Ibid.
43. Ibid., Act I. sc. 10.
44. Ibid.

RICHARD III IN THE
NINETEENTH CENTURY
੩੭

Drawing on and augmenting the late eighteenth-century interest in character analysis, the nineteenth century produced some astute and penetrating studies of the ways in which Richard's character evolves, including a further assessment of the reasons why he both repels and attracts his audience. Most significantly, the latter part of the century saw an emerging perspective that, for all of Richard's villainy, Shakespeare presents a credible human being. This insight represents a new psychological dimension that the twentieth century would seize on and take in new directions. Thus, there is a growing appreciation of Shakespeare's insight into and presentation of the human dimension in his reinterpretation of the remote historical past. At the same time, from the romantics onward there was a strong emphasis placed on viewing Shakespeare's *Richard III* in relation to his other work, an interest that generated many strong scholarly and comprehensive investigations into the political motivations behind the bard's presentation of historical events. These critical assessments emphasized the need to understand *Richard III* in the context of the three parts of *King Henry VI* as well as the great tragic figures of his later work. Equally as important, nineteenth-century critiques of *Richard III* also began to reveal an interest in the anachronistic character of Margaret, in addition to the role of women in general and the symbolic function of events.

As a further key to understanding the early nineteenth-century response to *Richard III*, Paul Prescott's book (including *The Shakepeare Handbooks: Richard III*) provides a rich discussion of the extent to which the romantic evaluation of the play was due to Edmund Kean's brilliant performance as Richard III in Colley Cibber's adaptation. An actor with a passionate and highly original style, Kean excelled at grotesque posturing and peculiar mannerisms and identified with those characters who had become outcasts from society. These personal attributes made him a natural for the part of Richard III. Prescott maintains that Kean's major contribution to the role was his ability to capture "the spirit of the age," which warmed to the character traits of an evil genius who possessed a daring individuality. William Hazlitt's commentary on *Richard III* attests to Kean's highly original performance in the title role in Cibber's revised play.

While applauding Kean's passionate portrayal of Shakespeare's brilliant and treacherous tyrant, however, Hazlitt declares Cibber's adaptation to be deficient in many ways, a glaring example of "[t]he manner in which Shakespeare's plays have been generally altered or rather mangled by modern mechanists . . . a disgrace to the English stage." Above all considerations, Hazlitt pays tribute to Shakespeare's incomparable imagination in fashioning a character who is both isolated from all others and in relentless competition with himself only, always striving to be greater than he actually is.

August Wilhelm Schlegel's early nineteenth-century analysis begins with a discussion of the enormous popularity of and interest in Richard III's character. Schlegel attributes the success of *Richard III* to the fine performance of many skilled actors who made the play accessible to readers who might not have appreciated Shakespeare's achievement if not for the transformative power of presenting the work on the stage. Nevertheless, Schlegel argues for a more comprehensive understanding of *Richard III* in stating that the protagonist's character can only be fully appreciated if understood within the context of the three parts of *Henry VI*, which chronologically precede the play. Schlegel maintains that in these earlier plays Richard III's character begins to take shape and, moreover, that his statements are a harbinger of the evil intentions that come to fruition in the play that bears his name. Schlegel also underscores the importance of two early soliloquies in *Henry VI, Part 3* in which Shakespeare skillfully and subtly offers evidence of Richard's hidden, yet fully conscious, malevolent agenda through the vehicle of a character revealing his innermost thoughts while alone on the stage. Having established Richard's full awareness and embrace of his own malicious nature, Schlegel nevertheless insists that Richard's acceptance of the truth must still find a "moral" construct on which to justify his actions. This is accomplished through a series of specious but utterly fallacious arguments based on the fact that Richard came into the world deprived of an attractive human form and thus denied the love and acceptance granted to all other mortals. Schlegel points out that Richard's rhetorical contortions are so vital to his existence that they become not only a means to seize power over others but a highly desirable and enjoyable end in itself. For skillfully eliciting this subtle fact of human nature, the poet deserves our utmost respect and admiration. Having praised Shakespeare's achievement in representing the complexities of Richard's character, Schlegel nonetheless believes that *Richard III* manifests aspects of Shakespeare's nascent artistry, as the tragic murders that Richard orchestrates are committed almost entirely offstage, except for Clarence. Schlegel contends that moving such key actions offstage seriously diminishes the full import of the many bloody sacrifices that take place. Nevertheless, despite this complaint, Schlegel has an abiding respect for Shakespeare's superb achievement in rendering the character of Richard III, a Machiavellian tyrant who despite all his monstrous acts continues to fascinate and disarm us through his brilliant machinations and, perhaps, even succeeds in eliciting a brief moment of admiration when he becomes a mere mortal, desperate and hopeless, about to engage Richmond on Bosworth Field. Most significantly for Schlegel, Shakespeare has transformed the chronicle of a historical figure into a vivid portrait of the irrepressible spiritual world, as a steady parade of Richard's victims haunt his last remaining hours.

In his commentary on *Richard III*, Nathan Drake sets forth the reasons why, paradoxically, we are drawn to such a morally reprehensible character such as Richard. Acknowledging that Shakespeare had a daunting task in creating a character both physically repugnant and devoid of all conscience and humanity, Drake maintains that Shakespeare had to create a being of such towering intellect in order to circumvent a response of utter revulsion from the audience. Drake notes that Shakespeare's endeavor in creating Richard was a far more difficult a task than Milton had in his conception of Satan, who he believes owes a great debt to Richard III's character, for Shakespeare had to contend with the prevailing prejudices of his time that understood physical deformity to be an outward manifestation of mental depravity. According to Drake, the most alluring aspect of Richard's many vices is his hypocrisy, because it is seen as an adroit exposition of his duplicitous skills. This particular quality, Drake maintains, contributed greatly to the popularity of the play, "both on the stage and in the closet" and, furthermore, afforded a great opportunity for the consummate actor to exercise his finest skills. In sum, Drake believes Richard III to be a unique Shakespearean character whose pre-eminence grants import and distinction to all the other characters to the extent that they deserve his attention. The exception, however, is Margaret, the one person over whom he has no control.

Samuel Taylor Coleridge focuses on the inherent danger of Richard's primary moral defect, namely his excessive pride of intellect. Citing Gloucester's first speech in act 2, in which the evil duke professes great love for both his brother, King Edward IV, and the royal retinue attending the king's deathbed, Coleridge maintains that there is a qualitative difference, as exemplified in this first scene, between Richard's superb and highly formal and duplicitous rhetorical skills in addressing a crowd and his far more direct manner of speaking with his "confidantes." In sum, Coleridge is focused on Richard's extreme vanity as he exults in his evil success at the expense of those who are of inferior intelligence. These latter characters, according to Coleridge, serve merely to augment Richard's feelings of pre-eminence above the drama's other participants and players.

Edward Dowden begins with the premise that *Richard III* contains certain elements and qualities to be found in Marlowe, namely, the presence of a towering figure distinguished by certain unique and excessive passions and personality traits. On the whole, though, he notes there is no element of surprise to be found within the play as the other characters often express a unified emotional response.

Citing the universal voice of the women who have been cruelly and irreparably harmed by Richard, Dowden identifies a strong element of collaborative response among them, which he refers to as the "lyrical-dramatic style." Dowden suggests that Shakespeare highlights Richard's outrageous villainy and audacious arguments by having other characters express a far more realistic and appropriate emotional reaction to his shameless evil, a "verisimilitude" or choral function in which he finds a sublime beauty that reminds him of Blake's illustrations for the book of Job. Dowden maintains that Margaret's function is to serve as Richard's nemesis. In other words, in setting up this contrast, Shakespeare creates a completely open-ended platform to display the full range of Richard's machinations and unabashed villainy.

Dowden is emphatic that Richard's character holds no surprises for us as he reveals his intentions from his opening soliloquy and spends the rest of his time manipulating people and orchestrating horrific events in order to advance his own self-interests. Unlike Hamlet, we do not witness the unfolding of a character in conflict with himself, a man who agonizes over difficult decisions or even has the capacity to form an intimate relationship with any other character. Nevertheless, Dowden suggests we are fascinated from first to last by the enactment of Richard's superhuman powers and malignity. Furthermore, with respect to his Herculean strength and abilities, Dowden maintains that Richard's pride is linked to his "daemonic" spirit rather than to his intellect, as Coleridge believed, and that, in his daemonic capacity, he is fundamentally human, a man with an insatiable appetite that requires great latitude to wreak havoc and fulfill his self-aggrandizing agenda. All other characters in the play serve as mere enablers for realizing Richard's goals.

In accordance with his perception of Richard as eminently human, Dowden maintains that Shakespeare has created a sublime character in the sheer strength of determination and exercise of a powerful intellect, a man who is at least justified in believing himself superior to all others, having compensated for his physical limitations in an extraordinary ability to manipulate people and events at will. In his admiration for Richard's character, Dowden goes as far as identifying a certain "bonhomie" or good-natured side to his personality, citing Richard's disarming sense of humor in the face of horrendous accusations by a chorus of grievously wronged women. Among the other traits that Dowden admires is Richard's ability to remain both focused and vigilant about his public "appearance," while plotting to eliminate his competition. To this end, Dowden cites Richard's meticulous attention to detail in ordering strawberries and concealing his murderous intentions toward the unsuspecting Lord Hastings. Even in Richard's final hours, when he is doomed to pay the price for all the chaos he has unleashed, Dowden praises him for his great display of courage, a warrior to the end who will not shrink from his military obligations. In the end, Richard is a man who, rather than being concerned with advancing his own interests, is simply bent on unleashing his indomitable will upon the world. In sum, Dowden has nothing but praise for Shakespeare's brilliant and poetic rendering of a historical figure, heretofore shrouded in myth by More and Holinshed, portrayed as a man diabolical rather than criminal in nature.

Denton Snider's essay is another important psychological interpretation of *Richard III*. It is written from the perspective of a late Victorian moralist interested in presenting the disintegration of the House of York on its most fundamental level of familial warfare and the ultimate restoration of domestic harmony in the marriage of Richmond and the young Elizabeth. Snider's perspective on the root problem that plagues *Richard III* can be characterized as an organic one in which the monarchy is a living entity that requires peace and concord within the extended royal family before it can positively administer state affairs. Snider begins with a presentation of Richard as the most extreme example of the pernicious retribution that has plagued the House of York from the start, for "it has within its own bosom the poisonous reptile which will sting it to death." Though Snider at first states his belief that since art is meant to give pleasure, *Richard III* does not live up to this standard, he presents a compelling argument that the situation is a complex one, as Richard is not merely the extreme monstrous manifestation of all the crimes that have preceded him, but more importantly he is the agent of retribution in the play, the "vindicator" of a primal law though he is not conscious of, an instrument through which judgment will be made. This primal law, according to Snider, places responsibility on mankind for their actions and the resulting punishment that is invoked for committing evil. Thus, from the standpoint of Richard as "the destroying Nemesis," a vehicle through which divine justice will be rendered, Snider maintains that *Richard III* ultimately provides consolation.

One of the most compelling aspects of Snider's thesis is in his somewhat "sympathetic" interpretation of Richard who has been wronged by nature and, most especially, by his mother. Born physically deformed, Richard has been placed by nature at an irremediable disadvantage. "Nature," Snider asserts, "was in a Satanic mood." However, when Snider turns his attention to Richard's mother, it is on her that he places the greatest responsibility for Richard's malignant personality. Having denigrated Richard from his earliest, formative years for his deformity and unnatural birth, Snider accuses the duchess of York of unremitting abuse toward him as a child without taking responsibility for his moral upbringing. Snider maintains that Richard's mother should have loved him even more because of his severe physical handicaps and, because she has utterly failed in her maternal duties, the result is that Richard became a man who revels in his villainy and "spiritual hideousness."

Richard Moulton views the play's central preoccupations as comparable to Dante's treatment of the battle between good and evil in the landscape of Hell and Milton's Satan, an epic study of a fiend. Moulton states that Shakespeare's delineation of a methodical villain needs to be viewed within the vast arena of a specific political and historical background. Moulton further makes the point that *Richard III* is a unique tale of crime, in that there is no space allotted for the audience to witness the progressive steps by which a criminal mind grows and develops. Except for his statements of outrage at his physical deformity and all the enjoyments from which he is precluded, Richard presents himself as a fully evolved and complete criminal from his opening soliloquy. Thus, rather than a conventional crime story, Moulton argues that the play must properly be understood as the portrait an artist of the highest order, a distinction that must be extended to the play's author as well. Rather than one who works from any clear motive other than anger about the circumstances of his birth, Richard enjoys carrying out his schemes as an exercise in pure intellect much as a painter delights in creating beauty from a skillful use of form and color. Given this perspective on Richard as an artist, Moulton accounts for Richard's objectivity and lack of sympathy, as he gazes on his work devoid of all emotion, as one who simply admires a job well done and exults in the knowledge that even the work of tyranny can be a creative act. However, for all his objectivity toward crime, Moulton maintains that Richard possesses an artist's enthusiasm for his work and, by extension, he is aware that crimes are being committed, though he acts without restraint or fear of reprisal. Instead, Moulton suggests that Richard is a "genius of intrigue" whose daring is irresistible to his audience.

1809—August Wilhelm von Schlegel. From *Lectures on Dramatic Art and Literature*

An important figure in German romanticism, August Wilhelm von Schlegel (1767-1845) was a poet, translator, and critic. In 1798, he was appointed extraordinary professor at the University of Jena and began his translation of Shakespeare, one of the finest in German.

The part of Richard III. has become highly celebrated in England from its having been filled by excellent performers, and this has naturally had an influence on the admiration of the piece itself, for many readers of Shakespeare stand in want of good interpreters of the poet to understand him properly. This admiration is certainly in every respect well founded, though I cannot help thinking there is an injustice in considering the three parts of Henry the Sixth as of little value compared with Richard the Third. These four plays were undoubtedly composed in succession, as is proved by the style and the spirit in the handling of the subject: the last is definitely announced in the one which precedes it, and is also full of references to it: the same views run through the series; in a word, the whole make together only one single work. Even the deep characterization of Richard is by no means the exclusive property of the piece which bears his name: his character is very distinctly drawn in the two last parts of Henry the Sixth; nay, even his first speeches lead us already to form the most unfavourable anticipations of his future conduct. He lowers obliquely like a dark thundercloud on the horizon, which gradually approaches nearer and nearer, and first pours out the devastating elements with which it is charged when it hangs over the heads of mortals. Two of Richard's most significant soliloquies which enable us to draw the most important conclusions with regard to his mental temperament, are to be found in The Last Part of Henry the Sixth. As to the value and the justice of the actions to which passion impels us, we may be blind, but wickedness cannot mistake its own nature; Richard, as well as Iago, is a villain with full consciousness. That they should say this in so many words, is not perhaps in human nature: but the poet has the right in soliloquies to lend a voice to the most hidden thoughts, otherwise the form of the monologue would, generally speaking, be censurable. Richard's deformity is the expression of his internal malice, and perhaps in part the effect of it: for where is the ugliness that would not be softened by benevolence and openness? He, however, considers it as an iniquitous neglect of nature, which justifies him in taking his revenge on that human society from which it is the means of excluding him. Hence these sublime lines:

And this word love, which graybeards call divine,
Be resident in men like one another,
And not in me. I am myself alone.

Wickedness is nothing but selfishness designedly unconscientious; however it can never do altogether without the form at least of morality, as this is the law of all thinking beings,—it must seek to found its depraved way of acting on something like principles. Although Richard is thoroughly acquainted with the blackness of his mind and his hellish mission, he yet endeavours to justify this to himself by a sophism: the happiness of being beloved is denied to him; what then remains to him but the happiness of ruling? All that stands in the way of this must be removed. This envy of the enjoyment of love is so much the more natural in Richard, as his brother Edward, who besides preceded him in the possession of the crown, was distinguished by the nobleness and beauty of his figure, and was an almost irresistible conqueror of female hearts. Notwithstanding his pretended renunciation, Richard places his chief vanity in being able to please and win over the women, if not by his figure at least by his insinuating discourse. Shakespeare here shows us, with his accustomed acuteness of observation, that human nature, even when it is altogether decided in goodness or wickeness, is still subject to petty infirmities. Richard's favourite amusement is to ridicule others, and he possesses an eminent satirical wit. He entertains at bottom a contempt for all mankind: for he is confident of his ability to deceive them, whether as his instruments or his adversaries. In hypocrisy he is particularly fond of using religious forms, as if actuated by a desire of profaning in the service of hell the religion whose blessings he had inwardly abjured.

So much for the main features of Richard's character. The play named after him embraces also the latter part of the reign of Edward IV., in the whole a period of eight years. It exhibits all the machinations by which Richard obtained the throne, and the deeds which he perpetrated to secure himself in its possession, which lasted however but two years. Shakespeare intended that terror rather than compassion should prevail throughout this tragedy: he has rather avoided than sought the pathetic scenes which he had at command. Of all the sacrifices to Richard's lust of power, Clarence alone is put to death on the stage: his dream excites a deep horror, and proves the omnipotence of the poet's fancy: his conversation with the murderers is powerfully agitating; but the earlier crimes of Clarence merited death, although not from his brother's hand. The most innocent and unspotted sacrifices are the two princes: we see but little of them, and their murder is merely related. Anne disappears without our learning any thing farther respecting her: in marrying the murderer of her husband, she had shown a weakness almost incredible. The parts of Lord Rivers, and other friends of the queen, are of too secondary a nature to excite a powerful sympathy; Hastings, from his triumph at the fall of his friend, forfeits all title to compassion; Buckingham is the satellite of the tyrant, who is afterwards consigned by him to the axe of the executioner. In the background the widowed Queen Margaret appears as the fury of the past, who invokes a curse on the future: every calamity, which her enemies draw down on each other, is a cordial to her revengeful heart. Other female voices join, from time to time, in the lamentations and imprecations. But Richard is the soul, or rather the daemon, of the whole tragedy. He fulfills the promise which he formerly made of leading the murderous Machiavel to school. Notwithstanding the uniform aversion with which he inspires us, he still engages us in the greatest variety of ways by his profound skill in dissimulation, his wit, his prudence, his presence of mind, his quick activity, and his valour. He fights at last against Richmond like a desperado, and dies the honourable death of a hero on the field of battle. Shakespeare could not change this historical issue, and yet it is by no means satisfactory to our moral feelings, as Lessing, when speaking of a German play on the same subject, has very judiciously remarked. How has Shakespeare solved this difficulty? By a wonderful invention he opens a prospect into the other world, and shows us Richard in his last moments already branded with the stamp of reprobation. We see Richard and Richmond in the night before the battle sleeping in their tents; the spirits of the murdered victims of the tyrant ascend in succession, and pour out their curses against him, and their blessings on his adversary. These apparitions are properly but the dreams of the two generals represented visibly. It is no doubt contrary to probability that their tents should only be separated by so small a space; but Shakespeare could reckon on poetical spectators who were ready to take the breadth of the stage for the distance between two hostile camps, if for such indulgence they were to be recompensed by beauties of so sublime a nature as this series of spectres and Richard's awakening soliloquy. The catastrophe of Richard the Third is, in respect of the external events, very like that of Macbeth: we have only to compare the thorough difference of handling them to be convinced that Shakespeare has most accurately observed poetical justice in the genuine sense of the word, that is, as signifying the revelation of an invisible blessing or curse which hangs over human sentiments and actions.

1817—Nathan Drake. "King Richard the Third: 1595," from *Shakespeare and His Times*

Nathan Drake (1766-1836) was an English essayist and physician. In 1780, he was apprenticed to a doctor in York in 1780 and, in 1786, entered Edinburgh University, where he took his medical degree in 1789. In 1790, he became a general practitioner at Sudbury, Suffolk, and, in 1792, he relocated to Hadleigh, where he died in 1836. Drake's works include several volumes of literary essays and some papers he contributed to medical periodicals, but his most important work was *Shakespeare and His Times* published in 1817.

Though two centuries have now elapsed, since the death of Shakspeare, no attempt has hitherto been made to render him the medium for a comprehensive and connected view of the Times in which he lived.

Yet, if any man be allowed to fill a station thus conspicuous and important, Shakspeare has undoubtedly the best claim to the distinction; not only from his pre-eminence as a dramatic poet, but from the intimate relation which his works bear to the manners, customs, superstitions, amusements of his age.

Struck with the interest which a work of this kind, if properly executed, might possess, the author was induced, several years ago, to commence the undertaking, with the express intention of blending with the detail of manners, etc. such a portion of criticism, biography, and literary history, as should render the whole still more attractive and complete.

In attempting this, it has been his aim to place Shakspeare in the foreground of the picture, and to throw around him, in groups more or less distinct and full, the various objects of his design; giving them prominency and light, according to their greater or smaller connection with the principal figure.

More especially has it been his wish, to infuse throughout the whole plan, whether considered in respect to its entire scope, or to the parts of which it is composed, that degree of unity and integrity, of relative proportion and just bearing, without which neither harmony, simplicity, nor effect, can be expected or produced.

With a view, also, to distinctness and perspicuity of elucidation, the whole has been distributed into three parts or pictures, entitled.—"SHAKSPEARE IN STRATFORD;"—"SHAKSPEARE IN LONDON;"—"SHAKSPEARE IN RETIRE- MENT;"—which, though inseparably united, as forming but portions of the same story, and harmonized by the same means, have yet, both in subject and execution, a peculiar character to support.

The first represents our Poet in the days of his youth, on the banks of his native Avon, in the midst of rural imagery, occupations, and amusements; in the second, we behold him in the Capital of his country, in the centre of rivalry and competition, in the active pursuit of reputation and glory; and in the third, we accompany the venerated bard to the shades of retirement, to the bosom of domestic peace, to the enjoyment of unsullied fame.

It has, therefore, been the business of the author, in accordancy with his plan, to connect these delineations with their relative accompaniments; to incorporate, for instance, with the first, what he has to relate of the country, as it existed in the age of Shakspeare; its manners, customs, and characters; its festivals, diversions, and many of its superstitions; opening and closing the subject with the biography of the poet, and binding the intermediate parts, not only by a perpetual reference to his drama, but by their own constant and direct tendency towards the development of the one object in view.

With the second, which commences with Shakspeare's introduction to the stage as an actor, is combined the poetic, dramatic, and general literature of the times, together with an account of metropolitan manners and diversions, and a full and continued criticism on the poems and plays of our bard.

After a survey, therefore, of the Literary world, under the heads of Bibliography, Philology, Criticism, History, Romantic and Miscellaneous Literature, follows a View of the Poetry of the same period, succeeded by a critique on the juvenile productions of Shakspeare, and including a biographical sketch of Lord Southampton, and a new hypothesis on the origin and object of the Sonnets.

Of the immediately subsequent description of diversions, etc. the Economy of the Stage forms a leading feature, as preparatory to a History of Dramatic Poetry, previous to the year 1590; and this is again introductory to a discussion concerning the Period when Shakspeare commenced a writer for the theatre; to a new chronology of his plays, and to a criticism on each drama; a department which is interspersed with dissertations on the Fairy Mythology, the Apparitions, the Witchcraft, and the Magic of Shakspeare; portions of popular credulity which had been, in reference to this distribution, omitted in detailing the superstitions of the country.

This second part is then terminated by a summary of Shakspeare's dramatic character, by a brief view of dramatic poetry during his connection with the stage, and by the biography of the poet to the close of his residence in London.

The third and last of these delineations is, unfortunately, but too short, being altogether occupied with the few circumstances which distinguish the last three years of the life of our bard, with a review of his disposition and moral character, and with some notice of the first tributes paid to his memory.

It will readily be admitted, that the materials for the greater part of this arduous task are abundant; but it must also be granted, that they are dispersed through a vast variety of distant and unconnected departments of literature; and that to draw forth, arrange, and give a luminous disposition to these masses of scattered intelligence, is an achievement of no slight magnitude, especially when it is considered, that no step in the progress of such an undertaking can be made, independent of a constant recurrence to authorities.

How far the author is qualified for the due execution of his design, remains for the public to decide; but it may, without ostentation, be told, that his leisure, for the last thirty years, has been, in a great degree, devoted to a line of study immediately associated with the subject; and that his attachment to old English literature has led him to a familiarity with the only sources from which, on such a topic, authentic illustration is to be derived.

He will likewise venture to observe, that, in the style of criticism which he has pursued, it has been his object, an ambitious one it is true, to unfold, in a manner more distinct than has hitherto been effected, the peculiar character of the poet's drama; and, lastly, to produce a work, which, while it may satisfy the poetical antiquary, shall, from the variety, interest, and integrity of its component parts, be equally gratifying to the general reader.

* * *

KING RICHARD THE THIRD: 1595. It is the conjecture of Mr. Malone, and by which he has been guided in his chronological arrangement, that this play, and King Richard the Second, were written, acted, registered and printed in the year 1597. That they were registered and published during this year, we have indisputable authority;[1] but that they were written and acted within the same period, is a supposition without any proof, and, to say the least of it, highly improbable.

Mr. Chalmers, struck by this incautious assertion, of two such plays being written, acted, and published in a few months;[2] reflecting that Shakspeare, impressed by the character of Gloucester, in his play of Henry the Sixth, might be induced to resume his national dramas by continuing the "Historie" of Richard, to which he might be more immediately stimulated by his knowledge that an enterlude, entitled the "Tragedie of Richard the Third," had been exhibited in 1593, or 1594; and ingeniously surmising that Richard the Second was a subsequent production, because it ushered in a distinct and concatenated series of history, has, tinder this view of the subject, given precedence to Richard the Third in the order of composition, and assigned its origin to the year 1595.

The description of a small volume of Epigrams by John Weever, in Mr. Beloe's Anecdotes of Literature, has since confirmed the chronology of Mr. Chalmers, so far as it proves that one of Shakspeare's Richards had certainly been acted in 1595.

The book in question, in the collection of Mr. Comb, of Henley, and supposed to be a unique, was published in 1599, at which period, according to the date of the print of him prefixed by Cecill, the author was twenty-three years old, but Weever tells us, in some introductory stanzas, that when he wrote the poems which compose this volume, he was not twenty years old; that he was one

That twenty twelve months yet did *never know*,"

consequently, these Epigrams must have been written in 1595, though not printed before 1599. They exhibit the following title: "Epigrammes in the oldest Cut and newest Fashion. A twise seven Houres (in so many Weekes) Studie. No longer (like the Fashion) not unlike to continue. The first seven, John Weever. At London: printed by V.S. for Thomas Rushell, and are to be sold at his shop, at the great North doore of Paules. 1599. 12mo."

Of this collection the twenty-second Epigram of the fourth Weeke, which we have formerly had occasion to notice, and which we shall now give at length, is addressed

"AD GULIELMUM SHAKSPEARE.
"Honie-Tongd Shakspeare, when I saw thine issue,
I swore Apollo got them, and none other.
Their rosie-tainted features clothed in tissue,
Some heaven-born goddesse said to be their mother.
Rose cheeckt Adonis with his amber tresses,
Faire fire-hot Venus charming him to love her,
Chaste Lucretia, virgine-like her dresses,
Proud lust-stung Tarquine seeking still to prove her,
Romeo, RICHARD, more whose names I know not,
Their sugred tongues and power attractive beauty,
Say they are saints, althogh that saints they shew not,
For thousand vowes to them subjective dutie,

They burn in love thy children Shakspeare let them
Go wo thy muse more nymphish brood beget them."[3]

We have no doubt that by the "Richard" of this epigram the author meant to imply the play of Richard the Third, which, according to our arrangement, was the immediately succeeding tragedy to Romeo, and may be said to have been almost promised by the poet in the two concluding scenes of the Last Part of King Henry the Sixth, a promise which, as we believe, was carried into execution after an interval of three years.[4]

The character of Richard the Third, which had been opened in so masterly a manner in the Concluding Part of Henry the Sixth, is, in this play, developed in all its horrible grandeur.

It is, in fact, the picture of a demoniacal incarnation, moulding the passions and foibles of mankind, with super-human precision, to its own iniquitous purposes. Of this isolated and peculiar state of being Richard himself seems sensible, when he declares—

"I have no brother, I am like no brother:
And this word love, which grey-beards call divine,
Be resident in men like one another.
And not in me: I am myself alone." Act v. sc. 6.

From a delineation like this Milton must have caught many of the most striking features of his Satanic portrait. The same union of unmitigated depravity, and consummate intellectual energy, characterises both, and renders what would otherwise be loathsome and disgusting, an object of sublimity and shuddering admiration.

Richard, stript as he is of all the softer feelings, and all the common charities, of humanity, possessed of "neither pity, love, nor fear," and loaded with every dangerous and dreadful vice, would, were it not for his unconquerable powers of mind, be insufferably revolting. But, though insatiate in his ambition, envious, and hypocritical in his disposition, cruel, bloody, and remorseless in all his deeds, he displays such an extraordinary share of cool and determined courage, such alacrity and buoyancy of spirit, such constant self-possession, such an intuitive intimacy with the workings of the human heart, and such matchless skill in rendering them subservient to his views, as so far to subdue our detestation and abhorrence of his villainy, that we, at length, contemplate this fiend in human shape with a mingled sensation of intense curiosity and grateful terror.

The task, however, which Shakspeare undertook was, in one instance, more arduous than that which Milton subsequently attempted; for, in addition to the hateful constitution of Richard's moral character, he had to contend also against the prejudices arising from personal deformity, from a figure

—"curtail'd of it's fair proportion,
Cheated of feature by dissembling nature,
Deform'd, unlinish'd, sent before it's time
Into this breathing world, scarce half made up;" Act i. sc. 1.

and yet, in spite of these striking personal defects, which were considered, also, as indicative of the depravity and wickedness of his nature, the poet has contrived, through the medium of the high mental endowments just enumerated, not only to obviate disgust, but to excite extraordinary admiration.

One of the most prominent and detestable vices indeed, in Richard's character, his hypocrisy, connected, as it always is, in his person, with the most profound skill and dissimulation, has, owing to the various parts which it induces him to assume, most materially contributed to the popularity of this play, both on the stage and in the closet. He is one who can "frame his face to all occasions," and accordingly appears, during the course of his career, under the contrasted forms of a subject and a monarch, a politician and a wit, a soldier and a suitor, a sinner and a saint; and in all with such apparent ease and fidelity to nature, that while to the explorer of the human mind he affords, by his penetration and address, a subject of peculiar interest and delight, he offers to the practised performer a study well calculated to call forth his fullest and finest exertions. He, therefore, whose histrionic powers are adequate to the just exhibition of this character, may be said to have attained the highest honours of his profession; and, consequently, the popularity of Richard the Third, notwithstanding the moral enormity of its hero, may be readily accounted for, when we recollect, that the versatile and consummate hypocrisy of the tyrant has been embodied by the talents of such masterly performers as Garrick, Kemble, Cook, and Kean.

So overwhelming and exclusive is the character of Richard, that the comparative insignificance of all the other persons of the drama may be necessarily inferred; they are reflected to us, as it were, from his mirror, and become more or less important, and more or less developed, as he finds it necessary to act upon them; so that our estimate of their character is entirely founded on his relative conduct, through which we may very correctly appreciate their strength or weakness.

The only exception to this remark is in the person of Queen Margaret, who, apart from the agency of Richard, and dimly seen in the darkest recesses of the picture, pours forth, in union with the deep tone of this tragedy, the most dreadful curses and imprecations; with such a wild and prophetic fury, indeed, as to involve the whole scene in tenfold gloom and horror.

We have to add that the moral of this play is great and impressive. Richard, having excited a general sense of indignation, and a general desire of revenge, and, unaware of his danger from having lost, through familiarity with guilt, all idea of moral obligation, becomes at length the victim of his own enormous crimes; he falls not unvisited by the terrors of conscience, for, on the eve of danger and of death, the retribution of another world is placed before him; the spirits of those whom he had murdered reveal the awful sentence of his fate, and his bosom heaves with the infliction of eternal torture.

NOTES

1. Richard the Second was entered on the Stationers' books, on August 29, 1597; and Richard the Third on October 20, 1597; and both printed the same year.

2. It must be recollected that Mr. Malone's "Chronological Order of Shakspeare's Plays," is founded, not on the period of their publication, but on that of their composition; it is "an attempt to ascertain tho order in which the Plays of Shakspeare were *written*,"

3. Anecdotes of Literature and Scarce books, vol. vi. p. 156, 158, 159.

4. The lines which seem to imply the future intentions of the poet, are these:—

> "*Glo.* Clarence, beware: thou keep'st me from the light;
> But I will sort a pitchy day for thee:
> For I will buz abroad such prophecies.
> That Edward shall be fearful of his life;
> And then to purge his fear. I'll be thy death.
> King Henry, and the prince his son, are gone:
> Clarence, thy turn is next, and then the rest."
> —*Henry VI. Part III.* act v. sc. 6.

> *Glo.* I'll blast his harvest, if your head were laid;
> For yet I am not look'd on in the world
> This shoulder was ordain'd so thick, to heave;
> And heave it shall some weight, or break my back:—
> Work thou the way,—and thou shall execute."
> —*Ibid,* act v. sc. 7.

1817—William Hazlitt. "The Character of Richard III," from *Characters of Shakespear's Plays*

William Hazlitt (1778–1830) was an English essayist and one of the finest Shakespearean critics of the nineteenth century. He is the author of *Lectures on the English Poets* (1818), *A View of the English Stage* (1818), and *The Spirit of the Age* (1825).

Richard III may be considered as properly a stage-play: it belongs to the theatre, rather than to the closet. We shall therefore criticise it chiefly with a reference to the manner in which we have seen it performed. It is the character in which Garrick came out: it was the second character in which Mr. Kean appeared, and in which he acquired his fame. Shakespeare we have always with us: actors we have only for a few seasons; and therefore some account of them may be acceptable, if not to our contemporaries, to those who come after us, if "that rich and idle personage, Posterity," should deign to look into our writings.

It is possible to form a higher conception of the character of Richard than that given by Mr. Kean: but we cannot imagine any character represented with greater distinctness and precision, more perfectly *articulated* in every part. Perhaps indeed there is too much of what is technically called execution. When we first saw this celebrated actor in the part, we thought he sometimes failed from an exuberance of manner, and dissipated the impression of the general character by the variety of his resources. To be complete, his delineation of it should have more solidity, depth, sustained and impassioned feeling, with somewhat less brilliancy, with fewer glancing lights, pointed transitions, and pantomimic evolutions.

The Richard of Shakespeare is towering and lofty; equally impetuous and commanding; haughty, violent, and subtle; bold and treacherous; confident in his strength as well as in his cunning; raised high by his birth, and higher by his talents and his crimes; a royal usurper, a princely hypocrite; a tyrant, and a murderer of the house of Plantagenet.

"But I was born so high:
Our aery buildeth in the cedar's top,
And dallies with the wind, and scorns the sun."

The idea conveyed in these lines (which are indeed omitted in the miserable medley acted for *Richard III*) is never lost sight of by Shakespeare, and should not be out of the actor's mind for a moment. The restless and sanguinary Richard is not a man striving to be great, but to be greater than he is; conscious of his strength of will, his power of intellect, his daring courage, his elevated station; and making use of these advantages to commit unheard-of crimes, and to shield himself from remorse and infamy.

If Mr. Kean does not entirely succeed in concentrating all the lines of the character, as drawn by Shakespeare, he gives an animation, vigour, and relief to the part which we have not seen equalled. He is more refined than Cooke; more bold, varied, and original than Kemble in the same character. In some parts he is deficient in dignity, and particularly in the scenes of state business, he has by no means an air of artificial authority. There is at times an aspiring elevation, an enthusiastic rapture in his expectations of attaining the crown, and at others a gloating expression of sullen delight, as if he already clenched the bauble, and held it in his grasp. The courtship scene with Lady Anne is an admirable exhibition of smooth and smiling villainy. The progress of wily adulation, of encroaching humility, is finely marked by his action, voice and eye. He seems, like the first

Tempter, to approach his prey, secure of the event, and as if success had smoothed his way before him. The late Mr. Cooke's manner of representing this scene was more vehement, hurried, and full of anxious uncertainty. This, though more natural in general, was less in character in this particular instance. Richard should woo less as a lover than as an actor—to shew his mental superiority, and power of making others the playthings of his purposes. Mr. Kean's attitude in leaning against the side of the stage before he comes forward to address Lady Anne, is one of the most graceful and striking ever witnessed on the stage. It would do for Titian to paint. The frequent and rapid transition of his voice from the expression of the fiercest passion to the most familiar tones of conversation was that which gave a peculiar grace of novelty to his acting on his first appearance. This has been since imitated and caricatured by others, and he himself uses the artifice more sparingly than he did. His by-play is excellent. His manner of bidding his friends "Good night," after pausing with the point of his sword, drawn slowly backward and forward on the ground, as if considering the plan of the battle next day, is a particularly happy and natural thought. He gives to the two last acts of the play the greatest animation and effect. He fills every part of the stage; and makes up for the deficiency of his person by what has been sometimes objected to as an excess of action. The concluding scene in which he is killed by Richmond is the most brilliant of the whole. He fights at last like one drunk with wounds; and the attitude in which he stands with his hands stretched out, after his sword is wrested from him, has a preternatural and terrific grandeur, as if his will could not be disarmed, and the very phantoms of his despair had power to kill.—Mr. Kean has since in a great measure effaced the impression of his *Richard III* by the superior efforts of his genius in *Othello* (his masterpiece), in the murder-scene in *Macbeth*, in *Richard II*, in Sir Giles Overreach, and lastly in *Oroonoko*; but we still like to look back to his first performance of this part, both because it first assured his admirers of his future success, and because we bore our feeble but, at that time, not useless testimony to the merits of this very original actor, on which the town was considerably divided for no other reason than because they *were* original.

The manner in which Shakespeare's plays have been generally altered or rather mangled by modern mechanists, is a disgrace to the English stage. The patch-work *Richard III* which is acted under the sanction of his name, and which was manufactured by Cibber, is a striking example of this remark.

The play itself is undoubtedly a very powerful effusion of Shakespeare's genius. The ground-work of the character of Richard, that mixture of intellectual vigour with moral depravity, in which Shakespeare delighted to shew his strength—gave full scope as well as temptation to the exercise of his imagination. The character of his hero is almost every where predominant, and marks its lurid track throughout. The original play is however too long for representation, and there are some few scenes which might be better spared than preserved, and by omitting which it would remain a complete whole. The only rule, indeed, for altering Shakespeare is to retrench certain passages which may be considered either as superfluous or obsolete, but not to add or transpose any thing. The arrangement and development of the story, and the mutual contrast and combination of the *dramatis personae*, are in general as finely managed as the development of the characters or the expression of the passions.

This rule has not been adhered to in the present instance. Some of the most important and striking passages in the principal character have been omitted, to make room for idle and misplaced extracts from other plays; the only intention of which seems to have been to make the character of Richard as odious and disgusting as possible. It is apparently for no other purpose than to make Gloucester stab King Henry on the stage, that the fine abrupt introduction of the character in the opening of the play is lost in the tedious whining morality of the uxorious king (taken from another play);—we say *tedious*, because it interrupts the business of the scene, and loses its beauty and effect by having no intelligible connection with the previous character of the mild, well-meaning monarch. The passages which the unfortunate Henry has to recite are beautiful and pathetic in themselves, but they have nothing to do with the world that Richard has to "bustle in." In the same spirit of vulgar caricature is the scene between Richard and Lady Anne (when his wife) interpolated without any authority, merely to gratify this favourite propensity to disgust and loathing. With the same perverse consistency, Richard, after his last fatal struggle, is raised up by some Galvanic process, to utter the imprecation, without any motive but pure malignity, which Shakespeare has so properly put into the mouth of Northumberland on hearing of Percy's death. To make room for these worse than needless additions, many of the most striking passages in the real play have been omitted by the foppery and ignorance of the prompt-book critics. We do not mean to insist merely on passages which are fine as poetry and to the reader, such as Clarence's dream, &c. but on those which are important to the understanding of the character, and peculiarly adapted for stage-effect. We will give the following as instances among several others. The first is the scene where Richard enters abruptly to the queen and her friends to defend himself:—

> *Gloucester.* They do me wrong, and I will not endure it.
> Who are they that complain unto the king,
> That I forsooth am stern, and love them not?
> By holy Paul, they love his grace but lightly,
> That fill his ears with such dissentious rumours:
> Because I cannot flatter and look fair,
> Smile in men's faces, smooth, deceive, and cog,
> Duck with French nods, and apish courtesy,
> I must be held a rancorous enemy.
> Cannot a plain man live, and think no harm,
> But thus his simple truth must be abus'd

With silken, sly, insinuating Jacks?
  Gray. To whom in all this presence speaks your grace?
  Gloucester. To thee, that hast nor honesty nor grace;
When have I injur'd thee, when done thee wrong?
Or thee? or thee? or any of your faction?
A plague upon you all!

Nothing can be more characteristic than the turbulent pretensions to meekness and simplicity in this address. Again, the versatility and adroitness of Richard is admirably described in the following ironical conversation with Brakenbury:

  Brakenbury. I beseech your graces both to pardon me.
His majesty hath straitly given in charge,
That no man shall have private conference,
Of what degree soever, with your brother.
  Gloucester. E'en so, and please your worship, Brakenbury.
You may partake of any thing we say:
We speak no treason, man—we say the king
Is wise and virtuous, and his noble queen
Well strook in years, fair, and not jealous.
We say that Shore's wife hath a pretty foot,
A cherry lip,
A bonny eye, a passing pleasing tongue;
That the queen's kindred are made gentlefolks.
How say you, sir? Can you deny all this?
  Brakenbury. With this, my lord, myself have nought to do.
  Gloucester. What, fellow, naught to do with mistress Shore?
I tell you, sir, he that doth naught with her,
Excepting one, were best to do it secretly alone.
  Brakenbury. What one, my lord?
  Gloucester. Her husband, knave—would'st thou betray me?

The feigned reconciliation of Gloucester with the queen's kinsmen is also a masterpiece. One of the finest strokes in the play, and which serves to shew as much as any thing the deep, plausible manners of Richard, is the unsuspecting security of Hastings, at the very time the former is plotting his death, and when that very appearance of cordiality and good-humour on which Hastings builds his confidence arises from Richard's consciousness of having betrayed him to his ruin. This, with the whole character of Hastings, is omitted.

Perhaps the two most beautiful passages in the original play are the farewell apostrophe of the queen to the Tower, where the children are shut up from her, and Tyrrel's description of their death. We will finish our quotations with them.

Queen. Stay, yet look back with me unto the Tower;
Pity, you ancient stones, those tender babes,
Whom envy hath immured within your walls;
Rough cradle for such little pretty ones,
Rude, rugged nurse, old sullen play-fellow,
For tender princes!

The other passage is the account of their death by Tyrrel:—

Dighton and Forrest, whom I did suborn
To do this piece of ruthless butchery,
Albeit they were flesh'd villains, bloody dogs,—
Melting with tenderness and mild compassion,
Wept like to children in their death's sad story:
O thus! quoth Dighton, lay the gentle babes;
Thus, thus, quoth Forrest, girdling one another
Within their innocent alabaster arms;
Their lips were four red roses on a stalk,
And in that summer beauty kissed each other;
A book of prayers on their pillow lay,
Which once, quoth Forrest, almost changed my mind:
But oh the devil!—there the villain stopped;
When Dighton thus told on—we smothered
The most replenished sweet work of nature,
That from the prime creation ere she framed.
These are some of those wonderful bursts of feeling, done to the life, to
the very height of fancy and nature, which our Shakespeare alone could
give. We do not insist on the repetition of these last passages as proper
for the stage: we should indeed be loth to trust them in the mouth of
almost any actor: but we should wish them to be retained in preference
at least to the fantoccini exhibition of the young princes, Edward and
York, bandying childish wit with their uncle.

1818—Samuel Taylor Coleridge. "Richard III," from *Shakspeare, with Introductory Remarks on Poetry, the Drama, and the Stage*

Samuel Taylor Coleridge (1772-1834) was a pre-eminent English poet,
critic, and philosopher. Along with his friend William Wordsworth, he

was one of the founders of the romantic movement in England and one of the Lake Poets. He is the author of *Biographia Literaria* (1817) and *Lectures and Notes on Shakespeare and Other English Poets* (delivered in 1818 and first published in 1883).

This play should be contrasted with Richard II. Pride of intellect is the characteristic of Richard, carried to the extent of even boasting to his own mind of his villany, whilst others are present to feed his pride of superiority; as in his first speech, act II. sc. 1. Shakespeare here, as in all his great parts, developes in a tone of sublime morality the dreadful consequences of placing the moral, in subordination to the mere intellectual, being. In Richard there is a predominance of irony, accompanied with apparently blunt manners to those immediately about him, but formalized into a more set hypocrisy towards the people as represented by their magistrates.

1875—Edward Dowden. "The English Historical Plays," from *Shakspere: A Critical Study of His Mind and Art*

Edward Dowden (1843–1913) was an Irish critic, university lecturer, and poet. His works include *New Studies in Literature* (1895), *The French Revolution and English Literature: Lectures Delivered in Connection with the Sesquicentennial Celebration of Princeton University* (1897), and *Shakespeare Primer* (1877).

Certain qualities which make it unique among the dramas of Shakspere characterize the play of King Richard III. Its manner of conceiving and presenting character has a certain resemblance, not elsewhere to be found in Shakspere's writings, to the ideal manner of Marlowe. As in the plays of Marlowe, there is here one dominant figure distinguished by a few strongly marked and inordinately developed qualities. There is in the characterization no mystery, but much of a daemonic intensity. Certain passages are entirely in the lyrical-dramatic style; an emotion which is one and the same, occupying at the same moment two or three of the personages, and obtaining utterance through them almost simultaneously, or in immediate succession; as a musical motive is interpreted by an orchestra, or taken up singly by successive instruments:—

Q. Eliz.: Was never widow had so dear a loss!
Children: Were never orphans had so dear a loss!
Duchess: Was never mother had so dear a loss! Alas! I am the mother of these griefs.

Mere verisimilitude in the play of King Richard III. becomes at times subordinate to effects of symphonic orchestration, or of statuesque composition. There is a Blake-like terror and beauty in the scene in which the three women,—queens and a duchess,—seat themselves upon the ground in their desolation and despair, and cry aloud in utter anguish of spirit. First by the mother of two kings, then by Edward's widow, last by the terrible Medusa-like Queen Margaret, the same attitude is assumed, and the same grief is poured forth. Misery has made them indifferent to all ceremony of queen-ship, and for a time to their private differences; they are seated, a rigid yet tumultuously passionate group, in the majesty of mere womanhood and supreme calamity. Readers acquainted with Blake's illustrations to the Book of Job will remember what effects, sublime and appalling, the artist produces by animating a group of figures with one common passion, which spontaneously produces in each individual the same extravagant movement of head and limbs.

The daemonic intensity which distinguishes the play proceeds from the character of Richard, as from its source and centre. As with the chief personages of Marlowe's plays, so Richard in this play rather occupies the imagination by audacity and force, than insinuates himself through some subtle solvent, some magic and mystery of art. His character does not grow upon us; from the first it is complete. We are not curious to discover what Richard is, as we are curious to come into presence of the soul of Hamlet. We are in no doubt about Richard; but it yields us a strong sensation to observe him in various circumstances and situations; we are roused and animated by the presence of almost superhuman energy and power, even though that power and that energy be malign.

Coleridge has said of Richard that pride of intellect is his characteristic. This is true, but his dominant characteristic is not intellectual; it is rather a daemonic energy of will. The same cause which produces tempest and shipwreck produces Richard; he is a fierce elemental power raging through the world; but this elemental power is concentrated in a human will. The need of action is with Richard an appetite to which all the other appetites are subordinate. He requires space in the world to bustle in; his will must wreak itself on men and things. All that is done in the play proceeds from Richard; there is, as has been observed by Mr Hudson, no interaction. "The drama is not so much a composition of co-operative characters, mutually developing and developed, as the prolonged yet hurried outcome of a single character, to which the other persons serve but as exponents and conductors; as if he were a volume of electricity disclosing himself by means of others, and quenching their active powers in the very process of doing so.'"

Richard, with his distorted and withered body, his arm shrunk like "a blasted sapling," is yet a sublime figure by virtue of his energy of will and tremendous power of intellect. All obstacles give way before him;—the courage of men, and the bitter animosity of women. And Richard has a passionate scorn of men, because they are weaker and more obtuse than he, the deformed outcast of nature. He practises hypocrisy not merely for the sake of success, but because his hypocrisy is a cynical jest, or a gross insult to humanity. The Mayor of London has a bourgeois veneration for piety and established forms of religion. Richard advances to meet him reading a book of prayers, and supported on each side by a bishop. The grim joke, the contemptuous insult to the citizen faith in church and king, flatters his malignant sense of power. To cheat a gull, a coarse hypocrisy suffices.[2]

Towards his tool Buckingham, when occasion suits, Richard can be frankly contemptuous. Buckingham is unable to keep pace with Richard in his headlong career; he falls behind and is scant of breath:

> The deep-revolving, witty Buckingham
> No more shall be the neighbour to my counsel;
> Hath he so long held out with me untired
> And stops he now for breath?

The duke, "his other self, his counsel's consistory, his oracle, his prophet," comes before the king claiming the fulfilment of a promise, that he should receive the Earldom of Hereford. Richard becomes suddenly deaf and, contemptuously disregarding the interpellations of Buckingham, continues his talk on indifferent matters. At length he turns to "his other self;"—

> Buck.: My lord!
> K. Rich.: Ay, what's o'clock?
> *Buck.:* I am thus bold to put your Grace in mind
> Of what you promised me.
> K. *Rich.:*   Well, but what's o'clock?
> *Buck.:* Upon the stroke of ten.
> K. Rich.:   Well, let it strike.
> *Buck.:* Why let it strike?
> K. *Rich.:* Because that like a Jack thou keep'st the stroke
> Betwixt thy begging and my meditation. I am not in the giving vein to-day.

Richard's cynicism and insolence have in them a kind of grim mirth; such a bonhomie as might be met with among the humourists of Pandemonium. His brutality is a manner of joking with a purpose. When his mother, with Queen Elizabeth, comes by "copious in exclaims," ready to "smother her damned son in the breath of bitter words," the mirthful Richard calls for a flourish of trumpets to drown these shrill female voices:

> A flourish trumpets! strike alarum, drums! Let not the heavens hear
> these tell-tale women Rail on the Lord's anointed. Strike, I say!

On an occasion when hypocrisy is more serviceable than brutality, Richard kneels to implore his mother's blessing, but has a characteristic word of contemptuous impiety to utter aside:

Duchess: God bless thee and put meekness in thy
breast, Love, charity, obedience, and true duty.
Richard: Amen! and make me die a good old man! That is the butt-end
of a mother's blessing; I marvel that her grace did leave it out.

He plays his part before his future wife, the Lady Anne, laying open his breast to the sword's point with a malicious confidence. He knows the measure of woman's frailty, and relies on the spiritual force of his audacity and dissimulation to subdue the weak hand, which tries to lift the sword. With no friends to back his suit, with nothing but "the plain devil, and dissembling looks," he wins his bride. The hideous irony of such a courtship, the mockery it implies of human love, is enough to make a man "your only jigmaker," and sends Richard's blood dancing along his veins.

While Richard is plotting for the crown, Lord Hastings threatens to prove an obstacle in the way. What is to be done? Buckingham is dubious and tentative:

Now, my lord, what shall we do, if we perceive Lord Hastings will not
yield to our complots?

With sharp detonation, quickly begun and quickly over, Richard's answer is discharged, "Chop off his head, man." There can be no beginning, middle, or end to a deed so simple and so summary. Presently Hastings making sundry small assignations for future days and weeks, goes, a murdered man, to the conference at the Tower. Richard, whose startling figure emerges from the background throughout the play with small regard for verisimilitude and always at the most effective moment, is suddenly on the spot, just as Hastings is about to give his voice in the conference as though he were the representative of the absent Duke. Richard is prepared, when the opportune instant has arrived, to spring a mine under Hastings' feet. But meanwhile a matter of equal importance concerns him,—my Lord of Ely's strawberries: the flavour of Holborn strawberries is exquisite, and the fruit must be sent for. Richard's desire to appear disengaged from sinister thought is less important to note than Richard's need of indulging a cynical contempt of human life. The explosion takes place; Hastings is seized; and the delicacies are reserved until the head of Richard's enemy is off. There is a wantonness of diablerie in this incident:

Talk'st thou to me of ifs? Thou art a traitor—Off with his head! Now by
Saint Paul I swear I will not dine until I see the same.[3]

The fiery energy of Richard is at its simplest, unmingled with irony or dissimulation in great days of military movement and of battle. Then the force within him expends itself in a paroxysm which has all the intensity of ungovernable spasmodic action, and which is yet organised and controlled by his intellect. Then he is engaged at his truest devotions, and numbers his Ave-Maries, not with beads but with ringing strokes upon the helmets of his foes.[4] He is inspired with "the spleen of fiery dragons;" "a thousand hearts are great within his bosom." On the eve of the battle of Bosworth Field, Richard, with uncontrollable eagerness, urges his enquiry into the minutiae of preparation which may ensure success. He lacks his usual alacrity of spirit, yet a dozen subalterns would hardly suffice to receive the orders which he rapidly enunciates. He is upon the wing of "fiery expedition:"

> I will not sup to-night. Give me some ink and
> paper. What, is my beaver easier than it was?
> And all my armour laid within my tent?
> *Catesby:* It is, my liege, and all things are in readiness.
> *K. Rich.:* Good Norfolk, hie thee to thy charge;
> Use careful watch, choose trusty sentinels.
> *Norfolk:* I go, my lord.
> *K. Rich.:* Stir with the lark to-morrow, gentle Norfolk.
> *Norfolk:* I warrant you, my lord.
> *K. Rich.:* Catesby!
> *Catesby:* My Lord?
> *K. Rich.:* Send out a pursuivant at arms
> To Stanley's regiment; bid him bring his power
> Before sun-rising, lest his son George fall
> Into the blind cave of eternal night.
> Fill me a bowl of wine. Give me a watch.
>   [Exit *Catesby.*
> Saddle White Surrey for the field to-morrow. Look that my staves be
> sound, and not too heavy, Ratcliff!

And learning from Ratcliff, that Northumberland and Surrey are alert, giving his last direction that his attendant should return at midnight to help him to arm, King Richard retires into his tent.

In all his military movements, as in the whole of Richard's career, there is something else than self-seeking. It is true that Richard, like Edmund, like Iago, is solitary; he has no friend, no brother; "I am myself alone;" and all that Richard achieves tends to his own supremacy. Nevertheless, the central characteristic of Richard is not self-seeking or ambition. It is the necessity of releasing and letting loose upon the world the force within him (mere force in which there is nothing moral), the necessity of deploying before himself and others the terrible resources of his will. One human tie Shakspere attributes to Richard; contemptuous to his mother, indifferent to the life or death of Clarence and Edward, except as their life or death may serve his own attempt upon the crown, cynically loveless towards his feeble and unhappy wife, Richard admires with an enthusiastic admiration his great father:

> Methinks 'tis prize enough to be his son.

And the memory of his father supplies him with a family pride which, however, does not imply attachment or loyalty to any member of his house.

> But I was born so high; Our aery buildeth in the cedar's top, And dallies with the wind and scorns the sun.

History supplied Shakspere with the figure of his Richard. He has been accused of darkening the colours, and exaggerating the deformity of the character of the historical Richard found in More and Holinshed. The fact is precisely the contrary. The mythic Richard of the historians (and there must have been some appalling fact to originate such a myth) is made somewhat less grim and bloody by the dramatist. Essentially, however, Shakspere's Richard is of the diabolical (something more dreadful than the criminal) class. He is not weak, because he is single-hearted in his devotion to evil. Richard does not serve two masters. He is not like John, a dastardly criminal; he is not like Macbeth, joyless and faithless because he has deserted loyalty and honour. He has a fierce joy, and he is an intense believer,—in the creed of hell. And therefore he is strong. He inverts the moral order of things, and tries to live in this inverted system. He does not succeed; he dashes himself to pieces against the laws of the world which he has outraged. Yet, while John is wholly despicable, we cannot refrain from yielding a certain tribute of admiration to the bolder malefactor, who ventures on the daring experiment of choosing evil for his good.

Such an experiment, Shakspere declares emphatically, as experience and history declare, must in the end fail. The ghosts of the usurper's victims rise between the camps, and are to Richard the Erinnyes, to Richmond inspirers of hope and victorious courage. At length Richard trembles on the brink of annihilation, trembles over the loveless gulf:—

> I shall despair; there is no creature loves me;
> And if I die, no soul shall pity me.

But the stir of battle restores him to resolute thoughts, "Come, bustle, bustle, caparison my horse," and he dies in a fierce paroxysm of action. Richmond conquers, and he conquers expressly as the champion and representative of the moral order of the world, which Richard had endeavoured to set aside:

> O Thou, whose captain I account myself,
> Look on my forces with a gracious eye;
> Put in their hands thy bruising irons of wrath,
> That they may crush down with a heavy fall
> The usurping helmets of our adversaries!
> Make us thy ministers of chastisement,
> That we may praise thee in thy victory.

The female figures of this play,—Queen Elizabeth, Queen Margaret, the Duchess of York, the Lady Anne; and with these the women of Shakspere's other historical plays, would form an interesting subject for a separate study. The women of the histories do not attain the best happiness of women. In the rough struggle of interests, of parties, of nations, they are defrauded of their joy, and of its objects. Like Constance, like Elizabeth, like Margaret, like the Queen of the Second Richard, like Katharine of Arragon, they mourn some the loss of children, some of husbands, some of brothers, and all of love. Or else, like Harry Percy's wife (who also lives to lament her husband's death, and to tremble for her father's fate),[6] they are the wives of men of action to whom they are dear, but "in sort or limitation," dwelling but in the suburbs of their husbands' good-pleasure,

> To keep with you at meals, comfort your bed,
> And talk with you sometimes.

The wooing of the French Katharine by King Henry V. is business-like, and soundly affectionate, but by no means of the kind which is most satisfying to the heart of a sensitive or ardent woman. That Shakspere himself loved in another fashion than that of Hotspur or Henry might be inferred, if no other sufficient evidence were forthcoming, from the admirable mockery of the love given by men of letters, and men of imagination—poets in chief—which he puts into Henry's mouth. "And while thou livest, dear Kate, take a fellow of plain and uncoined constancy; for he perforce must do thee right, because he hath not the gift to woo in other places; for these fellows of infinite tongue, that can rhyme themselves into ladies' favours, they do always reason themselves out again." Was this a skit by Shakspere against himself, or against an interpretation of himself for which he perceived there was a good deal to be said, from a point of view other than his own? While the poet was buying up land near Stratford, he could describe his courtier Osric as "very spacious in the possession of dirt." Is this a piece of irony similar in kind?

The figure of Queen Margaret is painfully persistent upon the mind's eye, and tyrannises, almost as much as the figure of King Richard himself, over the imagination. "Although banished upon pain of death, she returns to England to assist at the intestine conflicts of the House of York. Shakspere personifies in her the ancient Nemesis; he gives her more than human proportions, and represents her as a sort of supernatural apparition. She penetrates freely into the palace of Edward IV., she there breathes forth her hatred in presence of the family of York, and its courtier attendants. No one dreams of arresting her, although she is an exiled woman, and she goes forth, meeting no obstacle, as she had entered. The same magic ring, which on the first occasion opened the doors of the royal mansion, opens them for her once again, when Edward IV. is dead, and his sons have been assassinated in the Tower by the order of Richard. She came, the first time, to curse her enemies; she comes now to gather the fruits of her malediction. Like an avenging Fury, or the classical Fate, she has announced to each his doom."[7]

The play must not be dismissed without one word spoken of King Edward IV. He did not interest the imagination of Shakspere. Edward is the self-indulgent, luxurious king. The one thing which Shakspere cared to say about him was, that his pleasant delusion of peace-making shortly before his death, was a poor and insufficient compensation for a life spent in ease and luxury rather than in laying the hard and strong bases of a substantial peace. A few soft words, and placing of hands in hands will not repair the ravage of fierce years, and the decay of sound human bonds during soft, effeminate years. Just as the peace-making is perfect, Richard is present on the scene:—There wanteth now our brother Gloster here To make the blessed period of our peace. And Gloster stands before the dying king to announce that Clarence lies murdered in the Tower. This is Shakspere's comment upon and condemnation of the self-indulgent King.[8]

NOTES

1. H. N. Hudson, Shakespeare, His Life, Art and Characters, vol. ii.,p. 156.

2. The plan originates with Buckingham, but Richard plays his part with manifest delight. Shakspeare had no historical authority for the presence of the Bishops. See Skottowe's Life of Shakspeare, vol. i.,pp. 195, 96.

3. This scene, including the incident of the dish of strawberries, is from Sir T. More's history. See Courtenay's Commentaries on Shakspeare, vol. ii., pp. 84–87.

4. 3 Henry VI., Act ii., Scene 1.

5. See the detailed study of this play by W. Oechelhauser in Jahrbuch der Deutschen Shakespeare-Gesellschaft, vol. iii. pp. 37–39, and pp. 47, 53. Holinshed's treatment of the character of Richard is hardly in harmony with itself. From the death of Edward IV. onwards the Richard of Holinshed resembles Shakspere's Richard, but possesses fainter traces of humanity. "Wenn hiemach also thatsachlich zwei Holinshed'sche Versionen des Charakters und der Handlungen Richards vorliegen, so hat Shakespeare allerdings die auf More

basierte, also die schwarzere gewahlt; iiber diese ist er aber nicht, wie so vielfact behauptet wird, hinausgegangen, sondern er hat sie sogar gemildert, hat die Faden, welche das Ungeheuer noch mit der Menschheit verknipfen, verstarkt, start sie ganz zu losen."

6. See the pathetic scene, 2 Henry JV., Act ii., Scene 3.

7. A. Mexieres, Shakspeare, ses ceutres et ses critiques, p. 139.

8. Otto Ludwig notices the ideal treatment of time in King Richard 111. But does it differ from the treatment of time in other historical plays of Shakspere? "Wie in keinem anderen seiner Stucke die Be- gebenheiten gewaltsamer zusammenge-riickt sind, so ist auch in keinem anderen die Zeit so ideal behandelt als hier. Hier gibt es kein Gestern, kein Morgen, keine Uhr, and keinen Kalender."—Shakespeare-Studien, pp. 450, 451.

1889—Denton J. Snider. "Richard the Third," from *The Shakespearean Drama*

Denton Jacques Snider (1841–1925) was a writer, educator, and literary critic, an accomplished classicist, and one of the original members of the Saint Louis Philosophical Society. He is the author of *Homer in Chios: An Epopee* (1891), *Modern European Philosophy: The History of Modern Philosophy Psychologically Treated* (1904), and *Lincoln in the White House: A Dramatic Epos of the Civil War* (ca. 1913).

Not one member of the House of Lancaster remains; it has been torn up root and branch. It was begotten in revolution, in revolution it has perished. It had based its claim upon the competency of its rulers, and the nation had sanctioned this claim in the most emphatic manner; but it, too, has now furnished its incompetent monarch, to whom its own law must be applied with unswerving justice. But it would not submit to the principle which was the very origin of its existence—it resisted to the bitter end; nor does it cease the struggle till the last descendant of Bolingbroke is swept into the grave. The House of Lancaster, therefore, has decreed its own fate through its acts. Retribution is written in bloody letters over its corpse; let it now be buried out of sight of the world, which it will harass no more.

The House of York, the successful instrument of vengeance, is, however, left upon the face of the earth, and is sure to give trouble. It cannot stop in its bloody frenzy. But its enemies have perished; upon what object can it now fix its insatiate jaws? It will, indeed, find a most deserving object, namely, itself. Moreover, these furious sons of York, are they to be the rulers of England on the ground of competency—of fitness? Title they may have, but the nation declared in the great Lancastrian revolution something more than, title to be necessary. The triumph of a vindictive party is not the triumph of the country; there is no rest yet possible. The true reconciliation can only be national; both sides must be united and harmonized in the ruler. Down with the bloody party; the House of York must be cleared away, like the savage forest, by the sharp, swift axe of justice before the soil of England will be blessed with the harvest of peace.

But what is the instrument for bringing retribution home to the House of York? We do not have to look far; it has within its own bosom the poisonous reptile which will sting it to death. In the woeful throes of civil war it has begotten a monster—a fire-breathing, blood-drinking monster—whose delight is to prey upon its own kindred. This is the function of Richard, Duke of Gloster, in the drama before us. He is to annihilate his own House by murdering all who have the misfortune to be connected with him in ties of relationship. The tender bond of the Family, which usually softens even the most obdurate heart, for him marks out the victim of destruction; he cannot rest as long as one of his blood be left to claim the throne of England. A doomed House is this House of York, whose executioner is Richard, one of its own children. Most bitter, yet true, is the reproach cast by Queen Margaret upon his mother:

"From forth the kennel of thy womb hath crept
A hell-hound that doth hunt us all to death—
That dog that had his teeth before his eyes
To worry lambs and lap their gentle blood."

Such a character is not a delightful object of contemplation, and, if the end of art be to give pleasure, then here it has lost its end. But the deep, reconciling principle must never be forgotten. Richard is a necessity of this world's justice— he is the instrument of retribution. The House of York has done that before God which makes it doomed—it simply must be extirpated. Richard, therefore, is tolerated because he is executing a just decree—the edict of impartial, incorruptible Nemesis. To consider him as a villain, pure and simple, destroying the innocent, is a view altogether one-sided; let him also be taken, on the other hand, as a hero who carries out in full measure a divine judgment. The primal law of man here below is responsibility for the deed; violation must bring punishment, and Richard is the man who wields the bloody rod; he thus is the vindicator—unconscious, it is true, but still the vindicator of that primal law. He is wicked, inexpressibly wicked—an incarnate fiend, red-hot from Hell, if you wish; but is he not the genuine product of this age—of these Wars of the Roses, whose diabolical atrocity culminates in him? Indeed, is he not the true—the truest—child of this House of York, both in birth and in character? He, the arch-fiend, is come to destroy Pandemonium; to burn it up in its own sulphur, with all the devils in it, himself included.

For Richard as a moral man there is clearly no defense, and none will be attempted here; but for Richard as the instrument of retribution—as the burning purifier of England—there is defense, and we may derive from his career even consolation. As the pitiless executor of a world-justice he must be considered in the present drama, if we are to have any relief at all from his portraiture; so he is certainly drawn by the Poet. In art, as well as in morals, there is no justification for him considered merely as an individual; but Richard as the destroying Nemesis of Hell-on-Earth is a necessity of History, and, hence, must belong to its artistic representation in the Historical Drama.

The tone of the play of *Richard the Third* is in the deepest harmony with the character of its one leading personage. Retribution is its beginning, middle, and end—the ominous sound uttered by all living shapes here, from the highest to the lowest. An over-mastering power hovers in the air above and swoops down upon the guilty world, requiting the wicked deed often with immediate destruction. Human actions must return, and return at once, to the doer, is the spirit of the whole work. It is, indeed, the drama of Retribution—Retribution to the Nation, to the Family, to the Individual. This trait is even too rigidly and too intensely drawn; mankind seems on the point of being crushed beneath the mace of retributive justice; mercy has quite fled from the world. Yet it is the true medicine for the diseased age; the conviction must sink deep into the minds of men that guilt is followed by retribution with the speed and power of the whirlwind.

There is another peculiarity of the present drama which ought to be mentioned—the frequent use of the curse. It is a terrific weapon, and is employed here with terrific violence. It seems to be something above the individual, dwelling in the Heavens—a mighty God, who, being invoked, rushes down from his Olympian height and dashes the frail human being to speedy death. The curse, however, is the mere utterance of retribution. In order to result in true fulfillment, it must be declared in view of the universal nature of the deed; its spokesman is a seer who looks far down into the consequences of an action, often unconsciously including himself in its operation. Lady Anne, when she curses the future wife of Richard, utters the deepest truth of the situation; the wife of such a man must be accursed, because it lies in his character to make a woman wretched; still, Lady Anne marries him, and thus curses herself. A groundless imprecation is a monstrosity, to be excluded from every work of Art. The person who curses should only be a voice declaring judgment—the voice of Nemesis uttering the irrevocable penalty of the deed; petty personal spite is no ground for the curse.

The style of the drama will correspond to the matter. There is no rest to the impetuous torrent, dashing angrily down the sides of the mountain; grand, majestic movement of vast volume it has not. There is a terror in its expression— an unseen hand that almost smites to the earth. The language is mighty, furious, and feverish; it may be called frenzied at times. Titanic struggles and passions are hurled forth in words of Titanic strength and intensity. Human utterance has here reached its limit in some respects. It touches many chords, even the most diverse; at one moment the language of wrath and imprecation sends shudder after shudder through the soul, if not through the body; then follow the tenderest notes of sorrow, swelling into the loud wail of despair. Men gnash their teeth in agony, women weep for the slaughter of their innocent babes; but through all these cries is heard everywhere the demonic irony of Richard—a fiend scoffing over his victims. Many impurities of style may be pointed out—it is, indeed, the nature of the torrent to stir up the ooze and carry it along—but no grammatical cleansing process can possibly purify the torrent into the placid, crystalline brook.

Let us grasp the total action of play as it unfolds itself before us. It moves from party triumphant and using success for partisan purposes to the complete national restoration which united both parties and was superior to both parties. The victory of York was the victory of one side—of a fragment of the nation; the victory of Richmond was the victory of both sides—of the whole nation. The House of York, having overcome the Lancastrians, disintegrates within; both parties, therefore, are quite annihilated. The surviving leaders, a man and a woman, join in marriage, and thus unite the White and the Red Rose. So the Tetralogy comes to an end in a new constructive epoch.

There are two distinct movements in the play, though they are of unequal length. Their fundamental principles are, respectively, the Guilt and Retribution of Richard; or, what is the same thing from a different point of view, the Retribution of the House of York and the Retribution of Richard. The first movement portrays Richard destroying his own family; he turns against his relatives—even against his own mother; he tears asunder every domestic tie in order to reach the throne. Yet all these evils are the offspring of the guilty House—the consequences of its own deeds. Richard himself is its truest representative, though in punishing its crimes he is its greatest criminal. The second movement shows the Retribution brought home to Buckingham, Richard's worst satellite, and to Richard himself. The latter perishes on the battlefield, and his enemy mounts the throne.

Through all the folds and sinuosities of the action two threads can be seen moving, whose line of distinction is marked by sex. Among the men everywhere the central figure is Richard, who thus becomes the head of different groups, according to the different purposes which he is seeking to accomplish. One relation of the family after another is assailed by him, till every obstruction to his permanent possession of the crown seems to be removed—his brother Clarence, the Queen's kindred, Hastings, his little nephews; such are the subordinate groupings. The second thread is composed of the women of the drama. It is difficult to separate this thread from the rest of the play, but its employment is so peculiar and distinct that it must be looked at by itself. There are here four Queens, two belonging to the defeated Lancastrians and two belonging to the victorious Yorkists. Their chief function, it must be confessed, is to curse their enemies; then they have also to bewail their own unhappy lot. Being royal women, they unite the political and domestic relations; still, they represent here the Family in its manifold struggles and afflictions. All are wives and have lost husbands; three are mothers and have lost children; one has begotten the monster who is laying waste the country and devouring his own kindred. With every new misfortune is heard the echo of female lamentation and imprecation; some one of them is wronged and bereaved in these terrible times. The two Lancastrian women represent the lost House, but their loudest wail goes up for their lost families. Queen Margaret is the embodiment of the curse. Its substance is: As Lancaster has perished, so York will perish. The judgment is fulfilled to the letter; the aged Duchess of York, mother of monsters, will be brought to curse her own brood. Most sad and woeful is this chorus of high Queens, uttering the shrieks of the Family as it is ground to death between the contending elements of the nation.

I.

Following now our plan, let us grasp the character of Richard in its very germ. He is resolved to wear the crown of England. In his way to it stand two older brothers and their children; they must be removed, one and all—that is, he intends to destroy his kindred; his means are dissimulation and murder. The great types of deception he cites—Ulysses, Sinon, Proteus, Machiavel; these he can equal—indeed, surpass—in treachery and cruelty. The domestic emotion, strong even in the savage breast, he utterly abjures:

> "And this word, love, which gray beards call divine,
> Be resident in men like one another,
> And not in me; I am myself alone."

No feeling of affection, therefore, can swerve him from his purpose; he is now to be let loose upon his family.

1. The first victim is his brother Clarence. He works upon the weak, superstitious nature of King Edward, who is failing in health; by means of "lies well steeled with weighty arguments" Clarence is thrown into the Tower, while the odium of his imprisonment is deftly turned aside to the account of the Queen, Elizabeth—Richard pretending to sympathize deeply with Clarence. So he drives the two brothers against each other, that they may perish, while he is looking out for himself.

But this Clarence is by no means an innocent man, though he dies of a charge of which he is not guilty. His hands have been imbrued in blood during the civil wars; now retribution has come, though from an unexpected quarter. As he lies in prison, conscience begins to work upon him, and in a dream which he narrates there is beheld the dark picture of his guilt. Perjury and murder stain his soul, and, as he approaches the confines of the future world, he hears the dire voices of accusation. He is a member of the guilty House—he is to be cut down with his own vengeful instrument; his own deed is to be served up to him. Listen to his confession: "I have done those things, that now give evidence against my soul, for Edward's sake;" and Edward has already signed his death-warrant. The doomed family is executing judgment upon its own members—Clarence, the perjured murderer, is himself treacherously murdered. Richard has thus succeeded in his first attempt, and so let us pass to his next plan against his House.

This is directed against the family of his reigning brother, chiefly represented by the Queen, for this brother is already dying of sickness, and need not be proceeded against. She has two sons, still very young, by the present monarch, as well as sons by a former marriage; she has also brothers. These relatives of hers are the natural protectors and defenders of her small children; Richard must first get them out of the way. He has already excited much odium against them by representing them as greedy adventurers and intriguers at court. The dying Edward effects a hollow reconciliation between the two hostile parties; but upon this scene of peace there falls the sudden news of the death of Clarence.

Thereupon Edward is borne from the company in an expiring condition. This is the second death—rapid is the exit of these Yorkists. Edward falls by the torture of disease, aided by the worse torture of conscience. Before his departure he, too, opens his soul, and we behold the agony there. A brother—to whom, more than to any one else, he owed his throne—is murdered under his warrant. Retribution, again swooping down, infixes him; forebodings for his family may well fill his last moments with anguish, as he addresses those around him: "Oh, God, I fear thy justice will take hold on me and you, and mine and yours, for this." God's justice is truly much to be feared in a Yorkian world.

Two brothers are, therefore, gone—cleared out of the way of Richard. Now succeeds the chorus of women and children—the wild, piercing lament of the disrupted Family. The mother, aged Duchess of York, is there with two orphaned grandchildren—son and daughter of Clarence; then comes the bereaved wife, Queen Elizabeth, mourning for her husband. The domestic relation is all torn and mangled; the mother, the wife, the child, sad trio of lamentation, utter their respective sorrows. But even through their present grief pierces the dim premonition of worse that is to come; both the Duchess and the Queen have felt, and recognize, the diabolical spirit which is casting the events for the annihilation of their House. A reflection of the same presentiment is given in the conversation of the two citizens; the gloomy foreboding of the future has descended into the minds of the people. "O, full of danger is the Duke of Gloster," says one of these citizens; popular instinct points out the evil genius of the time with prophetic insight.

But Richard's work is far from being done. He thinks: Let me now knock down the supports of these orphaned heirs of Edward, Rivers, Grey, Vaughan—brother, son, friend of the Queen—are executed in prison. They, too, are caught in the net of the doomed House, for which they deserted their Lancastrian party; if not guilty participation, at least guilty indifference, is the charge against them. "Now Margaret's curse is fallen upon our heads, for standing by when Richard stabbed her son," is the penitent cry of Grey. Yes, you did not interfere to save an innocent boy from the butcher; on the contrary, you went over to the party of the murderers, and shared in their blood-dripping honors. Off with your heads; such men as you must be got out of England before it is again inhabitable by human beings. So shrieks Retribution, smiting anew with vengeful ire.

The family of the Queen is thus destroyed or scattered—Dorset, her other son, fleeing soon to France. Richard now takes a step further. Hastings was an enemy of the Queen's relatives; so far he could cooperate with the designs of Richard. But he is a firm supporter of Edward's young sons; at this point he stands in Richard's way to the throne, and must be removed. Hastings is doubly warned by his friend, Stanley, but he refuses to take the advice. Suddenly Richard trumps up a false charge against him, and demands his head before dinner. He, too, falls under the curse of Margaret, having shared in the bloody deeds of the Yorkists. He aided in destroying "the relatives of the Queen and exults in their death, holding himself to be "in better state than ere I was." He should have been their ally; he is slaughtered for the same offense as they—standing in Richard's way to the throne. It is a harsh punishment for simple, blind Hastings, yet it gives back his own merely; when he exults in the death of his enemies he is really exulting in his own death. Let him be satisfied, says Nemesis, handing him his deed. He sees, when it is too late, and repents:

"I now repent I told the pursuivant,
As too triumphing, how mine enemies
To-day at Pomfret bloodily were butcher'd,
And I myself secure in grace and favor.
Oh! Margaret, Margaret, now thy heavy curse
Is lighted on poor Hastings' head."

Now all the defenders are pretty much out of the way. But his assault upon his family is not yet ended; he orders, his tools to "infer the bastardy of Edward's children"—nay, to declare that Edward himself was illegitimate. Richard thus impugns the honor of his own mother—the very origin of the Yorkian family is nullified as far as possible; even his own claim perishes with the legal right of his House. But, to make his title certain, the young boys of Edward are murdered by his orders. Thus all that stand between him and the throne are removed. Richard has attained the pinnacle in his destructive career toward his family. He has violated almost every domestic relation, one after another; he has passed the summit—now he begins to descend with violent speed.

But the butchery of these young children—what ground can Nemesis have for entangling them in her inevitable net? Innocent babes, smiling in infantile joy, prattling in unconscious prattle—why immolate them? the reader sternly demands. Red-mouthed Nemesis, in a frenzy, answers him: They, too, belong to this House of York, which must be got rid of—they are the young demonic brood, offspring of a fiend-begetting House; burn up the young devils in this general conflagration of Pandemonium. "God's justice" does, then, visit the sins of the parents upon the children. Both these families—York and Lancaster—have, with a blood-dripping scourge, smitten every family and every child in England; let now all their branches be cut off and consumed, down to the smallest tendril. Insatiate Nemesis, this may be a justice, and a justice indispensable to a Yorkian world, but it is not a high justice—not a justice through institutions.

2. At these last acts the chorus of female lamentation has redoubled, and, indeed, the cause of grief is more than double what it was before. Yet these Queens have always a political element in their character which hardly consists with their domestic devotion. The loss of the throne affects Queen Elizabeth too deeply for a mother in great sorrow; "Ah, cut my lace asunder," she cries on hearing of Richard's usurpation. Still, the death of her two boys affects her maternal soul almost to distraction; but shortly afterwards her political ambition seems to get the upper hand, by Richard's proposition for her daughter. Strange woman, strange product of the age—the instinct of the mother and the ambition of the queen in eternal conflict, swaying from one side to the other in a tempest of passion. As wife and mother she has lost two husbands and two sets of children; still, she hopes to be—and, in fact, will be—Queen-mother. Her double nature rocks and tears her heart, but both principles remain in full force.

Then there is Queen Anne, wooed and won by Richard, the slayer of her husband, while she is weeping over the dead body of a father-in-law, slaughtered by the same hand. She is flattered by the wily suitor; nor can she resist his fair promises. She, too, is possessed with the demon of political ambition. To enter the domestic relation with a monster, it is a sacrifice of the woman in her to position. Domestic wretchedness has been hitherto her fate, but now death is the penalty of her choice. She takes to her bosom the destroyer of her family—hence of herself. A plaintive note she, too, utters in this female chorus, full of sad presentiment—then disappears:

"For never yet one hour in his bed
Did I enjoy the golden dew of sleep,
But with his timorous dreams was still awaked."

But the Duchess, mother of monsters, has doubtless the saddest lot. All the misfortunes of the rest of the family are hers, with others peculiar to herself. Husband, children, grandchildren, she has lost; besides, she is mother of Richard, the death-breathing dragon who drinks the blood of his kindred. To give birth to the destroyer of her own offspring would seem to be the direst fate of motherhood. "Eighty odd years of sorrow have I seen;" both in the quality and quantity of the affliction her case is the extreme. What is her deed which has brought this mountain of horrors upon her? She has given to the world the House of York; the whole era of calamities goes back to her as its natural origin. Yet, personally, she commits no offense; she appears here as the best woman of them all—quite free from political ambition. Nor does Retribution punish her with death, but the crimes of her family rend her innocent bosom; when the offspring of her body are struck by the axe of justice, she, too, feels the blow. Thus every deed, every punishment of her guilty House, sweeps back to her, thrilling with pain her aged heart-strings. That is the tragic woman, if ever she was portrayed. But her last words are the most painful part of her painful life; after seeing her house perish, almost to the last member, she is compelled to lay her curse upon her only surviving son. Laden with that curse, Richard sinks rapidly to his fate.

This terrific calamity—whence does it come? It seems horrible, monstrous, unnatural. But the Poet is going to give its ground—it is retribution; this is uttered through the mouth of Margaret. Everything which has befallen the House of York is a picture of what it did to the House of Lancaster. Margaret was wife and mother; her husband and son were cruelly butchered by the Yorkists. The Yorkian Queens are now what she is—shorn of family and of throne. Her curse has been fulfilled in every particular, being based upon "God's justice;" she gloats over the fall of her enemies, who are reduced to a level with herself for the same crimes. Well may she prophesy; in her own person already have prophecies been fulfilled; she has but to read her own history and fate to the proud victors. She has good reason to believe in retribution, and she easily transfers to others what has happened to herself.

So ends this wonderful chorus of Queens; it will be heard no more in the second movement—the measure of lamentation is full. A woeful undertone to the wicked deeds and swift punishment of the men, it echoes along the drama like fitful moans of the wind through forest; it is the wail of women weeping for their disrupted domestic ties. The chorus has two parts, of different sound, yet in deep harmony—both the Lancastrian and Yorkian Queens, though enemies to each other, suffer the same afflictions, and fundamentally sing the same song of sorrow. For Margaret's curse is merely her own grief, concordant to the grief of Elizabeth. Man is punished for his political deeds; woman, joined with him in the Family, suffers along with him, even though she be innocent.

II.

We are now ready for a rapid survey of the second movement—the descent of Richard, which appears to begin with his mother's curse. To ambition he has sacrificed his family, which now, in its supreme representative, prays for his sacrifice. Richard changes; he begins to woo the daughter of his brother, instead of slaying her—it is a new policy for him. Queen Elizabeth seems to yield to his suit, but afterwards we read that she has promised her daughter to Richmond. It is an obscure point in the Drama, but we may suppose that the Queen deceives the butcher of her sons; Richard fails in his new plan—the star of his destiny is beginning to set. The domestic tie, which lie has so deeply injured, revenges itself on him by a refusal.

Next, Richard destroys his most cunning and unprincipled tool, Buckingham, who hesitated at the murder of the young Princes. Buckingham had managed successfully many important transactions, particularly the coronation; it was folly in Richard to throw away such a useful servant. But retribution thereby rays out the more glaring light; Buckingham is treated to that which he has done to others—"underhand, corrupted, foul injustice," inflicted upon him by the very man for whose benefit his crimes were committed. He also sees the state of the matter too late, and expresses the justice of his punishment:

> "Thus Margaret's curse falls heavy on my neck,
> Wrong hath but wrong, and blame the due of blame."

But Richmond has landed on the shores of England. Let us give thanks, for he brings death to the monster, death to this age, and an end to this Tetralogy. Messenger after messenger reports bad news—Richard loses his poise amid danger; he feels himself sinking. He marches out to give battle; the hostile camps lie facing each other, when in the middle a strange vision passes before the mind of both captains. The ghostly forms of those whom Richard had murdered rise up before him and bid him think on their wrongs, that he may be unnerved and lose the battle. At the same time they give words of good will and encouragement to Richmond. The Poet has thus indicated that the hour of retribution is come; and the motives of the play, with its leading incidents, he summarizes in the vision.

Moreover, the scene will aid us in arriving at a judgment concerning Shakespeare's employment of ghosts and supernatural appearances. The conscious intention of the Poet is here so manifest that nobody can deny it, for the ghosts only reiterate what has been fully given in the play—without this unreal form. Richard's overthrow and Richmond's victory has been amply motived; here it is cast into the unconscious presentiment of both leaders. In sleep the foreboding of the soul moulds itself into the distinct image, and there results the dream. The subjective nature of both men is thus shown—one buoyed up with a just cause, the other weighed down with his crimes. What Richard really is comes out in the vision; he might be able to suppress himself when awake. In fact, sleep has relaxed his strong will and we now get a glimpse of his soul, with conscience working there. In like manner the poet broke the will of Lady Macbeth by sleep, before he could show her scourged by remorse. Already Richard's wife, Lady Anne, has spoken of his dreadful unrest during sleep, so that this vision of Richard has been suggested in her words.

Now he for the first time is frightened; the dream has fully revealed, not merely his character to himself—that he knew before—but the certainty of his punishment. It is the revelation of his own soul concerning his destiny, for Richard hitherto had no faith in retribution; his belief was in successful villainy. Hence his terror.

"By the apostle Paul, shadows to-night
Have struck more terror to the soul of Richard
Than can the substance of ten thousand soldiers
Armed in proof and led by shallow Richmond."

But he shuts his eyes, as it were, on the future; stamps out the rising remorse; "conscience is a word that cowards use." Utterly reckless, he gives the command to march on—"if not to Heaven, then hand in hand to Hell." So he rushes into the fight, seeking to drown conscience in death.

Can we, even in a partial degree, account for the development of such a character as Richard? Has he suffered any wrong which has made him unfold into such a moral monstrosity? Is he a victim? Let us put together what facts we can find, not for his defense but for his explanation.

1st. There is seen in him the wrong of Nature, if wrong is ever done by Nature. That deformity of his is an appearance, which hints of some primal malice, which takes shape in him; at least, he may well think so. He may say: In me the world is out of joint, being partial, wrongful, ugly, demonic; in my creation Nature was in a Satanic mood, which has passed over into me. Shall I not revenge it? There is in him an elemental malignity, which came with his birth, and which has been specially fostered and quickened by man.

2nd. Even greater than the wrong of Nature is the wrong of his mother, the earliest formative influence. It is clear that she has reproached him since infancy with his deformity; he has heard as a boy that he had his teeth before his birth, that he came feet foremost into the world, with all the dire prognostications of such unusual events. There can follow but one result from that kind of education; he has fulfilled the prophecy, which here forces its own fulfillment; he is driven into certain lines of character just in the tenderest period of development. Many echoes we catch of what his mother was in the habit of telling him:—

"A grievous burden was thy birth to me,
Tetchy and wayward was thy infancy,
Thy school-days frightful, desperate, wild, and furious,
Thy prime of manhood daring, bold, and venturous,
Thy age confirmed, proud, subtle, bloody, treacherous,
More wild, but yet more harmful, kind in hatred.
What comfortable hour canst thou name
That ever graced me with thy company?"

His own mother has looked upon him as a natural monstrosity, and thereby did her share to train him into being a moral monstrosity. She, too, has a touch of the Yorkian demon which has become incorporate in her son; she has reversed the native instinct of the mother who loves the deformed child with the greater love, as if to make good the wrong of nature, and to save the spiritual from the wreck of the physical element.

3rd. In the same line we continually read about another wrong, that of men, who heap Richard with personal abuse because of his deformity. A whole anthology of stinging epithets might be culled from these plays. Already in the *Second Part of Henry the Sixth* we hear him called, "Thou foul undigested lump, as crooked in thy manners as thy shape." Not one word of pity from man or woman, not even from his own mother, has ever been bestowed upon him; the result is, he is pitiless. He has been reared to abjure all human relations: "I am myself alone." The atmosphere which he has breathed has been that of scorn: can we wonder at his Mephistophelean scoff? But, chiefly, he has had to dissemble his feelings, and hide even the smoke of his malice; the outcome is a most adroit hypocrite. Finally, he has grown up in a time of civil broils and personal encounters; he is a soldier open and daring, as well as an assassin sly and merciless.

Now Richard pays all these wrongs back, to the extent of his ability, which is considerable. Even his own mother is not spared from his counter-stroke; he stands ready to besmirch in the presence of the world, her womanly honor. Not altogether without the penalty has she reared such a son. This is no defense of Richard, but we can see why he had no "love which gray beards call divine." He has been nurtured as the executioner of his family from his cradle.

Accordingly, in this weak piping time of peace, "when he cannot occupy himself with war, or amuse himself with love on account of his shape, he is "determined to prove a villain." He blames Nature, for he has been "cheated of feature by dissembling Nature," which has thus begun with a monstrous act of treachery in creating him

"Deformed, unfinished, sent before my time
Into this breathing world, scarce half made up—"

but how can he help himself? His grim irony can yet take some delight in seeing "my shadow in the sun," and descanting "on mine own deformity." This deformity is indeed the bitter source of all his thoughts and even of his villainy. He is worse off than another famous villain of Shakespeare, the illegitimate Edmund, who is handsome perchance, and can say "Thou, Nature, art my Goddess," not my devil, for Nature has done as well by him as by legitimate Edgar, his brother. But Richard at last comes to look upon his bodily deformity with a certain Satanic delight, just as he takes pleasure in his own spiritual hideousness. Still he has over women the fascination of the serpent that handed to mother Eve the original apple.

Richard is the humorist of Inferno, a human devil jesting with the moral principle of the Universe. The question which he unconsciously proposes to himself, is: Am I or the World's Order supreme? A demonic subtlety of intellect and a demonic strength of will are given to him, and he makes the trial. He must exploit himself in a worthy way, and so he concludes to have a tussle with the divine economy; this heaven-scaling audacity lends him enchantment. One can almost hear his defiant sneer: Of course I shall be hurled from the celestial battlements, but what of it?

In Richmond we have the religious—and, in a higher sense, the national—hero, who unites the two parties into the nation. He stands above the dissension which produced the Wars of the Roses; his object is not partisan, but patriotic. With the battle of Bosworth Field a solution is given to the Yorkian Tetralogy—a solution which is essentially tragic, though it points beyond to a reconciliation. Both Houses have perished in all their immediate representatives; their names descend to remote members of each line, who proceed to disown the titles—York and Lancaster—and to found a new House of their own. A man and a woman—the heir of the Lancastrians and the heiress of the Yorkists—unite in marriage, and thus transform the political hate of the hostile Houses into the domestic love of the Family. But this Yorkian Tetralogy is truly one great historical tragedy; in fact, we may go back and include the whole eight plays, beginning with *Richard the Second*. It was, indeed, the tragic period of English History, in which, not an individual, but the entire nation, became tragic. But such is not the true destiny of England; there must be a conclusion which is not tragic, as the nation is still surviving. The play of *Henry the Eighth*, therefore, is to follow; it will bring to a happy termination the English Historical series.

1893—Richard G. Moulton. From
Shakespeare as a Dramatic Artist

Richard G. Moulton (1849–1924) was an English author and critic who
also served as professor of literary theory and interpretation at the
University of Chicago (1891–1919). He is the author of *Shakespeare as
a Dramatic Artist: A Popular Illustration of the Principles of Scientific Criticism*
(1893), *The Moral System of Shakespeare: A Popular Illustration of Fiction as the
Experimental Side of Philosophy* (1903), and *The Literary Study of the Bible: An
Account of the Leading Forms of Literature Represented in the Sacred Writings:
Intended for English Readers* (1899).

I hope that the subject of the present study will not be considered by any reader
forbidding. On the contrary, there is surely attractiveness in the thought that
nothing is so repulsive or so uninteresting in the world of fact but in some way
or other it may be brought under the dominion of art beauty. The author of
L'Allegro shows by the companion poem that he could find inspiration in a rainy
morning; and the great master in English poetry is followed by a great master in
English painting who wins his chief triumphs by his handling of fog and mist.
Long ago the masterpiece of Virgil consecrated agricultural toil; Murillo's pictures have taught us that there is a beauty in rags and dirt; rustic commonplaces
gave a life passion to Wordsworth, and were the cause of a revolution in poetry;
while Dickens has penetrated into the still less promising region of low London
life, and cast a halo around the colourless routine of poverty. Men's evil passions have given Tragedy to art, crime is beautified by being linked to Nemesis,
meanness is the natural source for brilliant comic effects, ugliness has reserved
for it a special form of art in the grotesque, and pain becomes attractive in the
light of the heroism that suffers and the devotion that watches. In the infancy
of modern English poetry Drayton found a poetic side to topography and maps,
and Phineas Fletcher idealised anatomy; while of the two greatest imaginations
belonging to the modern world Milton produced his masterpiece in the delineation of a fiend, and Dante in a picture of hell. The final triumph of good over
evil seems to have been already anticipated by art.

The portrait of Richard satisfies a first condition of ideality in the scale
of the whole picture. The sphere in which he is placed is not private life, but
the world of history, in which moral responsibility is the highest: if, therefore,
the quality of other villainies be as fine, here the issues are deeper. As another
element of the ideal, the villainy of Richard is presented to us fully developed
and complete. Often an artist of crime will rely—as notably in the portraiture of
Tito Melema—mainly on the succession of steps by which a character, starting
from full possession of the reader's sympathies, arrives by the most natural
gradations at a height of evil which shocks. In the present case all idea of growth
is kept outside the field of this particular play; the opening soliloquy announces
a completed process:

I am determined to prove a villain.

What does appear of Richard's past, seen through the favourable medium of a mother's description, only seems to extend the completeness to earlier stages

A grievous burthen was thy birth to me
Tetchy and wayward was thy infancy;
Thy school-days frightful, desperate, wild, and furious,
Thy prime of manhood daring, bold, and venturous,
Thy age confirm'd, proud, subtle, bloody, treacherous,
More mild, but yet more harmful, kind in hatred.

So in the details of the play there is nowhere a note of the hesitation that betrays tentative action. When even Buckingham is puzzled as to what can be done if Hastings should resist, Richard answers:

Chop off his head, man; somewhat we will do.

His choice is only between different modes of villainy, never between villainy and honesty.

Again, it is to be observed that there is no suggestion of impelling motive or other explanation for the villainy of Richard. He does not labour under any sense of personal injury, such as Iago felt in believing, however groundlessly, that his enemies had wronged him through his wife; or Edmund, whose soliloquies display him as conscious that his birth has made his whole life an injury. Nor have we in this case the morbid enjoyment of suffering which we associate with Mephistopheles, and which Dickens has worked up into one of his most powerful portraits in Quilp. Richard never turns aside to gloat over the agonies of his victims; it is not so much the details as the grand schemes of villainy, the handling of large combinations of crime, that have an interest for him: he is a strategist in villainy, not a tactician. Nor can we point to ambition as a sufficient motive. He is ambitious in a sense which belongs to all vigorous natures; he has the workman's impulse to rise by his work. But ambition as a determining force in character must imply more than this; it is a sort of moral dazzling, its symptom is a fascination by ends which blinds to the ruinous means leading up to these ends. Such an ambition was Macbeth's; but in Richard the symptoms are wanting, and in all his long soliloquies he is never found dwelling upon the prize in view. A nearer approach to an explanation would be Richard's sense of bodily deformity. Not only do all who come in contact with him shrink from the 'bottled spider,' but he himself gives a conspicuous place in his meditations to the thought of his ugliness; from the outset he connects his criminal career with the reflection that he 'is not shaped for sportive tricks':

> Deform'd, unfinish'd, sent before my time
> Into this breathing world, scarce half made up,
> And that so lamely and unfashionable
> That dogs bark at me as I halt by them;
> Why, I, in this weak piping time of peace,
> Have no delight to pass away the time,
> Unless to spy my shadow in the sun
> And descant on mine own deformity.

Still, it would be going too far to call this the motive of his crimes: the spirit of this and similar passages is more accurately expressed by saying that he has a morbid pleasure in contemplating physical ugliness analogous to his morbid pleasure in contemplating moral baseness.

There appears, then, no sufficient explanation and motive for the villainy of Richard: the general impression conveyed is that to Richard villainy has become an end in itself needing no special motive. This is one of the simplest principles of human development—that a means to an end tends to become in time an end in itself. The miser who began accumulating to provide comforts for his old age finds the process itself of accumulating gain firmer and firmer hold upon him, until, when old age has come, he sticks to accumulating and foregoes comfort. So in previous plays Gloster may have been impelled by ambition to his crimes: by the time the present play is reached crime itself becomes to him the dearer of the two, and the ambitious end drops out of sight. This leads directly to one of the two main features of Shakespeare's portrait: Richard is an *artist in villainy*. What form and colour are to the painter, what rhythm and imagery are to the poet, that crime is to Richard: it is the medium in which his soul frames its conceptions of the beautiful. The gulf that separates between Shakespeare's Richard and the rest of humanity is no gross perversion of sentiment, nor the development of abnormal passions, nor a notable surrender in the struggle between interest and right. It is that he approaches villainy as a thing of pure intellect, a religion of moral indifference in which sentiment and passion have no place, attraction to which implies no more motive than the simplest impulse to exercise a native talent in its natural sphere.

Of the various barriers that exist against crime, the most powerful are the checks that come from human emotions. It is easier for a criminal to resist the objections his reason interposes to evildoing than to overcome these emotional restraints: either his own emotions, woven by generations of hereditary transmission into the very framework of his nature, which make his hand tremble in the act of sinning; or the emotions his crimes excite in others, such as will cause hardened wretches, who can die calmly on the scaffold, to cower before the menaces of a mob. Crime becomes possible only because these emotions can be counteracted by more powerful emotions on the other side, by greed, by thirst for vengeance, by inflamed hatred. In Richard, however, when he is surveying his works, we find no such evil emotions raised, no gratified vengeance or triumphant hatred. The reason is that there is in him no restraining emotion to be overcome. Horror at the unnatural is not subdued, but absent; his attitude to atrocity is the passionless attitude of the artist who recognises that the tyrant's cruelty can be set to as good music as the martyr's heroism. Readers are shocked at the scene in which Richard woos Lady Anne beside the bier of the parent he has murdered, and wonder that so perfect an intriguer should not choose a more favourable time. But the repugnance of the reader has no place in Richard's feelings: the circumstances of the scene are so many *objections*, to be met by so much skill of treatment. A single detail in the play illustrates perfectly this neutral attitude to horror. Tyrrel comes to bring the news of the princes' murder; Richard answers:

Come to me, Tyrrel, soon at after supper,
And thou shalt tell the process of their death.

Quilp could not have waited for his gloating till after supper; other villains would have put the deed out of sight when done; the epicure in villainy reserves his *bonbouche* till he has leisure to do it justice. Callous to his own emotions, he is equally callous to the emotions he rouses in others. When Queen Margaret is pouring a flood of curses which make the innocent courtiers' hair stand on end, and the heaviest curse of all, which she has reserved for Richard himself, is rolling on to its climax,

Thou slander of thy mother's heavy womb!
Thou loathed issue of thy father's loins!
Thou rag of honour! thou detested—

he adroitly slips in the word 'Margaret' in place of the intended 'Richard,' and thus, with the coolness of a schoolboy's small joke, disconcerts her tragic passion in a way that gives a moral wrench to the whole scene. His own mother's curse moves him not even to anger; he caps its clauses with bantering repartees, until he seizes an opportunity for a pun, and begins to move off: he treats her curse, as in a previous scene he had treated her blessing, with a sort of gentle impatience as if tired of a fond yet somewhat troublesome parent. Finally, there is an instinct which serves as resultant to all the complex forces, emotional or rational, which sway us between right and wrong; this instinct of conscience is formally disavowed by Richard:

> Conscience is but a word that cowards use,
> Devised at first to keep the strong in awe.

But, if the natural heat of emotion is wanting, there is, on the other hand, the full intellectual warmth of an artist's enthusiasm, whenever Richard turns to survey the game he is playing. He reflects with a relish how he does the wrong and first begins the brawl, how he sets secret mischief abroach and charges it on to others, beweeping his own victims to simple gulls, and, when these begin to cry for vengeance, quoting Scripture against returning evil for evil, and thus seeming a saint when most he plays the devil. The great master is known by his appreciation of details, in the least of which he can see the play of great principles: so the magnificence of Richard's villainy does not make him insensible to commonplaces of crime. When in the long usurpation conspiracy there is a moment's breathing space just before the Lord Mayor enters, Richard and Buckingham utilise it for a burst of hilarity over the deep hypocrisy with which they are playing their parts; how they can counterfeit the deep tragedian, murder their breath in the middle of a world, tremble and start at wagging of a straw:—here we have the musician's flourish upon his instrument from very wantonness of skill. Again:

> Simple, plain Clarence! I do love thee so
> That I will shortly send thy soul to heaven—

is the composer's pleasure at hitting upon a readily workable theme. Richard appreciates his murderers as a workman appreciates good tools

> Your eyes drop millstones, when fools' eyes drop tears:
> I like you, lads.

And at the conclusion of the scene with Lady Anne we have the artist's enjoyment of his own masterpiece:

> Was ever woman in this humour woo'd?
> Was ever woman in this humour won? . . .
> What! I, that kill'd her husband and his father,
> To take her in her heart's extremest hate,
> With curses in her mouth, tears in her eyes,
> The bleeding witness of her hatred by;
> Having God, her conscience, and these bars against me,
> And I nothing to back my suit at all,
> But the plain devil and dissembling looks,
> And yet to win her, all the world to nothing!

The tone in this passage is of the highest: it is the tone of a musician fresh from a triumph of his art, the sweetest point in which has been that he has condescended to no adventitious aids, no assistance of patronage or concessions to popular tastes; it has been won by pure music. So the artist in villainy celebrates a triumph of *plain devil*!

This view of Richard as an artist in crime is sufficient to explain the hold which villainy has on Richard himself; but ideal villainy must be ideal also in its success; and on this side of the analysis another conception in Shakespeare's portraiture becomes of first importance. It is obvious enough that Richard has all the elements of success which can be reduced to the form of skill: but he has something more. No theory of human action will be complete which does not recognise a dominion of will over will operating by mere contact, without further explanation so far as conscious influence is concerned. What is it that takes the bird into the jaws of the serpent? No persuasion or other influence on the bird's consciousness, for it struggles to keep back; we can only recognise the attraction as a force, and give it a name, fascination. In Richard there is a similar fascination of irresistibility, which also operates by his mere presence, and which fights for him in the same way in which the idea of their invincibility fought for conquerors like Napoleon, and was on occasions as good to them as an extra twenty or thirty thousand men. A consideration like this will be appreciated in the case of *tours de force* like the Wooing of Lady Anne, which is a stumblingblock to many readers—a widow beside the bier of her murdered husband's murdered father wooed and won by the man who makes no secret that he is the murderer of them both. The analysis of ordinary human motives would make it appear that Anne would not yield at points at which the scene represents her as yielding; some other force is wanted to explain her surrender, and it is found in this secret force of irresistible will which Richard bears about with him. But, it will be asked, in what does this fascination appear? The answer is that the idea of it is furnished to us by the other scenes of the play. Such a consideration illustrates the distinction between real and ideal. An ideal incident is not an incident of real life simply clothed in beauty of expression; nor, on the other hand, is an ideal incident divorced from the laws of real possibility. Ideal implies that the transcendental has been made possible by treatment: that an incident (for example) which might be impossible in itself becomes possible through other incidents with which it is associated, just as in actual life the action of a public personage which may have appeared strange at the time becomes intelligible when at his death we can review his life as a whole. Such a scene as the Wooing Scene might be impossible as a fragment; it becomes possible enough in the play, where it has to be taken in connection with the rest of the plot, throughout which the irresistibility of the hero is prominent as one of the chief threads of connection. Nor is it any objection that the Wooing Scene comes early in the action. The play is not the book, but the actor's interpretation on the stage, and the actor will have collected even from the latest scenes elements of the interpretation he throws into the earliest: the actor is a lens for concentrating the light of the whole play upon every single detail. The fascination of irresistibility, then, which is to act by instinct in every scene, may be arrived at analytically when we survey the play as a whole—when we see how by Richard's innate genius, by the reversal in him of the ordinary relation of human nature to crime, especially by his perfect mastery of the successive situations as they arise, the dramatist steadily builds up an irresistibility which becomes a secret force clinging to Richard's presence, and through the operation of which his feats are half accomplished by the fact of his attempting them.

To begin with: the sense of irresistible power is brought out by the way in which the unlikeliest things are continually drawn into his schemes and utilised as means. Not to speak of his regular affectation of blunt sincerity, he makes use of the simple brotherly confidence of Clarence as an engine of fratricide, and founds on the frank familiarity existing between himself and Hastings a plot by which he brings him to the block. The Queen's compunction at the thought of leaving Clarence out of the general reconciliation around the dying king's bedside is the fruit of a conscience tenderer than her neighbours': Richard adroitly seizes it as an opportunity for shifting on to the Queen and her friends the suspicion of the duke's murder. The childish prattle of little York Richard manages to suggest to the bystanders as dangerous treason; the solemnity of the king's deathbed he turns to his own purposes by outdoing all the rest in Christian forgiveness and humility; and he selects devout meditation as the card to play with the Lord Mayor and citizens. On the other hand, amongst other devices for the usurpation conspiracy, he starts a slander upon his own mother's purity; and further—by one of the greatest strokes in the whole play—makes capital in the Wooing Scene out of his own heartlessness, describing in a burst of startling eloquence the scenes of horror he has passed through, the only man unmoved to tears, in order to add:

> And what these sorrows could not thence exhale,
> Thy beauty bath, and made them blind with weeping.

There are things which are too sacred for villainy to touch, and there are things which are protected by their own foulness: both alike are made useful by Richard.

Similarly it is to be noticed how Richard can utilise the very sensation produced by one crime as a means to bring about more; as when he interrupts the King's dying moments to announce the death of Clarence in such a connection as must give a shock to the most unconcerned spectator, and then draws attention to the pale faces of the Queen's friends as marks of guilt. He thus makes one crime beget another without further effort on his part, reversing the natural law by which each criminal act, through its drawing more suspicion to the villain, tends to limit his power for further mischief. It is to the same purpose that Richard chooses sometimes instead of acting himself to foist his own schemes on to others; as when he inspires Buckingham with the idea of the young King's arrest, and, when Buckingham seizes the idea as his own, meekly accepts it from him:

I, like a child, will go by thy direction.

There is in all this a dreadful *economy* of crime: not the economy of prudence seeking to reduce its amount, but the artist's economy which delights in bringing the largest number of effects out of a single device. Such skill opens up a vista of evil which is boundless.

The sense of irresistible power is again brought out by his perfect imperturbability, of mind: villainy never ruffles his spirits. He never misses the irony that starts up in the circumstances around him, and says to Clarence:

This deep disgrace in brotherhood
Touches me deeply.

While taking his part in entertaining the precocious King he treats us to continual asides—

So wise so young, they say, do never live long—

showing how he can stop to criticise the scenes in which he is an actor. He can delay the conspiracy on which his chance of the crown depends by coming late to the council, and then while waiting the moment for turning upon his victim is cool enough to recollect the Bishop of Ely's strawberries. But more than all these examples is to be noted Richard's *humour.* This is *par excellence* the sign of a mind at ease with itself: scorn, contempt, bitter jest belong to the storm of passion, but humour is the sunshine of the soul. Yet Shakespeare has ventured to endow Richard with unquestionable humour. Thus, in one of his earliest meditations, he prays, 'God take King Edward to his mercy,' for then he will marry Warwick's youngest daughter:

What though I killed her husband and her father!
The readiest way to make the wench amends
Is to become her husband and her father!

And all through there perpetually occur little turns of language into which the actor can throw a tone of humorous enjoyment; notably, when he complains of being 'too childish-foolish for this world,' and where he nearly ruins the effect of his edifying penitence in the Reconciliation Scene, by being unable to resist one final stroke:

I thank my God for my humility!

Of a kindred nature is his perfect frankness and fairness to his victims: villainy never clouds his judgment. Iago, astutest of intriguers, was deceived, as has been already noted, by his own morbid acuteness, and firmly believed—what the simplest spectator can see to be a delusion—that Othello has tampered with his wife. Richard, on the contrary, is a marvel of judicial impartiality; he speaks of King Edward in such terms as these—

If King Edward be as true and just
As I am subtle, false and treacherous;

and weighs elaborately the superior merit of one of his victims to his own:

Hath she forgot already that brave prince,
Edward, her lord, whom I, some three months since,
Stabb'd in my angry mood at Tewksbury?
A sweeter and a lovelier gentleman,
Framed in the prodigality of nature,
Young, valiant, wise, and, no doubt, right royal,
The spacious world cannot again afford
And will she yet debase her eyes on me,
That cropped the golden prime of this sweet prince,
And made her widow to a woful bed?
On me, whose all not equals Edward's moiety?

Richard can rise to all his height of villainy without its leaving on himself the slightest trace of struggle or even effort.

Again, the idea of boundless resource is suggested by an occasional recklessness, almost a slovenliness, in the details of his intrigues. Thus, in the early part of the Wooing Scene he makes two blunders of which a tyro in intrigue might be ashamed. He denies that he is the author of Edward's death, to be instantly confronted with the evidence of Margaret as an eye-witness. Then a few lines further on he goes to the opposite extreme:

Anne. Didst thou not kill this king?
Glouc. I grant ye.
Anne. Dost grant me, hedgehog?

The merest beginner would know better how to meet accusations than by such haphazard denials and acknowledgments. But the crack billiard-player will indulge at the beginning of the game in a little clumsiness, giving his adversaries a prospect of victory only to have the pleasure of making up the disadvantage with one or two brilliant strokes. And so Richard, essaying the most difficult problem ever attempted in human intercourse, lets half the interview pass before he feels it worth while to play with caution.

The mysterious irresistibility of Richard, pointed to by the succession of incidents in the play, is assisted by the very improbability of some of the more difficult scenes in which he is an actor. Intrigue in general is a thing of reason, and its probabilities can be readily analysed; but the genius of intrigue in Richard seems to make him avoid the caution of other intriguers, and to give him a preference for feats which seem impossible. The whole suggests how it is not by calculation that he works, but he brings the *touch* of an artist to his dealing with human weakness, and follows whither his artist's inspiration leads him. If, then, there is nothing so remote from evil but Richard can make it tributary; if he can endow crimes with power of self-multiplying; if he can pass through a career of sin without the taint of distortion on his intellect and with the unruffled calmness of innocence; if Richard accomplishes feats no other would attempt with a carelessness no other reputation would risk, even slow reason may well believe him irresistible. When, further, such qualifications for villainy become, by unbroken success in villainy, reflected in Richard's very bearing; when the only law explaining his motions to onlookers is the lawlessness of genius whose instinct is more unerring than the most laborious calculation and planning, it becomes only natural that the *opinion* of his irresistibility should become converted into a mystic *fascination*, making Richard's very presence a signal to his adversaries of defeat, chilling with hopelessness the energies with which they are to face his consummate skill.

The two main ideas of Shakespeare's portrait, the idea of an artist in crime and the fascination of invincibility which Richard bears about with him, are strikingly illustrated in the wooing of Lady Anne. For a long time Richard will not put forth effort, but meets the loathing and execration hurled at him with repartee, saying in so many words that he regards the scene as a 'keen encounter of our wits.' All this time the mysterious power of his presence is operating, the more strongly as Lady Anne sees the most unanswerable cause that denunciation ever had to put produce no effect upon her adversary, and feels her own confidence in her wrongs recoiling upon herself. When the spell has had time to work then he assumes a serious tone: suddenly, as we have seen, turning the strong point of Anne's attack, his own inhuman nature, into the basis of his plea—he who never wept before has been softened by love to her. From this point he urges his cause with breathless speed; he presses a sword into her hand with which to pierce his breast, knowing that she lacks the nerve to wield it, and seeing how such forbearance on her part will be a starting-point in giving way. We can trace the sinking of her will before the unconquerable will of her adversary in her feebler and feebler refusals, while as yet very shame keeps her to an outward defiance. Then, when she is wishing to yield, he suddenly finds her an excuse by declaring that all he desires at this moment is that she should leave the care of the King's funeral

> To him that hath more cause to be a mourner.

By yielding this much to penitence and religion we see she has commenced a downward descent from which she will never recover. Such consummate art in the handling of human nature, backed by the spell of an irresistible presence, the weak Anne has no power to combat. To the last she is as much lost in amazement as the reader at the way it has all come about

> Lo, ere I can repeat this curse again,
> Even in so short a space, my woman's heart
> Grossly grew captive to his honey words.

To gather up our results. A dramatist is to paint a portrait of ideal villainy as distinct from villainy in real life. In real life it is a commonplace that a virtuous life is a life of effort; but the converse is not true, that he who is prepared to be a villain will therefore lead an easy life. On the contrary, 'the way of transgressors is hard.' The metaphor suggests a path, laid down at first by the Architect of the universe, beaten plain and flat by the generations of men who have since trodden it: he who keeps within this path of rectitude will walk, not without effort, yet at least with safety; but he who 'steps aside' to the right or left will find his way beset with pitfalls and stumbling blocks. In real life a man sets out to be a villain, but his mental power is deficient, and he remains a villain only in intention. Or he has stores of power, but lacks the spark of purpose to set them aflame. Or, armed with both will to plan and mind to execute, yet his efforts are hampered by unfit tools. Or, if his purpose needs reliance alone on his own clear head and his own strong arm, yet in the critical moment the emotional nature he has inherited with his humanity starts into rebellion and scares him, like Macbeth, from the half-accomplished deed. Or, if he is as hardened in nature as corrupt in mind and will, yet he is closely pursued by a mocking fate, which crowns his well-laid plans with a mysterious succession of failures. Or, if there is no other limitation on him from within or from without, yet he may move in a world too narrow to give him scope: the man with a heart to be the scourge of his nation proves in fact no more than the vagabond of a country side.—But in Shakespeare's portrait we have infinite capacity for mischief, needing no purpose, for evil has become to it an end in itself; we have one who for tools can use the baseness of his own nature or the shame of those who are his nearest kin, while at his touch all that is holiest becomes transformed into weapons of iniquity. We have one whose nature in the past has been a gleaning ground for evil in every stage of his development, and who in the present is framed to look on unnatural horror with the eyes of interested curiosity. We have one who seems to be seconded by fate with a series of successes, which builds up for him an irresistibility that is his strongest safeguard; and who, instead of being cramped by circumstances, has for his stage the world of history itself, in which crowns are the prize and nations the victims. In such a portrait is any element wanting to arrive at the ideal of villainy?

The question would rather be whether Shakespeare has not gone too far, and, passing outside the limits of art, exhibited a monstrosity. Nor is it an answer to point to the 'dramatic hedging' by which Richard is endowed with undaunted personal courage, unlimited intellectual power, and every good quality not inconsistent with his perfect villainy. The objection to such a portrait as the present study presents is that it offends against our sense of the principles upon which the universe has been constructed; we feel that before a violation of nature could attain such proportions nature must have exerted her recuperative force to crush it. If, however, the dramatist can suggest that such reassertion of nature is actually made, that the crushing blow is delayed only while it is accumulating force: in a word, if the dramatist can draw out before us a Nemesis as ideal as the villainy was ideal, then the full demands of art will be satisfied. The Nemesis that dominates the whole play of *Richard III* will be the subject of the next study.

RICHARD III: How Shakespeare Weaves Nemesis into History. A Study in Plot.

I have alluded already to the dangerous tendency, which, as it appears to me, exists amongst ordinary readers of Shakespeare, to ignore plot as of secondary importance, and to look for Shakespeare's greatness mainly in his conceptions of character. But the full character effect of a dramatic portrait cannot be grasped if it be dissociated from the plot; and this is nowhere more powerfully illustrated than in the play of *Richard III*. The last study was devoted exclusively to the Character side of the play, and on this confined view the portrait of Richard seemed a huge offence against our sense of moral equilibrium, rendering artistic satisfaction impossible. Such an impression vanishes when, as in the present study, the drama is looked at from, the side of Plot. The effect of this plot is, however, missed by those who limit their attention in reviewing it to Richard himself. These may feel that there is nothing in his fate to compensate for the spectacle of his crimes: man must die, and a death in fulness of energy amid the glorious stir of battle may seem a fate to be envied. But the Shakespearean Drama with its complexity of plot is not limited to the individual life and fate in its interpretation of history; and when we survey all the distinct trains of interest in the play of *Richard III*, with their blendings and mutual influence, we shall obtain a sense of dramatic satisfaction amply counterbalancing the monstrosity of Richard's villainy. Viewed as a study in character the play leaves in us only an intense craving for Nemesis: when we turn to consider the plot, this presents to us the world of history transformed into an intricate design of which the recurrent pattern is Nemesis.

This notion of tracing a pattern in human affairs is a convenient key to the exposition of plot. Laying aside for the present the main interest of Richard himself, we may observe that the bulk of the drama consists in a number of minor interests—single threads of the pattern—each of which is a separate example of Nemesis. The first of these trains of interest centres around the Duke of Clarence. He has betrayed the Lancastrians, to whom he had solemnly sworn fealty, for the sake of the house of York; this perjury is his bitterest recollection in his hour of awakened conscience, and is urged home by the taunts of his murderers; while his only defence is that he did it all for his brother's love. Yet his lot is to fall by a treacherous death, the warrant for which is signed by his brother, the King and head of the Yorkist house, while its execution is procured by the bulwark of the house, the intriguing Richard. The centre of the second nemesis is the King, who has thus allowed himself in a moment of suspicion to be made a tool for the murder of his brother, seeking to stop it when too late. Shakespeare has contrived that this death of Clarence, announced as it is in so terrible a manner beside the King's sick bed, gives him a shock from which he never rallies, and he is carried out to die with the words on his lips:

> O God, I fear Thy justice will take hold
> On me; and you, and mine, and yours, for this.

In this nemesis on the King are associated the Queen and her kindred. They have been assenting parties to the measures against Clarence (however little they may have contemplated the bloody issue to which those measures have been brought by the intrigues of Gloster). This we must understand from the introduction of Clarence's children, who serve no purpose except to taunt the Queen in her bereavement:

> *Boy.* Good aunt, you wept not for our father's death;
> How can we aid you with our kindred tears!
> *Girl.* Our fatherless distress was left unmoan'd;
> Your widow-dolour likewise be unwept!

The death of the King, so unexpectedly linked to that of Clarence, removes from the Queen and her kindred the sole bulwark to the hated Woodville family, and leaves them at the mercy of their enemies. A third Nemesis Action has Hastings for its subject. Hastings is the head of the court-faction which is opposed to the Queen and her allies, and he passes all bounds of decency in his exultation at the fate which overwhelms his adversaries:

> But I shall laugh at this a twelvemonth hence,
> That they who brought me in my master's hate,
> I live to look upon their tragedy.

He even forgets his dignity as a nobleman, and stops on his way to the Tower to chat with a mere officer of the court, in order to tell him the news of which he is full, that his enemies are to die that day at Pomfret. Yet this very journey of Hastings is his journey to the block; the same cruel fate which had descended upon his opponents, from the same agent and by the same unscrupulous doom, is dealt out to Hastings in his turn. In this treacherous casting off of Hastings when he is no longer useful, Buckingham has been a prime agent. Buckingham amused himself with the false security of Hastings, adding to Hastings's innocent expression of his intention to stay dinner at the Tower the aside

> And supper too, although thou know'st it not;

while in the details of the judicial murder he plays second to Richard. By precisely similar treachery he is himself cast off when he hesitates to go further with Richard's villainous schemes; and in precisely similar manner the treachery is flavoured with contempt.

> *Buck.* I am thus bold to put your grace in mind
> Of what you promised me.
> *K. Rich.* Well, but what's o'clock?
> *Buck.* Upon the stroke of ten.
> *K. Rich.* Well, let it strike.
> *Buck.* Why let it strike?
> *K. Rich.* Because that, like a Jack, thou keep'st the stroke
> Betwixt thy begging and my meditation.
> I am not in the giving vein to-day.
> *Buck.* Why, then resolve me whether you will or no.
> *K. Rich.* Tut, tut,
> Thou troublest me; I am not in the vein.
> [*Exeunt all but Buckingham.*
> *Buck.* Is it even so? rewards he my true service
> With such deep contempt? made I him king for this?

O, let me think on Hastings, and be gone
To Brecknock, while my fearful head is on!

These four Nemesis Actions, it will be observed, are not separate trains of incident going on side by side, they are linked together into a system, the law of which is seen to be that those who triumph in one nemesis become the victims of the next; so that the whole suggests a 'chain of destruction,' like that binding together the orders of the brute creation which live by preying upon one another. When Clarence perished it was the King who dealt the doom and the Queen's party who triumphed: the wheel of Nemesis goes round and the King's death follows the death of his victim, the Queen's kindred are naked to the vengeance of their enemies, and Hastings is left to exult. Again the wheel of Nemesis revolves, and Hastings at the moment of his highest exultation is hurled to destruction, while Buckingham stands by to point the moral with a gibe. Once more the wheel goes round, and Buckingham hears similar gibes addressed to himself and points the same moral in his own person. Thus the portion of the drama we have so far considered yields us a pattern within a pattern, a series of Nemesis Actions woven into a complete underplot by a connecting-link which is also Nemesis.

Following out the same general idea we may proceed to notice how the dramatic pattern is surrounded by a fringe or border. The picture of life presented in a play will have the more reality if it be connected with a life wider than its own. There is no social sphere, however private, but is to some extent affected by a wider life outside it, this by one wider still, until the great world is reached the story of which is History. The immediate interest may be in a single family, but it will be a great war which, perhaps, takes away some member of this family to die in battle, or some great commercial crisis which brings mutation of fortune to the obscure home. The artists of fiction are solicitous thus to suggest connections between lesser and greater; it is the natural tendency of the mind to pass from the known to the unknown, and if the artist can derive the movements in his little world from the great world outside, he appears to have given his fiction a basis of admitted truth to rest on. This device of enclosing the incidents of the actual story in a framework of great events—technically, the 'Enveloping Action'—is one which is common in Shakespeare; it is enough to instance such a case as *A Midsummer Night's Dream*, in which play a fairy story has a measure of historic reality given to it by its connection with the marriage of personages so famous as Theseus and Hippolyta. In the present case, the main incidents and personages belong to public life; nevertheless the effect in question is still secured, and the contest of factions with which the play is occupied is represented as making up only a few incidents in the great feud of Lancaster and York. This Enveloping Action of the whole play, the War of the Roses, is marked with special clearness: two personages are introduced for the sole purpose of giving it prominence. The Duchess of York is by her years and position the representative of the whole house; the factions who in the play successively triumph and fall are all descended from herself; she says:

> Alas, I am the mother of these moans!
> Their woes are parcell'd, mine are general.

And probabilities are forced to bring in Queen Margaret, the head and sole rallying-point of the ruined Lancastrians: when the two aged women are confronted the whole civil war is epitomised. It is hardly necessary to point out that this Enveloping Action is itself a Nemesis Action. All the rising and falling, the suffering and retaliation that we actually see going on between the different sections of the Yorkist house, constitute a detail in a wider retribution: the presence of the Duchess gives to the incidents a unity, Queen Margaret's function is to point out that this unity of woe is only the nemesis falling on the house of York for their wrongs to the house of Lancaster. Thus the pattern made up of so many reiterations of Nemesis is enclosed in a border which itself repeats the same figure.

The effect is carried further. Generally the Enveloping Action is a sort of curtain by which our view of a drama is bounded; in the present case the curtain is at one point lifted, and we get a glimpse into the world beyond. Queen Margaret has surprised the Yorkist courtiers, and her prophetic denunciations are still ringing, in which she points to the calamities her foes have begun to suffer as retribution for the woes of which her fallen greatness is the representative—when Gloster suddenly turns the tables upon her:

> The curse my noble father laid on thee,
> When thou didst crown his warlike brows with paper
> And with thy scorns drew'st rivers from his eyes,
> And then, to dry them, gavest the duke a clout
> Steep'd in the faultless blood of pretty Rutland,—
> His curses, then from bitterness of soul
> Denounced against thee, are all fall'n upon thee;
> And God, not we, hath plagu'd thy bloody deed.

And the new key-note struck by Gloster is taken up in chorus by the rest, who find relief from the crushing effect of Margaret's curses by pressing the charge home upon her. This is only a detail, but it is enough to carry the effect of the Enveloping Action a degree further back in time: the events of the play are nemesis on York for wrongs done to Lancaster, but now, it seems, these old wrongs against Lancaster were retribution for yet older crimes Lancaster had committed against York. As in architecture the vista is contrived so as to carry the general design of the building into indefiniteness, so here, while the grand nemesis, of which Margaret's presence is the representative, shuts in the play like a veil, the momentary lifting of the veil opens up a vista of nemeses receding further and further back into history.

Once more. All that we have seen suggests it as a sort of law to the feud of York and Lancaster that each is destined to wreak vengeance on the other, and then itself suffer in turn. But at one notable point of the play an attempt is made to evade the hereditary nemesis by the marriage of Richard and Lady Anne. Anne, daughter to Warwick—the grand deserter to the Lancastrians and martyr to their cause—widow to the murdered heir of the house and chief mourner to its murdered head, is surely the greatest sufferer of the Lancastrians at the hands of the Yorkists. Richard is certainly the chief avenger of York upon Lancaster. When the chief source of vengeance and the chief sufferer are united in the closest of all bonds, the attempt to evade Nemesis becomes ideal. Yet what is the consequence? This attempt of Lady Anne to evade the hereditary curse proves the very channel by which the curse descends upon herself. We see her once more: she is then on her way to the Tower, and we hear her tell the strange story of her wooing, and wish the crown were 'red hot steel to sear her to the brain'; never, she says, since her union with Richard has she enjoyed the golden dew of sleep; she is but waiting for the destruction, by which, no doubt, Richard will shortly rid himself of her.

An objection may, however, here present itself, that continual repetition of an idea like Nemesis, tends to weaken its artistic effect, until it comes to be taken for granted. No doubt it is a law of taste that force may be dissipated by repetition if carried beyond a certain point. But it is to be noted, on the other hand, what pains Shakespeare has taken to counteract the tendency in the present instance. The force of a nemesis may depend upon a fitness that addresses itself to the spectator's reflection, or it may be measured by the degree to which the nemesis is brought into prominence in the incidents themselves. In the incidents of the present play special means are adopted to make the recognition of the successive nemeses as they arise emphatic. In the first place the nemesis is in each case pointed out at the moment of its fulfilment. In the case of Clarence his story of crime and retribution is reflected in his dream before it is brought to a conclusion in reality; and wherein the bitterness of this review consists, we see when he turns to his sympathising jailor and says:

O Brackenbury, I have done those things,
Which now bear evidence against my soul,
For Edward's sake: and see how he requites me!

The words have already been quoted in which the King recognises how God's justice has overtaken him for his part in Clarence's death, and those in which the children of Clarence taunt the Queen with her having herself to bear the bereavement she has made them suffer. As the Queen's kindred are being led to their death, one of them exclaims:

Now Margaret's curse is fall'n upon our heads
For standing by when Richard stabb'd her son.

Hastings, when his doom has wakened him from his infatuation, recollects a priest he had met on his way to the Tower, with whom he had stopped to talk about the discomfiture of his enemies:

O, now I want the priest that spake to me!

Buckingham on his way to the scaffold apostrophises the souls of his victims:

If that your moody discontented souls
Do through the clouds behold this present hour,
Even for revenge mock my destruction.

And such individual notes of recognition are collected into a sort of chorus when Margaret appears the second time to point out the fulfilment of her curses, and sits down beside the old Duchess and her daughter-in-law to join in the 'society of sorrow' and 'cloy her' with beholding the revenge for which she has hungered.

Again, the nemeses have a further emphasis given to them by prophecy. As Queen Margaret's second appearance is to mark the fulfilment of a general retribution, so her first appearance denounced it beforehand in the form of curses. And the effect is carried on in individual prophecies: the Queen's friends as they suffer foresee that the turn of the opposite party will come:

You live that shall cry woe for this hereafter;

and Hastings prophesies Buckingham's doom:

They smile at me that shortly shall be dead.

It is as if the atmosphere cleared for each sufferer with the approach of death, and they then saw clearly the righteous plan on which the universe is constructed, and which had been hidden from them by the dust of life.

But there is a third means, more powerful than either recognition or prophecy, which Shakespeare has employed to make his Nemesis Actions emphatic. The danger of an effect becoming tame by repetition he has met by giving to each train of nemesis a flash of irony at some point of its course. In the case of Lady

Anne we have already seen how the exact channel Nemesis chooses by which to descend upon her is the attempt she made to avert it. She had bitterly cursed her husband's murderer:

> And be thy wife—if any be so mad—
> As miserable by the life of thee
> As thou hast made me by my dear lord's death!

In spite of this she had yielded to Richard's mysterious power, and so, as she feels, proved the *subject of her own heart's curse*. Again, it was noticed in the preceding study how the Queen, less hard than the rest in that wicked court, or perhaps softened by the spectacle of her dying husband, essayed to reverse, when too late, what had been done against Clarence; Gloster skilfully turned this compunction of conscience into a ground of suspicion on which he traded to bring all the Queen's friends to the block, and thus a moment's relenting was made into a means of destruction. In Clarence's struggle for life, as one after another the threads of hope snap, as the appeal to law is met by the King's command, the appeal to heavenly law by the reminder of his own sin, he comes to rest for his last and surest hope upon his powerful brother Gloster—and the very murderers catch the irony of the scene:

> *Clar.* If you be hired for meed, go back again,
> And I will send you to my brother Gloster,
> Who shall reward you better for my life
> Than Edward will for tidings of my death.
>   *Sec. Murd.* You are deceived, your brother Gloster hates you.
>   *Clar.* O, no, he loves me, and he holds me dear:
> Go you to him from me.
>   *Both.* Ay, so we will.
>   *Clar.* Tell him, when that our princely father York
> Bless'd his three sons with his victorious arm,
> And charg'd us from his soul to love each other,
> He little thought of this divided friendship
> Bid Gloster think of this, and he will weep.
>   *First Murd.* Ay, millstones; as he lesson'd us to weep.
>   *Clar.* O, do not slander him, for he is kind.
>   *First Murd.* Right,
> As snow in harvest. Thou deceivest thyself:
> 'Tis he that sent us hither now to slaughter thee.
>   *Clar.* It cannot be; for when I parted with him,
> He hugg'd me in his arms, and swore, with sobs,
> That he would labour my delivery.

Sec. Murd. Why, so he doth, now he delivers thee
From this world's thraldom to the joys of heaven.

In the King's case a special incident is introduced into the scene to point the irony. Before Edward can well realise the terrible announcement of Clarence's death, the decorum of the royal chamber is interrupted by Derby, who bursts in, anxious not to lose the portion of the King's life that yet remains, in order to beg a pardon for his follower. The King feels the shock of contrast:

Have I a tongue to doom my brother's death,
And shall the same give pardon to a slave?

The prerogative of mercy that exists in so extreme a case as the murder of a 'righteous gentleman,' and is so passionately sought by Derby for a servant, is denied to the King himself for the deliverance of his innocent brother. The nemesis on Hastings is saturated with irony; he has the simplest reliance on Richard and on 'his servant Catesby,' who has come to him as the agent of Richard's treachery; and the very words of the scene have a double significance that all see but Hastings himself.

Hast. I tell thee Catesby,—
Cate. What, my lord!
Hast. Ere a fortnight make me elder
I'll send some packing that yet think not on it.
  Cate. 'Tis a vile thing to die, my gracious lord,
When men are unprepared, and look not for it.
  Hast. O monstrous, monstrous! and so falls it out
With Rivers, Vaughan, Grey: and so 'twill do
With some men else, who think themselves as safe
As thou and I.

As the scenes with Margaret constituted a general summary of the individual prophecies and recognitions, so the Reconciliation Scene around the King's dying bed may be said to gather into a sort of summary the irony distributed through the play; for the effect of the incident is that the different parties pray for their own destruction. In this scene Buckingham has taken the lead and struck the most solemn notes in his pledge of amity; when Buckingham comes to die, his bitterest thought seems to be that the day of his death is All Souls' Day.

This is the day that, in King Edward's time,
I wish'd might fall on me, when I was found
False to his children or his wife's allies;

This is the day wherein I wish'd to fall
By the false faith of him I trusted most;....
That high All-Seer that I dallied with
Hath turn'd my feigned prayer on my head
And given in earnest what I begg'd in jest.

By devices, then, such as these; by the sudden revelation of a remedy when it is just too late to use it; by the sudden memory of clear warnings blindly missed; by the spectacle of a leaning for hope upon that which is known to be ground for despair; by attempts to retreat or turn aside proving short cuts to destruction; above all by the sufferer's perception that he himself has had a chief share in bringing about his doom:—by such irony the monotony of Nemesis is relieved, and fatality becomes flavoured with mockery.

Dramatic design, like design which appeals more directly to the eye, has its perspective: to miss even by a little the point of view from which it is to be contemplated is enough to throw the whole into distortion. So readers who are not careful to watch the harmony between Character and Plot have often found in the present play nothing but wearisome repetition. Or, as there is only a step between the sublime and the ridiculous, this masterpiece of Shakespearean plot has suggested to them only the idea of Melodrama,—that curious product of dramatic feeling without dramatic inventiveness, with its world in which poetic justice has become prosaic, in which conspiracy is never so superhumanly secret but there comes a still more superhuman detection, and however successful villainy may be for a moment the spectator confidently relies on its being eventually disposed of by a summary 'off with his head.' The point of view thus missed in the present play is that this network of Nemesis is all needed to give dramatic reality to the colossal villainy of the principal figure. When isolated, the character of Richard is unrealisable from its offence against an innate sense of retribution. Accordingly Shakespeare projects it into a world of which, in whatever direction we look, retribution is the sole visible pattern; in which, as we are carried along by the movement of the play, the unvarying reiteration of Nemesis has the effect of *giving rhythm to fate*.

What the action of the play has yielded so far to our investigation has been independent of the central personage: we have now to connect Richard himself with the plot. Although the various Nemesis Actions have been carried on by their own motion and by the force of retribution as a principle of moral government, yet there is not one of them which reaches its goal without at some point of its course receiving an impetus from contact with Richard. Richard is thus the source of movement to the whole drama, communicating his own energy through all parts. It is only fitting that the motive force to this system of nemeses should be itself a grand Nemesis Action, the *Life and Death*, or crime and retribution, of *Richard III*. The hero's rise has been sufficiently treated in the preceding study; it remains to trace his fall.

This fall of Richard is constructed on Shakespeare's favourite plan; its force is measured, not by suddenness and violence, but by protraction and the perception of distinct stages—the crescendo in music as distinguished from the fortissimo. Such a fall is not a mere passage through the air—one shock and then all is over—but a slipping down the face of the precipice, with desperate clingings and consciously increasing impetus: its effect is the one inexhaustible emotion of suspense. If we examine the point at which the fall begins we are reminded that the nemesis on Richard is different in its type from the others in the play. These are (like that on Shylock) of the *equality* type, of which the motto is measure for measure: and, with his usual exactness, Shakespeare gives us a turning-point in the precise centre of the play, where, as the Queen's kindred are being borne to their death, we get the first recognition that the general retribution denounced by Margaret has begun to work. But the turning-point of Richard's fate is reserved till long past the centre of the play; his is the nemesis of *sureness*, in which the blow is delayed that it may accumulate force. Not that this turning-point is reserved to the very end; the change of fortune appears just when Richard has *committed himself* to his final crime in the usurpation—the murder of the children—the crime from which his most unscrupulous accomplice has drawn back. The effect of this arrangement is to make the numerous crimes which follow appear to come by necessity; he is 'so far in blood that sin will pluck on sin'; he is forced to go on heaping up his villainies with Nemesis full in his view. This turning-point appears in the simple announcement that 'Dorset has fled to Richmond.' There is an instantaneous change in Richard to an attitude of defence, which is maintained to the end. His first instinct is action: but as soon as we have heard the rapid scheme of measures—most of them crimes—by which he prepares to meet his dangers, then he can give himself up to meditation; and we now begin to catch the significance of what has been announced. The name of Richmond has been just heard for the first time in this play. But as Richard meditates we learn how Henry VI prophesied that Richmond should be a King while he was but a peevish boy. Again, Richard recollects how lately, while viewing a castle in the west, the mayor, who showed him over it, mispronounced its name as 'Richmond'—and he had started, for a bard of Ireland had told him he should not live long after he had seen Richmond. Thus the irony that has given point to all the other retributions in the play is not wanting in the chief retribution of all: Shakespeare compensates for so long keeping the grand nemesis out of sight by thus representing Richard as *gradually realising that the finger of Nemesis has been pointing at him all his life and he has never seen it!*

From this point fate never ceases to tantalise and mock Richard. He engages in his measures of defence, and with their villainy his spirits begin to recover:

The sons of Edward sleep in Abraham's bosom,
And Anne my wife hath bid the world good night;

young Elizabeth is to be his next victim, and

To her I go, a jolly thriving wooer.

Suddenly the Nemesis appears again with the news that Ely, the shrewd bishop he dreads most of all men, is with Richmond, and that Buckingham has raised an army. Again, his defence is completing, and the wooing of Elizabeth—his masterpiece, since it is the second of its kind—has been brought to an issue that deserves his surprised exultation

Relenting fool, and shallow, changing woman!

Suddenly the Nemesis again interrupts him, and this time is nearer: a puissant navy has actually appeared on the west. And now his equanimity begins at last to be disturbed. He storms at Catesby for not starting, forgetting that he has given him no message to take. More than this, a little further on *Richard changes his mind*! Through the rest of the long scene destiny is openly playing with him, giving him just enough hope to keep the sense of despair warm. Messenger follows messenger in hot haste: Richmond is on the seas—Courtenay has risen in Devonshire—the Guildfords are up in Kent.—But Buckingham's army is dispersed.—But Yorkshire has risen.—But, a gleam of hope, the Breton navy is dispersed—a triumph, Buckingham is taken.—Then, finally, Richmond has landed! The suspense is telling upon Richard. In this scene he strikes a messenger before he has time to learn that he brings good tidings. When we next see him he wears a false gaiety and scolds his followers into cheerfulness; but with the gaiety go sudden fits of depression:

Here will I lie to-night;
But where to-morrow?

A little later he becomes nervous, and we have the minute attention to details of the man who feels that his all depends upon one cast; he will not sup, but calls for ink and paper to plan the morrow's fight, he examines carefully as to his beaver and his armour, selects White Surrey to ride, and at last calls for wine and *confesses* a change in himself:

I have not that alacrity of spirit,
Nor cheer of mind, that I was wont to have.

Then comes night, and with it the full tide of Nemesis. By the device of the apparitions the long accumulation of crimes in Richard's rise are made to have each its due representation in his fall. It matters not that they are only apparitions. Nemesis itself is the ghost of sin: its sting lies not in the physical force of the blow, but in the close *connection* between a sin and its retribution. So Richard's victims rise from the dead only to secure that the weight of each several crime shall lie heavy on his soul in the morrow's doom. This point moreover must not be missed—that the climax of his fate comes to Richard in his *sleep*. The supreme conception of resistance to Deity is reached when God is opposed by God's greatest gift, the freedom of the will. God, so it is reasoned, is omnipotent, but God has made man omnipotent in setting no bounds to his will; and God's omnipotence to punish may be met by man's omnipotence to endure. Such is the ancient conception of Prometheus, and such are the reasonings Milton has imagined for his Satan: to whom, though heaven be lost,

> All is not lost, the unconquerable will . . .
> And courage never to submit or yield.

But when that strange bundle of greatness and littleness which makes up man attempts to oppose with such weapons the Almighty, how is he to provide for those states in which the will is no longer the governing force in his nature; for the sickness, in which the mind may have to share the feebleness of the body, or for the daily suspension of will in sleep? Richard can to the last preserve his will from faltering. But, like all the rest of mankind, he must some time sleep: that which is the refuge of the honest man, when he may relax the tension of daily care, sleep, is to Richard his point of weakness, when the safeguard of invincible will can protect him no longer. It is, then, this weak moment which a mocking fate chooses for hurling upon Richard the whole avalanche of his doom; as he starts into the frenzy of his half-waking soliloquy we see him, as it were, tearing off layer after layer of artificial reasonings with which the will-struggles of a lifetime have covered his soul against the touch of natural remorse. With full waking his will is as strong as ever: but meanwhile his physical nature has been shattered to its depths, and it is only the wreck of Richard that goes to meet his death on Bosworth field.

There is no need to dwell on the further stages of the fall: to the last the tantalising mockery continues. Richard's spirits rise with the ordering of the battle, and there comes the mysterious scroll to tell him he is bought and sold. His spirits rise again as the fight commences, and news comes of Stanley's long-feared desertion. Five times in the battle he has slain his foe, and five times it proves a false Richmond. Thus slowly the cup is drained to its last dregs and

Richard dies. The play opened with the picture of peace, the peace which led
Richard's turbid soul, no longer finding scope in physical warfare, to turn to
the moral war of villainy; from that point through all the crowded incidents has
raged the tumultuous battle between Will and Nemesis; with Richard's death it
ceases, and the play may return to its keynote:

Now civil wounds are stopp'd, peace lives again.

RICHARD III IN THE
TWENTIETH CENTURY
❧

Twentieth-century criticism of *Richard III* ranges from allegorical and generic concerns to in-depth psychoanalytical analyses of character and detailed examinations of the ways in which history, philosophy, politics, and gender relate to the play. Though critics continue to investigate many of the issues raised in the prior century, their analyses present an increasingly broader and more refined consideration of those critical themes. Scholarly thinking on *Richard III* has branched out in so many directions that an overview of the ways in which those themes are elaborated during a period of approximately one hundred years, rather than following a strict chronological overview, might offer the best approach to understanding the ways in which various interpretive trajectories have evolved.

In the opening decade of the century, Stopford Brooke's 1905 essay presents a typological interpretation of Richard's character along the lines of the medieval allegorical tradition, but he is careful to contextualize Richard III's character as representative of the political strife that had been evolving in the preceding historical plays. Brooke's critique essentially casts the play in terms of an avenging justice, which is the real authority that controls events and the ultimate power that determines the outcome. Accordingly, Richard merely encapsulates, historically, all the political turmoil and civil strife that has been accumulating with the reign of Richard II. As a personification of chaos, Richard III is the embodiment of pride and the attendant dangers of one who believes he is above divine law, his primary adversary being the figure of Margaret, a supernaturally powerful being who exists solely to torment her arch enemy. Having outlived humanity in her return from the *Henry VI* plays, she serves as the prognosticator of Richard's terrible fate while "her curses have the intensity of an immortal's passion." With respect to characterization, however, Stopford Brooke pays tribute to Shakespeare's superb poetic skills in refashioning these historical personages, admiring his delineation of Richard as a type of master puppeteer, forever causing suspicion and strife, setting one character against another for his own ends. Brooke describes Richard as a supernatural being in that he functions outside the boundaries of human love, living only for himself. In this respect,

Brooke argues that Richard III is unique to Shakespeare and indeed separates him from some of the bard's most famous villains such as Macbeth, a man who deliberates before murdering Duncan. Brooke concludes that *Richard III* is an adept rendering of the process of working out divine justice, while Richard and Margaret serve as its instruments, an aspect that he identifies with Greek drama. At the same time, Brooke argues that, despite its beautiful poetry, the play remains somewhat mediocre, a defect that he attributes to Shakespeare's weariness with the limitations of historical representation.

While Brooke maintains that that Shakespeare is exhibiting weariness with the limitations of the historical genre, E.M.W. Tillyard, writing some forty years later, sees Shakespeare's primary motivation in writing *Richard III* as providing a conclusion to the three preceding parts of *Henry VI*. Tillyard argues that, despite our fascination with Richard's character, Shakespeare was determined to complete the narrative contained in the three previous parts of *Henry VI* and thus demonstrate the presence of a divine plan for the restoration of peace and prosperity in England. Having set forth the argument that Shakespeare intended to bring this particular narrative to a conclusion in *Richard III*, Tillyard is nevertheless left with the task of bridging a gap that exists between this last play and its three predecessors, for *Richard III* suffers from a lack of continuity in the events that have taken place much earlier as, for instance, the memory of Queen Margaret crowning York with a paper crown before stabbing him at Wakefield. Tillyard argues for the unity of all four plays based on the common political/theological theme where order must be imposed on chaos and God's imposition of justice is tempered by mercy. Most especially, Tillyard sees a pivotal role for Margaret as she creates a strong link between *Henry VI, Part 1* and *Richard III*, for in both plays she functions as both a strong Frenchwoman and Richard's primary adversary. Finally, having set forth Shakespeare's primary focus on political and theological issues, Tillyard sees the characterizations of both Richard and Richmond as vehicles through which these themes are expressed. Ultimately, his essay is full of praise for Shakespeare's exquisite artistry in *Richard III*.

Madonne Miner argues for an equality of power for the male and female characters. In her critique of the relationship between men and women in *Richard III*, Miner makes the argument that, by the end of the play, there is an equality of power between the sexes that has been slowly evolving. Miner posits the question of why Richard's character is so fully delineated while other characters are greatly "atrophied" and attenuated figures. The first section of her essay discusses Richard's antagonism toward women as expressed in his opening soliloquy, as he rails against the feminine qualities of peace and sets himself at odds with nature and women. Having established this abiding resentment, Miner offers a multitude of examples of the way in which Richard allocates guilt along sexual lines such as his specious explanation to Clarence that women are responsible for things going wrong at court and attributing his imprisonment to scheming women. Equally audacious is Richard's seduction of Anne—whose husband, Edward, and father-in-law, Henry VI, he has slaughtered—and exculpation of his crimes by stating that her beauty caused him to remove all obstacles. Thus, Richard again maneuvers the argument so that women are to blame for his actions. Nevertheless, while enumerating the many instances in which Richard denigrates or falsely accuses women, Miner points out that the male characters are always victimized by his actions at the same time. One such example cited is in act 3 when Richard decides to eliminate all those who oppose his coronation. Lord Hastings, because he is involved with Mistress Shore, is implicated when he questions the validity of Richard's outrageous charge that Shore has used witchcraft against him; he is summarily sentenced to a beheading. In sum, Richard III is shown to be an equal-opportunity abuser with one qualification, namely that women become the vehicle through which he implicates men. "Richard blames women in order to benefit himself and, in so doing, he creates or destroys associational bonds between men." In the following sections of her essay, Miner explains the ascending power of women, which she marks as the evolving camaraderie among Margaret, Elizabeth, and the duchess of York who, though initially competing with one another as to who has suffered the most, gradually form a bond, a "new humanity" in act 4. Here, the women are transformed into a communal sympathy toward one another. When Elizabeth is denied visitation privileges to see her young sons, for example, the duchess and Anne are supportive of her rights as a mother. As Miner goes on to explain, the women form a communal bond and begin to function as a chorus when they join Margaret in her inimitable cursing of Richard. Thus, Miner concludes, women ultimately cannot be silenced despite Richard's best efforts and, as a result, they become as "round" and fully delineated as Richard himself.

Perhaps most important to twentieth-century criticism of the play is the continued interest in Richard as a human subject and the increasingly sophisticated interpretation of his character in this context. W. H. Auden, adopting philosophical and psychological paradigms, respectively, has made important contributions to our understanding of Richard's subjectivity. In his attempt to identify Richard III's personality, Auden's 1946 essay presents a complex analysis of a particular type of villain and provides a unique philosophical explanation of Richard's particular variety of pathological behavior. Auden's argument can be broken down into two categories, beginning with a discussion of Richard as a fascinating literary personality and, secondly, as a particular type of man whose primary motivation is to guarantee his continued existence. As to the first aspect, Auden maintains that Richard is a physically deformed man, outside the normal realm of human nature, and is thoroughly conscious of his evil actions. Moreover, in order to capture our interest, Shakespeare endows him with a superhuman intelligence. Auden contends that the representation of brilliant, depraved characters are especially interesting to artists because they are poetic creations that exist in the realm of language and, therefore, must necessarily exhibit an acute mental awareness of how they will manipulate others in accomplishing their goals. This is especially true of drama and even more so for Elizabethan conventions, as characters speak in soliloquies, revealing their true thoughts, and thus function as their own chorus. As to the second part of his argument about the type of man Richard represents, Auden makes a distinction between the essential man, an individual who is incomplete but always striving to achieve his potential, one who has a particular set of values by which he lives and who needs to communicate with others, and the existential man, like Richard III, who is complete in himself. Rather than working toward realizing a potential, the existential man is already complete though isolated and forever strives against himself in trying to become stronger than he actually is. In other words, the existential man, ever distrustful of others and highly anxious within himself, must conjure up a fictional self to which he can fasten his sense of security. Needless to say, Richard III falls into this latter category, a man who lives in a state of negativity, who thrives on war and dissension, and, above all, is only satisfied when he can manipulate people to act contrary to their beliefs and desires. "[H]e must always make enemies, for then he can be sure he exists."

Other important twentieth-century critics such as Wolfgang Clemen have exhibited a deep appreciation of Shakespeare's originality in creating a history play unique to Renaissance dramatic conventions and ways of perceiving physical deformity. In his essay, "Tradition and Originality in Shakespeare's *Richard III*," Clemen argues for the brilliant way in which Shakespeare worked within dramatic conventions of his day while, at the same time, exhibited an exceptional talent for experimenting with those same literary and dramatic genres that succeeded in creating theatrical literature quite modern for its time. Clemen begins with a discussion of the inherent restrictions of the Renaissance chronicle play, which sought to present a vast amount of fact and historical material and often forfeited structure and plot, given its main focus. Clemen further points out that the in the earliest chronicle plays, though the audience likewise expected to learn about English history, the playwright often fused a series of colorful, spectacular episodes drawn from documented sources, with the result that the plays lacked unity and dramatic interest. Moreover, as Clemen points out, the earlier chronicle plays often intertwined comic material with their serious theme (a point that becomes important for Clemen's examination of the Senecan influence). However, in *Richard III*, Clemen maintains that Shakespeare has adapted his sources to and woven certain select details into an intricate and fascinating plot, while still remaining faithful to the original purpose of the chronicle play. One of the main points of Clemen's essay is the way in which Shakespeare worked within the classical tradition of Seneca and yet transformed many characteristics of this particular genre of ancient tragedy. For purposes of Clemen's essay, the essential features of Senecan tragedy are elaborate rhetoric, a slow-moving plot with little concern for issues of stage performance and with an abiding interest in reflection, excessive moralizing, and expression of emotion. Additionally, Seneca's plays also focused on ideas such as revenge, violence, and the supernatural. For Clemen, Shakespeare's innovations incorporated these same elements into a faster-paced narrative that paid more attention to issues of representation on the stage, including increased change of setting and shorter dialogues, while utilizing more characters and events. Thus, Shakespeare created a unified play that no longer required comic material to capture the audience's interest. Having outlined the fundamental differences between these two dramatists, Clemen examines some important instances that highlight Shakespeare's unique contribution to the tragic history of Richard III. One of those instances concerns Shakespeare's elevation of the Senecan theater of blood to a study of a superhumanly intellectual villain. Thus, only one murder, Clarence's, needs to be staged, since the audience is instead captivated by the workings of Richard's evil mind rather than the spectacle of execution. Another important instance cited is Clarence's dream, though it contains the introspective meditation characteristic of Seneca, goes far beyond it in its vivid description of his nightmare as an underwater hell. Clemen contends that Shakespeare balances mythological and biblical elements with psychological interest in the experience of dreams and, thus, forces us to exercise our imaginations. In this, Shakespeare made *Richard III* a thoroughly modern play.

1905—Stopford A. Brooke. "Richard III," from *On Ten Plays of Shakespeare*

Stopford A. Brooke (1832–1916) was an Irish churchman who wrote extensively on a wide range of literary matters. He is the author of *The History of Early English Literature* (1892), *The Poetry of Robert Browning* (1902), and *Theology in the English Poets: Cowper, Coleridge, Wordsworth & Burns* (1910).

Richard III. completes the vast drama, carried on through eight plays, which was begun in *Richard II.* It is, as it were, the fifth act, the winding up of the varied threads of the action of ninety years, the coming home to roost of all their curses, hatreds, and crimes, the accomplishment of the work of avenging Justice, and, in Richmond's victory, the initiation of a new England, purged from guilt.

In *Richard III.*, then, the long tragedy is closed. It brings to death those who, having torn the heart out of their country, have tried to govern England for their own advance, and sacrificed to that the welfare of the people.

Richard's figure embodies all the civil evil in himself. He is it, incarnate; and
he dominates the play. Over against him, and towering, is Margaret, who is
the embodied Destiny of the play. Her worn and wasted figure hovers above
it like a bird of doom. Her curse pervades its atmosphere and enters into all
its action. One by one the guilty—Clarence, Hastings, Rivers, Vaughan,
Buckingham, all save Richard; one by one the innocent—the two boy-princes,
Anne, Elizabeth, are forced to feel her presence in the hour they meet their
fate, and to recognise in her the impersonated vengeance of natural law in the
quarrel which has defiled England with fraternal blood. Richard himself is
made her avenger in his bloody passage to the throne, and having finished this
work, he is himself destroyed by the evil he has done. Nothing can be finer
than this knitting of all the avenging forces round the supernatural image of
Margaret, who is herself the prophetess and the victim of Justice. It clasps all
the persons and all the action of the play into unity. It incarnates the judgment
of moral law.

Within this main purpose of Justice working out the penalties due to
those hatreds of great families which in their exercise injure the people—the
conception which is at the back of *Romeo and Juliet*—is the final evolution of
Richard's character and of his doom. When this play begins that character
has been already fully formed. His long soliloquy in the third part of *Henry
VI.* (Act III. Sc. ii.) is Shakespeare's sketch of what Richard is when the new
drama opens. The passion at the root of him is, like Macbeth's, ambition for the
crown, with tenfold more steadfastness in ambition than Macbeth possessed.
Macbeth's ambition does not deliberately premeditate the murder of Duncan.
It may have occurred to him at intervals, but it is only a sudden opportunity
which lures him into it. When he is in it, he debates the crime, hesitates, fears,
thinks of his honour, is imaginative with dark superstition. None of these
things touch Richard. He plots all his murders beforehand with a certain joy,
with unblenching resolution. He has no hesitation, nor does he debate with
his honour, conscience, fear, or affection. He condemns his brothers as well as
his enemies. Every means to his aim is right. 'Would,' he cries, 'Edward were
wasted, marrow, bones, and all,' and Clarence, Henry, and young Edward
dead. They are in my way, they shall be cleared away. What other pleasure in
the world but sovereignty is there for me? Love? Why, love forswore me in my
mother's womb. Therefore 'I'll make my heaven to dream upon the crown.'
Shall I attain it with all those lives between it and me?

> And I, like one lost in a thorny wood,
> That rents the thorns and is rent with the thorns,
> Seeking a way and straying from the way;
> Not knowing how to find the open air,
> But toiling desperately to find it out,

Torment myself to catch the English crown
And from that torment I will free myself,
Or hew my way out with a bloody axe.
Why, I can smile, and murder while I smile,
And cry, 'Content,' to that which grieves my heart,
And wet my cheeks with artificial tears,
And frame my face to all occasions.
I'll drown more sailors than the mermaid shall;
I'll slay more gazers than the basilisk;
I'll play the orator as well as Nestor,
Deceive more slily than Ulysses could,
And, like a Sinon, take another Troy.
I can add colours to the chameleon,
Change shapes with Proteus for advantages,
And set the murd'rous Machiavel to school.
Can I do this, and cannot get a crown?
Tut! were it further off, I'll pluck it down.

Fierce ambition, cold cunning, finished hypocrisy, ruthless murder, conscience-less resolve—these are his powers. And he keeps his word. He stabs Prince Edward after the battle with a savage scoff—

Sprawl'st thou! take that, to end thine agony.

When the others after Tewksbury are talking, he has ridden from the field to London, entered the Tower, and slain King Henry, mocking and rejoicing. And over the dead body of the King he plans the murder of his brother Clarence—

Clarence, thy turn is next, and then the rest,
Counting myself but had till I be best.

A masterful person whose iron will makes and leads events! He is, on the contrary, the servant of Justice, and Shakespeare rarely did a closer piece of work than when, without any special insisting on this, he makes us conscious of it. Richard thinks he makes and guides the storm in which so many lives are shipwrecked. He is really the chief victim of the storm, driven from shoal to shoal, till he is wrecked inevitably.

But the most remarkable thing in his character, as Shakespeare conceived it, is that he is devoid of the least emotion of love. Not one trace of it exists, and it places him outside of humanity. It is not the absence of conscience which is at the root of his evil. Of course, he who has no love has no true sense of right and wrong, and the absence of conscience in Richard is rooted in the absence of love in him. The source of all his crime is the unmodified presence of self alone. As he stabs Henry, he cries—

> Down, down to hell; and say, I sent thee thither,
> I, that have neither pity, love, nor fear.

This creation of a character absolutely devoid of love is deliberately done by Shakespeare. The Richard of the original play of *Henry VI.* is not without some power or grace of love. Ambition for the crown is also the leading element in this Richard's character; these lines which must be Marlowe's tell us that;

> And, father, do but think
> How sweet a thing it is to wear a crown;
> Within whose circuit is Elysium,
> And all that poets feign of bliss and joy.

But such an ambition would not alone make him the monster he is in *Richard III.*—a man incapable of love. It does not: he feels a passionate grief when he thinks that his father is dead. He has no joy till he hears he is alive. His very revenge is coloured by love: it is the wrath of affection. What feeling of love this earlier Richard has is natural, wholly unlike the semblance of it which Shakespeare puts upon the lips of the Richard of this play, who himself mocks at the words of love which he uses. Nor do we see anything in the original Richard of the mask of hypocrisy, our Richard wears; nothing of the intellectual power, the mastery of guile, the love of guile for its own sake, the chuckling pleasure in his cunning, the deliberate contempt of God and man, the deliberate self-contempt, the deep scorn of women because they loved, the pitilessness, the self-isolation—all of which Shakespeare has added to the Richard of this play; and none of which could have been so complete, so unmodified, if any touch of love had belonged to his character.

This is a unique attempt in Shakespeare's work. Richard is entirely isolated by this absence of love from humanity. He is deprived even of a great number of the passions—all those which are derived from love or opposed to love. Richard has no good passions, but neither has he the evil passions of hatred, envy, or jealousy. Any passion that he has—if the word passion may justly be applied to ambition—is the servant of his intellect. Of course, without love, and the qualities that depend on it, he has no conscience, no repentance, no fear of God. What seems at times remorse in him at the end is the agony of failure, is fury at the breaking down of his intellectual power. When a sense of the existence of conscience occurs to him, it intrudes in dreams only, not in real life. Awake, he passes from one crime to another without one touch of emotion, without one moment of morality.

This separates him even from Iago, whose malignity is partly accounted for, who at least attempts to account for his curious, self-gratulating pleasure in torturing Othello by pretending jealousy. This also accounts for the unhesitating swiftness with which crime follows crime in Richard's course, which otherwise would be unnatural Macbeth before Duncan's murder is not half so rapid The sense of honour which serves Macbeth for conscience makes him pause again and again before the murder, but Richard never hesitates. Old affections, admiration for Duncan's character, the chieftain's sense of honour, hinder Macbeth's quickness in guilt. Macbeth has some love in his heart; he loves his wife; he would not have murdered Clarence nor rejoiced when Edward died. He was naturally full of the milk of human-kindness of which Richard had not one drop. When he acts swiftly, and he is hurried by his love for his wife as well as by his ambition, his haste is lest his sense of honour, of which he is always conscious, should get the better of him. It is only when he has realised that honour is irrevocably violated that he becomes the reckless murderer. Guilt is not his natural element, because he is not mere intellect unbalanced by any affection. One with Richard in ambition, he differs from him by the presence of love in his nature. Richard is loveless intellect, ambitious of unchallenged power—absolute self with cunning—an awful solitary.

Shakespeare felt obliged to account for this supernatural devilry in man; and he does so by making Richard a monster from his mother's womb. At his birth Nature rebelled;

> The owl shrieked at thy birth, an evil sign;
> The night-crow cried, aboding luckless time;
> Dogs howl'd, and hideous tempests shook down trees!
> The raven rook'd her on the chimney's top,
> And chattering pies in dismal discord sung.
> Thy mother felt more than a mother's pain,
> And yet brought forth less than a mother's hops;
> To wit, an indigest deformed lump,
> Not like the fruit of such, a goodly tree.

And his mother confirms the tale when she lays her curse upon him. But Shakespeare does not think this enough to motive the unnaturalness of the character. Therefore he further dwells on Richard's belief that all the world hates him for his misshapen person, and that heaven—the only touch of religion in Richard—has made him in its anger;

> Then, since the heavens have shap'd my body so,
> Let hell make crook'd my mind to answer it.
> I have no brother, I am like no brother

And this word 'love,' which grey-beards call divine,
Be resident in men like one another
And not in me: I am myself alone.

'I am myself alone'; that is the keynote of Richard's character as conceived by Shakespeare; intellect without love, like Goethe's Mephistopheles; and by the absence of love outside of human nature.

Be resident in men like one another,
And not in me.

It is this incapacity to even conceive love which makes him try to do things which would seem impossible to any one who loved. No other man could have wooed Lady Anne as he did, or asked Elizabeth for her daughter, yet both are not out of character in one who is wholly ignorant of love.

What though I kill'd her husband and her father,
The readiest way to make the wench amends
Is to become her husband and her father;

is a speech incredible on the lips of any one who has ever loved. It is only when he has won Anne that he is astonished; and in the astonishment a faint gleam of belief in the existence of moral right and wrong for others comes upon him. 'She has God,' he says, 'and her conscience against her.' But this only serves to make him proud of his own isolation in lovelessness from other men. His scorn of himself and of others, and the mixture of bitterness, pride, contempt, fierce self-knowledge, and isolation in the long soliloquy which begins

Was ever woman in this humour woo'd?

is a splendid example of the power by which Shakespeare felt and shared within himself a thousand others than himself, and even dared, as here, to paint the nature of one who was set aside by him from all mankind.

This is followed by that masterly scene in the palace where Richard, the lord here of politic intellect, puts himself forward as 'the plain man,' and then as 'too soft and pitiful and childishly foolish for the world'; and so sets all his enemies at loggerheads, plays the interests and passions of each against those of the others, and makes use even of Margaret, the foe of all, to develop and win his schemes. His soulless cunning is triumphant, and he has a certain pleasure, even joy, in his devilment, such as we have in the unhindered exercise of any natural force we possess. In his case, however, the force exercised by absolute want of love is an unnatural force; and the result is—that the will and the intellectual cunning which exercise it are finally broken down. It is lovelessness which spoils his cunning, causes him to make mistakes, and finally destroys his aim. Again we get back to the root of his character; he is self alone.

The second idea of the drama comes in (Act I. Sc. iii.) with the presence of Margaret, the incarnate Fury of the Civil Wars, who has been their incessant urger, and is now the Pythoness of their punishment. 'Small joy have I,' cries Elizabeth, 'in being England's queen.' And Margaret, her first entrance into the action, mutters from the background—

And lessen'd be that small, God, I beseech him.

She is a terrible figure, the Fate and Fury together of the play. She does nothing for its movement; she is outside of that. But she broods above its action, with hands outstretched in cursing. Worn, like 'a wrinkled witch,' her tongue edged with bitter fire, with all the venom of the Civil Wars bubbling in her heart; grey-haired, tall, with the habit of command, she has not been, like Richard, without love or exiled from human nature. But all she loved are dead. She has outlived humanity, and passed into an elemental Power, hopeless, pitiless, joyless save for the joy of vengeance. It is not till she finds the Duchess of York and Edward's queen sunk in their hopeless pain that she feels herself at one, even for a moment, with any human creature. She sits down and curses with them, but soon leaves them, as one removed; towering over them as she flings back on them her parting curse, incensed that she has been even for that moment at one with their feeble wrath. Her eloquence is that of primeval sorrow and hate. Her curses have the intensity of an immortal's passion.

'O, well skilled in curses,' cries the Queen Elizabeth, 'teach me how to curse.' 'Life is her shame,' Margaret says, but she will not die till she has vengeance. 'Tis the only thing which brings a smile to her withered lips. And her vengeance is felt, like an actual presence in the air, by all who die. Shakespeare takes pains to mark that out. She is not only Margaret and hate to them, but the spirit through whom divine justice works its wrath upon them. And when she sees the end, she passes away, still alive, like one who cannot die; departs in an awful joy—

These English woes will make me smile in France.

Immediately after her first appearance, the curse and punishment begin to act. Richard is left alone on the stage, and the murderers of Clarence enter to receive his command to slay. These are the only persons in the play with whom Richard is at his ease. With murderers he drops his mask. He hails them as if they were comrades;

> How now, my hardy, stout-resolved mates!
> Are you now going to dispatch this thing?
> . . . .
> I like you, lads; about your business straight;
> Go, go, dispatch.

This murder fills the fourth scene. Shakespeare does not expose it unrelieved. He feels that the passion in the last scene has been too loud and furious, as indeed it has. He therefore lowers the note, and introduces, not to lessen but to deepen the tragedy, the wonderful piteousness, the wonderful beauty of the dream of Clarence.

Nevertheless, he does not let loose his main conception. The murder is itself a crime, but it is also part of the great punishment, of the working out of the law that greed produces greed, and the sword the sword. Clarence confesses that his death is morally just.

> O God! if my deep prayers cannot appease thee,
> And thou wilt be aveng'd on my misdeeds,
> Yet execute thy wrath on me alone.

Immediately, pat on the point, and done in Shakespeare's way of setting over against a grave thought the same thought in a grotesque or ghastly framework, there is now a parody, with a grim earnestness in it, of this same question of the vengeance of conscience. Is there that in us which punishes with thought? Is there a wrath beyond ourselves? An imperative command within us? If so, is it worth regarding? The murderers debate the question from their rude stand-point, and settle the matter as the robbing and murdering kings and nobles had settled it. They have a warrant for their crime; it is done on command. But these considerations are indifferent, of these conscience might get the better; but the reward, the gain—that conquers conscience; and arguing to and fro with extraordinary variety of base and cunning thought and phrase, they end by attacking conscience as the most dangerous enemy of states and societies.

> Sec. Murd. 'Zounds! he dies: I had forgot the reward.
> First Murd. Where's thy conscience now?
> Sec. Murd. In the Duke of Gloucester's purse.
> . . . .
> I'll not meddle with it; it makes a man a coward; a man cannot steal, but it
> accuseth him; a man cannot swear, but it checks him; a man cannot lie with
> his neighbour's wife, but it detects him; 'tis a blushing, shamefast spirit, that
> mutinies in a man's bosom; it fills one full of obstacles; it made me once
> restore a purse of gold that I found; it beggars any man that keeps it; it is

turned out of all towns and cities for a dangerous thing; and every man that means to live well endeavours to trust to himself and live without it.

This is exactly Richard's point of view, put coarsely. Yet these two are not as bad as Richard. They do feel the pull of conscience. He could not.

The same elements of division appear in the second act. The hatreds of all parties underlie the hollow reconciliation at the deathbed of the King. Buckingham concentrates the falsehood of them all in his perjurous vow. By that falsehood, as a moral matter, his coming death is accounted for. But Shakespeare, though here in his sternest mood, awakens the pity of the audience by the form in which he casts Buckingham's oath. He prays for the very fate which falls upon him. Whenever Buckingham doth turn his hate (he speaks to the Queen) on you or yours

> God punish me
> With hate in those where I expect most love!
> When I have most need to employ a friend,
> And most assured that he is a friend,
> Deep, hollow, treacherous, and full of guile,
> Be he unto me!

And so it falls out. The words make us think of Richard, and Shakespeare answers our thought. 'We only want Gloucester,' says the king,

> To make the blessed period of this peace.

He enters, and flings into their false calm, like a shell, the news of the death of Clarence.

Then, Clarence being the first, Edward is the second to feel the judgment which descends on those guilty of the blood of England. His conscience awakens, and he dies, feeling that God's justice is taking hold on men.

It is characteristic of Shakespeare's work that the form of Edward's confession (recalling Clarence and his kindness) throws back a new light of pity on the scene of Clarence's death, and keeps up the continuity of the dramatic action and the dramatic pity. And the pity is made almost terrible by the picture Edward's confession contains of the universal selfishness of the court, where not one has thought of Clarence, only of himself.

> My brother kill'd no man; his fault was thought:
> And yet his punishment was bitter death.
> Who sued to me for him? Who, in my wrath,
> Kneel'd at my feet, and bade me be advis'd?

Who spoke of brotherhood? Who spoke of love?
Who told me how the poor soul did forsake
The mighty Warwick, and did fight for me?
Who told me, in the field at Tewksbury,
When Oxford had me down, he rescu'd me,
And said, 'Dear brother, live, and be a king'?
Who told me, when we both lay in the field
Frozen almost to death, how he did lap me
Even in his garments; and did give himself,
All thin and naked, to the numb cold night?
All this from my remembrance brutish wrath
Sinfully pluck'd, and not a man of you
Had so much grace to put it in my mind! . . .
　　　The proudest of you all
Have been beholding to him in his life,
Yet none of you would once beg for his life.
O God! I fear thy justice will take hold
On me and you and mine and yours for this.
Come, Hastings, help me to my closet. O! poor Clarence!

Nor is the main scope of the play lost sight of in the next scene between the boys and their aunt and grandam—a quiet moment in this tempest of crime. The fate of the young princes is shadowed forth in the talk of their cousins. The fate which overglooms the play is heard in the grief of the women. The gloom is deepened when the Queen enters wailing her husband's death, and she and the Duchess (who, with Margaret, serve the uses, in some sort, of the Greek chorus) toss their sorrow to and fro with the children of Clarence, till the whole world seems full of weeping. Then Gloucester, sheathed in hypocrisy and mocking inwardly the sorrow he has caused, adds poignancy to the tragic pain the audience feels.

　　The act ends with the arrest by Buckingham and Gloucester of the kinsmen of the Queen. 'Ah me,' she cries, 'I see the ruin of my house'; and then the Duchess, sick even to death of strife and slaughter, gathers together all the woes of the long quarrel as they have touched the house of York.

Accursed and unquiet wrangling days,
How many of you have mine eyes beheld!
My husband lost his life to get the crown,
And often up and down my sons were toss'd,
For me to joy and weep their gain and loss:
And being seated, and domestic broils
Clean over-blown, themselves, the conquerors,
Make war upon themselves; brother to brother,

Blood to blood, self against self: O! preposterous
And frantic outrage, end thy damned spleen;
Or let me die, to look on death no more.

Amidst an astonishing variety of circumstance and character which the
Greek dramatists would have repudiated as injurious to unity, the third act
keeps close to the tragic development of the work of Justice. The audience knows
what fate hangs over the princes on their arrival in London. It expects to have
it presaged. And it is. Touch after touch, in their graceful prattle, awakes our
pity. Some are even put into the mouth of Gloucester. The gallant bearing of the
prince, his hopes to be a famous warrior like Caesar, while his murderer stands
by; his misliking of the Tower; the light, peevish, innocent talk of York; his scoff
at Gloucester's deformity; the sudden overshadowing of his heart also when he
hears of the Tower—all deepen the tragic darkness. And now Richard, having
resolved on the murder of the princes, murders all who stand in the way of his
design. Yet it is not he who really slays the new victims. It is avenging Justice,
wading, as usual, to her conclusion through the blood of the innocent as well
as of the guilty. Richard is her blind instrument. Rivers, Grey, Vaughan are
now slain, the third, fourth, and fifth after Clarence and Edward who feel the
sentence of conscience and the curse of Margaret. Their last words remember her.
Next Hastings meets his unexpected fate. While he is talking of Gloucester's
friendly face (Shakespeare is at home in these bitter contrasts of life) Gloucester
breaks in suddenly, 'Off with his head.' 'He's sudden, if a thing comes in his
head,' said King Edward—and Hastings also sees Margaret as he dies. Richard
slays them, but Justice holds his sword.

The scenes which follow, where Richard is induced to accept the crown, as it
were by force, and where he apparently persuades Elizabeth to give him her daughter
are weakened by their great length, and almost trench on farce. Richard between
the two bishops, with the prayer-book in his hand, is ridiculous; and the scene
drags on without Shakespeare's crispness, clearness, or concentration of thought.
It is a worse blot on the play than the scenes between Richard and Lady Anne,
between Richard and Elizabeth. Richard's dissimulation, in spite of the variety
of the dramatic talk, seems in these scenes to pass the bounds of nature. Yet it is
difficult to find just fault with Shakespeare. It may be that he desired to mark by
their strained unnaturalness that weakness in the intellect of Richard which arises
from the absence of love in his character. Intellectual power, without love, grows
abnormal, unbalanced, and weak through pride of itself. Nay more, Shakespeare
felt that it would not only lose its power, but finally itself. It would be sure to make
mistakes in dealing with mankind and with the movements of the world; to overdo
its cunning; to end like the plotting of Mephistopheles, in folly and failure. The
common-sense of mankind has decided that long ago. In all folklore stories the
Devil—intellect without love—is invariably made a hare of in the end.

In the fourth act the coronation of Richard brings about the first movement towards his overthrow. Elizabeth sends Dorset to Richmond, and we scent from afar the ruin of Richard; and, like the rest, she, when anticipating doom, remembers the curse of Margaret.

As the speakers of this scene depart, they are standing in front of the Tower. Shakespeare, who always prepares his audience, does not let these sorrowful women leave the stage without hinting at the murder of the princes, and with an exquisite tenderness speaks—

> Stay yet, look back, with me unto the Tower.
> Pity, you ancient stones, those tender babes
> Whom envy hath immur'd within your walls,
> Rough cradle for such little pretty ones!
> Rude ragged nurse, old sullen playfellow
> For tender princes, use my babies well.
> So foolish sorrow bids your stones farewell.

Imagine that! What a playwright was Shakespeare! How effective for the stage is that farewell!

And now, in the next scene (Act IV. Sc. ii.), the disintegration of Richard's intellectual power continues. Anne has already told how in sleep he is not able to beat back superstitious fear. Even his physical courage is then, as we see afterwards, in abeyance.

> For never yet one hour in his bed
> Did I enjoy the golden dew of sleep,
> But with his timorous dreams was still awak'd.

Richard is represented by Shakespeare as without a soul, being without love. But this is when he is awake, and his will at the helm of his life. When he is asleep, Shakespeare, with his belief that in the far background of an evil nature the soul lives, but unknown, unbelieved in, by its possessor, shows how it awakens at night when the will sleeps, and does its work on the unconscious man. Then, and only then, conscience stirs in Richard. Then, and only then, fear besets him. The day-result of this work of the soul at night in Richard is plainly suggested in the dialogue. He is represented at all points as in a state of nervous strain of which he does not know the cause; and this ignorance, irritating the intensity of his wrath with any obstacle, throws not only his intellect, as I have said above, but his management of men and events out of gear. His intellect is no longer clear, for his body is no longer sane. All his powers, even his hypocrisy, are decaying. His doom has begun.

Moreover, he now begins to feel the steady pull of the universe against immoderate crime. To escape this hitherto unknown terror he is driven, as it were by necessity, to add crime to crime. He proposes the death of the princes to Buckingham—'I wish the bastards dead.' Buckingham retreats from this, with a courtier's words—

BUCK. Your grace may do your pleasure.
K. RICH. Tut, tut! thou art all ice, thy kindness freezes.

And this hesitation dooms him—

CATES. The King is angry: see, he gnaws his lip.
K. RICH. I will converse with iron-witted fools
And unrespective boys: none are for me
That look into me with considerate eyes.
High-reaching Buckingham grows circumspect.

And when the princes are dead, Anne his wife shall die, and he will marry Elizabeth. 'Murder her brothers, and then marry her—uncertain way of gain.' This is the wild hurry of crime—Justice driving its victim—

But I am in
So far in blood, that sin will pluck on sin:
Tear-falling pity dwells not in this eye.

To double this guilty speed, the news comes of Richmond preparing a power, and the news abides, stings and irritates within him. Its inward insistence breaks out in short soliloquies, even when alone with Buckingham. The accomplished mask-wearer drops his mask; betrays himself. His self-control is giving way; and with that, his intellect fails still more; fails so much that he is touched with superstition. He talks of prophecies—of warnings given by a bard of Ireland. All through this little scene with Buckingham (Act IV. Sc. ii.) he has lost his coolness of temper and his hypocrisy in irritability. His nerve is gone, like Macbeth's, but, also like Macbeth, his courage lives on. The affection is of the mind, not of the body.

And now, just at the turn of things, when Richmond begins to increase and Richard to decrease, Margaret fitly appears for the last time, and at first alone, to concentrate their curse, and hers. Two splendid lines introduce the vengeful Queen.

So, now prosperity begins to mellow
And drop into the rotten mouth of death.

To her enter the Queen Elizabeth and the Duchess of York; and they join in the doom Margaret pronounces on Richard. Had Shakespeare written this scene with his matured power and concentration, it would have been a matchless scene. As it is, it is of an extraordinary force—mightily conceived and shaped. One after another, these three, whose darlings Richard has slain, sit down, with sorrow, like three Fates, on the earth of England 'unlawfully made drunk with innocent blood.' Hooded, old, grey with grief, are Margaret and the Duchess; Elizabeth, though not yet old, is one with them in sorrow, a prey of time. Under the palace walls, all three, royal yet huddled in the dust, prophesy the wrath and the decrees of justice. They concentrate, not only the misery of their own grief, but all the woe of the Civil Wars, into their speech; and bring the whole weight of their sorrow and sin to a point in Richard, on whom falls their accumulated curse. Margaret rises above the others in the joy of revenge, and leaves them to their session on the earth. 'Forbear,' she cries to Elizabeth, who asks for help in cursing—

> Forbear to sleep the night, and fast the day;
> Compare dead happiness with living woe;
> Think that thy babes were fairer than they were,
> And he that slew them fouler than he is:
> Bettering thy loss makes the bad causer worse:
> Revolving this will teach thee how to curse.

Their curse is deep, but it is deepened when Nature herself retreats before it, when it is stronger than motherhood. The scene closes when on Richard's head—who now, in fine dramatic contrast to this almost solitary scene, comes marching by with warlike sound and pomp on his way to overthrow Buckingham—falls his mother's curse. And the curse is a prophecy, as it were, of all his victims will say to him the night before Bosworth field. It is often Shakespeare's habit to anticipate in a short passage a scene which he means to give in full, a sketch of the picture to be completed;

> Therefore, take with thee my most grievous curse,
> Which, in the day of battle, tire thee more
> Than all the complete armour that thou wear'st!
> My prayers on the adverse party fight;
> And there the little souls of Edward's children
> Whisper the spirits of thine enemies
> And promise them success and victory.
> Bloody thou art, bloody will be thy end;
> Shame serves thy life and doth thy death attend.

The scene with Elizabeth which follows is of that cunning which overreaches its aim. Richard thinks he has persuaded Elizabeth to give him her daughter—

Relenting fool, and shallow changing woman!

But it is he who has been deceived, he whom the woman has played with. She pretends to consent, but is already in communication with Richmond, to whom she does give her daughter. From this point of view, which I think Shakespeare meant,[1] the unnaturalness of the scene (the far too great length of which is only excused by the impossible effort Richard makes) is modified; and the weakness which has come on Richard's intellect is more than suggested. All is breaking down in him; his self-control, his temper, intelligence, his clear sight of things, his foresight, his power to keep men and subdue them to his will.

The art is excellent with which this is shown in Richard's talk with Catesby, Ratcliff, Stanley, and the messengers. He is no longer the calm, smooth, cautious, deliberate, unimpassioned politician, all his powers held in hand. He gives half-orders, and stops short, yet thinks he has fully given them, as with Catesby. He gives orders and withdraws them, suspicion darting into his mind, as with Ratcliff—

> K. RICH. Catesby, fly to the duke.
> CATES. I will, my lord, with all convenient haste.
> K. RICH. Ratcliff, come hither. Post to Salisbury:
> When thou com'st thither,—[To CATESBY] Dull, unmindful villain,
> Why stay'st thou here, and go'st not to the duke?
> CATES. First, mighty liege, tell me your highness' pleasure,
> What from your Grace I shall deliver to him.
> K. RICH. O! true, good Catesby: bid him levy straight
> The greatest strength and power he can make,
> And meet me suddenly at Salisbury.
> CATES. I go. [*Exit.*
> RAT. What, may it please you, shall I do at Salisbury?
> K. RICH. Why, what would'st thou do there before I go?
> RAT. Your highness told me I should post before.
> [*Enter* STANLEY.
> K. RICH. My mind is chang'd.

He flies into a passion with Stanley, but in the end believes in him; yet Stanley is the only one of his followers who is deceiving him. Richmond's name makes him as fierce in words as Macbeth was when his doom had come. The nerve-storm is speaking:

STAN. Richmond is on the seas.
  K. RICH. There let him sink and be the seas on him!
White-liver'd runagate! What doth he there?

Speech after speech his fury increases. Messenger after messenger comes in
with bad news. The third brings good tidings. Richard anticipates it as misfortune, and strikes him down—

  Out on ye, owls! nothing but songs of death.

The furies are upon him.

* * *

The fifth act opens with the death of Buckingham. He also feels that divine
justice has descended on him. His false oath has come home; and, like the rest,
he sees Margaret as he dies.

  'When he,' quoth she, 'shall split thy, heart with sorrow,
  Remember Margaret was a prophetess.'

  And now all the interest centres around Richard. He has been used by Justice
to punish the rest. His own doom (now that he is with himself in a terrible
solitude) is close at hand. Richmond, who is here only a shadow, brings with him
the just sentence of God.

  God and good angels fight on Richmond's side.

But though justice is to be done, yet Shakespeare will not quite degrade Richard
out of the sympathy of the audience. Action and its need have partly healed his
fluttering temper. His native courage, his pride of birth, his natural joy in battle, have dispersed his dreams for a time. His orders are sharply, clearly given.
He speaks again like a great commander, and he dies a soldier and a king.
  Shakespeare knew the relief which the crisis, having come, gives to a
courageous man. He knew also that no amount of crime could do away with
physical courage, or make a man forget that he was of high lineage, if that had
ever been a power in his life. And it was deep in Richard:

  Our aëry buildeth in the cedar's top,
  And dallies with the wind, and scorns the sun.

Yet, neither courage nor pride are what they were.

So, I am satisfied. Give me a bowl of wine:
I have not that alacrity of spirit,
Nor cheer of mind, that I was wont to have.

The phrase prepares us for the well-known scene in which the courage of
Richard when he is asleep trembles before the ghosts of all whom he has slain.
It is equally prepared for by the prayer of Richmond for the help of God whose
captain he accounts himself, the minister of whose chastisement he is. Night
falls, and each ghost, rising one after another—Prince Edward, Henry VI.,
Clarence, Rivers, Grey, Vaughan, Hastings, the young Princes, Lady Anne,
Buckingham—speaks to Richmond of victory, lays a curse on Richard. Each
bids him 'Despair and die.'

In this, the predominant idea of the drams—the working out into catastrophe
of all the evil of the Civil Wars—is brought into full prominence, since Richard
is the incarnation of that evil. The connected idea of the supremacy of justice
in the course of the world is also brought out so forcibly that Richard, for one
brief hour, recognises the lordship of conscience, though he argues that it ought
to have none over him. The supernatural world can alone convince him of his
guilt, and he fights against the conviction. It is only in the half-conscious state,
between sleep and waking when one is scarcely one's self, that Richard gives
way to conscience and to fear, and in that state speaks that wonderful soliloquy,
which—if we take it as the confused utterances of a man who is half asleep and
half awake, half in the supernatural terror of his dreams and half in his reaction
from them, half himself, half not himself—is an amazing piece of subtle analysis,
only not succeeding altogether because it was more difficult to shape in words
than mortal man could manage. None but Shakespeare would even have tried
to put it into form.

> K. RICH. Give me another horse! bind up my wounds!
> Have mercy, Jesu! Soft! I did but dream.
> O coward conscience, how dost thou afflict me.
> The lights burn blue. It is now dead midnight.
> Cold fearful drops stand on my trembling flesh.
> What! do I fear myself? there's none else by:
> Richard loves Richard; that is, I am I.
> Is there a murderer here? No. Yes; I am:
> Then fly: what! from myself? Great reason why
> Lest I revenge. What! myself upon myself?
> Alack! I love myself. Wherefore? for any good
> That I myself have done unto myself?
> O! no: alas! I rather hate myself

For hateful deeds committed by myself.
I am a villain: Yet I lie; I am not.
Fool, of thyself speak well: fool, do not flatter,
My conscience hath a thousand several tongues
And every tongue brings in a several tale,
And every tale condemns me for a villain.
Perjury, perjury, in the high'st degree:
Murder, stern murder, in the dir'st degree;
All several sins, all us'd in each degree
Throng to the bar, crying all, 'Guilty! guilty!'
I shall despair. There is no creature loves me;
And if I die, no soul will pity me:
Nay, wherefore should they, since that I myself
Find in myself no pity to myself?
Methought the souls of all that I had murder'd
Came to my tent: and every one did threat
To-morrow's vengeance on the head of Richard.

On this Ratcliff breaks in and, for a minute or two, the dream, lingering as dreams
linger, still holds Richard in its grip. Then, fully awake, he shakes it off—

By the apostle Paul, shadows to-night
Have struck more terror to the soul of Richard
Than can the substance of ten thousand soldiers,
Armed in proof, and led by shallow Richmond.

The momentary weakness of fear, the momentary belief in conscience, which,
with all that guilt behind, might make him die ignobly, pass away. He scorns
his dreams, he mocks at conscience.

Go, gentlemen; every man unto his charge:
Let not our babbling dreams affright our souls;
Conscience is but a word that cowards use,
Devis'd at first to keep the strong in awe:
Our strong arms be our conscience, swords our law.
March on, join bravely, let us to't pell mell;
If not to heaven, then hand in hand to hell.

And his speech to his army is a masterpiece of bold mockery of the foe, and
of appeal to the pride of England; the words of a fighting partisan, of a king
at bay. As we read it, we should sit in his soul, below the words. I wonder if
Shakespeare meant the overstrain I seem to detect in it to express the hungry

despair which so lately had clutched his heart, and which he strove by passionate words to beat under. He bluffs himself. It is impossible not to sympathise
with his self-conquest and courage; and Shakespeare meant us to do so. Since
justice is done, pity may steal in; and circumstance has made Richard its victim,
as well as his own will. He goes to battle with a joyful courage, as to a banquet.
Macbeth's courage was intermingled with the despondencies of crime and of
loss of honour, for he had loved and sorrowed, and of old had resisted evil.
Richard's courage has no tenderness, no sense of violated honour to trouble it,
for he has never loved. It has no despondency, no philosophising on life and
death, when the crisis comes. There is a physical rapture in it.

> A thousand hearts are great within my bosom:
> Advance our standards! set upon our foes!
> Our ancient word of courage, fair Saint George,
> Inspire us with the spleen of fiery dragons!
> Upon them! Victory sits on our helms.

But there is no victory for him—

> The day is ours, the bloody dog is dead.

Yet, he perishes like a king, slaying five Richmonds in the throat of death. His
death would be the death of despair, were he not greater than despair itself. The
drama closes with that speech of Richmond's, in which the wrong, the fraternal
slaughter, the misery of the Civil Wars are dwelt on, resumed, and absolved in
the reconciliation of the white rose and the red, in the union of Richmond and
Elizabeth—

> Smile, heaven, upon this fair conjunction,
> That long hath frown'd upon their enmity!

Justice has done her work; and she retires, well pleased.

* * *

In this play there is the same conception of an overruling Justice as we have
found in *Romeo and Juliet*. Punishment, not arbitrary, but the direct consequence of crime against humanity, falls on all those who have caused the Civil
Wars. This is clearly an artistic conception, and has its parallels in the Greek
drama, as for example in the *Seven against Thebes*.

As a dramatic subject, *Richard III.* did not afford sufficient opportunity for
the representation of the manifold varieties of human life which now began

to allure Shakespeare. It was confined within a limited set of people—kings, queens, the noblesse and their dependants—within their selfish quarrels and ambitions. And what a set they are! And the women, if we exclude the Duchess of York, are nearly as bad as the men. Nor, with the exception of Richard and Margaret, is any one of them seriously intelligent or interesting. Shakespeare must have been tired of the odiousness of it all, tired even of his conception of Justice working out her law on states; anxious to live among a brighter and more varied class of characters, and freely to develop them.

Moreover he was, I think, weary of the limitations laid upon him by the close following of history. Of this last weariness he got rid, as I have said, in *Henry IV.* by entering into the life of the people.[2] I am not sure that he did not begin to break loose from both these limits by the writing of *Richard II.*, where, while following the main lines of history, he develops out of his own imagination, and apart from history, the character of Richard after his return from Ireland. The Richard of the castle scenes and of the rest of the drama is not the Richard of history. He is Shakespeare's own, as complex in character as Richard III. is simple. It is this outbreak of Shakespeare's into pure invention which seems to suggest that *Richard II.* was written after *Richard III.* Richard II. has no ambition to be greater than he is. He desires to be let alone to enjoy himself. Richard III is ambition incarnate. The one has only one desire, the other has a hundred; and the hundred desires make his character as complex as the other is simple. The one is devoid of love, and therefore devoid of imagination. The other has tenderness, pity, sweetness, and thoughtfulness, when he has gone through sorrow; and because he loves and desires to love, he is capable of imagination. Shakespeare makes him more than capable of it. He gives it to him after his fall, and in his hands he becomes the shaper of poetry.

Then, again, the character of Richard II. grows into nobility; at every change he gains; he is noblest before death; but the character of Richard III. loses power day by day, loses even intellectual power, and he ends as only a royal bravo. There is also far more characterisation and invention in *Richard II.* than in *Richard III.*, and I think this suggests at least that the former was written after the latter. Moreover, the characters who are of vital interest are much more numerous in *Richard II.*, more vivid, more distinct, more complex. The Queen in *Richard II.* is only touched, yet she is alive and distinct, and so is the Duchess of Gloucester. Anne and the Duchess of York in *Richard III.* are not clearly, though they are elaborately, drawn. In *Richard II.* Gaunt is extremely interesting; Old York and Bolingbroke, even Mowbray, are all clearly individualised; but Buckingham, Rivers, Hastings, and Grey in *Richard III.* are not. The only creature, save Margaret and Richard, who is specialised into a greater vitality than the others in *Richard III.* is Clarence in the Tower before his death.

The play itself is unequal, strangely unequal. Its conduct wavers from excellence to mediocrity. The over-length of such scenes as that before the coronation, and that between Richard and Elizabeth, wearies an audience, and the first of these is not redeemed by brilliancy of thought or dramatic play. Shakespeare had not yet learned concentration or moderation. There is none of his plays in which one more regrets the Greek measure, and the Greek power to say enough and no more.

Its finer poetry is of less impressiveness because it is the poetry of cursing—a matter somewhat naturally apart from beauty. And the cursing is too long to be intense, to have that closely knitted passion which lifts the curse into the world of art. Margaret rarely reaches that: Lear reaches it in a few sentences. Only one passage in the whole play rises into a splendour of poetry, so piteous and so beautiful that it will live for ever. It is the dream of Clarence.

NOTES

1. See Act IV. Sc. v., where Stanley says to sir Christopher Urswiok Richmond's emissary—

> So, get thee gone, commend me to thy lord.
> Withal, say that the Queen hath heartily consented
> He should espouse Elizabeth her daughter.

2. We may see this desire to represent the people even in *Richard III*. The little sketch of the Scrivener, Act in. Sc. vi., is done by a master. hand. We see and feel the man. The three citizens who meet and discuss the political situation in the second act belong to the honest, god-fearing, steadfast, commonplace burghers of London. Their talk is representative, yet each of them is quite distinct in character.

1944—E.M.W. Tillyard. "Richard III," from *Shakespeare's History Plays*

E.M.W. Tillyard (1889–1962) was a classical scholar, literary critic, and master at Jesus College, Cambridge University. The list of his scholarly works include *Shakespeare's Last Plays* (1938), his influential essay titled *The Elizabethan World Picture* (1943), *The Miltonic Setting: Past and Present* (1949), *Shakespeare's Problem Plays* (1950), and *The Nature of Comedy and Shakespeare* (1958).

If in *3 Henry VI* Shakespeare was at times hesitant, impatient, bored, and explanatory, he did in compensation succeed in putting his whole heart into *Richard III*. He was to do better when he matured, but in *Richard III* he delivered himself of what he was good for at that time. Not being the fully accomplished artist he had to labour prodigiously and could not conceal the effort. But of the sheer accomplishment there can be no doubt.

If *Titus Andronicus*, the *Comedy of Errors*, and *1 Henry VI* show the full scope of his earliest powers, *Love's Labour's Lost* joins with *Richard III*, which unites the strains of tragedy and history, to do the same thing later. This comedy is a splendid laboured affair, massive like *Richard III*, though in its own different way. The two plays have other things too in common. They abound in formal balance; they are both strong in the ritual element described in the last chapter. The scenes of formal wit in *Love's Labour's Lost* are strongly and powerfully worked out like the complicated political scenes in *Richard III*. And in both plays Shakespeare is constantly starting out of the easier security of an accepted norm (easier, however much heightened and embellished beyond the capacities of any of his contemporaries) into his own unique utterance. Thus the discourse of Clarence's Second Murderer on conscience is in its freshness like the spring and winter songs at the end of *Love's Labour's Lost*:

> I'll not meddle with it. It is a dangerous thing. It makes a man a coward:
> a man cannot steal but it accuseth him; he cannot swear but it checks
> him; he cannot lie with his neighbour's wife but it detects him. 'Tis a
> blushing shamefast spirit that mutinies in a man's bosom. It fills one full
> of obstacles. It made me once restore a purse full of gold that I found: it
> beggars any man that keeps it. It is turned out of all towns and cities for
> a dangerous thing; and every man that means to live well endeavours to
> trust to himself and to live without it.

This is prose as easy and exquisite in its way as the lyrics in the comedy.

In spite of the eminence of Richard's character the main business of the play is to complete the national tetralogy and to display the working out of God's plan to restore England to prosperity.

In its function of summing up and completing what has gone before, *Richard III* inevitably suffers as a detached unit. Indeed it is a confused affair without the memory of Clarence's perjury to Warwick before Coventry, of Queen Margaret's crowning York with a paper crown before stabbing him at Wakefield, and of the triple murder of Prince Edward at Tewkesbury. The play can never come into its own till acted as a sequel to the other three plays and with the solemnity that we associate rather with the Dionysia at Athens and the Wagner Festival at Bayreuth than with the Shakespeare Festival at Stratford. I advisedly include all four plays, because, though for immediate understanding of incident a memory of *3 Henry VI* is sufficient, there are many links with the other two parts. Thus *Richard III*, after the temporary boredom of *3 Henry VI*, regains the interest, so powerful in *2 Henry VI*, in the massive scene of political intrigue: for instance in Act I Scene 3, where Richard makes trouble with the queen and her relations and Queen Margaret appears, to curse all; or in Act III Scene 7, where Richard is jockeyed into the throne. In the first of these there is even a direct reference back to *2 Henry VI*. Margaret, advancing to the front of the stage where Richard and Queen Elizabeth's kindred have been quarrelling, says:

> Hear me, you wrangling pirates, that fall out
> In sharing that which you have pill'd from me.

This is the metaphor York had used in his first soliloquy in *2 Henry VI*, quoted above, pp. 186–7. Only now the position has changed, and it is the house of Lancaster that watches the Yorkists fighting over the spoil. With *1 Henry VI* the resemblances are closer and different, and they have to do with the plot. Both *1 Henry VI* and *Richard III*, unlike the other plays, contain an outstanding character having a Frenchwoman as his chief opponent. Talbot stands for order and Richard for its contrary, chaos, and whereas Joan prospers in her efforts to humiliate England, Margaret through her curses unwittingly creates the unity of the land she has so terribly injured. Again, in *1 Henry VI* the nobles are wantonly disunited, while in *Richard III* they are schooled by their sufferings into a unity otherwise unattainable. When there is already so much evidence that Shakespeare wrote his tetralogy deliberately and academically and that he was deeply influenced by the Morality tradition with its medieval passion for equivalences, it is not pressing things to assert that Shakespeare fully intended the above cross-references between the first and last plays of his series.

However, the greatest bond uniting all four plays is the steady political theme: the theme of order and chaos, of proper political degree and civil war, of crime and punishment, of God's mercy finally tempering his justice, of the belief that such had been God's way with England.

I noticed that in each part of *Henry VI* there was some positive, usually very formal or stylised reference to the principle of order. In *1 Henry VI* there was the scene of Talbot doing homage to his king, in *2 Henry VI* the blameless conduct of Iden and his perfect contentment with his own station in life, in *3 Henry VI* Henry's pathetic longing for the precisely ordered life of a shepherd. In *Richard III* Shakespeare both continues this technique by inserting the choric scene of the three citizens, mentioned above, p. 156, and at the end of the play comes out with his full declaration of the principle of order, thus giving final and unmistakable shape to what, though largely implicit, had been all along the animating principle of the tetralogy. His instrument, obviously and inevitably, is Richmond; and that this instrument should be largely passive, truly an instrument (hence likely to be overlooked or made little of by the modern reader) was also inevitable in the sort of drama Shakespeare was writing. In the tremendous evolution of God's plans the accidents of character must not be obtruded. Every sentence of Richmond's last speech, today regarded as a competent piece of formality, would have raised the Elizabethans to an ecstasy of feeling.) Richmond gets everything right and refers to all the things they minded about. He is conventionally pious, his first words after the victory being, "God and your arms be prais'd, victorious friends"; just as Talbot after his capture of Rouen had said "Yet heavens have glory for this victory." Then he thinks of the immediate problems and asks about the dead. Hearing of them, he begins his last speech,

> Inter their bodies as becomes their birth,

and thereby implies: after thanks to God, the keeping of due degree on earth. And again he duplicates Talbot, who in the same scene; after thanking God, said

> let's not forget
> The noble Duke of Bedford late deceas'd,
> But see his exequies fulfill'd in Roan.

Then, after degree, mercy:

> Proclaim a pardon to the soldiers fled
> That in submission will return to us.

And lastly an oath, taken with full religious solemnity and duly observed, and the healing of the wounds of civil war, with an insensible and indeed very subtle transfer of reference from the epoch of Bosworth to the very hour of the play's performance, from the supposed feelings of Richmond's supporters to what Shakespeare's own audience felt so ardently about the health of their country. The reference to father killing son and son killing father served at a single stroke both to recall the battle of Towton and to take the audience out of the Wars of the Roses to the wider context of civil wars in general: to Israel, France, and Germany; to the writers of chronicles and the Homilies; to what they had heard endlessly repeated on the subject by fireside or in tavern.

> And then, as we have ta'en the sacrament,
> We will unite the White Rose and the Red.
> Smile heaven upon this fair conjunction,
> That long have frown'd upon their enmity!
> What traitor hears me and says not amen?
> England hath long been mad and scarr'd herself:
> The brother blindly shed the brother's blood;
> The father rashly slaughter'd his own son;
> The son, compell'd, been butcher to the sire.

All this divided York and Lancaster,
Divided in their dire division,
O now let Richmond and Elizabeth,
The true succeeders of each royal house,
By God's fair ordinance conjoin together;
And let their heirs, God, if thy will be so,
Enrich the time to come with smooth-fac'd peace,
With smiling plenty and fair prosperous days.
Abate the edge of traitors, gracious Lord,
That would reduce these bloody days again,
And make poor England weep in streams of blood.
Let them not live to taste this land's increase
That would with treason wound this fair land's peace.
Now civil wars are stopp'd, peace lives again:
That she may long live here God say amen.

An Elizabethan audience would take the dramatist's final amen with a transport of affirmation.

But Richmond's final speech not only voiced popular opinion, it showed Shakespeare fulfilling his old debt to Hall, when he invested the very practical and politic match between Richmond and Elizabeth with a mysterious and religious significance. True, Shakespeare quite omits the Tudors' ancient British ancestry; but his references to the marriage are in the very spirit of Hall's title: *The Union of the two noble and illustre Families of Lancaster and York* and his statement in his preface of the "godly matrimony" being "the final end of all dissensions titles and debates." Nor is this the only place in the play that sends us back to Hall and Tudor conceptions of history. There are some rather queer lines in III.i, where Edward V, Richard, and Buckingham talk about oral and written tradition. They serve to bring out Edward's precociousness but they also take us into the centre of contemporary opinions on history. Edward, before the Tower, asks if Julius Caesar built it. Buckingham tells him that Julius Caesar began it; and Edward asks:

Is it upon record, or else reported
Successively from age to age, he built it?

Buckingham answers it is "upon record," and Edward goes on:

But say, my lord, it were not register'd,
Methinks the truth should live from age to age,
As 'twere retail'd to all posterity,
Even to the general all-ending day.

His words take us to the familiar medieval and renaissance context of fame: its capriciousness, its relation to all history and to all time. And he goes on to a more specifically historical commonplace:

> That Julius Caesar was a famous man.
> With what his valour did enrich his wit,
> His wit set down to make his valour live.
> Death makes no conquest of this conqueror,
> For now he lives in fame though not in life.

It was a stock saying in discussions on history that Caesar provided both the material of history and its memorial. Shakespeare was telling his audience that they must put his tetralogy among other solemn documents of history, that he is striving to continue the high tradition of Polydore and Hall.

Above, I put the theme of *Richard III* partly in terms of God's intentions. As it is usual to put it in terms of Richard's character, I had better expand my thesis. But it is a delicate matter. People are so fond of Shakespeare that they are desperately anxious to have him of their own way of thinking. A reviewer in the *New Statesman* was greatly upset when I quoted a passage in *Measure for Measure* as evidence that Shakespeare was familiar with the doctrine of the Atonement: he at once assumed I meant that Shakespeare believed the doctrine personally. And if one were to say that in *Richard III* Shakespeare pictures England restored to order through God's grace, one gravely risks being lauded or execrated for attributing to Shakespeare personally the full doctrine of prevenient Grace according to Calvin. When therefore I say that *Richard III* is a very religious play, I want to be understood as speaking of the play and not of Shakespeare. For the purposes of the tetralogy and most obviously for this play Shakespeare accepted the prevalent belief that God had guided England into her haven of Tudor prosperity. And he had accepted it with his whole heart, as later he did not accept the supposed siding of God with the English against the French he so loudly proclaimed in *Henry V.* There is no atom of doubt in Richmond's prayer before he falls asleep in his tent at Bosworth. He is utterly God's minister, as he claims to be:

> O Thou, whose captain I account myself,
> Look on my forces with a gracious eye;
> Put in their hands thy bruising irons of wrath,
> That they may crush down with a heavy fall
> The usurping helmets of our adversaries.
> Make us thy ministers of chastisement,
> That we may praise thee in the victory.
> To thee I do commend my watchful soul,

Ere I let fall the windows of mine eyes.
Sleeping and waking, O, defend me still.

In the same spirit Shakespeare drops hints of a divine purpose in the mass
of vengeance that forms the substance of the play, of a direction in the seemingly endless concatenation of crime and punishment. In *3 Henry VI*, York at
Wakefield, Young Clifford at Towton, Warwick at Barnet, and Prince Edward
at Tewkesbury die defiantly without remorse. In *Richard III* the great men die
acknowledging their guilt and thinking of others. Clarence, before his murderers enter, says:

O God, if my deep prayers cannot appease thee,
But thou wilt be aveng'd on my misdeeds,
Yet execute thy wrath in me alone:
O spare my guiltless wife and my poor children.

Edward IV, near his death, repents his having signed a warrant for Clarence's
death and while blaming others for not having restrained him blames himself
the most:

But for my brother not a man would speak,
Nor I, ungracious, speak unto myself
For him, poor soul. The proudest of you all
Have been beholding to him in his life;
Yet none of you would once plead for his life.
O God, I fear thy justice will take hold
On me and you and mine and yours for this.

The Duchess of York, who once rejoiced when her family prospered, now in
humility acknowledges the futility of ambitious strife.

Accursed and unquiet wrangling days,
How many of you have mine eyes beheld.
My husband lost his life to get the crown,
And often up and down my sons were toss'd,
For me to joy and weep their gain and loss.
And, being seated and domestic broils
Clean overblown, themselves, the conquerors,
Make war upon themselves: blood against blood,
Self against self. O, preposterous
And frantic outrage, end thy damned spleen.

All this penitence cannot be fortuitous; and it is the prelude to forgiveness and regeneration. But the full religious temper of the play only comes out in the two great scenes in the last third of the play: the lamentations of the three queens after Richard has murdered the princes in the Tower, and the ghosts appearing to Richard and Richmond before Bosworth. These are both extreme and splendid examples of the formal style which I suggested above (p. 197) should be considered the norm rather than the exception in the tetralogy. Both scenes are ritual and incantatory to a high degree, suggesting an ecclesiastical context; both are implicitly or explicitly pious; and both are archaic, suggesting the prevalent piety of the Middle Ages. The incantation takes the form not only of an obvious antiphony like Queen Margaret's balancing of her own woes with Queen Elizabeth's—

> I had an Edward, till a Richard kill'd him;
> I had a Harry, till a Richard kill'd him;
> Thou hadst an Edward, till a Richard kill'd him;
> Thou hadst a Richard, till a Richard kill'd him—

but of a more complicated balance of rhythmic phrases and of varied repetitions, as in the Duchess of York's self-address:

> Blind sight, dead life, poor mortal living ghost,
> Woe's scene, world's shame, grave's due by life usurp'd,
> Brief abstract and record of tedious days,
> Rest thy unrest on England's lawful earth,
> Unlawfully made drunk with innocents' blood.

The piety in this scene is implicit rather than explicit, and the two passages just quoted will illustrate it. Queen Margaret is thinking of Richard's crimes and the vengeance he will incur, yet by repeating a phrase in four successive lines she expresses unconsciously the new and fruitful unity that God is to construct out of Richard's impartial wickedness. The Duchess's mention of England's *lawful* earth is in itself an assertion of the principle of order and an implicit prayer for a juster age. The medievalism and its accompanying suggestion of piety comes out in Margaret's great speech to Elizabeth, itself an example of incantation and antiphony. She refers to her prophecies made earlier in the play and no fulfilled.

> I call'd thee then vain flourish of my fortune.
> I call'd thee then poor shadow, painted queen;
> The presentation of but what I was;
> The flattering index of a direful pageant;
> One heav'd a-high, to be hurl'd down below;

A mother only mock'd with two sweet babes;
A dream of what thou wert, a breath, a bubble,
A sign of dignity, a garish flag,
To be the aim of every dangerous shot;
A queen in jest, only to fill the scene.
Where is thy husband now? where be thy brothers?
Where are thy children? wherein dost thou joy?
Who sues to thee and cries 'God save the queen'?
Where be the bending peers that flatter'd thee?
Where be the thronging troops that follow'd thee?—
Decline all this and see what now thou art:
For happy wife a most distressed widow;
For joyful mother one that wails the name;
For queen a very caitiff crown'd with care;
For one being sued to one that humbly sues;
For one that scorn'd at me now scorn'd of me;
For one being fear'd of all now fearing one;
For one commanding all obey'd of none.
Thus hath the course of justice wheel'd about
And left thee but a very prey to time;
Having no more but thought of what thou wert
To torture thee the more being what thou art.

The speech takes us back to the Middle Ages; to the laments of the fickleness of fortune, to the constant burden of *Ubi sunt,* and to the consequent contempt of the world. It contains the same matter as the verses attributed to St. Bernard, of which the following is a specimen in Elizabethan translation:

Where is that Caesar now, whose high renowned fame
Of sundry conquests won throughout the world did sound?
Or Dives rich in store and rich in richly name,
Whose chest with gold and dish with dainties did abound?
Where is the passing grace of Tully's pleading skill?
Or Aristotle's vein, whose pen had wit and will?

Or still more apt, because narrowing the general passing of the great to the loss of a single person's treasures, is the complaint of Henryson's Cressida:

Quhair is thy garding with thir greissis gay
And fress flouris, quhilk the quene Floray
  Had paintit plesandly in every pane,
Quhair thou was wont full merily in May

To walk and tak the dew be it was day
　And heir the merle and mavis mony ane;
　With ladyis fair in carrolling to gane
And see the royal rinkis in thair array.
　In garmentis gay garnishit on every grane?[1]

The scene of the ghosts of those Richard has murdered follows immediately
on Richmond's solemn prayer, quoted above. It is essentially of the Morality
pattern. Republic of England is the hero, invisible yet present, contended for
by the forces of heaven represented by Richmond and of hell represented by
Richard. Each ghost as it were gives his vote for heaven, Lancaster and York
being at last unanimous. And God is above, surveying the event. The medieval
strain is continued when Richard, awaking in terror, rants like Judas in the
Miracle Plays about to hang himself. The scene, like Richmond's prayer and
his last speech, is very moving. It may have issued from Shakespeare's official
self, from Shakespeare identifying himself with an obvious and simple phase of
public opinion. But the identification is entirely sincere, and the opinion strong
and right, to be shared alike by the most sophisticated and the humblest. The
scene becomes almost an act of common worship, ending with Buckingham's
assertion:

God and good angels fight on Richmond's side;
And Richard falls in height of all his pride.

And just because he participates so fully, because he holds nothing of himself
back, Shakespeare can be at his best, can give to his language the maximum of
personal differentiation of which he was at the time capable. This differentiation he achieves, not as in some of the other great places in the play by surprising conjunctions of words or new imagery but by subtle musical variations
within a context of incantation. He seems indeed to have learnt and applied the
lessons of Spenser. At the same time the substance of what each ghost says is
entirely appropriate to the speaker and by referring back to past events in the
tetralogy serves to reinforce the structure of the plot There may be better scenes
in Shakespeare, but of these none is like this one. Of its kind it is the best.

That the play's main end is to show the working out of God's will in English
history does not detract from the importance of Richard in the process and from
his dominance as a character. And it is through his dominance that he is able
to be the instrument of God's ends. Whereas the sins of other men had merely
bred more sins, Richard's are so vast that they are absorptive, not contagious.
He is the great ulcer of the body politic into which all its impurity is drained
and against which all the members of the body politic are united. It is no longer
a case of limb fighting limb but of the war of the whole organism against an

ill which has now ceased to be organic. The metaphor of poison is constantly applied to Richard, and that of beast, as if here were something to be excluded from the human norm. Queen Margaret unites the two metaphors when she calls him "that poisonous hunch-back'd toad" and that "bottled spider," the spider being proverbially venomous.

In making Richard thus subservient to a greater scheme I do not deny that for many years now the main attraction of the play has actually been Richard's character in itself, like Satan's in *Paradise Lost*. Nor was this attraction lacking from the first. Indeed it antedates the play, going back to More's *History of Richard III*, which was inserted with trifling modifications into Hall's chronicle and repeated thence by Holinshed. Shakespeare in singling out Richard III and later Henry V for special treatment as characters is not therefore departing from tradition but following closely his own main teacher of the philosophy of history, Hall.

One would like to think of Shakespeare hailing More (through Hall) as a kindred spirit and using his charm as an inspiration. Actually, though Shakespeare accepts More's heightened picture of Richard as an arch-villain, he can very coolly reject the episodes of which More made much. He quite omits Edward's wonderful speech on his deathbed and the most moving scene of all, the Archbishop persuading Queen Elizabeth to give up her younger son out of sanctuary. It may be however that More's abundant sense of humour encouraged Shakespeare to add to Richard that touch of comedy that makes him so distinguished a villain. His aside after he has gone on his knees to ask his mother's blessing is very much in More's spirit:

> *Duch.* God bless thee, and put meekness in thy mind,
> Love, charity, obedience, and true duty.
>   *Rich.* Amen; and make me die a good old man.
> That is the butt-end of a mother's blessing
> I marvel why her grace did leave it out.

A number of people have written well on the character of Richard: in one place or another all has been said that need be said. It remains now to think less in terms of alternatives and to include more than is usually done in Richard's character, even at the sacrifice of consistency. Lamb, for instance, who in his brief references raised most of the pertinent questions, wants to exclude the melodramatic side:

> Shakespeare has not made Richard so black a monster as is supposed. Wherever he
> is monstrous, it was to conform to vulgar opinion. But he is generally a Man.

Actually Shakespeare was already at one with vulgar opinion and willingly makes him a monster. But only in some places; in others he keeps him human.

Similarly we need not choose between Richard the psychological study in compensation for physical disability and Richard the embodiment of sheer demonic will, for he is both. It is true that, as Lamb notes, Richard in the allusions to his deformity

> mingles . . . a perpetual reference to his own powers and capacities, by which he is enabled to surmount these petty objections; and the joy of a defect conquered, or turned into an advantage, is one cause of these very allusions, and of the satisfaction, with which his mind recurs to them.

But Dowden also is right when he says of Richard that

> his dominant characteristic is not intellectual; it is rather a daemonic energy of will. . . . He is of the diabolical class. . . . He is single-hearted in his devotion to evil. . . . He has a fierce joy, and he is an intense believer,—in the creed of hell. And therefore he is strong. He inverts the moral order of things, and tries to live in this inverted system. He does not succeed; he dashes himself to pieces against the laws of the world which he has outraged.

It might be retorted that the above distinction is superfluous, because an extreme manifestation of demonic will can only arise from the additional drive set in motion by an unusual need to compensate for a defect. But the point is that Shakespeare does actually make the distinction and that Richard, within the limits of the play, is psychologically both possible and impossible. He ranges from credibly motivated villain to a symbol, psychologically absurd however useful dramatically, of the diabolic.

This shift, however, is not irregular. In the first two scenes, containing his opening soliloquy, his dealings with Clarence, his interruption of the funeral of Henry VI with his courtship of Ann Nevil, he is predominantly the psychological study. Shakespeare here builds up his private character. And he is credible; with his humour, his irony, and his artistry in crime acting as differentiating agents, creating a sense of the individual. After this he carries his established private character into the public arena, where he is more than a match for anyone except Queen Margaret. Of her alone he is afraid; and her curse establishes, along with the psychologically probable picture just created, the competing and ultimately victorious picture of the monstrosity, the country's scapegoat, the vast impostume of the commonwealth. She makes him both a cosmic symbol, the "troubler of the poor world's peace," and sub-human, a "rooting hog," "the slave of nature and the son of hell." She calls on him the curse of insomnia, which later we find to have been fulfilled. Clearly this does not apply to the exulting ironic Richard: *he* must always have slept with infant tranquillity. Thus Margaret's curse is prospective, and though he continues to pile up the materials for the construction of his monstrosity, it is the credible Richard, glorying in his will and his success in compensating his disabilities, who persists till the end of the third act and the attainment of the throne. Thenceforward, apart from his outburst of energy in courting Queen Elizabeth for her daughter's hand, he melts from credible character into a combination of sheer melodrama villain and symbol of diabolism. His irony forsakes him; he is unguarded not secretive in making his plans; he is no longer cool but confused in his energy, giving and retracting orders; he *really* does not sleep; and, when on the eve of Bosworth he calls for a bowl of wine because he has not "that alacrity of spirit nor cheer of mind that I was wont to have," he is the genuine ancestor of the villain in a nineteenth-century melodrama calling for whiskey when things look black. Then, with the ghosts and his awakening into his Judas-like monologue, psychological probability and melodramatic villainy alike melt into the symbol of sheer denial and diabolism. Nor does his momentary resurrection at Bosworth with his memorable shout for a horse destroy that abiding impression. That a character should shift from credible human being to symbol would not have troubled a generation nurtured on Spenser. Richard in this respect resembles one of Spenser's masterpieces, Malbecco, who from a realistic old cuckold is actually transformed into an allegorical figure called jealousy.

Finally we must not forget that Richard is the vehicle of an orthodox doctrine about kingship. It was a terrible thing to fight the ruling monarch, and Richard had been crowned. However, he was so clearly both a usurper and a murderer that he had qualified as a tyrant; and against an authentic tyrant it was lawful to rebel. Richmond, addressing his army before Bosworth, makes the point absolutely clear:

> Richard except, those whom we fight against
> Had rather have us win than him they follow.
> For what is he they follow? truly, gentlemen,
> A bloody tyrant and a homicide;
> One rais'd in blood and one in blood establish'd;
> One that made means to come by what he hath
> And slaughter'd those that were the means to help him;
> One that hath ever been God's enemy.
> Then if you fight against God's enemy,
> God will injustice ward you as his soldiers;
> If you do sweat to put a tyrant down,
> You sleep in peace, the tyrant being slain.

And Derby, handing Henry the crown after the battle, calls it "this long-usurped royalty."

I have indicated in outline the course of the play: the emerging of unity from and through discord, the simultaneous change in Richard from accomplished villain to the despairing embodiment of evil. Shakespeare gives it coherence through the dominant and now scarcely human figure of Queen Margaret: the one character who appears in every play. Being thus a connecting thread, it is fitting that she give structural coherence to the crowning drama. As Richard's downfall goes back to her curse, so do the fates of most of the characters who perish in the play go back to her curses or prophecies in the same scene, I.3. Nor are her curses mere explosions of personal spite; they agree with the tit-for-tat scheme of crime and punishment that has so far prevailed in the tetralogy. She begins by recalling York's curse on her at Wakefield for the cruelty of her party to Rutland and the penalty she has paid; and then enumerates the precisely balanced scheme of retribution appointed for the house of York:

> If not by war, by surfeit die your king,
> As ours by murder, to make him a king.
> Edward thy son, which now is Prince of Wales,
> For Edward my son, which was Prince of Wales,
> Die in his youth by like untimely violence.
> Thyself a queen, for me that was a queen,
> Outlive thy glory like my wretched self.

Curses on minor characters follow, but Richard, as befits, has a speech to himself. His peculiar curse is the gnawing of conscience, sleeplessness, and the mistake of taking friends for enemies and enemies for friends. I have spoken of the sleeplessness above, how it could not apply to the Richard of the first three acts. Similarly it is not till Bosworth that the curse of thinking his enemies friends comes true. We are meant to think of it when Richmond says in lines quoted above that "those whom we fight against had rather have us win than him they follow." The man with the best brain in the play ends by being the most pitifully deceived. For a detailed working out of the different curses I refer the reader to A. P. Rossiter's study of the play. But it is worth recording that Margaret in her last lines before she goes out unconsciously forecasts the larger theme of the plays. Talking of Richard she says:

> Let each of you be subject to his hate,
> And he to yours, and all of you to God's.

Margaret does not realise that this grouping of Yorkists against Richard will unite them to the Lancastrians similarly opposed, and that the just vengeance of God had even then given way to his mercy.

In style the play is better sustained than its predecessor. There is less undifferentiated stuff, and the finest pieces of writing (as distinguished from the finest scenes) are more dramatic. The quiet concentration of the Duchess of York's last words to Richard is beyond anything in the other three plays:

Either thou wilt die, by God's just ordinance,
Ere from this war thou turn a conqueror,
Or I with grief and extreme age shall perish
And never look upon thy face again.
Therefore take with thee my most heavy curse;
Which, in the day of battle, tire thee more
Than all the complete armour that thou wear'st!
My prayers on the adverse party fight;
And there the little souls of Edward's children
Whisper the spirits of thine enemies
And promise them success and victory.
Bloody thou art, bloody will be thy end;
Shame serves thy life and doth thy death attend.

Richard's plotting with Buckingham and his acquisition of the throne though strongly organised must have tired Shakespeare. There are even signs of strain in the last stage of the process when Richard appears between the two bishops; the verse droops somewhat. After this (and it is here that Richard begins his change of nature) the vitality flags, except in patches, till the great scene when the three queens get together to join in lamentation. The courting of Elizabeth for her daughter is a prodigious affair, but not at all apt at this point. It leads nowhere; for in the very next scene (IV.5) Elizabeth is reported to have consented to her daughter's union with Richmond. Are we to think, with E. K. Chambers, that Elizabeth had outwitted Richard and had consented, only to deceive? This is so contrary to the simple, almost negative character of Elizabeth and so heavily ironical at Richard's expense that I cannot believe it. A better explanation is that Elizabeth was merely weak and changeable and that Richard's comment on her as she goes from him, having consented,

Relenting fool and shallow, changing woman,

was truer than he thought, forecasting the second change. It is fitting that Richard, having been so often ironical at the expense of others, should himself be the occasional victim of the irony of events. Even so, the scene is far too elaborate and weighty for its effect on the action. Indeed I suspect an afterthought, a mistaken undertaking to repeat the success of the earlier scene of courtship. It would have been better to have gone quickly on to the great finale of the ghosts and of Bosworth, to that consummate expression, achieved here once and for all, of what I have ventured to call Shakespeare's official self.

NOTE

1. "Where is your garden with its gay lawn and fresh flowers, which Queen Flora has painted delightfully in every bed; where you used to walk so merrily in May and take the dew before daylight, and bear all the blackbirds and thrushes; where you used to go singing with fair ladies and see the throng of courtiers dressed in gay clothes of all colours?"

1946—W. H. Auden. "Richard III"
from *Lectures on Shakespeare*

W. H. Auden (1907-73) was a renowned English-born American poet, essayist, and lecturer, considered by many to be one of the greatest writers of the twentieth century. In the 1930s, Auden became famous when literary journalists referred to him as the leader of the so-called Oxford Group, a circle of young English poets influenced by literary modernism, most particularly the work of T. S. Eliot. From 1956 to 1961, Auden was Professor of Poetry at Oxford University. His works include *Another Time: Poems* (1940), *The Age of Anxiety: A Baroque Eclogue* (1948), *The Enchafed Flood* (1950), and *The Shield of Achilles* (1955), for which he won the National Book Award for poetry in 1956.

Henry VI is a general history. *Richard III* concerntrates on an individual character: the character of a villain. There is a difference between a villain and one who simply commits a crime. The villain is an extremely conscious person and commits crime consciously, for its own sake. Aaron in *Titus Andronicus* is an early example of the villain in Shakespeare. Barabas in *The Jew of Malta*, another crude villain, is an example in Marlowe. In appearance these characters—a Jew, a Moor, a hunchback—are all outside the norm. Barabas announces,

> As for myself, I walk abroad o' nights
> And kill sick people groaning under walls:
> Sometimes I go about and poison wells.

Aaron, after his capture, wishes he had done a "thousand more" evils:

> Even now I curse the day (and yet I think
> Few come within the compass of my curse)
> Wherein I did not some notorious ill:

As kill a man, or else devise his death;
Ravish a maid, or plot the way to do it;
Accuse some innocent, and forswear myself;
Set deadly enmity between two friends;
Make poor men's cattle break their necks;
Set fire on barns and haystacks in the night
And bid the owners quench them with their tears.

    (V.i.125–34)

And Richard boasts, as we have seen, in his long soliloquy in the third part of *Henry VI*, that he "can smile, and murther whiles I smile," "drown more sailors than the mermaid shall," "slay more gazers than the basilisk," "and set the murtherous Machiavel to school" (III.ii.182, 186–87, 193).

    Richard's opening monologue in *Richard III* is similar to the earlier soliloquy, though there is a slight difference in tone. Saying he is "rudely stamp'd" and wants "love's majesty," he announces that he is not made "to court an amorous looking glass," and has "no delight to pass away the time,"

Unless tos eemy shadown in the sun
And descant on mine own deformity.
And therefore, since I cannot prove a lover
To entertain these fair well-spoken days,
I am determined to prove a villain
And hate the idle pleasures of these days.

    (I.i.14–16, 25–31)

Richard III's monologue is not unlike Adolf Hitler's speech to his General Staff on 23 August 1939, in its utter lack of self-deception. The lack of self-deception is striking because most of us invent plausible reasons for doing something we know is wrong. Milton describes such rationalization in *Paradise Lost* in Eve, both before she eats the fruit of the forbidden tree and afterwards, when she justifies inducing Adam to eat:

So dear I love him, that with him all deaths
I could endure, without him live no life.

    (*PL*.IX.832–33)

Eve makes this profession of love for Adam at the moment when she is, in effect, planning to kill him.

    Villains are of particular interest to artists, and there are more examples of them in art than in life. Because language is the medium of literature, people who are usable in literary works have to be conscious people. They are one of two types: (1) people who are not really conscious but who are made to be so, and (2) actually educated people, for whom artists have a natural basis. That's why most works about peasants are boring—literary works consist mostly of people's remarks. Movies do a better job with less articulate people. Drama accentuates the literary problem: characters in plays must be more verbally explicit than in novels or in life, and if they rationalize, they confuse an audience. Elizabethan drama, in addition, has the convention of characters stepping outside themselves and becoming a chorus. This puts an additional premium on highly aware characters. Richard always displays a consciousness of his ultimate goal as he is getting rid of his enemies. "My thoughts aim at a further matter. I / Stay not for love of Edward but the crown" (*3 Henry VI*, IV.i.125–26). There is a premium on villains as interesting bad characters rather than on simple people.

Let's look now at Richard's soliloquy in *Richard III* when he awakens at Bosworth Field, after dreaming of the ghosts of people whom he has killed:

> What do I fear? Myself? There's none else by.
> Richard loves Richard; that is, I and I.
> Is there a murderer here? No. Yes, I am.
> Then fly! What, from myself? Great reason why:
> Lest I revenge. What, myself upon myself?
> Alack, I love myself. Wherefore? For any good
> That I myself have done unto myself?
> O, no! Alas, I rather hate myself
> For hateful deeds committed by myself.
> I am a villain. Yet I lie. I am not.
> Fool, of thyself speak well. Fool, do not flatter.
> My conscience hath a thousand several tongues,
> And every tongue brings in a several tale,
> And every tale condemns me for a villain.
> Perjury, perjury, in the high'st degree;
> Murther, stern murther, in the dir'st degree;
> All several sins, all us'd in each degree,
> Throng to the bar, crying all, "Guilty! guilty!"
> I shall despair. There is no creature loves me,
> And if I die no soul will pity me.
> And wherefore should they, since that I myself
> Find in myself no pity to myself?
>
>   (V.iii.183–204)

This soliloquy needs to be glossed. There are two different senses to Richard's continual use of the terms "I" and "myself," and some light can be thrown on how to distinguish them by looking at Ibsen's *Peer Gynt*. When Peer is in the

Troll Kingdom seeking to marry the Troll King's daughter, the King tells him that the common saying among men is, "Man, to thyself be true!" but that among the Trolls the saying is "Troll, to thyself be—enough!" The trolls tie a tail on Peer, they serve him strange food, and they put on a show of ugly dances for him. When Peer reacts by telling the truth about what he sees despite his best intentions, the Troll King tries to persuade him to have his eye cut out in order to become like the Trolls and "cure this troublesome human nature." Peer refuses. He is only willing to do something that he can undo. Truth always creeps in.

There are two poles of the self: the essential self and the existential self. Hunter Guthrie remarks that when he talks of the essence of a thing, he means its nature. The essential self has a personal responsibility to its name and must live up to it. The essential self is always potential, a self in the process of realization. It is also a self that, since it is based on a common human nature, is central for communication and is mutually comprehensible and universal. Existence is not necessary to the essential self—characters in books have essential selves, our dead friends have essential selves. It is a characteristic of essence to want to come into being, into existence, and this characteristic is displayed in the anxiety of the weak to become strong, of the potential to become actual. The essential self wishes to be self-sufficient—internally, from compassion, externally, from other selves. Its method for dealing with external threats is to absorb, annihilate, or flee. It desires self-realization. As hunger is to food, and the desire for knowledge is to knowledge, so is the essential self to the potential it wishes to realize. It wants admiration and fears a stronger external object. The ideals of the essential self are also relative. For the Greeks, the ideals of the self were strength, beauty, and freedom from sorrow. The purpose of religious practices, for the essential self, is to prevent the hostile interest of stronger external objects.

The existential self is different: it is aware of being in the world now, it is complete, not potential, and it is contingent and unstable. Existence is not mine, a given, but depends on others. Its anxiety is different as well. The existential self is a lonely self that seeks a stronger other self to which it wishes to be attached. It seeks an infinitely strong outside appearance, it fears other objects as too weak, and it wants to be loves as it is now. Its God is not Greek, but the Absolute, and the gourn of its Absolute is not logical—the Aristotelian self-sufficient, unknowable, uncarning Unmoved Mover—but an Absolute that cares infinitely. Hatred is not better than love for the existential self, but it is better than indifference. It has an admiration of quality and love for a qualitative self. The existential self wants to be known. The essential self wants to know, and it asks for ability, not ethical importance, which is the quest of the existential self.

Look in the mirror. What does one see? One sees an object known by others, an essence. The image lacks the anxiety of the original because its existence is derived from me. What is the fascination of acting? The actor is an existing individual who expresses an essence other than his, but this essence is not anxious and does not need to become real, since the role that is played is only a possibility. Most of us make a compromise between our essential and existential selves. Parents give us affection and respect our merits, so our existential anxiety is assuaged. We seek public approval or love, and avoid public disapproval. In return for that, we abandon some objective of the essential self so as to be loved. Most of us, most of the time, avoid the anxiety of making real choices, either by making our surroundings varied and exciting enough to keep us in a state of passion that can dictate what we do—we have our cake and eat it too—or by repressing all but one alternative so that no choice is available because all others have been repressed. Choice means willing unhappiness.

What about a person in an exceptional situation? As a hunchback, Richard III is exceptionally aware of his loneliness because his self is rejected by others and he despairs of attachment. He must either seek a real absolute to surrender to or he must make one up—make his essential self a not-self and absolutely strong so that he can worship it. His essential self is pushed into competition because it must constantly be tested to see whether it's strong enough. The existential drive of Don Giovanni is indifferent to the individuality of the girls he seduces. He keeps an impersonal list of them. The Greek gods were more selective: people they seduced had to be beautiful, and they forgot about their previous affairs. The existential drive devolves into an infinite series, not to satisfy the essential self, which wants only relief from tension, but—despite corns, tiredness—to satisfy the need for other selves, acquired either by absorption or murder.

Murder is different from other injuries: the thief may repent in a theft, the victim may forgive in a rape. Neither is possible in murder. There is a difference between anti-Negroes and anti-Semites. To anti-Semites, Jews represent a threat to existence, to anti-Negroes, Negroes are a threat to the essential self. The Southerner doesn't wish to destroy all Negroes. He is anxious that they should exist as servants. The anti-Semite wishes Jews not to be. If the essential self despairs of the possibility of becoming strong, its recourse is the opposite of Don Giovanni's—it wishes suicidally, like Tristan, to annihilate the self and be absorbed into another.

What about Richard III? In the beginning he is a hunchback with a strong physique for whom people feel either pity or fear—fear because his physical appearance must reflect his inner nature. He is the opposite of the actor, who deliberately projects a different personality from his own. Here people draw conclusions that Richard doesn't intend. In the beginning he attempts to imitate his father, whom he admires: "Methinks 'tis prize enough to be his son" (*3 Henry VI,* II.i.20). But he overcompensates. Because he feels people will believe what they see him do, not what they hear him say—how could they believe him, looking as he does?—he first distrusts words and believes only in deeds. Thus, as he ostentatiously throws down Somerset's head, he says, "Speak thou for me, and tell them what I did" (*3 Henry VI*, I.i.16), and in the scene in which he kills Somerset, he declares, "Priests pray for enemies, but princes kill" (*2 Henry VI*, V.ii.71).

Richard discovers the power of words when his father decides not to seize the crown from Henry because of an oath he had sworn to him "that he should quietly reign." Richard playfully makes up a specious verbal justification for him to violate his oath:

> An oath is of no moment, being not took
> Before a true and lawful magistrate,
> That hath authority over him that swears.
> Henry had none, but did usurp the place;
> Then, seeing 'twas he that made you to depose,
> Your oath, my lord, is vain and frivolous.
> Therefore, to arms!
>
> (*3 Henry VI*, I.ii.15, 22–28)

His father immediately grasps at this speech. He watches his brother Edward have a similar initial hesitation when news is brought of their father's death. Edward, for whom the news is horrible and who does not like to think of its advantage to him, says to the messenger, "O, speak no more, for I have heard too much!" But Richard declares, "Say how he died, for I will hear it all" (*3 Henry VI*, II.i.47–48), and he soon persuades his brother to take arms as well:

> Shall we go throw away our coats of steel
> And wrap our bodies in black mourning gowns,
> Numb'ring our Ave-Maries with our beads?
>
> (*3 Henry VI*, II.i.160–62)

There is a complete difference between Richard's monologues and his conversations with others. He starts out his career with people thinking him other than he is—he's fairly decent. *Then* he makes people think him good when he's really bad. Instead of being a true mirror to his self, he is a false mirror, one that makes people look and see what they want to see, as Hastings does in *Richard III*, for example, just moments before Richard has him executed:

> I think there's never a man in Christendom
> Can lesser hide his love or hate than he,

For by his face straight shall you know his heart.

> (III.iv.51–53)

As a hunchback, Richard doesn't court people to be liked. He knows you exist anyway. "I'll make my heaven," he says,

> to dream upon the crown
> And, whiles I live, t'account this world but hell
> Until my misshap'd trunk that bears this head
> Be round impaled with a glorious crown.

> (*3 Henry VI*, III.ii.168–71)

His brother Edward allays his anxiety by chasing one girl after another. Richard is not envious of Edward's success itself—he eventually has his own success with Anne. What he does envy is Edward's easy satisfaction with a love that has nothing to do with his nonqualitative self. Richard really wants to be loved for himself alone—not for his beauty, if he had it, or his cleverness, but for his essential self. Each person desires that. What people are in the habit of calling love is the reflection of their self-love, which is why we love or want to love people like us or like what we want to be. This is impossible for Richard, since he will not ever look like other people.

Following his realization of how his father needs a rationalization for action comes Richard's great soliloquy of the "thorny wood" (*3 Henry VI*, III.ii.124ff.), where he hasn't yet made any plans but is trying to find out what he wants. The problem is crucial for him because what he calls "this weak piping time of peace" in *Richard III* (I.i.24) is near at hand. War solves existential anxiety. The number of suicides declines in wartime. There is a Charles Addams cartoon of a little man with an umbrella—his bourgeois umbrella suggesting a magician's wand—engaged in a life-and-death struggle with a large octopus that has emerged from a manhole in the middle of a residential street in New York. A crowd watches, saying nothing. Behind the crowd, two men with briefcases are walking along without bothering to turn their heads, and one is saying "It doesn't take much to collect a crowd in New York." The individual exists because he is struggling for existence, the crowd exists by watching—they have both *Schadenfreude* and the feeling that "nothing ever happens to me." The two men exist negatively: whatever the crowd does, they do the opposite. In time of war Richard is needed. His postwar planning is more acute because he is more isolated and even more conscious than usual.

Richard is not ambitious in an ordinary sense. He's not interested in becoming king for the position of power, but because becoming king is so difficult. He is not so much interested in simply making people do what he wants them to do:

what excites him is that they themselves don't want to do it. The wooing of Anne is a good example. The first stage of his seduction is his frank admission of his murders of members of her family, which appeals to Anne's desire for strength—her existential character. Second, he dares her to kill him and offers to kill himself at her orders, thereby treating her as infinitely strong, with his own existence deriving from hers:

> Then bid me kill myself, and I will do it.
> [*Rises, and takes up his sword.*]
> *Anne.* I have already.
> *Rich.* That was in thy rage:
> Speak it again, and, even with the word,
> That hand, which, for thy love, did kill thy love,
> Shall, for thy love, kill a far truer love;
> To both their deaths thou shalt be accessary.
> *Anne.* I would I knew thy heart.
> *Rich.* 'Tis figured in my tongue.
>
> (I.ii.186–93)

When Anne succumbs, Richard exults not in the prospect of possessing her, but in having won her against such odds:

> Was ever woman in this humour woo'd?
> Was ever woman in this humour won?
> I'll have her; but I will not keep her long.
> What! I, that kill'd her husband and his father,
> To take her in her heart's extremest hate,
> With curses in her mouth, tears in her eyes,
> The bleeding witness of her hatred by;
> Having God, her conscience, and these bars against me,
> And I nothing to back my suit at all,
> But the plain devil and dissembling looks,
> And yet to win her, all the world to nothing!
> Ha! . . .
> I do mistake my person all this while!
> Upon my life, she finds (although I cannot)
> Myself to be a marv'llous proper man.
> I'll be at charges for a looking glass,
> And entertain some score or two of tailors,
> To study fashions to adorn my body:
> Since I am crept in favour with myself,

Will maintain it with some little cost.
But first I'll turn yon fellow in his grave;
And then return lamenting to my love.
Shine out, fair sun, till I have bought a glass,
That I may see my shadow as I pass.

    (I.ii.227–38, 252–63)

Richard is superstitious. He is anxious about being named Duke of Gloucester: "Let me be Duke of Clarence, George of Gloucester; / For Gloucester's dukedom is too ominous" (*3 Henry VI*, IV.vii.106–7). He sees a bad omen in the gates of York being locked:

The gates made fast? Brother, I like not this!
For many men that stumble at the threshold
Are well foretold that danger lurks within.

    (*3 Henry VI*, IV.vii.10–12)

And he is very troubled that the sun is not shining at Bosworth Field:

Who saw the sun to-day?
  Rat.   Not I. My lord.
  Rich. Then he disdains to shine; for by the book
He should have brav'd the East an hour ago.
A black day will it be to somebody.

    (V.iii.278–81)

    Superstition treats inanimate objects and accidents as if they were intentional. The greater the success a man has in mastering the wills of others, the greater becomes the importance of the unintentional, the uncontrollable. Very strong-willed people are apt to believe in fate and signs—Carmen reading the cards, for example. In playing cards, if I lose because of my own mistakes in play, I do not mind. But if I lose because of consistently bad cards, I get mad because I am not getting the cards I think I should get. I consider it a good omen for the day if a subway train pulls in just in time for me to board it. If it pulls out of the station just as I come in, I regard it as a bad omen. But I do not think it is the driver who is responsible. I blame the train. For thinking beings are obviously controllable, but inanimate objects are not. Richard is doomed to failure in proportion to his success because ultimately if he controlled all souls, he'd be thrown back on existential anxiety: what support can he have for his own existence? So he must always make enemies, for then he can be sure he exists.

1954—Wolfgang H. Clemen. "Tradition and Originality in Shakespeare's *Richard III*"

Wolfgang Clemen (1909–90) was a German scholar and critic. He was also a professor at the University of Munich from 1946 to 1974. He is the author of *English Tragedy Before Shakespeare: The Development of Dramatic Speech* (1961), *Shakespeare's Dramatic Art: Collected Essays* (1972), *The Development of Shakespeare's Imagery* (1977), and *Shakespeare's Soliloquies* (1987).

The[1] relation between the originality of a dramatist and the tradition from which his work derives is an interesting subject in the case of any playwright. But it is of particular and indeed fascinating importance in the study of Shakespeare's dramas. This is due not only to the fact that Shakespeare is just a greater dramatist than the others. For we could well imagine a great dramatist very soon developing his own individual style and no longer caring about tradition, in fact discarding and ignoring tradition to such an extent that the interplay between tradition and originality could be studied only at the very outset of his career. But Shakespeare appears to have been intensely aware of the dramatic traditions around him throughout his whole career; he was more given over to experiment than any other dramatist of his time (excepting, perhaps, Greene), and he was also more interested in the fusion, transmutation, and evolution of existing literary and dramatic genres than anybody else. He sought his own way and his own style not by developing exclusively his own idiosyncrasies and his own once-discovered devices but by an ever-renewed encounter with existing modes of dramatic expression. Thus the astounding originality of his plays is balanced by the equally amazing integration and amalgamation of dramatic tradition; and these two do not appear as hostile forces but as friends, supplementing and stimulating each other.

In this paper I should like to consider *Richard III* as an early example of this relationship. Criticism of this play seems to have been guided from the very beginning by certain likes and dislikes and also certain modern dramatic criteria rather than by an attempt at finding out what kind of play Shakespeare wanted to write and an endeavor to appreciate Shakespeare's achievement in terms of the drama existing before and during his time. Admiration for Shakespeare's creation of Richard's character, recognition of the play's effectiveness on the stage, appraisal of certain fine passages or great dramatic moments on the one hand, but discontent with the play's so-called faults and improbabilities on the other hand[2]—these "evaluations" in terms of modern dramatic criticism may have blinded our eyes to the fact that here is a play which marks a decisive step in the history of English drama, a play which in its structure, style and character constitutes a very peculiar and revealing compound of various elements, a play in which Shakespeare succeeded in solving a difficult problem that each dramatist of his time, trying his hand at chronicle plays, had to face.

In the chronicle play the wealth of facts and of historical material to be covered was likely to hinder the attainment of unity of structure and clarity and coherence of plot (if indeed such an effort had been made at all).[3] The audience's express wish to learn the facts of English history through the chronicle play was a minor factor in convincing the dramatist that a chronicle play which included a great many historical circumstances, persons and names was better than one which presented only a rather limited phase of history. Hence we find that the first history plays are dramatized chronicle rather than genuine drama, a series of spectacular scenes with much episodic matter interspersed, knit together by an exterior interest rather than by inner necessity. The sequence of events, in adhering too closely to that of the chronicle, is epic rather than dramatic, and the variety and disconnectedness of episodes treated and of characters introduced in such a play (again following the chronicle source) accounts for the sense of confusion which these dramas leave in the minds of most readers. For an audience which saw them presented on the stage this effect was perhaps outweighed by the enjoyment of so much colorful variety and spectacular panorama of "pageantry on the stage," the importance of which has recently been demonstrated to us in Miss Venezky's book *Pageantry on the Shakespearean Stage*.[4] But for a dramatist of Shakespeare's calibre it must have been clear that this was not and could not remain his ultimate aim. That in *Richard III* Shakespeare gave roundness, unity and coherence to the chronicle play, that he overcame its formlessness by creating a closely and well-knit plot is a statement which is to be found in many accounts of the English drama. And even if substantial evidence should one day force us to wholly accept Professor F. P. Wilson's challenging new theory that there were no chronicle plays based on English history before Shakespeare and that Shakespeare was in fact the first to write them, we could still subscribe to this statement in so far as the sequence of the plays in Shakespeare's first tetralogy of histories from *Henry VI* up to *Richard III* reveals to us this very process—Shakespeare's development from the more epic and episodic dramatization to his grasp of a play's dramatic unity in the tragic history of *Richard III*. And this step of course also involved a freer, more selective handling of his source material.

Moreover, it was not only the chronicle play which in its structure showed this diffuseness and diversity, this predominance of colorful variety and wealth over unity and coherence. For most of the popular plays were marked by the mixture of heterogeneous elements, by the juxtaposition of farcical incident and serious pathos, of colloquial and rhetorical language, in fact by this whole naive and wonderful jostle of divergent modes and styles of dramatic expression. But unity, reached by the observance of decorum and other means was far more a characteristic of the *coterie plays,* to adopt Professor Harbage's distinction.[5] The new unity and coherence Shakespeare achieved in *Richard III* therefore means a decisive stage in view of the whole development of the popular drama and not only with regard to the chronicle play. And we shall see that this unity was attained by Shakespeare without sacrificing the rich potentialities inherent in that multi-colored and diversified dramatic form of the popular play.

I should like to indicate by a few examples how this process of unifying and tightening the play's structure goes on, as it were, on several levels, how it means far more than merely focussing our interest on one central figure, and how it involves a new and original integration of traditional dramatic forms and elements. I should also like to show how different this new unity is from what we see in Marlowe's *Tamburlaine,* which is usually, but wrongly, taken as the decisive model and influence under which Shakespeare wrote *Richard III.*

Every fresh study of the play of *Richard III* will reveal how extraordinarily well-planned and closely knit is its plot, how the events follow each other with necessity, how each scene is a unit within a larger unit, a link in a logical chain which runs from the beginning to the end and comes to its inevitable conclusion when the "wheel has come full circle." The logic of this well-wrought plot is however at the same time an inner logic. Each new event, each new character introduced into the action has a meaning beyond that of outward circumstance and sequence of facts. *Richard III* seems to be the first play of Shakespeare's in which the machinery of plot, the course of the outward action is raised to a higher level of inner significance. Events and characters have become at the same time more concrete and specific, but also more meaningful and significant in a sometimes almost symbolic way. It is remarkable that Shakespeare has in most scenes attained this greater significance of character and situation without becoming more abstract and without sacrificing the vividness and concreteness of detail.

Furthermore in the structure of this play, unlike that of almost all plays before Shakespeare, there are no "loose threads." Each motive of the action, once it has been introduced, each minor character and each detail is never lost sight of but taken up again at a later moment and made use of in connection with the major issue. This is all the more admirable as Shakespeare has not achieved this tightness of construction by restricting, as the early English classical tragedies had done, the number of persons and of events to be covered in his play but by retaining the large number of characters and incidents which usually figured in a chronicle play. This elaborate and well-considered construction of the play is generally attributed to Shakespeare's superior dramaturgical skill. But it is more than that. Shakespeare has given it a deeper significance by reflecting through this well-planned action Richard's intellectual superiority in planning and scheming, his immense power of will, his clarity of purpose. Richard is the secret agent of the action, and all its threads eventually converge in his hands

even if he is not on the stage. Again this is different from Tamburlaine's role
in Marlowe's play. For in *Tamburlaine* the whole action is a kind of façade for
Tamburlaine's conquering advance and the repetition of parallel episodes of
victory over different sets of enemies in their lack of interconnectedness is epic
rather than dramatic. In Shakespeare's play we can see how it is Richard who
secretly and cunningly watches the movements and actions of his enemies to
weave them into his spider's web before they are aware of it and then to wait for
the advantageous moment at which he can overcome them. Thus the movements
and indeed even the words and the thoughts of Richard's victims are made use
of by him for his diabolical intents, are integrated into his plans. The plot is thus,
in a manner very different from *Tamburlaine*, of Richard's doing, it is or rather it
becomes in the course of the play, *his*, the master-plotter's plot. And though the
play is centered in him, all other characters being subordinated and dependent
on him and all reacting on him in different ways, this does not mean that it is,
like *Tamburlaine*, an egocentric play. For *Tamburlaine* is indeed a play around a
superhuman figure who overrides and overshadows all his enemies and all other
characters; for these are only feeble foils to serve as interchangeable material for
the illustration of his victorious passage. This, however, we cannot say of *Richard
III*. Far more than in *Tamburlaine* we are allowed to enter the mind and world of
his victims, not only in that scene for which Shakespeare found no foundation
in the source, Clarence's dream and murder, but also in several other scenes of
which mention shall be made later on. These so-called "minor characters" in
Richard III, though in themselves vivid and individual portraits, are in a much
higher degree than the characters in *Tamburlaine* or even in *Edward II* indirect
means of characterizing the main hero. Each of them discloses to us a different
and a new facet of Richard's complex personality. They do not merely repeat
the same portrait-picture (as in *Tamburlaine*), for Richard behaves differently
towards each of them, and consequently their reaction is different. Moreover
they are not merely characterized through their different relation towards
Richard, but some of them are independently of this relation individualized
by subtle touches. And lastly Richard himself, to be sure, is no superman, no
"overreacher" in H. Levin's phrase,[6] but a realist carefully calculating how far he
can go, a man who knows the world of men and weighs the realities of this world
before he proceeds to action.

But the aim of this paper is not to enlarge upon Richard's character (a subject
too much talked of for more than a century) but to suggest how there is a relation
between the form of the play and the mood of its hero. Nor is this the only way
by which the form and composition of the play ceases to be merely a technical
matter of dramaturgical skill but is raised to a level of symbolic significance.
Even if we cannot today entirely adopt Moulton's ingenious system of several
parallel nemesis—actions in *Richard III*, we can still safely speak—in O. J.
Campbell's words—of the play's "carefully wrought moral architecture"[7] which,

superimposed on and corresponding to its external architecture, illustrates the operation of Nemesis. For we are made to realize how every murder is both crime and punishment for crime, until at the end Richard pays the final penalty. As this idea is brought home to us by recurring similar situations and episodes, we expect this end as a necessary consummation, with the same kind of simultaneous tension and absolute certainty with which we watch "the wheel coming full circle." Again we can see in this case how Shakespeare has transformed a basic conception of tragedy into a structural principle of composition. Not only has he thus modified and in a way elevated the crude treatment of the revenge-motif in the conventional revenge-tragedies, he has also given to this Nemesis-idea—for which he found only a very faint suggestion in the chronicle's account of the York–Lancaster struggle—a dramatic expression on various levels.

Curses and forebodings belonged to the conventional apparatus of Senecan tragedy. Their use in *Richard III* would therefore not be original in itself. But if we look into Seneca and into the early English classical tragedies such as *Misfortunes of Arthur*, or even popularized Seneca such as the *Spanish Tragedy* or *Locrine*, we find that these curses occur as emotional outcries, so to speak, as conventional gestures at moments of despair or wrath. But they have no bearing on the course of the action, no place in the dramatic structure. In *Richard III*, however, these curses are all fulfilled, they are not "loose threads" or mere figures of speech, but they will be remembered at decisive moments later on. Contrary to their form in pre-Shakespearian drama, the curses in *Richard III* refer to concrete events in the past and prepare for concrete events in the future. They are thus, as in the case of Margaret's curses, an important link with the past, in fact with *Henry VI*. The memory of the past is embodied in them and, pronounced by Margaret who comes into the play as from a world far remote in the past, these curses impress on us the feeling that the action we are watching transcends this present encounter between individuals and carries with it the impact of that hundred-year old struggle between York and Lancaster.

The same integration of rhetorical outbursts into the course of the action applies to the lamentations which come mainly from the lips of the three women, Anne, Elizabeth, and the Duchess. For whereas these laments in Senecan drama are like interchangeable formulae which give conventional expression to moments of distress, Shakespeare concretizes and makes specific these complaints in making these women on this occasion sum up all that so far has been done by Richard and all that so far has been suffered by his victims. In Shakespeare's hands these lamentations, looking back into the past and forward into the future, become another of his numerous means of binding his play together and of giving it inner coherence and unity. A rhetorical figure is made to form a connecting link in the dramatic structure.

Other means to serve this purpose of unifying and tightening can only very briefly be summed up here. Tragic irony, found as a rare device here and there in pre-Shakespearian drama, becomes in *Richard III* a deliberately applied instrument of foreshadowing and cross-referencing. Presentiment, forecast, omen, and prophecy as well as announcement of future intent are further means of continually connecting the past with the present and the present with the future, of establishing a whole network of interwoven threads throughout this play.[8] With regard to these features and to several others which cannot be dwelt upon, we can speak of Shakespeare's conscious art of preparation in this play—a subject which in all his plays would deserve more attention. The art of suggesting the play's central theme through leading motives in the imagery, also a contribution to unity, is as yet slightly developed in *Richard III*, but we find that another technique of leading motives is very effectively used. Certain abstract words that bear relation to the play's moral issues are repeated in different contexts and through the mouths of different characters (love, hate, conscience, fear, God). And lastly, mention should be made of Shakespeare's new and original treatment of time which—as shown in a Yale dissertation[9]—not only consists in his frequent allusions to hours and days, which creates the effect of a rapid passing of time, but also in his extraordinary condensation of time into a very few days. (The material of the chronicle covered in fact ten years.)

But we must look once again at Shakespeare's modification of features of Senecan tragedy. Margaret has already been mentioned. She has been justly called a descendant of the Furies of a Senecan tragedy, an embodiment of Nemesis or Ate, and of the chorus in tragedy.[10] We could call her a humanized or individualized Nemesis, but she is still superhuman enough to fill us with awe and an intimation of destiny that will "shape our ends rough hew them how we will." In fitting Margaret into the pattern of his play, Shakespeare has given to his chronicle play another tragic ingredient, at the same time avoiding the obvious use of the conventional chorus or of the Ghost calling for revenge.[11] And would not a play which has in it this figure of a Margaret allow and indeed demand a diction very different from the chronicle play's usual language? We can again see how the high formality of language, the abundant use of balanced and antithetical rhetorical figures, of solemn lament and execration find their equivalent in the static form and the symmetrical pattern of the mourning scenes (IV.i; IV.iv), in the statuesque or tableau-like grouping of the lamenting women, in the superpersonal choric complaints. But even these scenes in which we can clearly trace the Senecan influence are in a sense original. For this Senecan diction is no longer an "over-all style" covering the whole play and thus achieving unity through monotony and uniformity, but an appropriate medium for situation and figures which by their very nature would demand heightened language.

The combination of artificial and natural styles was, to be sure, a characteristic feature of quite a few plays before Shakespeare. We find it in plays such as *Locrine*, *Edward I*, *James IV*, and even in the *Spanish Tragedy*. But it appears as though these different levels of style were either rigidly kept apart from each other or mixed with little feeling for the innate appropriateness of these different media of expression. Shakespeare's *Richard III* is—as far as I can see—the first play in which a successful attempt is being made at reconciling and fusing the language of Senecan tragedy with that of the popular play. The transition from one style to another in most scenes seems natural and easy. By means of this alteration the stylized and rhetorically heightened passages can be counterbalanced by the more natural utterance of quick dialogue and colloquial phrase. This humanizing and normalizing influence of natural language is most apparent in Richard's own speech, which again and again drops from the rhetorical attitude to an outspoken directness and a stark colloquialism which is unique in the whole range of tragic heroes in the drama before and during Shakespeare's time.[12]

The blending of the styles of Senecan tragedy and popular chronicle play involves not only differences of language but also different modes of dramatic expression and representation. It involves the combination of two dramatic styles; on the one hand, one which is more static, slow moving and without much regard to stage business, emphasizing reflection, retrospection, narrative, description, elaborate expression of emotion; and a very different dramatic style on the other hand which makes us watch the progress of the action *on the stage*, entailing more acting and gesticulation, more change of place, more short dialogue, more characters and more circumstance and event dramatized in the scenes themselves. Kyd not unsuccessfully tried to combine these two dramatic methods, but a close comparison with *Richard III* would again reveal how great is Shakespeare's advance in this direction. By this I do not mean to suggest that Shakespeare has succeeded in completely harmonizing these two styles. He will do so in the two Parts of *Henry IV*, where by the inclusion of comic material he reaches an even wider range of different styles than in any of his previous history plays. In *Henry IV* he gave harmony to the contrasting dramatic moods of farce and tragedy, of the serious and the comic element which we find side by side in earlier drama from *Cambises* up to Peele's and Greene's plays. Shakespeare thus realized and fulfilled the rich potentialities latent in this unique compound of tragicomedy so characteristic of Elizabethan drama. In appreciating this achievement of *Henry IV* we can better understand Shakespeare's wisdom in failing to include any comic material in *Richard III* such as he had tentatively introduced in the Jack Cade episodes in *Henry VI*. He probably knew that the dramatic unity he was aiming at in *Richard III* would have been upset if at that phase of his dramatic career he had introduced comic material.

One scene only should be mentioned where we can watch the effect of this juxtaposition of pathos and realism: The long scene IV.iv often blamed for its tiresome, long-drawn-out dialogue between Richard and Elizabeth in which he asks for her daughter's hand,[13] in similar method as in Act I.ii. The scene begins with that sublime picture of mourning, reminiscent of Attic tragedy, in which the three royal women sitting down on the floor one after the other join in a symphonic chorus of lament, imprecation and curse. This passage is a striking example of that essentially static and melodramatic Senecan style involving highly formalized and rhetorical language, with this chief difference, however, that nowhere in Seneca would we find that kind of masterful distribution of choric lament among three voices, giving us the effect of simultaneousness as in a symphony. This first picture is followed by the equally "static" scene between Richard and Elizabeth, a scene which still relies entirely on words and not on action. Here Shakespeare in a manner similar to that of Richard's wooing of Anne, makes use of the technique of stichomythia for the sake of persuasion, enhancing the speed of dialogue by the use of broken lines, sudden interruption, interrogation, and exclamation. We do not find these irregularities in typical Senecan drama, and here they may suggest the transition from artificiality to naturalness. But at the end of this scene, after Queen Elizabeth's exit, full reality, action and movement break in and counterbalance the static tableau of the choric lamentations and the brilliant word-encounter between Richard and Elizabeth. For one breathless messenger after the other rushes in, carrying alarming news of the growing revolt against the King and we now see Richard facing a new situation, new realities which in fact threaten to upset his hitherto preserved balance of mind. For he beats the third messenger before the latter is able to deliver his news (which happens to be the only good news on that day), and even his language reflects this gradual loss of control over himself ("My mind is changed, sir, my mind is changed"). These last hundred lines of the scene not only make up for the previous lack of realism but also constitute the answer and reaction of the real world to the wishes and curses previously expressed by the mourning women. The device of the messenger's report, in Senecan drama used for the insertion of retrospective narrative and consequently contributing to slowing down the tempo of the action, is here used by Shakespeare just in the opposite way: it enhances the speed of the action and brings realism into the play.[14]

In Senecan tragedy the messenger had primarily the function of reporting events which could not be acted on the stage, and the Elizabethans adopted this convention—ignoring the fact that it derived from *closet* drama—in their own Senecan imitations, to drop it again in the popularized Senecan play such as the *Spanish Tragedy*. Shakespeare, in *Richard III*, seems to steer a middle course, allowing only one murder—namely that of Clarence—to be acted on the stage, the remaining murders being referred to or being reported. In this we may see an endeavor to raise the so-called tragedy of blood to a higher level, not consisting so much in atrocities and acts of sheer force as in villainous plotting which springs from intellectual superiority. To make us realize this intellectual superiority and audacity of mind as the first and foremost thing about Gloucester was surely also the reason why Shakespeare placed the wooing of Anne, for which the chronicle gave us foundation, near the beginning of the play in the second scene.

This scene has often been criticized as outrageously improbable, and it certainly is one of the greatest extremes to which Shakespeare ever went. But it affects us as less extreme and also as less improbable when we see it well acted in a good performance of the play. And does not this scene, viewed against the background of pre-Shakespearian drama, also reveal to us certain conventions handled in an entirely new manner? The verbal technique of the wooing scene in comedy with its quick repartee, its puns and its brilliant dialogue is here transferred to tragedy and suffused with grim pathos and terrible paradox. The figures of rhetoric are here used in their original function, namely as means of persuasion. Moreover, Richard slyly characterizes himself through this rhetorical dialogue. He who uses these figures like a virtuoso and who enjoys this "keen encounter of our wits" with such sarcasm and cynical pleasure appeals to us as the kind of man in whose command over words and people we begin to believe, the master-actor who watches himself and applauds himself while acting and talking, a man who can play with words just as he can play with people. This virtuosity in language and the conscious enjoyment of it, through which this great dissembler can adjust himself to very diverse situations and persons gives more credibility or, shall we say, a more "organic function" to the use of the "arts of language" not only in this scene. Richard's rhetoric is effectively set off by the brusque colloquialism of his diction on other occasions. In fact, Richard's peculiar speech seems to be the first example of Shakespeare's characterizing a person through language—another feature of his art which we do not find in the drama before him.

I mentioned the scene of Clarence's murder, and I should now like to say a few words about it, as it offers a particularly illuminating example of the relation between tradition and originality. The narrative Clarence gives of his dream is—according to its type—the kind of introspective and retrospective piece of narrative to be found in Senecan tragedy. But it differs from all extant and all possible parallels and models in important respects. It is more imaginative, more poetic, and at the same time more concrete, because richer in graphic detail.[15] The sublime imaginative vision of hell and of the realm deep below the surface of the sea with its strange fusion of mythological, biblical, and legendary elements is counterbalanced by the psychological realism with which the actual dream-experience is conveyed. Nowhere in any sixteenth-century description of a dream do we find this instinctive rendering of what we feel and what we are likely to experience when dreaming. Besides, the dream motif is handled here in an entirely new and original manner compared to pre-Shakespearian drama. For the usual procedure was to give a brief matter-of-fact account of the dream and then to add its interpretation or explanation, which was the chief thing. This method was actually followed by Shakespeare in Act III, Scene ii, in the account of Stanley's dream. But here no moral is drawn, no interpretation is added. Through this dream Shakespeare wanted to act on our imagination, not on our rational or logical understanding. By this evocative series of images he wished to bring home to us the atmosphere of suffering, sudden assault, threatening death which we shall see spreading out into reality in the next acts.

It is significant that these lines, surely the most poetical and imaginative in this play (which is otherwise so full of keen rationalism), come from the lips of Gloucester's first victim but not from Gloucester himself. Besides, this dream is a prelude and foreboding not only to the murder of Clarence himself but also to the whole series of dark catastrophes following. Theodore Spencer was the first to point this out,[16] and he drew the attention to the dramatic function of this passage, comparing it to an equally startling and imaginative, but *undramatic* description of hell in *Tamburlaine* II.iii.

From the moving pathos and the sublime vision of Clarence's dream the tone drops to the realistic prose dialogue between the two murderers. Being "low characters," murderers had to speak in prose, and being of a low and at the same time mischievous extraction, murderers were apt to be put into the role of witty clowns. So much for the "tradition" in this case. But it would be difficult to find two low characters conversing with each other so wittily and so philosophically, at the same time in their dialogue carrying on one of the play's major themes. The murderers' talk about conscience and especially the second murderer's definition of it anticipate Falstaff's remarks about honor and are an early example of Shakespeare's art of integrating this kind of low, clownish prose (in pre-Shakespearian plays a comic digression but rarely ever to the point) into the structure and meaning of his drama. It must be admitted, however, that in this scene the murderers' later lines, spoken in solemn and sonorous blank verse, are not in keeping with their preceding prose-dialogue and indicate that here Shakespeare has used them as a mouthpiece for the verdict on Clarence's guilt which he wished to bring home to us. Besides, their roles are confused and there is the ironical contradiction of Clarence being first stabbed and then drowned in a Malmsey butt, as tradition would have it. In the period of *Henry IV* Shakespeare would have escaped these pitfalls. But even if we admit this, the scene is a fine example of how Shakespeare tried to combine pathos and realism, high and low style, in one single scene; how he managed to find the transition from the poetic vision of the dream narrative to the absorbing acting of the murder at the end of the scene.

We could thus go through the play scene by scene and would find that at the basis of almost each scene there is a typical situation of pre-Shakespearian drama, or a typical convention, or a conventional motif. We should then realize that the full current of dramatic tradition is reflected in *Richard III* and that without this wealth of already existing models and modes of dramatic representation the play could not have been written. But we should also become aware that there is always something new and original in Shakespeare's treatment of this heritage of tradition which goes beyond the usual modification to be found in any dramatist's adoption of conventional material. Generalizations are always hazardous in a matter as complex as a Shakespearian play. But I suggest that Shakespeare's original handling of tradition takes three main directions. One is his superior sense of dramatic form and art, his feeling for essentially dramatic values, for the inner unity and coherence of the drama, and his consequent endeavor to integrate heterogeneous elements in the play. The second is his conscious and deliberate use of dramatic conventions, figures of speech and single elements which, to be sure, had all existed before, but which are here coordinated and made use of with a view to their contribution to the joint effect within the framework of just this drama. And the third direction is that the new element which we can trace in Shakespeare's use of tradition is very often the human aspect which he emphasized, added, or rediscovered in the conventional patterns or forms. This ranges from his rediscovery of the inherent psychological function of certain figures of speech to his achievement in arousing a genuine human interest in the hero, who is more than a compound of the three stock figures of the Senecan tyrant, the Machiavellian villain, and the Dissembler of the Morality Play. Again, we may admit that the human vividness of Richard does not come out in all scenes of his appearance on the stage. But it certainly appears in the play's total effect and is conveyed to us in a most striking, unusual, and again "original" manner in his famous speech toward the end of the play when he starts out of his dream: "Give me another horse, bind up my wound." For here he is not only "cut off from the rest of mankind," as Theodore Spencer put it,[17] but cut off even from himself in that terrible experience of the dissociation of his personality.[18] I have deliberately used the term "direction," to suggest that the achievement of *Richard III* is not yet fulfilment but a milestone on Shakespeare's way. This statement must further be qualified by saying that from *Richard III* we cannot even infer in what direction Shakespeare would go next. For in *Richard II* he adopted a style entirely different from that in *Richard III*. In our play Shakespeare appears to have tried out what this particular dramatic form would yield him, and after having achieved a certain perfection in this specific manner he dropped it again to turn to quite another way of writing a chronicle play. Again, this perfection which we find in *Richard III* is still to a large extent a perfection that lies on the surface. However, a perfection of form and of expression, and even an original and effective handling of conventional material is not yet everything. It seems as if Shakespeare knew how to write a good and effective play before he had within his reach that full and profound experience of tragic human existence which he will present to us in dramatic form in his tragedies. It is for this reason, too, that with *Richard III* a study of the means of dramatic expression, of form and structure in their relation to the tradition, is particularly interesting and fruitful.[19]

NOTES

1. This paper was delivered as Theodore Spencer Memorial Fund Lecture at Harvard University 17 April 1953. It is published here with only minor alterations.

2. For examples see Appendix to Variorum Edition of *Richard III* but also the respective passages in more recent monographs on Shakespeare.

3. On the English chronicle play see F. E. Schelling, *The English Chronicle Play* (1902). One of the best recent discussions of the English chronicle play before Shakespeare is A. P. Rossiter's introduction to his edition of *Woodstock* (1946).

4. New York, 1951.

5. *Shakespeare and the Rival Traditions* (New York, 1952).

6. Harry Levin, *The Overreacher A Study of Christopher Marlowe* (1952).

7. *The Living Shakespeare*, ed. O. J. Campbell (New York, 1949). p. 116.

8. See the present author's article, "Anticipation and Foreboding in Shakespeare's Early Histories," *Shakespeare Survey* 6 (1953).

9. Mable Buland, The *Presentation of Time in the Elizabethan Drama*. Yale Studies in English, XLIV (New York, 1912).

10. Cf. *The Living Shakespeare*, p. 117.

11. Cf. P. Simpson, *The Theme of Revenge in Elizabethan Tragedy*. Annual Sh. Lecture of the Brit. Acad. (1935)

12. Cf. A. H. Thorndike, *Tragedy* (London, 1908), p. 123.

13. For a textual criticism of this scene of which the Quarto contains only a small part and therefore may be a later addition see L. L. Schücking, *Über einige Nachbesserringen bei Shakespeare*. Berichte über die Verhandlungen der Sächs. Akademie der Wissenschaften Phil.-histor. Masse. 95. Bd. (1943).

14. For Shakespeare's use of the messenger's report see the present author's *Wandlung des Botenberichts bei Shakespeare*. Sitzungsberichte der Bayer. Akademie der Wissenschaften, Phil. histor. Klasse (1952).

15. For a comparison of Clarence's dream-narrative with Barabas' description of his jewels see F. P. Wilson, *Marlowe and the Young Shakespeare* (1953), p. 122.

16. *Death and Elizabethan Tragedy* (Cambridge, Mass., 1936), p. 118.

17. *Shakespeare: and the Nature of Man* (New York, 1949), p. 72.

18. For a comparison of this speech with the use of the Doppelgänger-motiv in a Dutch play about Richard III see O. J. Campbell, *The Position of the Roode en Witte Roos in the Saga of King Richard III* (Madison, 1919).

19. In a forthcoming interpretative commentary on *Richard III* the ideas advanced in this brief essay will be more fully illustrated and expanded.

1980—Madonne M. Miner. "'Neither Mother, Wife, nor England's Queen': The Roles of Women in *Richard III*," from *The Woman's Part: Feminist Criticism of Shakespeare*

Madonne M. Miner is professor of English at Texas Tech University. She is the author of *Insatiable Appetites: Twentieth-Century American Women's*

Bestsellers (1984), "'Trust Me': Reading the Romance Plot in Margaret Atwood's The Handmaid's Tale" (1991) and "Horatio Alger's Ragged Dick: Projection, Denial and Double-Dealing" (1990).

Richard sufficiently dominates the play so that analyses of his personality virtually exhaust the play's possibilities.

Psychoanalysis and Shakespeare

Although Norman Holland[1] speaks here primarily with reference to psychoanalytic interpretations of Shakespeare's *Richard III*, his comment actually serves as indication of the initial assumption behind almost all critical readings of the play; literary critics generally indulge in an a priori and unacknowledged Forsterian division of characters into round (Richard) and flat (everyone else), focus upon the former, and then weave their own particular analytic threads according to patterns perceived in the character of Richard.[2] Such threads comprise the traditional web of literary criticism—and deservedly so—but, because of the initial division of character and limitation of focus, certain questions raised by *Richard III* tend to fall outside the critical web. Why does one figure appear to assume a roundness of dimension while others, suffering from advanced anorexia, appear to atrophy? What is the nature of the interaction *among* "atrophied" figures as well as *between* such figures and the other, more "substantial" figure? This essay, organized into three sections, considers such questions with respect to one group of formerly ignored "flat characters": the women of *Richard III*. Section I studies the interaction between Richard and women, an interaction characterized by his determination to cast women in unattractive roles: as scapegoat for men, currency of exchange between men, and cipher without men. Section II suggests that interaction occurs among the women of the play, and Section III further substantiates the integrity of female figures with an analysis of the way in which metaphors of birth and pregnancy are used and abused throughout the play.

I

Richard III opens with a soliloquy, in which Richard, Duke of Gloucester, distinguishes time past, time present, and what he perceives to be time future:

> Grim-visaged War hath smoothed his wrinkled front,
> And now, instead of mounting barbed steeds
> To fright the souls of fearful adversaries,
> He capers nimbly in a lady's chamber
> To the lascivious pleasing of a lute.
> . . .
> Why, I, in this weak piping time of peace,

Have no delight to pass away the time.

. . .

And therefore, since I cannot prove a lover
To entertain these fair well-spoken days,
I am determinèd to prove a villain. (I.i.9–13, 24–25, 28–30)[3]

Out of step with his time, Richard determines to force it into closer conformity
with his own nature. Implicitly, the quality of the present which Richard finds
so onerous is its femininity; present days belong to "wanton ambling nymphs,"
not to marching warriors, not to hunchbacked younger brothers.[4] The opposition between war and peace is expressed as opposition between male and
female; "male" is associated with "bruised arms," "stern alarums," and "barbed
steeds," and "female" with "merry meetings," "delightful measures," and "sportive tricks."[5] It makes no difference whether we agree or disagree with Richard's
sexual collocations; what is of importance is Richard's exclusive identification
with one side of the antithesis and his determination to obliterate those who
represent the opposite—those who, according to the imagery of Richard's
soliloquy, are women.

In addition to introducing the poles of opposition in *Richard III*, Gloucester's
opening soliloquy also introduces a tactic that Richard employs throughout:
an allocation of guilt along sexual lines so that women are invariably at fault.
Within the soliloquy it is apparent that women are to blame for effacing the
countenance of "Grim-visaged War" and, immediately following the soliloquy,
Richard explains to brother Clarence that women are to blame for other things
as well. Even though Richard has just told us that he has spun "inductions
dangerous" so as to set Clarence and Edward "in deadly hate the one against the
other," when Clarence enters, under guard, Richard maintains that women are
at the root of his woes:

Why, this it is when men are ruled by women.
'Tis not the king that sends you to the Tower.
My Lady Grey his wife, Clarence, 'tis she
That tempers him to this extremity. (I.i.62–65)

Richard's allegation not only deflects suspicion from himself and onto Elizabeth,
but also tends to unite the two brothers against an intruder (the sister-in-law,
the "Other"). While challenging bonds of marriage, Richard appears to be
reaffirming bonds of consanguinity. Clarence catches the impulse of Richard's
comment and carries it yet further, naming Mistress Shore as another female
force undermining the throne; if one woman is not to blame, another may be
found. Clarence cites Shore's intervention in favor of Hastings and Richard
agrees: "Humbly complaining to her deity / Got my Lord Chamberlain his

liberty" (I.i.76–77). Obviously, according to Richard, when prostitutes capture the ear of kings, when wives wield more power than brothers, the time is out of joint.[6]

In the subsequent exchange with Anne, who follows the corpse of her father-in-law Henry to Chertsey, as in that with Clarence, Richard directs culpability from himself and onto the female figure.[7] He greets the recently widowed woman as "sweet saint" (I.ii.49), and bolsters this greeting with a string of compliments, to which she responds with curses. When Anne charges him with the slaughter of her father-in-law, Henry VI, and her husband, Edward, Richard initially scrambles for a surrogate (blaming Edward IV and Margaret) but then hits upon a far more effective line, accusing Anne as the primary "causer" of the deaths:

Your beauty was the cause of that effect;
Your beauty, that did haunt me in my sleep
To undertake the death of all the world,
So I might live one hour in your sweet bosom.

    (I.ii.121–24)

Thus, Anne is responsible; her beauty serves as incentive for murder. Richard, of course, lies; he kills Edward and Henry so as to come closer to the throne, and he woos Anne for the same reason. By the end of the scene, however, this hunchbacked Machiavellian is able to acknowledge his role in the murders of Edward and Henry, to offer Anne his sword to use against him, and to smile in the knowledge of his victory as she refuses to take vengeance.

Nay, do not pause, for I did kill King Henry,
But 'twas thy beauty that provoked me.
Nay, now dispatch; 'twas I that stabbed young Edward,
But 'twas thy heavenly face that set me on.
Take up the sword again, or take up me. (I.ii.179–83)

By focusing on her beauty, Richard insists that Anne fit the very flat definition of "womankind" he articulated in his opening soliloquy—a definition that divides the world into male and female provinces, denying the latter any possibility of communion with emblems (such as swords) of the former. Focusing upon Anne's guilt, Richard deflects responsibility from himself, and constructs a bond of alliance between Anne and himself, against the House of Lancaster, rendering her powerless.

While the exchange between Richard and Anne may be the most dramatic example of Richard's aptitude with respect to sexual dynamics and the allocation of guilt, it is by no means a final example. Another variation occurs in Act III, scene iv, when Richard determines to weed out the ranks of those in opposition to his coronation. Because Hastings is involved with Mistress Shore, all Richard need do is accuse Shore, implicate Hastings (guilt by association) and be rid of him. Thus, in the midst of an assembly meeting, Richard draws forth his withered arm and announces: "And this is Edward's wife, that monstrous witch, / Consorted with that harlot strumpet Shore, / That by their witchcraft thus have marked me" (III.iv.69–71). Hastings's reply, "If they have done this deed, my noble lord" (72), is twisted by an enraged Richard into unimpeachable evidence of guilt: "If! Thou protector of this damned strumpet, / Talk'st thou to me of ifs? Thou art a traitor. / Off with his head!" (73–75). In spite of the incredible and illogical nature of Richard's accusation (his arm has always been withered; the association of Elizabeth and Mistress Shore as conspirators is extremely unlikely), it holds: Hastings loses his head on the basis of his involvement with a woman. Although the dynamics in the three examples cited above vary considerably, in each instance Richard blames women in order to benefit himself and, in so doing, he creates or destroys associational bonds between men.

If, in the scenes above, Richard is able to manipulate women and blame so as to cut or spin associational threads, his tailoring skills appear yet more impressive when he sets himself to matchmaking—an activity which appears to encourage the reduction of female status from "person" to "thing exchanged." As Lévi-Strauss observes in *Structural Anthropology*, marriage functions as the lowest common denominator of society; based as it has been on the exchange of a woman between two men, marriage brings together two formerly independent groups of men into a kinship system.[8] Richard takes advantage of these associational possibilities, but, interestingly enough, the impulse behind his marital connections most often appears to be one of destruction rather than creation; society is wrenched apart rather than drawn together. We see Richard play the role of suitor twice, with Lady Anne and with Queen Elizabeth (whom he approaches to request the hand of her daughter Elizabeth). To be sure, in formulating his marital plans, Richard approaches women—an eligible widow and a widowed mother—but in both cases, Richard actually focuses on men behind the women. Before meeting Anne en route to Chertsey, he reveals his designs on her:

> For then I'll marry Warwick's youngest daughter.
> What though I killed her husband and her father?
> The readiest way to make the wench amends
> Is to become her husband and her father. (I.i.153–56)

"To make the wench amends"? Such, of course, is not the actual motivation behind Richard's system of substitution; he realizes that in order to substantiate his claims to the position previously held by Henry VI, it is politic to align himself with Henry's daughter-in-law. Further, maneuvering himself into Anne's bedchamber, Richard moves closer to replacing Edward, former occupant thereof, and former heir to the throne. Thus, after killing Anne's "husband and father," Richard can assume their sexual and political roles.[9] Finally, Richard's speech clarifies the function of women in the marital game: whether the game be one of exchange or one of substitution, the female serves as a piece to be moved by others, and a piece having value only *in relation* to others.

Political values, however, like those of the stock market, fluctuate wildly, and by Act IV, Richard (now king) recognizes that Anne has outlived her usefulness to him. After instructing Catesby to rumor it abroad that Anne is "very grievous sick," Richard ruminates alone: "I must be married to my brother's daughter, / Or else my kingdom stands on brittle glass. / Murder her brothers and then marry her!" (IV.ii.58–60). As in his earlier choice of bride, Richard here pursues a woman from whom he has taken all male relatives; although not fully responsible for the death of Elizabeth's father, Richard conspires to lessen the natural term of Edward's life, and he employs more direct measures with respect to Clarence (Elizabeth's uncle) and the two princes (Elizabeth's brothers). However, not all possible rivals have been obliterated: Richmond also seeks the hand of Edward's daughter, and Richard's awareness of a living male rival sharpens his desire to legitimize his claim:

> Now, for I know the Britain Richmond aims
> At young Elizabeth, my brother's daughter,
> And by that knot looks proudly on the crown,
> To her go I, a jolly thriving wooer. (IV.iii.40–43)

Elizabeth, of course, has been a loose end; with the young princes dead ("cut off") she remains the only legitimate possibility of access to the throne. By tying his own knots, Richard plans to exclude Richmond from making any claims to the kingdom. In sum, Richard woos both Anne and Elizabeth because of the position they occupy with respect to men. However, in proposing marriage (which might lead to a bonding of male to male through female, Richard does not seek a union *with* other men but rather *replaces* them by assuming their roles with respect to women.

In considerations of the way Richard employs women as scapegoats and currency, younger female figures have received most attention. However, when we consider how Richard uses women as ciphers, three older women— Queen Elizabeth, Margaret, and the Duchess of York—step, reluctantly, into the foreground. All of these women suffer, on one level, a loss of definition at the hand of Richard. Caught in a society that conceives of women strictly in relational terms (that is, as wives to husbands, mothers to children, queens to kings), the women are subject to loss of title, position, and identity, as Richard destroys those by whom women are defined: husbands, children, kings.[10] Early in the play, Queen Elizabeth perceives the precarious nature of *her* position as her husband, King Edward, grows weaker and weaker. "The loss of such a lord includes all harms" (I.iii.8), she tells her son Grey. Elizabeth's words find verification not only in later scenes, but also, here, before Edward's death, in the figure of Margaret, England's former queen. Margaret, hiding in the wings, listens as Richard taunts Elizabeth and accuses her of promoting her favorites. When Elizabeth replies, "Small joy have I in being England's Queen" (109), Margaret can barely restrain herself; she says in an aside: "As little joy enjoys the queen thereof; / For I am she, and altogether joyless" (154–55). Margaret's aside pinpoints the confusion that results when women must depend upon men for identity and when Richard persists in removing these men. Is a woman to be considered "queen" after her "king" has been killed? Does one's title apply only as long as one's husband is alive? And, after her husband's death, what does the "queen" become? Margaret serves, of course, as model for the women of *Richard III*; she enters in Act I and shows Elizabeth and the Duchess of York what they have to expect from the future; like her, they are destined to years of sterile widowhood. But the women of York do not yet perceive Margaret's function; with Richard, they mock her and force her from the stage. Before leaving, however, Margaret further clarifies her relationship to Elizabeth by underlining the similarity of their woes:

> Thyself a queen, for me that was a queen,
> Outlive thy glory like my wretched self!
> Long mayst thou live to wail thy children's death;
> . . .
> Long die thy happy days before thy death,
> And, after many length'ned hours of grief,
> Die neither mother, wife, nor England's Queen! (I.iii.201–3, 206–8)

Alive—but neither mother, wife, nor England's queen: the description may apply to Margaret, Elizabeth, and the Duchess. Only a very short time elapses between the day of Margaret's curse and the day Elizabeth suffers the death of her lord. Addressing the Duchess, the twice-widowed woman cries: "Edward, my lord, thy son, our king, is dead! / Why grow the branches when the root is gone? / Why wither not the leaves that want their sap?" (II.ii.40–42). Elizabeth's questions forecast her upcoming tragedy.

Not only does Richard subvert the role of queen, he also undermines roles of mother and wife. For example, while the death of Edward robs Elizabeth of a husband, it robs the Duchess of York of a son. Having lost son Clarence earlier, the Duchess's "stock" suffers a depletion of two-thirds. She turns to Elizabeth, commenting that years ago she lost a worthy husband,

And lived with looking on his images;
But now two mirrors of his princely semblance
Are cracked in pieces by malignant death,
And I for comfort have but one false glass
That grieves me when I see my shame in him.
Thou art a widow, yet thou art a mother
And hast the comfort of thy children left. (II.ii.50–56)

Stressing Elizabeth's yet-current claim to motherhood, the Duchess appears to abjure her own; it is as if she no longer wants to assume the title of mother if Richard is the son who grants her this right; accepting "motherhood" means accepting responsibility for "all these griefs," for the losses sustained by Elizabeth and by Clarence's children.

It is not enough for one mother to abandon her claim to the title of mother; Richard pursues a course of action that eventually forces Elizabeth to relinquish her claim also (note that as the play proceeds, Elizabeth comes to bear a closer resemblance to Margaret). The process leading to Elizabeth's forfeiture of her title is more complicated than that of the Duchess and is accomplished in a series of steps: Buckingham and Richard override maternal authority and, parenthetically, the right of sanctuary, by "plucking" the Duke of York from the sheltering arms of his mother; Brakenbury, under order from Richard, denies Elizabeth entrance to the Tower, thereby denying her right to see her children; Richard casts doubt on the legitimacy of Edward's marriage to Elizabeth, and hence, on the legitimacy of her children; Richard preys upon Elizabeth to grant him her daughter in marriage while Elizabeth knows that to do so would be to sentence her daughter to a living death.

As this process is set in motion, the "Protector" refuses to grant Elizabeth her status as mother; as it comes to a close, Elizabeth freely abjures her motherhood in an attempt to protect her remaining child. Up until the murder of her sons, Elizabeth insists, often futilely, upon her maternal rights. When, for example, Brakenbury refuses to admit her to the Tower, she protests violently upon the grounds of familial relation: "Hath he set bounds between their love and me? / I am their mother; who shall bar me from them?" (IV.i.20–21). Almost as if she were determined actively to dispute Richard's allegations that her children are illegitimate, Elizabeth reiterates, time and time again, the status of her relationship and that of her children to Edward. After the deaths of young Edward and Richard, however, Elizabeth is forced to perform an about-face. Because of Richard's manipulations, a "mother's name is ominous to children"; hence, she must deny her title of mother in order to express her genuine identity as a mother concerned for her children's welfare. She dispatches her son Dorset to France—"O Dorset, speak not to me, get thee gone!" (IV.i.38)—and expresses her willingness to deny the legitimacy of young Elizabeth's birth to save her from marriage to Richard.

> And must she die for this? O, let her live,
> And I'll corrupt her manners, stain her beauty,
> Slander myself as false to Edward's bed,
> Throw over her the veil of infamy;
> So she may live unscarred of bleeding slaughter,
> I will confess she was not Edward's daughter. (IV.iv.206–11)

It is the love of a mother for her daughter which prompts Elizabeth's offer; she willingly renounces her titles both of wife and legitimate mother.

In the examples cited above, Richard's general course of action is such to encourage women to abandon traditional titles, to de-identify themselves. Richard more specifically encourages this cipherization by confounding the integrity of titular markers: that is, by juggling titles without regard for the human beings behind these titles (although Richard does not restrict himself to female markers, females suffer more grievously from these verbal acrobatics than do males, who may draw upon a wider range of options with respect to identifying roles). Richard's changing choice of title for his sister-in-law Elizabeth most clearly exemplifies his policy of confoundment. Richard's first reference to Elizabeth occurs in a conversation with Clarence, in which Richard promises that he will employ any means to procure his brother's freedom: "And whatsoe'er you will employ me in, / Were it to call King Edward's widow sister, / I will perform it to enfranchise you" (I.i.108–10). Several things are happening here. First, as the wife of Edward, Richard's brother, Elizabeth is Richard's sister (sister-in-law); she need not solicit the title from Richard, although Richard certainly implies that it is his prerogative to grant or withhold the title at will. Second, the title Richard actually bestows on Elizabeth is "King Edward's widow," an equivocation of marvelous subtlety; Elizabeth is the widow of Grey but Richard's phrasing makes it possible to read this description as a prediction: Elizabeth will wear weeds again. And finally, when Richard and Elizabeth meet in the following scene, it is Elizabeth who twice addresses Richard as "Brother Gloucester"; Richard refuses to call her anything, because, at this time, he has nothing to gain by doing so. Later, in Act II, following the convenient demise of Edward IV, Richard, as if to ensure a smooth transference of power, attempts to placate Elizabeth: he calls her "sister." In Act IV, however, after Richard has approached Elizabeth for the hand of young Elizabeth, he calls her "mother": "Therefore, dear mother—I must call you so—/ Be the attorney of my love to her" (IV.iv.412–13). The exchange between Richard and Elizabeth also supplies a rather startling example of Richard's indifference to the human beings who actually give substance to the titles he juggles with such apparent ease. Richard insists that he will provide substitutes for the children Elizabeth has lost at his hand:

> To quicken your increase I will beget
> Mine issue of your blood upon your daughter.
> A grandam's name is little less in love
> Than is the doting title of a mother. (IV.iv.297–300)

Focusing exclusively upon a "grandam's *name*" and the "*title* of a mother," Richard attempts to obscure the very real difference between these two positions; he attempts to confound all meaning attached to female position markers—a policy in keeping with his determination to confound women altogether.

II

Given Richard's perception of woman as enemy, as "Other," we should not be surprised that the action of the play depends upon a systematic denial of the human identity of women. Richard's apparently successful attempts to obscure Elizabeth's titular "sense of self" and Elizabeth's rejection of both her own identity and that of her daughter exemplify, on one level, the progression of women in *Richard III*: from mother to nonmother, wife to widow, queen to crone. However, this "progression" does not take into account a less obvious and more positive progression of women from a condition of bickering rivalry to a condition of sympathetic camaraderie. In the midst of loss, the women turn to each other. Thus, an interesting, but generally ignored, countermotion of interaction *among* women is introduced; having been reduced to the condition of nothing, Margaret, Elizabeth, and the Duchess evidence a new humanity, a humanity apparent nowhere else in the play. We need only explore the progression in the four scenes in *Richard III* in which women confront each other (I.iii; II.ii; IV.i; IV.iv) to see this countermotion. Act I, scene iii, opens with Elizabeth and Richard at each other's throat; with the entrance of Margaret, however, Richard is able to direct all hostility toward her. Even Elizabeth joins with crook-backed Gloucester in condemning the widow of Lancaster; angry words fly across the stage. When Elizabeth applauds Richard for turning Margaret's curse back on herself, Margaret chides the "poor-painted queen":

> Why strew'st thou sugar on that bottled spider
> Whose deadly web ensnareth thee about?
> Fool, fool, thou whet'st a knife to kill thyself.
> The day will come that thou shalt wish for me
> To help thee curse this poisonous bunch-backed toad. (I.iii.241–45)

Margaret's prediction proves true, but the women must suffer first.

If the preceding scene depicts the hostility between women of different Houses, Act II, scene ii, depicts hostility between women of the same House. Instead of coming together in sympathy upon learning of the deaths of Clarence and Edward, the women of York and the children of Clarence engage in a chorus of moans, each claiming the greater loss. An appalling absence of empathy characterizes this meeting. A few lines may serve to indicate the mood of the entire scene:

> Duch. O, what cause have I,
> Thine being but a moi'ty of my moan,
> To overgo thy woes and drown thy cries!
> Boy. Ah, aunt, you wept not for our father's death.
> How can we aid you with our kindred tears?
> Daughter. Our fatherless distress was left unmoaned;
> Your widow-dolor likewise be unwept!
> Elizabeth. Give me no help in lamentation;
> I am not barren to bring forth complaints. (II.ii.59–67)

Obviously, the tendency here is away from commiseration and toward a selfish indulgence. It is not until Act IV, scene i, that a reversal of this tendency begins to make itself felt, the result of the women's sympathy as their position continues to erode. Elizabeth, the Duchess of York, Anne, and Clarence's daughter meet en route to the Tower to greet the young princes. When Elizabeth is denied visitation privileges, the Duchess and Anne support her maternal rights. Even when Stanley announces that Anne is to be crowned queen, the bond of sympathy between Anne and Elizabeth is not destroyed. Given her history of suffering, Elizabeth can respond now with feeling to Anne as Margaret could not when she was replaced by Elizabeth. When the new queen expresses her wish that the "inclusive verge of golden metal" were "red-hot steel to sear me to the brains," Elizabeth attempts to console her: "Go, go, poor soul! I envy not thy glory. / To feed my humor wish thyself no harm" (IV.i.63–64). The Duchess of York adds her blessing also: "Go thou to Richard, and good angels tend thee!" (92). How different from the feeling of Act II, scene ii! Even though this union of sympathy may not generate any practical power (Richard continues to confound the women) it does prompt a revision in our responses to them: they attain a tragic dignity.

The most moving example of women-aiding-women, however, occurs in Act IV, scene iv, where the women of York join Margaret of Lancaster in cursing Richard. This union is achieved only gradually. Old Queen Margaret enters alone and withdraws to eavesdrop on Elizabeth and the Duchess of York, who sit down together to lament the death of the princes and lament their uselessness:

"Ah that thou wouldst as soon afford a gravel As thou canst yield a melancholy seat" (IV.iv.31–32). When Margaret comes forward and joins the two women on the ground, she first claims that her griefs "frown on the upper hand" and it seems the scene will be a reiteration of the earlier contest.

> If sorrow can admit society,
> Tell o'er your woes again by viewing mine.
> I had an Edward, till a Richard killed him;
> I had a husband, till a Richard killed him.
> Thou hadst an Edward, till a Richard killed him;
> Thou hadst a Richard, till a Richard killed him. (IV.iv.38–43)

The Duchess, catching the rhythm of Margaret's refrain, interrupts in order to wail a few lines of her own. Margaret, however, regains voice, reminding the Duchess that it is her womb that has bred the cause of all their sorrows: "From forth the kennel of thy womb hath crept / A hellhound that doth hunt us all to death" (IV.iv.47–48). These words signal a reversal in the dynamics of the scene; no longer willing to recognize the legal ties to men which prohibit a communion between women of different parties, these women join together in sorrow, in suffering; it is easy enough to imagine the three of them, seated on the earth, hand in hand. The Duchess abandons her competition with Margaret for the title of most grief-stricken, and turns, in commiseration, to her: "O Harry's wife, triumph not in my woes! / God witness with me I have wept for thine" (59–60). Elizabeth, too, moves toward Margaret, admitting that the prophesied time has come for her to request Margaret's help in cursing the "foul bunch-backed toad" (81) Richard. Thus, the exchange among the women leads to the decision to arm themselves (to assume a male prerogative) with words; Margaret provides lessons in cursing and the Duchess suggests that they smother Richard in "the breath of bitter words" (133); no more wasted or feeble words—instead, the women now use words as weapons. Accordingly, when Richard enters a short while after Margaret's departure, Elizabeth and the Duchess verbally accost and accuse him. Unaccustomed to such noise, an indignant Richard commands: "Either be patient and entreat me fair,/ Or with the clamorous report of war / Thus will I drown your exclamations" (152–54). Richard's response to these insistent female voices is worthy of note as it reiterates the alliance of Richard with war and against women, and as it serves as summary statement of Richard's policy with respect to women—they must be silenced. The Duchess, however, finds voice, and her final words to Richard take the form of a curse; she turns against her own House, prays for the adverse party, and damns her son Richard to a death of shame. Her ability to do so with such strength is surely a result of the communion of sympathy shared by the three women. If, in previous scenes, a meeting of women merely leads to angry words and altercation, the meeting of Act IV, scene iv, leads to the formation of bonds among the women against a single foe.[11] When the progression of female characters is charted on this level, it becomes apparent that they do not deserve the a priori dismissal they too frequently receive. Although attenuated by Richard, women take on an emotional solidity, a roundness of true humanity.

<h1 style="text-align:center">III</h1>

A consideration of birth metaphor clarifies, yet further, the paradoxically double presentation of women in *Richard III*; specifically, perversion of birth metaphors suggests the negative condition of women articulated in Section I (from mother to nonmother, etc.), while the persistence and importance of these metaphors suggest the very positive condition of women articulated in Section II (as individuals having considerable power and human value). Although examples of the birth metaphor are so numerous as to render selection a problem, three categories may be arbitrarily distinguished: metaphor as descriptive of the condition of the times; as descriptive of Richard's activities and of Richard himself from the perspective of other characters; and as descriptive of Richard's mind as revealed in his own comments.

As mentioned previously, Richard "declares war" on the present time in his opening soliloquy; the extent to which he realizes this declaration may be felt in comments made by other characters throughout the play about the changed condition of the times—comments which most often work through a distortion of imagery usually associated with birth. When a group of citizens gathers to discuss the recent death of Edward and the probable confusion that will result, one compares his apprehension of ensuing danger to the swelling of water before a boisterous storm (II.iii.42–45). Although "swelling" is not, by any means, a term associated exclusively with pregnancy, it almost always conveys a feeling of pregnant expectation. Here, and at all other times throughout *Richard III*, that which is expected, that which swells the body, is something ominous, something negative. This consistently pejorative use of the term "swelling" stands in contrast to a possible positive application of the word: that is, swelling as indicative of a generous fertility.[12] A similarly pejorative application of usually positive terms occurs in the speech of Elizabeth when she, like the citizens, is informed of Edward's death. Refusing all offers of sympathy from others, she cries: "I am not barren to bring forth complaints. / All springs reduce their currents to mine eyes, / That I . . . / May send forth plenteous tears to drown the world" (II.ii.67–68, 70). Two aspects of Elizabeth's choice of metaphor are worthy of note. First, the widow asserts her fertility, but a fertility that gives birth to complaints, instead of children. Second, the "children" that Elizabeth does produce assume the shape of tears, tears which, under normal conditions, might function as springs of life. Given the corruption of conditions under Richard, however, Elizabeth sends forth her tears to destroy life, "to drown the world."

Examination of Richard's specific activities reveals more explicitly his perversion of regenerative processes. When the thugs employed to murder Clarence attempt to convince him that Richard is the father of this deed, Clarence shakes his head in disbelief: "It cannot be, for he bewept my fortune / And hugged me in his arms and swore with sobs / That he would labor my delivery" (I.iv.247–49). While Clarence assumes that Richard will "deliver" him from prison, to freedom, Richard intends to deliver Clarence from prison to death. Thus, Richard reverses the normal delivery process; instead of drawing Clarence forth from the womb, two midwives push him back into a yet darker womb (specifically, into a butt of malmsey). The speech of Tyrrel, another murderer employed by Richard, provides a second commentary on Richard's activities. Having commissioned the execution of the young princes, he tells the king: "If to have done the thing you gave in charge / Beget your happiness, be happy then, / For it is done" (IV.iii.25–27). "The thing" given in charge is the murder of two children; once more, begetting and killing are conjoined. The comments of Margaret and the Duchess affirm this unnatural conjunction, transferring it to the literal level: Richard's unnatural birth. Margaret attacks Richard as "Thou slander of thy heavy mother's womb! / Thou loathed issue of thy father's loins!" (I.iii.230–31). Similarly, because of son Richard, the Duchess of York cries out against her own womb, revealing an extreme of female debasement and acceptance of guilt: "O my accursed womb, the bed of death! / A cockatrice hast thou hatched to the world, / Whose unavoided eye is murderous" (IV.i.53–55). Richard, forcing an association of the womb with "the bed of death," succeeds, at least *partially*, in debasing the value of women, these creatures with wombs.

One final category of defective birth imagery is that employed by Richard in describing his own activities. After the general altercation of Act I, scene iii, for example, Richard steps off alone and comments: "I do the wrong, and first begin to brawl. / The secret mischiefs that I *set abroach* / I lay unto the grievous charge of others" (I.iii.323–25, emphasis added). Or, just a short time later, when Edward, unaware of Richard's expeditious execution of Clarence, informs his court that peace has been made "between these swelling wrong-incensed peers," Richard replies: "A blessed *labor* my most sovereign lord" (II.i.52–53, emphasis added). But undoubtedly the most graphic of the many examples of debasement of the language of birth occurs in Act IV, scene iv, as Richard encourages Elizabeth to allow him to right previous wrongs by marrying her daughter. When Elizabeth protests, "Yet thou didst kill my children," Richard counters: "But in your daughter's womb I'll bury them, / Where in that nest of spicery they will breed / Selves of themselves, to your recomforture" (IV.iv.423–25). Richard will bury old Elizabeth's children in young Elizabeth's womb? Could Richard hit upon a line of argument any more perversely unnatural? Up to this point, most birth metaphors have been constructed so as to suggest that the womb breeds no good (as, for example, that the Duchess's womb breeds a cockatrice); here, Richard forces the metaphor to work in reverse as well: the womb serves as tomb, functioning as both sprouting ground and burial plot. In forcing this perverse alliance of terms, Richard reaffirms, on a linguistic level, the impulse behind all of his activities with respect to women—the impulse to silence, to negate. Yet, paradoxically, the persistence with which Richard acts upon this impulse gives the lie to the possibility of its fulfillment: Richard's *need* to debase birth imagery implies that women (those capable of giving birth) have a power which finally cannot be devalued or eliminated; further, his repeated attempts, on a larger level, to rob women of their identity as mothers, wives, or queens, are doomed to frustration in that he cannot rob women of their identity as creative, regenerative human beings.

Richard III opens with a series of complaints directed, implicitly, against women. It is women who tame "Grim-visaged War," who caper to lutes, who play Love's games—and who govern the times. *Richard III* ends with a series of scenes on the battlefield; men engage in combat with men, and women are nowhere to be found (the last female on stage appears in Act IV). On one level, the process of the play is one of denial and deflation; as Richard destroys husbands, kings, and children, as he confounds traditionally stable sources of identity and subjects women to an unnatural association with the forces of death, he suggests that women are without value—or, even worse, that they are destructive of value. But a reading of *Richard III* on just this one level does an injustice to the play; running parallel to the process described above is a counterprocess, one that insists upon the inherently positive value of women. We see evidence of this counterprocess in the progression of women from a condition of rivalry, battling amongst themselves, to a condition of camaraderie, sympathizing with each other, and in the persistence of the attack that Richard feels compelled to wage, both in life and in language, against these powerful foes. Even Richmond's final speech contributes to our sense of the invincibility of these females; after describing the bloody hatred between brothers which has divided England, Richmond proposes a reunification through his conjunction with the young woman Elizabeth. Hence, the argument of *Richard III* moves in two directions. The first insists that women are purely media of exchange and have no value in themselves; the second, overriding the first, insists that even when used as currency, women's value cannot be completely destroyed.

NOTES

1. Norman Holland, *Psychoanalysis and Shakespeare* (New York: McGraw-Hill, 1966), p. 261.

2. Just to cite a few of the major examples: see Wolfgang H. Clemen, *A Commentary on Shakespeare's "Richard III,"* trans. Jean Bonheim (London: Methuen and Co., 1968), and E. M. W. Tillyard, *Shakespeare's History Plays* (New York: Macmillan, 1946); as representative of historical-political interpretations, see

John Palmer, *Political Characters of Shakespeare* (London: Macmillan, 1961) or M. M. Reese, *The Cease of Majesty* (New York: St. Martin's Press, 1961); for psycho-analytic interpretations, see essays in M. D. Faber, *The Design Within* (New York: Science House, 1970), or Holland, *Psychoanalysis and Shakespeare*; as representative of "type criticism" see Bernard Spivack, *Shakespeare and the Allegory of Evil* (New York: Columbia University Press, 1958). All of these works offer something to the history of criticism of *Richard III*, but all, initially, take their cue from the star performer-cum-director, Richard. The exception to this generalization is Leslie Fiedler. In *The Stranger in Shakespeare* (New Fork: Stein and Day, 1972), he shows his sensitivity to the "problem of woman" in Shakespeare: "Obviously, the beginning for Shakespeare is the problem of woman, or more exactly perhaps, his problem with women. Certainly, in his first plays, members of that sex are likely to be portrayed as utter strangers" (p. 43). The only other critic from the list above who makes any more than cursory mention of the women is Reese.

3. All citations are from *The Complete Signet Classic Shakespeare*, gen. ed. Sylvan Barnet (New York: Harcourt Brace Jovanovich, 1963, 1972).

4. Although this soliloquy has elicited comment from a wide range of critics, most of them appear oblivious to its misogynic thrust. Focusing upon Richard's statement that he is "determined to prove a villain," they ignore the motivation behind his determination. William B. Toole, for example, insists that we should *not* "seek a modern psychological explanation for Richard's behaviour on the basis of this passage. The main purpose of this part of the soliloquy [1.i.1–30] is to indicate that the protagonist has freely chosen to be a villain" ("The Motif of Psychic Division in *Richard III*," *Shakespeare Survey*, 27 [1974], p. 25). A more interesting reading that appears closer to the text than Toole's, is Sigmund Freud's in "Some Character-Types Met with in Psycho-Analytic Work," included in Faber, *The Design Within*. Freud explains that we accept Richard's articulation of his disadvantages in the soliloquy because we identify with him: "And now we feel that we ourselves might become like Richard ... Richard is an enormous magnification of something we find in ourselves as well. We all think we have reason to reproach Nature and our destiny for congenital and infantile disadvantages" (p. 345). Remaining true to both Freud and Richard, we might emend Freud's comment: "We all think we have reason to reproach women (the "Great Mothers") for our disadvantages."

5. See also Richard's soliloquy in *Henry VI*, Part 3, III.ii.124–95, in which the sexual opposition is more explicit.

6. Interestingly enough, although Shore may have a hand in Hastings's release, the evidence against Elizabeth's involvement in Clarence's imprisonment is such that we must dismiss all charges against her—but the probable guilt of one and the certain innocence of the other make no difference; when Richard requires a scapegoat, any woman will serve.

7. Again, although critical response to this scene has been abundant, it has also been very narrow in focus. Palmer, *Political Characters*, p. 81, maintains that the prime purpose of Richard's wooing "is to show Richard's insolent virtuosity in persuasion, his delight in the exercise of his mind and will, his pride in attempting the impossible and his triumph in its achievement." Palmer does not choose to see the sexual ramifications of the *contents* of Richard's virtuosity, delight, pride, and triumph. Similarly, Reese, *The Cease of Majesty*, pp. 217–18, notes that Shakespeare invents most of the first act in order to "show off (Richard's) powers," but does not comment on the fact that these powers are directed against women.

8. Claude Lévi-Strauss, *Structural Anthropology*, trans. Claire Jacobson and Brooke Grandfest Schoepf (New York: Basic Books, 1976), I, 46: "a man obtains a woman from another man who gives him a daughter or a sister."

9. See Otto Rank, *Das Inzest Motiv in Dichtung und Sage* (Leipzig: Franz Deuticke, 1926), pp. 211–12, for a more complete analysis of incest motifs in *Richard III*. Also see Charles A. Adler, "Richard III—His Significance as a Study in Criminal Life-Style," *International Journal of Individual Psychology*, 2, No. 3 (1936), 55–60, for a brief, and rather crude, commentary on the way Richard attempts to conquer his murdered opponents by "possessing their ladies" (p. 59).

10. Although guilty of several murders throughout the play, Richard never raises his sword against a woman; he does not need to; instead, he effectively disposes of women by disposing of the "primary terms" according to which they identify themselves. (Richard's wife Anne is the possible exception; it is questionable whether her death should be attributed to poison from the hand of Richard or to the equally lethal experience of marriage to him.)

11. Very few critics pay much attention to this scene. Fiedler provides an especially sympathetic reading of the way in which Margaret, "squatting on the ground with Queen Elizabeth and the Duchess of York . . . has helped project the image of the Triple Goddess in darkest form" (*The Stranger in Shakespeare*, p. 50). As Fiedler explains a while later, this Triple Goddess is comprised of "Hera, Aphrodite, Persephone: mother, mistress and queen of the underworld," but in Shakespeare, "the first two functions blur into the third [which is why] . . . in that terrible scene of *Richard III* in which Queen Margaret, Queen Elizabeth, and the Duchess of York gather together, the second two are portrayed as mere shadows of the first, who, we suspect, will disappear when she leaves the land which has never really been hers" (p. 73). Richard Wheeler, in "History, Character, and Conscience in *Richard III*," *Comparative Drama*, 5 (1971–72), 314, also takes note of the scene, observing that although Richard virtually makes a career out of killing men, "the real suffering of the play comes to be focused in the voices of widowed mothers." Reese, on the other hand, is completely unsympathetic. Although he believes scenes with the women are important ones—"They provide a formal setting for Richard's crimes and epitomise the Elizabethan reading of history" (*The Cease of Majesty*, p. 209), he insists that the women's indifference to Richard's immortal soul "shows how low these women themselves have fallen. Except in an emptily rhetorical way, they are not touched by the finer issues" (p. 223). Finer issues?! Must such issues revolve around the eternal salvation of the male figure?

12. Shakespeare consistently chooses to use the terms "swell" and "swelling" in a pejorative fashion. Cf. *The Winter's Tale*, II.i.62; *Timon of Athens*, III.v.102; *Troilus and Cressida*, I.ii.276; *Othello*, II.iii.57. In each case, swelling promises something undesirable in the future or is evidence of ugliness in the past.

RICHARD III IN THE
TWENTY-FIRST CENTURY
❧

Twentieth-first-century criticism of *Richard III* identifies many tensions and ambiguities inherent in the play, including the inherent ambivalence within Richard's psyche, the various breaches of time both within the actual play and its deviations from a sequential presentation of historical events, and the conflicting attitudes toward the correlation between physical deformity and moral character. With respect to the issue of time, Jeremy Lopez does a close reading of the extraordinary temporal and poetic distinctions of Clarence's dream from the rest of *Richard III*, arguing that this peculiar scene functions independently from the rest of the play. Nevertheless, despite this tendency to highlight the various temporal disjunctures within the text, there are critics who return to the perennial question of why Shakespeare exaggerated Richard's deformity, and defend those distortions on the grounds that while he was interested in presenting the far-reaching moral consequences of a corrupt ruler, he nevertheless proved himself a consummate artist in reworking a popular medieval convention.

Michael Torrey's essay, "'The plain devil and dissembling looks': Ambivalent Physiognomy and Shakespeare's *Richard III*" adds yet a further dimension to the issue of bodily disfigurement by pointing out that a degree of indeterminacy in both ancient and medieval writings on the subject. Though modern critics themselves have generally held to the belief that Richard's deformity is a manifestation of a severe character disorder on a personal level or a diseased body politic experiencing the historical trauma of civil war, Torrey investigates a wide variety of treatises that reveal contradictory opinions on whether physical aberrations are a reliable indication of the psyche. Torrey makes the astute observation that even within Shakespeare's *Richard III*, there is no simple way to read his body for, though he is severely disfigured, Richard's intellect is so powerful that others forget this while in the process of being manipulated by him.

Jeremy Lopez's essay presents a compelling discussion of the atypical features of Clarence's murder in act 1, scene 4. Lopez maintains that Shakespeare affords far more attention and time to the circumstances of Clarence's execution—the only one to appear onstage, other than Richard's death in act 5—than either

Raphael Holinshed or St. Thomas More. Lopez also lends his attention to
the fact that the death is rendered entirely in prose. According to Lopez, this
execution scene is enigmatic and replete with temporal inconsistencies and
mutable characterizations, beginning with Clarence's elaborate dream and its
relentless shifts between past, present, and future, from which Clarence awakens
and falls asleep again. This episode is followed by the prolonged execution
during which the murderers first deliberate whether to awaken Clarence and
then discuss their feelings of cowardice, fear, and even guilt for the crime
they are about to commit. Lopez argues that this particular scene functions
somewhat autonomously from the rest of the play in that Richard does not
appear. Lopez discusses at great length the significance of Clarence's dream
with its numerous temporal disjunctions where one event slowly flows into
another, blurring our sense of a sequential ordering of events. Moreover, Lopez
argues that Clarence's reference to "the tempest to my soul" likewise effaces the
boundary lines between the literal and figurative meaning of a tempest. Though
on its metaphoric level, the tempest of the soul signals his troubled conscience
and the judgment he will meet after death, on a literal level it refers directly
to the physical act of drowning as the terrifying sound of the swelling waters
engulf him. In conclusion, Lopez believes that the confusion of time in this
scene must be understood extemporarily, which is to say outside our expectations
of an orderly narrative, as the disruptions are meant to highlight Shakespeare's
concern with political issues and the absolute necessity of restoring order to the
state. To this end, Lopez maintains that Shakespeare violates "the temporal
verisimilitude it simultaneously insist upon, in order to heighten the audience's
sense of anxiety." What makes *Richard III* so unique to Renaissance drama is
the fact that this scene, which is unusual in its inefficiency and inclusion of
garrulous murderers, is located in the genre of the history play, a feature that
Lopez suggests is probably only to be found in Shakespeare.

2000—Michael Torrey. "'The plain devil and dissembling looks': Ambivalent Physiognomy and Shakespeare's *Richard III*"

Micheal Torrey received his Ph.D. from the University of Virginia and
has been an assistant professor at La Salle University. He has contributed articles to *English Literary Renaissance* and reviews to *Shakespeare
Quarterly.*

What does Richard III's deformity mean? In his opening soliloquy, Richard
himself cites his having been "Cheated of feature by dissembling Nature, /
Deform'd, unfinish'ed, sent before my time / Into this breathing world scarce

half made up" as the principal reason for his being "determined to prove a villain."[1] For Anne and Margaret, his deformity is a clear sign that he is odious and wicked: Anne rebukes him as a "foul lump of deformity" (1.2.57), while Margaret declares that "Sin, death, and hell have set their marks on him, / And all their ministers attend on him" (1.3.293–94).[2] Likewise, critics routinely assert that Richard's misshapen body reveals not only his own moral condition but that of the state and the world as well,[3] while for Freud, Richard's deformity represents the origin of his psychological motivation.[4] Beyond these relatively straightforward views, recent critics have also invested Richard's deformity with more subtle theoretical implications. Marjorie Garber connects it to the process by which history is produced, claiming that his "twisted and misshapen body encodes the whole strategy of history as a necessary deforming and *un*forming—with the object of *re*forming—the past" (p. 36).[5] Similarly, Linda Charnes discusses Richard's deformity in relation to historiographical "over-emplotment" and its need to produce cultural symptoms—in particular, monstrous bodies—in the process of confronting historical trauma (in this case, the Wars of the Roses) (pp. 26–28). In a different vein, Ian Frederick Moulton argues that Richard's deformity embodies the "unruly masculinity" that patriarchy inevitably produces: "this unregulated, destructive masculine force," he states, "is personified in the twisted and deformed body of Richard III."[6]

Despite their different inflections, each of the above views assumes that Richard's deformity communicates important truths or ideas to its observers, and at least to some degree each view follows the fundamental assumption of physiognomy, which is that the visible features of the body are important signs to be interpreted. Given how frequently Richard's deformity is interpreted as a meaningful sign, and given that physiognomy represented an available, if not dominant, discourse in the early modern period,[7] we might expect that *Richard III* would have been examined in relation to actual physiognomical theory. Surprisingly, even though both characters and critics assert that Richard's body discloses his inner nature (or other things), the physiognomical assumption implied in such claims has not been explored in detail.[8] Perhaps this is because the issue might at first glance seem simple; after all, according to physiognomy, in order to know a man you had only to look at him closely, and in Richard's case, the truth about him is there for all to see—his crooked back, his misaligned shoulders, and his withered arm identify him as the villain that he proves to be. But complicating any simple correlation between Shakespeare's play and physiognomy is the fact that Richard is a successful deceiver; despite the obvious signs of his wickedness, he repeatedly ensnares his victims, using lies and histrionics to mask his seemingly obvious villainy as he relentlessly pursues the crown. In the course of the play, his body alternately does and does not seem to give him away. At times his victims seem to know what he is, and at other times they do not. Consequently, the play's relationship to physiognomy is more nuanced than we might initially assume. Although Richard's deceptions might at first seem a rejection of physiognomy, a refutation of its assumptions about the signifying capacity of the body, they actually mirror an uncertainty about appearances that physiognomy itself betrays. Richard's construction as a *deformed deceiver*, in other words, reproduces the surprising ambivalence of physiognomical discourse.

II

I say "surprising" because one might not expect to encounter ambivalence in a discourse that promises to reveal the secrets of bodily form and appearance. Without question, both ancient and early modern physiognomical texts confidently proclaim the correspondence between body and soul as the basis of their practice. The pseudo-Aristotelian *Physiognomics*, for example, begins, "Dispositions follow bodily characteristics and are not in themselves unaffected by bodily impulses" and describes instances in which the body affects the soul (drunkenness, illness) and the soul affects the body (love, fear, grief, and pleasure).[9] This assertion of a reciprocal relationship between body and soul persists in early modern physiognomy, as James Ferrand writes in Erotomania (1640) that "all Physiognomy is grounded, as Aristotle saies, on the Sympathy that is betwixt the Body and the Mind,"[10] and the astrologer Arcandam includes a section on physiognomy in his 1592 book because, as he states on that section's title-page, "the maners of the minde do followe the temperature of the bodie."[11] As a result of this correspondence, the body's appearance could be read as the indicator of the soul's condition, and physiognomers could offer their knowledge as a means for discerning the state of others' souls.[12] According to Thomas Hill's *The Contemplation of Mankind* (1571), moreover, one could practice "semiotical medicine" not only because "all the workings and passions of the spirite, appeare to be matched and ioyned with the bodie" (sig. *iiii) but also because "such marueylous differences of countenances, such diuers lineaments of the body" were attributable not to "hap, casualtie, or fortune, but onelye to the great prouidence and will of almight GOD."[13] Since the "outward notes of the bodie," as Hill later puts it, are not the product of accident, physiognomy is clearly "a necessarie and lawdable science, seing by the same a man may so readily pronounce and foretell the natural aptness unto the affections, and conditions in men" (sig. *i^v). Most importantly, though, foretelling the inclinations and conditions of men is eminently desirable because it provides a means of personal security: after reviewing examples of its use among the ancients, Hill writes,

> Seeing this knowledge hath so long time bene obserued and exercised of so excellent and famous men, what shall it let or staye me, not to applye my study and penne thereto, and the rather for that it is lawfull for euery man to decerne, as farre as he can, the qualitie and condicions of the hart: seeing the secret matters

lying deepe in the breast, are many times bewrayde by the outward gestures, what singular co[m]moditie the knowledge of this Arte bringeth with it, may euidently appeare in this, that oftentimes men happening into acquaintances and friendshippes, such as they suppose to be most friendly, most sounde, and most faythfull: for the more part are founde dissemblers, unfaithfull, turnecotes most hurtfull, and most peruerse in their doinges. And without this Arte, a man can not so well detect their falshoode and doings (Epistle, sig. vi^v).

Hill stresses the value of physiognomy as a tool of detection and thus a means of self-protection; with it, one can more easily spot dissemblers, since the wicked intentions of a corrupt soul will inevitably manifest themselves in the body that houses it.

To early modern physiognomers, one of physiognomy's principal benefits lies in its ability to expose liars and discover evil men. Any number of individual features are said to signify wickedness, and the frequent claims that bodies display visible signs of moral corruption seem intended to provide confidence about detecting the vicious nature of others. Ferrand explains that men who have little beards "are for the most part inclined to basenesse, cruelty, and deceitfulnesse," and that if they are lean and have hollow cheeks, "these marks denote [that] man to be of a filthy, lustfull disposition," as well as "Envious, Crafty, and consequently a knave" (sigs. L8–L8v). Similarly, a man with a wrinkled face is a liar; a man with a "lytell vysage and yelowe of colour is a deceyuer, dronken, and euyll"; and a man with "waueryng eyes" and a "lo[w] face" is full of guile, has a "rennynge mynde," and is "untrusty" (*Secreta*, sig. H4v). Other features that disclose untrustworthiness include the way in which the eyes are moved, the color and texture of hair, the thickness and breadth of eyebrows, the shape and color of teeth, and the size of feet.[14] This relentless identification of symptoms of deceitfulness and wickedness indicates how important early modern physiognomers thought their ability to unmask vice was.

Not surprisingly, they also look unfavorably upon deformity. Citing Plotinus, Ferrand states that "whatsoever is Faire and Beautifull, is also Good" and that the Greeks used one word to express both concepts because "the externall beauty of the Body, depend[s] on the Internall Forme" (sigs. L2v–L3). The pseudo-Aristotelian *Physiognomics* associates virtues with visible strength and health while correlating vices with signs of weakness or misproportion.[15] Likewise, Hill identifies proportionality as "a sure note in this Art": "the formes of the members well proportioned, doe denote vertue: but euill fashioned, doe argue an euill conditioned person" (sigs. Ff6v–Ff7). Because ugliness and vice are equated, therefore, the *Secreta* urges the reader to "Beware of hym . . . that is mysshapen" (sig. H4), and it observes, "He [that] hath his brest and backe egall, is a token of honeste. Hye reysed sholdres, is a toke[n] of lytell fydelyte, nought, and sharpe" (sig. I1). Noting that even unlearned commoners are wise enough to spurn "bunch backed, and gogle eyed persons" (sig. *iii^v), Hill affirms that "The crookednesse of the backe, doth innuate the wickednesse of conditions: but an equalitie of the backe, is then a good note" (sig. Bb2v).[16] In a lengthy analysis of the "shoulder points," he elaborates on the significance. of deformity:

> The phisiognomer Cocles uttereth of experience knowne, [that] he sildom saw any person, being crooke. backed, which were of a good nature: but that these hauing the like bearing out, or bunche on the shoulders, were rather trayterous, and verie wicked in their actions. And such (sayth the Phisiognomer) were knowne in his time, to be the founders of all wicked deceites, yea wylie under myners and gropers of the people, and had a deepe retching wyt, and wylie fetches,[17] in wicked actions. So that it seemeth impossible after nature, that such deformed persons shoulde possesse in them laudable actions . . . For which cause, a man ought carefully to beware and take heede, of fellowshipping or keeping company with such infortunate persons, for the abouesayde reason, and worke of nature. For these (sayth the Phisiognomer) are the lyke to be eschewed, as a man of skill would refuse and shunne the company of a person lacking any principall member of the bodye. (sigs. X8v–Y1)

If various bodily traits indicate wickedness and deceitfulness, there can be no more certain sign of evil than deformity. A misaligned body denotes a misaligned soul.

Yet even as it offers such certainties, physiognomy occasionally falters in its pronouncements. Considering the difficulties in drawing conclusions from the pitch of a subject's voice, the *Physiognomics* cautions that "On occasions when the signs are evidently not in agreement with each other but are contradictory, it is better to make no assumption, unless they belong to differences of class, in which some are more reliable than others" (pp. 97–99). Sometimes the moral significance of a trait remains unclear, as when Arcandam states equivocally that an overlarge head is a "playne signe of goodnes *or* of wickednes" (sig. M3, emphasis added). In other instances, a variety of symptoms reveals the same essential temperament, until nearly all signs seem to point in the same direction. Cataloguing the kinds of faces, for example, Arcandam states that a "full and fat face" denotes "a lyar, a deuourer" who is "not very wise," that a "very little" face signifies "naughtiness, craft, flattery," that a "crooked face" shows a "naughty [and] wicked disposition," and that a face "hollow like a valley, more leane than fat . . . signifieth the man to be iniurious, enuious, a her, a riotter, cruell" (sigs. O2v–O3). Similarly, Hill claims that stature reveals numerous characteristics but threads a motif through his list of types: a stature "long, and sufficient upright, and rather leane than fatte" indicates that the person is "sometimes lying, and in many thinges malicious [sic]"; a "long, and sufficient fat" stature shows that he is "lightly unfaythfull, [and] deceytfull," but a "very long, leane, and slender" stature indicates that the person is "often lying" (sig. Ff5v). Whether fat or lean, crooked or little, many faces reveal the untrustworthiness of their owners, just as a long stature, whether fat, lean or slender, indicates a penchant for lying— and again, the texts keep returning to the claim that physiognomy can uncover deceitfulness.

If multiple symptoms sometimes reveal the same basic disposition, however, at other times they reveal contradictory things. The *Secreta* claims that wide nostrils show a man to be slothful, boisterous, and quickly angered (sig. H4v), for instance, while Arcandam claims that they show him to have large testicles and to be "a whoremonger, a traitor, false, audacious, a her, enuious, couetous, a niggard, and but a little fearfull, and of a grosse understanding" (sigs. O3v– O4, O5v). Physiognomical texts, then, are frequently incoherent, primarily because physiognomy has, as Juliana Schiesari puts it, an "ad hoc quality": "its construction through compilation, typical of much Renaissance thought, favors the listing of particulars, no matter how contradictory, over the conceptual rigor of the logic of non-contradiction" (p. 66).

Even more telling than this lack of rigor, however, are the admissions of uncertainty by the authors themselves. Each of them cautions the reader not to rely on only one sign when making a physiognomical diagnosis; as Hill puts it, "a man may not hastily pronounce iudgement, of any one note alone, but [must] gather and marke diligently the testimonies of all the members" (sigs. Ff6–Ff6v).[18] But beyond advocating thoroughness in interpretation, they also admit the possibility of error, even when one considers all the signs together. Hill advises that one "pronounce iudgement . . . not firmely, but coniecturally" (sig. *iii), and he warns that errors can occur not only by considering only one sign but also by mistaking "notes, which sometimes declare the matter rather past," for signs of things "to come," and by giving too much credence to signs on the "hinder part" of the body, which are not as reliable as signs on the "fore part" (sigs. Ff7–Ff7v). More generally, Ferrand recalls that Alcibiades was beautiful but vicious, and Socrates ugly but virtuous (sig. H4v), so the general equation between beauty and virtue does not always hold. Socrates had been wrongly judged by a physiognomer to be lustful, in fact, but according to Ferrand and Hill, he admitted that he was inclined to lust, and therefore the physiognomer was right to judge him so; he was just more virtuous than the physiognomer could have known.[19] Misdiagnoses, physiognomers stress, do not necessarily reveal the diagnostic bankruptcy of physiognomy; instead, they can reveal how the virtuous simply overcome those inclinations to which their temperaments naturally dispose them, inclinations which their physical appearance, if not their actual behavior, shows them to have.[20] The following passage from Hill illustrates how virtue is the physiognomer's best friend, since it can be cited to explain away the physiognomer's seeming misjudgments: "if any hath the notes of a wicked person, [and is] threatened to come unto a miserable end: yet if such wickednesse doth then but little moue him, then may it be coniectured, that such a person hath well maystred his wicked affections: contrarye to others, which (for the more part) happen to come unto cruell torments, or sustaine long imprisonment. And an other example, that if anye hath the notes of an yrefull person, and that anger doth then but little disquiet him: then is it to be thought and fudged, that he hath well repressed and brideled the passions of yre: and eue[n] like iudgement may be giuen, in all others" (sig. Ff6v). The fact that people can overcome impulses to which they appear to be inclined leads Hill to note, at the end of his book, that the physiognomical judgments he has offered in it more readily apply to "the brutish sort," since they are unredeemed and therefore "mooued to follow their sensuall will and appetites" (sig. Hh2).[21] The physiognomers are well aware, then, of the difficulties involved in judging by appearances, so they create a convenient excuse for their failures by qualifying the deterministic implications of their claims. As Ferrand rather sheepishly puts it, he would not have his reader think that "these Physiognomicall signes doe alwaies necessarily discover the Passions and Affections of the mind, but *only for the most part, and Probably*" (sig. L5, emphasis added).

Given that explicitly physiognomical texts betray such ambivalence about the reliability of the "science" they describe, perhaps it is not surprising that both Michel de Montaigne and Francis Bacon also write in equivocal ways about the signifying capacity of the body. In his "Of Physiognomy," for instance, Montaigne, like the physiognomers cited above, considers the problem of Socrates' ugliness: "About Socrates, who was a perfect model in all great qualities, it vexes me that he hit on a body and face so ugly as they say he had, and so incongruous with the beauty of his soul, he who was so madly in love with beauty. Nature did him an injustice. There is nothing more likely than the conformity and relation of the body to the spirit."[22] The contrasting sentiments expressed in these sentences—the belief that body and spirit correspond (although this belief is qualified by the admission that nothing could be "more likely" as opposed to "more certain"), and the vexation and surprise at the "incongruity" and "injustice" of a virtuous man's having been ugly—suggest how conflicted the effort to think physiognomically can be. Montaigne acknowledges a notorious example of the discrepancy between outer appearance and inner character even as he reaches for physiognomy's principal tenet.[23]

Such contradictions, however, soon prove to be part of the very texture of his discussion, as he circles around the question of what can be learned from the body. Ruminating on the issue of ugliness, for instance, he distinguishes between minor unattractiveness and more significant disfigurement and concludes the following about them: "This superficial ugliness, which is very imperious for all that, is less prejudicial to the state of the spirit and not very certain in its effect on men's opinion. The other, which is more properly called deformity, is more substantial and more apt to strike home inwardly. Not every shoe of smooth leather but every well-formed shoe shows the form of the foot within" (p. 810). At first glance his argument seems clear enough: superficial ugliness, by virtue of its superficiality, has little impact on either the person in question or the opinion of others, while more severe deformity alters the soul and by implication reveals that alteration. In the final sentence's metaphor, however, the ambiguity of the "well-formed shoe" confuses the issue, for if by "well-formed" he means "beautiful," then he seems to suggest that the most *attractive* rather than the most ugly body reveals the most about the soul, even though he has just asserted that deformity is "more apt to strike home inwardly." By contrast, if "well-formed shoe" means "shoe that fits very well," then he seems to be arguing, tautologically, that only those bodies that reveal the soul are the bodies that reveal the soul. Either way, he has moved away from his initial point, which was to stress that deformity, the more severe form of ugliness, reveals more about the inner character than minor blemishes do. In seeking to stress how clearly ugliness reveals the soul, then, Montaigne chooses an analogy that simply clouds the picture, as if he were actually uncertain about what he thinks the body reveals.[24]

Such ambivalence persists in the remainder of his discussion. After emphasizing how advantageous beauty can be ("It holds the first place in human relations; it presents itself before the rest, seduces and prepossesses our judgment with great authority and a wondrous impression") and recalling that "the same word in Greek embraces the beautiful and the good" (p. 810), Montaigne turns in a very different direction:

> Yet it seems to me that the cast and formation of the face and those lineaments from which people infer certain inward dispositions and our fortunes to come, are things that do not fall very directly and simply under the heading of beauty and ugliness; any more than every good odor and clear air promises health, or every closeness and stench promises infection, in time of pestilence. Those who accuse the ladies of belying their beauty by their character do not always hit the mark. For in a not too well formed face there may dwell an air of probity and trustworthiness; as, on the contrary, I have sometimes read between two beautiful eyes threats of a malignant and dangerous nature. There are favorable physiognomies; and in a crowd of victorious enemies you will instantly choose, among men unknown to you, one rather than another to whom to surrender and entrust your life; and beauty has no real part in the choice. (pp. 810–11)

Here, considering the revelatory function of beauty and ugliness simply leads Montaigne to dispense with them as categories altogether, given the (explicitly gendered) examples he can cite of how these categories can fail to deliver what they promise.[25] But as the final sentence quoted reveals, to discard beauty and ugliness is not to discard physiognomy; it is simply to acknowledge that

physiognomical decisions will be made along different—and here unspeci-
fied—lines. What is interesting about this conclusion, however, is the urgency
Montaigne supplies it with: the assertion that "favorable physiognomies" do
exist leads him immediately into the life-threatening scenario of being surrounded by "victorious enemies" and having to choose, from among menacing
strangers, the one who will preserve one's life. Beauty may have no part in this
choice, but the choice is crucial nonetheless, and it will follow from what one
can see in the appearance of others, from what one can glean from their physiognomies. Alternately intrigued by but mistrustful of the significance of beauty
and ugliness, Montaigne both would and would not rely on appearances: hence
his ambivalent assertion in the next paragraph that "The face is a weak guarantee; yet it deserves some consideration"; hence his claim that if he "had to whip
the wicked," he would "punish malice more harshly when it was hidden under
a kindly appearance"; and hence his conclusion regarding prognostication from
the qualities of the face—"those are matters that I leave undecided" (p. 811).
Characteristically, he is skeptical of the credulous claim that the body reveals
the soul, but at the same time he would not abandon the proposition completely,
because of its apparent value in moments of crisis.[26]

III

For his part, Francis Bacon also vacillates on the question of physiognomy,
although with a different emphasis. His essay "Of Deformity" not only focuses
on the more specific issue of disfigurement but also approaches it in psychological terms. "Deformed persons," his opening sentence famously states, "are
commonly even with nature: for as nature hath done ill by them, so do they by
nature, being for the most part (as the Scripture saith) *void of natural affection;*
and so they have their revenge of nature."[27] Anticipating Freud, Bacon initially
sees deformity as producing rancor and an incessant desire to seek compensation
for the arbitrary curse that it represents. But he also views deformity physiognomically, adding, "Certainly there is a consent between the body and the
mind, and *where nature erreth in the one, she ventureth in the other: Ubi peccat in
uno, periclitatur in altero*" (p. 191). This last assertion, however, raises the question of exactly how nature might be seen as "venturing" or "running a risk" in
the mind after deforming the body. Presumably he means to suggest that when
the body is poorly formed, the mind is more fully endowed, that deformed
persons are granted uncommon shrewdness as compensation for their disfigurement. But if so, then this proposition places pressure on the word "consent,"
which would have to mean *not* that the body and mind directly correspond, as
we might expect, but rather that they have an inverse relationship, a weak or
inferior body thereby signifying a strong or superior mind. In any case, Bacon
pursues this ambiguity further in the next section of the essay by questioning
the extent to which deformity can be considered a sign of some inner quality:

But because there is in man an election [choice] touching the frame of his mind, and a necessity in the frame of his body, the stars of natural inclination are sometimes obscured by the sun of discipline and virtue. Therefore it is good to consider of deformity, not as a sign, which is more deceivable [deceptive], but as a cause, which seldom faileth of the effect. Whosoever hath anything fixed in his person that doth induce contempt, hath also a perpetual spur in himself to rescue and deliver himself from scorn. Therefore all deformed persons are extreme bold—first, as in their own defence, as being exposed to scorn, but in process of time, by a general habit. Also, it stirreth in them industry, and especially of this kind, to watch and observe the weakness of others, that they may have somewhat to repay" (p. 191).

Like the physiognomers, then, Bacon acknowledges that "necessity" can be overcome by "election," that inclinations signified by the body can be restrained by "virtue" and "discipline"; unlike the physiognomers, however, he responds to this idea by redefining deformity as a cause rather than a sign (which can be "more deceivable"), his notion of the "perpetual spur" thus returning his discussion to the realm of motivation. But in attempting to veer away from physiognomy, he actually does not get very far, for even if deformity is understood as a cause rather than a sign, it remains nonetheless a thoroughly *visible* cause, an obvious symptom of the motives and behavior that he describes. Whether the deformity is a sign or the cause of boldness, industry, and watchfulness, one can still be certain, according to Bacon's argument, that deformed people will be bold, industrious, and watchful.

Yet even as he seems to reaffirm that deformity is a symptom of morally dubious qualities and implies that one should beware of misshapen people, Bacon adds a further wrinkle to his account: "Again, in their superiors, it [deformity] quencheth jealousy towards them, as persons that they think they may at pleasure despise; and it layeth their competitors and emulators asleep, as never believing they should be in possibility of advancement, till they see them in possession. So that upon the matter, in a great wit deformity is an advantage to rising" (p. 191). Here, in contrast to physiognomical doctrine, Bacon describes how deformity *disarms* rather than arouses the suspicions of others; it functions not as a sign of wickedness, nor even of boldness or industry, but instead as a quality which lulls observers into a false sense of security, misleading them into assuming that they can easily "despise" the deformed person as someone incapable of "rising." Physiognomic sign and psychological symptom are thus transformed into a kind of beneficial camouflage, and the certainty that the essay initially provides (deformed people, we can be sure, *will* seek vengeance on nature) gives way to a more doubtful sense that deformity can actually aid rather than hinder a person's advancement (deformed people need not be feared, we sometimes foolishly think, because they are deformed).

Finally, comparing the deformed to eunuchs, Bacon concludes the essay by stating that both types "seek to free themselves from scorn, which must be *either by virtue or malice*. And therefore let it not be marvelled if sometimes they prove excellent persons" (pp. 191–92; emphasis added).[28] By the end of his essay Bacon has thus arrived at an entirely equivocal perspective: he has asserted the "consent" between body and mind yet inverted their relationship; he has described deformity as a physiognomical sign but then redefined it as a psychological cause; most importantly, he has portrayed the deformed as dangerously bold, then as quite possibly excellent, but ultimately as capable of either malice *or* virtue. For Bacon, deformity signifies *something*, but he remains open to the possibility that it can have multiple or even contradictory significance.

For all his ambivalence, however, Bacon is simply akin to Montaigne, to early modern physiognomers, and ultimately to Shakespeare as well. In early modern England contemplation of the body as a visible signifier inevitably produces such ambivalence, if for no other reason than that physical appearance will always fail to yield reliable insights about inner character. Even as physiognomy indulges the fantasy that appearances reveal character, it refrains in its more hesitant moments from promising that they do so absolutely. It claims that people live within a discernible semiotic order,[29] yet it acknowledges that this order can be misinterpreted and can sometimes fail to reveal the hidden truths that it supposedly displays. Yet this ambivalence in turn simply mirrors a broader pattern within early modern culture. As Katharine Eisaman Maus has shown, even though early modern thinkers of all sorts are painfully aware of the unreliability of appearances and the consequent difficulty of gaining access to others' interiors, they conclude that only some appearances are unreliable.[30] Similarly, Maus adds, early modern English culture articulates two fantasies: "one, that selves are obscure, hidden, ineffable; the other, that they are fully manifest or capable of being made fully manifest. These seem to be contradictory notions, but again and again they are voiced together, so that they seem less self-canceling than symbiotically related or mutually constitutive" (pp. 28–29). In similar fashion, physiognomy presupposes that selves are—to the untrained eye at least—obscure, but it offers a body of knowledge that would allegedly make those selves fully manifest. It claims that by analyzing appearances, it can discover the seemingly hidden truths of temperament and moral disposition; yet it also admits that some appearances are misleading. By qualifying its claims about appearances, by admitting the possibility of error, and by using people's virtue and rational self-control as screens to mask its own interpretive failures, physiognomy betrays an inevitable ambivalence, thereby casting doubt upon its promise to decode the semiotics of bodily form.

IV

It is precisely such ambivalence that we can see in *Richard III*'s treatment of deformity and deception. Shakespeare's portrayal of Richard follows the contours of Tudor historiography, which constructed Richard as a deformed villain.[31] His ability to deceive also stems both from this mytho-historical tradition and from a number of influences beyond it. Like his deformity, Richard's dissembling derives from the partisan imaginations of Tudor writers,[32] but as numerous critics have shown, it also reflects not only the stage traditions of the Vice and the Machiavel, but also broader anxieties about theater and rhetoric that troubled early modern England. As a latter-day Vice, a ruthless Machiavel, a histrionic improvisationalist, and a shameless sophist, Richard embodies several ways in which early modern England worried about duplicity.[33] More importantly, though, the confluence of these various traditions in Shakespeare's Richard reflects the dialectic of epistemological optimism and pessimism in early modern culture that Maus identifies and that physiognomy reproduces. By making Richard deformed, Shakespeare optimistically suggests that Richard's self was fully manifest, that his evil was easily known; but by making him a dissembler, Shakespeare pessimistically admits that Richard's self may actually have been obscure and his evil hidden. By combining deformity and deception, Shakespeare sets these two elements of Richard's character against each other; his ability to deceive repeatedly complicates the semiotic status of his deformity. On the one hand, the visible signs of evil on Richard's body make his metaphysical status available for all to see; on the other hand, in deceiving others Richard shows that his deformity sometimes fails to signify his evil to them. In a sense, *Richard III* implicitly asks the question, "What would a Vice (machiavel/usurping actor/shameless sophist), if transplanted into a drama of political history, actually look *like*?" And in keeping with both Tudor tradition and physiognomic logic, the question appears to have an immediate answer in Richard: "He would be deformed, and his deformity would clearly signal his vicious nature."[34] Yet the play goes on to qualify this answer by showing Richard deceiving numerous victims, thereby raising the question of how such an obviously wicked man—that is, a deformed man—could deceive anyone at all.

To see how this contradictory dynamic works, we might first note some of the ways in which Richard's deformity is explicitly referred to as a revelatory sign. Several moments in the first tetralogy call attention to Richard's deformity: Clifford denounces Richard as a "heap of wrath, foul indigested lump, / As crooked in thy manners as thy shape" (*2H6*, 5.1.157–58); King Henry calls him "an indigested and deformed lump" (*3H6*, 5.6.51); and Richard himself says that his deformity makes him "Like to a chaos, or an unlick'd bear-whelp / That carries no impression like the dam" (*3H6*, 3.2.161–62). Similarly, in his speech immediately after he has killed King Henry, Richard asserts that his deformed birth and body not only exclude him from all social bonds but also offer him a determined role which he will energetically embrace:

Indeed 'tis true that Henry told me of,
For I have often heard my mother say

I came into the world with my legs forward.
Had I not reason, think ye, to make haste,
And seek their ruin that usurp'd our right?
The midwife wonder'd and the women cried,
"O, Jesus bless us, he is born with teeth!"
And so I was, which plainly signified
That I should snarl, and bite, and play the dog.
Then since the heavens have shap'd my body so,
Let hell make crook'd my mind to answer it.

    (*3H6*, 5.6.69–79)

Beyond acknowledging that he has been marked as evil, Richard also suggests, with the word "signified," that others may read and interpret his body, that they may see in its crookedness and distorted birth the deformity of his soul. In *Richard III*, Margaret rebukes Richard as an "elvish-mark'd, abortive, rooting hog / . . . that wast seal'd in thy nativity / The slave of Nature, and the son of hell," and as a "bottled spider" (1.3.228–30, 242). Elizabeth refers to him as "that foul bunch-back'd toad" (4.4.81) and later tells him that he cannot marry her daughter "Unless thou couldst put on some other shape, / And not be Richard" (4.4.286–87). We might also note the more general way in which nearly everyone in *Richard III* views Richard with mistrust and suspicion. Since he is designated by his deformity as a dangerous man, most of the other characters respond to him with fear and loathing, and only those such as Buckingham who are actively colluding with him, or who are most deluded about him (Clarence and Hastings, for example) welcome any association with him. When Margaret later refers to him as "hell's black intelligencer" (4.4.71), however, she inadvertently points to the curious inconsistency of his deformity's signifying power. She means to identify Richard as a demonic agent, yet since "intelligencer" means both "one who conveys intelligence or information . . . a bringer of news; a messenger; an informant" and "one employed to obtain secret information, an informer, a spy, a secret agent,"[35] the doubleness of the word suggests how Richard both conceals and reveals his moral status. His deformity conveys information and discloses that he is wicked and has hellish designs; yet as a dissembler, a gatherer and manipulator of secrets, the secret agent of his own political ascension, he also succeeds in masking that wickedness and those hellish designs.

    His success in such deceptions frequently depends upon his ability either to nullify or to alter the signifying capacity of his body—his ability, as he himself puts it, to "clothe [his] naked villainy" (1.3.336) and to dress his deformity in flattering robes. As Marjorie Garber comments, Richard "turns his chaotic physical condition into a rhetorical benefit, suggesting that he can 'change shapes with Proteus for advantages' (*3H6*, 3.2. 192)" (p. 35). Linda Charnes describes how in order to acquire authority, Richard "must combat the play's politics of vision with an alternative strategy, one that negates the ideology of the visual by realigning the significance of his body with an ideology for the *invisible* body" (p. 31).[36] In crucial scenes his deceptions redefine the meaning of his deformity as he bends the semiotic power of his body to his own purposes, making it signify what he wants it to signify.

The seduction of Anne is a case in point. In the course of this scene Richard gradually overcomes Anne's initially hostile resistance to him, resistance that is predicated not only on her awareness of his past murders of her husband and father-in-law but also on her consciousness of his obvious deformity: "Blush, blush, thou foul lump of deformity" (1.2.57). By the end of the scene, however, when she begins to waver, she seems to realize that he is distorting her perceptions of him. When she cannot stab him, she says, "Arise, dissembler" (1.2. 188), indicating that she recognizes but cannot reverse his effect on her; and several lines later, she murmurs, "I would I knew thy heart" (l. 196), suggesting that she dimly perceives, even as she succumbs to him, that she cannot see his true intentions figured in his body but instead must see into his interior. Allowing him to slip his ring onto her finger, she makes physical contact with the body that she seemingly found repulsive when the scene began, and her responses to Richard just before her exit are flirtatious and even tenderly intimate.[37] She exits both charmed and temporarily free of the revulsion toward Richard that she formerly felt. For the moment, at least, his body no longer disgusts her, nor does it represent for her a signal of his villainy.

Equally important is Richard's exultant soliloquy after she exits, for in it he celebrates the realignment of her perception of him which he has just achieved. First he savors the fact that he caught her "in her heart's extremest hate" and yet won her with "no friends to back my suit / But the plain devil and dissembling looks" (1.2.232–42), and this last phrase nicely alludes both to the love-struck glances he bestowed upon her and to the way in which he made his "looks," his bodily appearance itself, dissemble. He then compares himself to her dead husband Edward and marvels that she has transferred her love from Edward, who was "sweet" and "lovely," to himself (1.2.244–50). Gloating, he asks,

And will she yet debase her eyes on me,
That cropp'd the golden prime of this sweet prince,
And made her widow to a woeful bed?
On me, whose all not equals Edward's moiety?
On me, that halts and am misshapen thus?
My dukedom to a beggarly denier,
I do mistake my person all this while!
Upon my life, she finds—although I cannot—
Myself to be a marvellous proper man.

I'll be at charges for a looking-glass,
And entertain a score or two of tailors
To study fashions to adorn my body:
Since I am crept in favour with myself,
I will maintain it with some little cost.
Shine out, fair sun, till I have bought a glass,

. . .

That I may see my shadow as I pass.

    (1.2.251–64, 267–68)

Both the contrast that Richard draws between Edward's appearance and his own, and the surprised delight that he expresses about his seduction of her, emphasize that he has altered her understanding of his deformity. He stresses that she finds him attractive even though he "halts" and is "misshapen" and his "all" does not "equal Edward's moiety." Earlier, when he responded to her lament, "I would I knew thy heart" by saying, "'Tis figured in my tongue" (l. 197), he insisted that his words accurately reflected his true feelings, and the audience could see how his disingenuity masked his actual motives. But here in this soliloquy, he points to an even greater rhetorical power—namely, his ability to make his body "marvellous proper" to Anne rather than an indicator of his evil.[38] His exuberant review of his accomplishment celebrates not only his conquest of her but also the fact that he has prevented an initially hostile reader from correctly interpreting the signs of treachery that are literally standing in front of her.[39]

In disposing of Hastings, Richard again redefines the significance of his body, and he even makes it an asset to his purposes rather than a hindrance. To some extent, of course, Hastings can be seen as deserving what he gets: he is as tainted by the political conflicts as anyone else, and after Richard has ordered his execution, he laments that he has pursued "the momentary grace of mortal men" more than the grace of God (3.5.96–101). The scenes leading up to his death, however, principally stress his inability to interpret the signs of doom that confront him. He fails to appreciate the implications of Stanley's dream and misgivings, the significance of Catesby's sounding him out about Richard's becoming king, and the ominous nature of his encounters with a priest and with the pursuivant whom he saw before his previous trip to the Tower. His impercipience about these omens, however, is less fatal than his misplaced confidence in his ability to interpret Richard's thoughts. Even though he admits to the Council that he does not know Richard's plan for the coronation (3.4.15–20), he blithely says of Richard, "I know he loves me well" (3.4.14); and just before Richard condemns him, he rhapsodizes about the transparency of Richard's visage:

His Grace looks cheerfully and smooth today:
There's some conceit or other likes him well
When that he bids good morrow with such spirit.
I think there's never a man in Christendom
Can lesser hide his love or hate than he,
For by his face straight shall you know his heart.

　　(3.4.48–53)

This emphasis on Hastings' shortcomings as an interpreter serves as an appropriately ironic prelude to his death, which Richard engineers by means of the most obvious sign that Hastings has ignored. Entering the Council chamber clamoring of witchcraft, Richard offers the following "proof." of his enchantment:

Then be your eyes the witness of their evil.
See how I am bewitch'd! Behold, mine arm
Is like a blasted sapling wither'd up!
And this is Edward's wife, that monstrous witch,
Consorted with that harlot, strumpet Shore,
That by their witchcraft thus have marked me.

　　(3.4.67–72)

By ostentatiously calling attention to his deformity (he is presumably waving his withered arm in his onlookers' faces), Richard not only achieves his political end—the elimination of Hastings—but also succeeds, as he did with Anne, in redefining the significance of his deformity. Where it previously signified his dangerousness and evil, he now makes it the mark of his vulnerability to, and victimization by, the conspiratorial actions of others.[40] That he does so just after Hastings, the most uncareful of readers, has claimed to see his heart in his face seems hardly accidental; if for no other reason, Hastings dies because he thinks he knows how to read Richard's appearance when in fact he does not. By redefining his deformity as a symptom of his innocence and merit, moreover, Richard again demonstrates that for the other characters in the play if not for the audience, he can refashion his deformity into a sign of anything but the inward truth about him that it supposedly represents.

Perhaps the most impressive transformation of his deformity's meaning, and certainly the funniest, comes when he and Buckingham slyly suggest that his bodily shape provides justification for his becoming king. Midway through the play Richard instructs Buckingham to circulate the rumor that Edward's children are bastards, and he even encourages Buckingham to suggest that Edward himself was illegitimate (3.5.71–89). To support the latter claim, Richard suggests, Buckingham can assert that Edward's illegitimacy "well

appeared in his lineaments, / Being nothing like the noble Duke, my father"
(3.5.90–91).[41] When Buckingham attempts to persuade the citizens of London
that Richard should be king, however, he takes this idea one step further: as
he later reports to Richard, he not only described to the people how both the
princes and Edward were bastards but also added the following: "Withal, I did
infer your lineaments—/ Being the right idea of your father, / Both in your form
and nobleness of mind" (3.7.12–14, emphasis added). Although the assertion that
Richard resembles his father seems too absurd to be spoken publicly, let alone
put forward as part of Richard's claim to the throne, Buckingham does not stop
there. Standing with the Lord Mayor and citizens and beseeching Richard to
accept the crown, he says,

> The noble isle doth want her proper limbs;
> Her face defac'd with scars of infamy,
> Her royal stock graft with ignoble plants,
> And almost shoulder'd in the swallowing gulf
> Of dark forgetfulness and deep oblivion;
> Which to recure, we heartily solicit
> Your gracious self to take on you the charge
> And kingly government of this your land . . .
>
>   (3.7.124–31)

In claiming that England will remain deformed until Richard becomes king,
Buckingham apparently cannot resist the puns on "proper limbs," "defac'd," and
"shoulder'd." Not to be outdone, Richard himself says, when he finally assents
to being king,

> Cousin of Buckingham, and sage grave men,
> Since you will buckle fortune on my back
> To bear her burden whe'er I will or no,
> I must have patience to endure the load
>
>   (3.7.226–29).

Critics have long commented on Richard's abilities as a "diabolic humorist,"[42]
and the play is certainly sprinkled with Richard's subtle jokes,[43] but this playing upon his deformity is outrageous, even for him. More surprising is the fact
that he would call attention to his deformity at all in this situation, since it is an
obvious sign that he should not become king.[44] But as we have seen, Richard
does not let the physiognomical significance of his deformity hinder him, and
it is in keeping with his manipulations of his body's significance, as well as with
his sardonic sense of humor, that he and Buckingham should turn his appearance into an argument in favor of his rule.[45]

At such crucial moments Richard succeeds in making his body signify something other than what it presumably does, and in doing so, he reproduces the epistemological ambivalence of physiognomy. As I have argued, in its most confident mode physiognomy asserts that appearances tell all, but at other times it confesses that they do not always do so. Likewise, Richard roves throughout the world of his play with the marks of his metaphysical status written all over him, yet through his duplicity, he sometimes demonstrates that for some of his fellow characters, if not for the audience, the significance of his appearance is manipulable, and therefore less than absolutely certain. The audience is never uncertain about what Richard is and what he represents, but the audience does see that some characters are uncertain about him, that his appearance fails to signify as consistently for these characters as it does for them. Watching such characters be deceived, the audience sees physiognomy fail, and in seeing it fail, the audience is consequently encouraged to ask whether physical appearances really reveal anything at all.

V

They are encouraged to ask this question because the play implicitly asks it not only of Richard's appearance but of the appearances of other characters as well. When Hastings is condemned, for instance, the text of the play does not clearly indicate how the men present in the Council chamber actually respond to Richard's ploy; it offers no stage directions about how they should conduct themselves as they leave. An audience will wonder whether those present actually believe what Richard says about his arm, or whether they recognize his claim to be a fatuous charge trumped up to eliminate Hastings. We can easily imagine that actors playing the Bishop of Ely, Stanley, Norfolk, and the rest would glance nervously but knowingly at each other, indicating that they understand exactly what has happened but fear retribution should they speak out against it. But the playtext lacks the definitive description of their states of mind that a prose narrative like Thomas More's *History of King Richard III* can provide. About Hastings's arrest, More writes: "And thereupon every man's mind sore misgave them, *well perceiving that this matter was but a quarrel*, for well they wist that the queen was too wise to go about any such folly. And also, if she would, yet would she, of all folk, least make Shore's wife of counsel, whom of all women she most hated, as that concubine whom the king, her husband, had most loved. *And also no man was there present but well knew that his arm was ever such since birth.*"[46] More's account not only exposes the preposterous nature of Richard's allegations about witchcraft, but also indicates that everyone knew that Richard's arm had always been malformed. Shakespeare's text, however, is not nearly so clear, even though he could have given any one of the lords an exit line which explains that he has not been fooled for one moment. But Shakespeare does not do so; instead, he keeps all the lords silent on the question of Richard's ruse, and consequently the audience can look to nothing other than the lords' appearances in trying to discern what the lords actually think. If the lords understand that Richard's claim is bogus, then they apparently understand as well that they cannot say that it is bogus. If they do not understand that it is bogus, then they must think that Richard's withered arm signals his victimization rather than his evil. But either way, the audience can only try to guess what they are thinking based on how they look, because unlike More's *History*, the play gives its audience only appearances to go on.

As it is with these lords, so it is with the citizens of London. In Act 3, scene 7, the stage again holds a group of silent people watching one of Richard's bogus performances. As Buckingham woos Richard into "accepting" the crown, the crowd of citizens—who did not respond to Buckingham's previous orations on Richard's behalf (3.7.24–41)—look on but say nothing until at the end of the scene, when the usurpation is a foregone conclusion, they offer an ambiguous "Amen" (l. 240). As Anne Righter points out, the text of Shakespeare's play "gives no indication whatsoever" if the citizens' response is sincere or simply the product of intimidation, but the scene does seem to fit Stephen Greenblatt's definition of power as "the ability to impose one's fictions upon the world."[47] Greenblatt adds that "the point" of a performance like Richard's and Buckingham's "is not that anyone is deceived by the charade, but that everyone is forced either to participate in it or to watch it silently" (p. 13). Both he and Righter refer in making their claims to the same famous passage in More's *History*:

> But much [the people] talked and marvelled of the manner of this dealing; that the matter was on both parts made so strange, as though neither had ever communed with other thereof before, when that themself well wist *there was no man so dull that heard them but he perceived well enough that all the matter was made between them.* Howbeit, some excused that again and said all must be done in good order though. *And men must sometime for the manner sake not be aknowen what they know.* For at the consecration of a bishop, every man woteth well, by the paying for his bulls, that he purposeth to be one, and though he pay for nothing else. And yet must he be twice asked whether he will be bishop or no, and he must twice say nay, and at the third time take it as compelled therunto by his own will. And in a stage play all the people know right well that he that playeth the sowdaine [sultan] is percase a sowter [shoemaker]. Yet if one should can so little good [be so foolish as] to show out of season what acquaintance he hath with him and call him by his own name while he standeth in his majesty, one of his tormenters might hap to break his head, and worthy, for marring of the play. And so they said that these matters be kings' games, as it were, stage plays, and for the more part played upon scaffolds, in which poor men be but the lookers-on. And they that wise be will meddle no farther. For they that

sometime step up and play with them, when they cannot play their parts, they disorder the play and do themself no good. (pp. 82–83, emphasis added)

Writing a prose narrative, More can omnisciently tell the reader what an entire group of people actually perceive and think. Writing a play, by contrast, Shakespeare chooses to leave them virtually silent and in doing so leaves the audience uncertain as to whether they can see through the charade that Richard offers them. On stage, they are simply a host of blank faces and silent bodies which may or may not tell the audience what thoughts he behind them; and where More describes the people's response to this fatuous but intimidating piece of political theater, Shakespeare does not clearly indicate what the onstage audience thinks about Richard and Buckingham's performances. Again, he could easily make this matter absolutely clear—he could give the crowd voices beyond their simple "Amen," as he does in Act 2, scene 3 when the three Citizens speak, the Third Citizen describing clear signs of trouble—but here he does not do so. Instead he fills the stage with bodies that, in this instance at least, signify nothing.[48]

If the lords in Act 3, scene 4 and the citizens in Act 3, scene 7 remain frustratingly silent, however, the Scrivener does tell the audience exactly what he knows and thinks. Yet his candor about Richard's duplicity simply transfers the problem of appearances back into the world of the play. Holding the indictment of Hastings in his hand, he says,

Here's a good world the while! Who is so gross
That cannot see this palpable device?
Yet who's so bold but says he sees it not?
Bad is the world, and all will come to naught
When such ill-dealing must be seen in thought.

    (3.6.10–14)

Since the knowledge that he possesses could prove fatal if revealed, he implies, he must remain silent and must "see" only in "thought"—a phrase that uncannily recalls More's observation, "men must sometime for the manner sake not be aknowen what they know." The Scrivener talks to the audience about how he cannot talk about what he knows, and since he cannot divulge that he recognizes the "palpable device" for what it is, he will henceforth take refuge in silence, thereby making himself inscrutable to others.[49] Unlike the lords in Act 3, scene 4 and the citizens in Act 3, scene 7, the Scrivener tells the audience that Richard's deceit has not fooled him, yet he also reveals that when he reenters the offstage world of the play, his thoughts, like those of the lords and citizens, will be veiled behind his appearance. His allusion to his enforced silence, coupled with the silence of the lords and the citizens, seems designed to show how knowing the thoughts of others quickly devolves into an exercise in guessing by appearances. Others, the Scrivener implies, may see through Richard's "palpable device" as easily as he has, but they will not say that they do, just as he will not, and their insight will remain hidden behind their blank faces and within their inscrutable bodies. Likewise, although the audience can know how the Scrivener has responded to one of Richard's deceptions, with the lords and the citizens, the audience can only guess what they are thinking by scrutinizing their appearances, which may or may not reveal anything, just as whoever subsequently encounters the Scrivener will have to guess at what he thinks, based on his impenetrable appearance. Thus the guessing by appearances will necessarily continue, even though, as the physiognomers admit and Richard shows, appearances can make such guessing quite difficult.

But this pattern of guessing is just one of the ways that the play calls attention—as physiognomy does—to the vexed relationship between outward appearances and inward reality, between surfaces and interiors. By reproducing the tradition of Richard's deformity and its implications, by incorporating various influences that highlight the problem of deception, by showing Richard manipulating the significance of his deformity, and by withholding from the audience the very information that a chronicler like More makes available to his reader, *Richard III* takes up the question of what surfaces can reveal about depths; and as the physiognomers do, it ultimately offers an ambivalent answer. Because of his deformity, Richard is often assumed to be the villain that he is, yet because of his deceptions, he can either render his deformity temporarily irrelevant or use it to his advantage. Likewise, his ability to mask his malicious motives corresponds to the indeterminate silence of various subjects who appear onstage, because in both cases, the body communicates nothing about the interior that it contains. The process that the play represents, whereby Richard's presumably significant deformity is shown to be at best an inconsistent sign of his wickedness, is in fact remarkably similar to what Devon Hodges has demonstrated about Renaissance efforts at anatomy: "the procedure of delving into forms," she writes, "collapses distinctions as depths are turned into ever more surfaces."[50] If anatomists, as she argues, are ultimately frustrated in their attempts to uncover unseen truths hidden beneath surfaces, so too are physiognomists stymied in their efforts to discern with certainty such truths in those surfaces themselves. Likewise, as Richard's deceptions and deformity work at cross purposes, the former concealing and the latter revealing who and what he is, Shakespeare's *Richard III* at once indulges and frustrates the desire that animates physiognomy: the desire for a world in which appearances signify reliably, in which surfaces illuminate depths, in which moral truths are visible and obvious—the desire for a world that has never existed.

NOTES
I would like to thank the audiences at the 1998 Group for Early Modern Cultural Studies and 1999 International Congress on Medieval Studies for their

helpful responses to versions of this essay. I am also indebted to Patricia Haberstroh, Linda Merians, and Katharine Maus for their generous comments on the full manuscript.

1. *King Richard III*, ed. Antony Hammond (London and NY, 1981) 1.1.19–21, 30. Quotations from all other plays are taken from *The Riverside Shakespeare*, ed. G. Blakemore Evans (Boston, 1974).

2. Margaret has previously expressed the idea that deformity is a sign of predetermined villainy: in *The Third Part of Henry VI*, she calls Richard "a foul misshapen stigmatic, / Mark d by the destinies to be avoided" (*3H6* 2.2.136–37). Since "stigmatic" can mean both "A person marked with some physical deformity or blemish" and "A person branded as a criminal; a profligate, [a] villain" (*OED*, B. sb. 1 and 2), Margaret's words link Richard's wickedness to his deformity. She sees the second definition of "stigmatic" as being implied by the first: "a person marked with some physical deformity" will indisputably be "a person branded as a criminal . . . [a] villain."

3. In *Shakespeare's Ghost Writers: Literature as Uncanny Causality* (New York, 1987), Marjorie Garber notes that Shakespeare's portrayal of Richard is "often viewed as a consequence . . . of the move by Tudor historians to classify Richard III as self-evidently a villain, his deformed body a readable text" (p. 30). Linda Charnes similarly points out that "Shakespeare's audience would immediately have recognized Richard's physical deformity and moral depravity as a synecdoche for the state," since in early modern England "[t]he body was one signifier in an elaborate network of signification in which God's 'signature' could be read in the physical world." See *Notorious Identity: Materializing the Subject in Shakespeare* (Cambridge, Mass., 1993) pp. 30, 22. For similar comments, see Peggy Endel, "Profane Icon: The Throne Scene of Shakespeare's *Richard III*," *Comparative Drama* 20 (Summer 1986), 120; Maurice Hunt, "Ordering Disorder in *Richard III*," *South Central Review* 6 (Winter 1989), 13; Richard Marienstras, "Of a Monstrous Body," *French Essays on Shakespeare and His Contemporaries: "What would France with us?"* ed. Jean-Marie Maguin and Michele Willems (Newark and London, 1995), pp. 159–60; and Moody E. Prior, *The Drama of Power* (Evanston, 1973), p. 301.

Behind such observations lies the idea of correspondence between macrocosm and microcosm, which requires that Richard's individual deformity be seen as the symptom of a larger disorder. As Leonard Barkan has shown in *Nature's Work of Art: The Human Body as Image of the World* (New Haven, 1975), analogies between the human body and the cosmos, and more particularly the human body and the state, have ancient origins (p. 61). Richard's deformity thus provides a local habitation for all that is wrong in Richard, in England, and in the cosmos; and critics' emphasis upon it has illuminated the effort, in both Shakespeare and Tudor historiography, to condense larger disruption into the visible body of a single figure.

4. Freud famously includes Richard III in his discussion of "The Exceptions," people who consider themselves excused, because of previous suffering, from the need to forego certain pleasures. He also insists that Richard is "an enormous magnification of something we find in ourselves," since "we all demand reparation for early wounds to our narcissism, our self-love" (p. 315). In this view Richard's deformity becomes a sign of "universal" inadequacy and the rancor that it produces. See "Some Character-Types Met with in Psycho-Analytic Work," *The Standard Edition of the Complete Psychological Works of Sigmund Freud*, trans. James Strachey,

24 vols., XIV, 309–33. For comments on Freud's view of Richard, see Garber, *Shakespeare's Ghost Writers*, p. 33. For similarly psychological interpretations of Richard's deformity, see Hunt, p. 11, and Janet Adelman, *Suffocating Mothers: Fantasies of Maternal Origins in Shakespeare's Plays* (New York and London, 1992), p. 2.

5. Garber's chapter on *Richard III* examines the connection between deformity and the production of history, and sees "Richard III—and *Richard III*—as the dramatization of the power of deformity in both tragedy and history" (p. 51).

6. Ian Frederick Moulton, "'A Monster Great Deformed': The Unruly Masculinity of Richard III," *Shakespeare Quarterly* 47.3 (1996), 258. Moulton later adds, "The alienation of Richard's masculinity from the patriarchal order that ought to channel its energies gives his physical deformity significance; indeed it is only after his father's death that he begins to lament his condition and to devise various explanations and genealogies for it (*3HVI*, 3.2.146–95; 5.6.68–83)," p. 262.

7. In *The Third volume of Chronicles, beginning at duke William the Norman* (1587), Holinshed may have prompted Shakespeare to view Richard III in a physiognomical light. Holinshed reproduces much of Thomas More's *History of King Richard III*, including the following passage, but added to More's description of Richard the final sentence below (which I have italicized): "Richard the third sonne [of Richard, Duke of York], of whome we now intreat, was in wit and courage equall with either of them, in bodie and prowesse farre under them both, litle of stature, ill featured of limmes, crooke backed, his left shoulder much higher than his right, hard fauoured of visage, and sich as is in states called warlie, in other men otherwise; he was malicious, wrathfull, enuious, and from afore his birth euer froward. It is for truth reported, that the duchesse his mother had so much adoo in hit trauell, that she could not be deliuered of him uncut; and that he carne into the world with the feet forward, as men be borne outward, and (as the fame runneth also) not untoothed, whether men of hatred report aboue the truth, or else that nature changed his course in his beginning, which in the course of his life manie things unnaturallie committed. *So that the full confluence of these qualities, with the defects of fauour and amiable proportion, gaue proofe to this rule of physiognomie: Distortum vultum sequitur distorsio morum*" (p. 712). As Hammond points out, "There is no doubt whatever that Shakespeare knew Holinshed, in the edition of 1587" (p. 79), so if Shakespeare read this section of Holinshed, he would have encountered not only More's description of Richard's birth and deformity, but also the allusion to physiognomy that it elicited from Holinshed.

8. Carroll Camden provides an overview of physiognomy in the early modern period and describes how it was viewed by various Elizabethan writers and dramatists, including Shakespeare, although he does not discuss *Richard III*. "The Mind's Construction in the Face," *Renaissance Studies in Honor of Hardin Craig*, ed. Baldwin Maxwell, et al. (Stanford, n.d.) pp. 208–20. Critics routinely assign significance to Richard's deformity, but they have not specifically connected Shakespeare's representation of it to physiognomy. Charnes is an exception, mentioning physiognomy several times (pp. 31, 53, 64n) and analyzing at great length the ideological function of deformity in the construction of Richard's subjectivity, but she does not examine specific physiognomic texts, nor does she analyze the peculiar ambivalence of physiognomical discourse. Similarly, Marie A. Plasse illuminates "the play's characteristic mode of representing in corporeal images and references Richard's impressive power over people and events" (p. 11) and even

discusses how Richard works as "a self-conscious manipulator of corporeal signs" (pp. 14ff.), but she does not place her analysis of "corporeality" within the context of physiognomy. See "Corporeality and the Opening of *Richard III*," *Entering the Maze: Shakespeare's Art of Beginning*, ed. Robert P. Willson, Jr. (New York, 1995) pp. 11–25.

9. Aristotle, *Physiognomics, Minor Works*, trans. W. S. Hat, Loeb Classical Library, 1936 (Cambridge, Mass., 1955), p. 85. Aristotle was often claimed to be the originator of physiognomy, but he is no longer thought to be the author of the *Physiognomics*. For the history of physiognomy in the medieval and early modern periods, see Lynn Thorndike, *A History of Magic and Experimental Science*, 8 vols. (New York, 1923–1958) IV, 190–07; V, 50–68; and VIII, 448–75; Graeme Tytler, *Physiognomy in the European Novel: Faces and Fortunes* (Princeton, 1982), pp. 35–48; J. B. Bamborough, *The Little World of Man* (London, 1952), pp. 30–31, 129–32, 134–40; and Camden.

10. James Ferrand, *Erotomania, or A Treatise Discoursing of the Essence, Causes, Symptomes, Prognosticks, and Cure of Love, or Erotique Melancholy*, trans. Edmund Chilmead (1640) sig. L4v. According to Bamborough's bibliography, the first French edition of this book was published in 1612.

11. Arcandam, The most excellent, *Profitable and pleasant book, of the famous Doctor and expert Astrologian Arcandam or Aleandrin . . . With an addition of Phisiognomy, very pleasant to reade*, trans. William Warde (1592).

12. In its chapter "Of the physonomy of people," the *Secreta Secretorum* calls physiognomy "a noble and meruaylous scye[n]ce . . . by the which thou shalt knowe the nature and condycyo[n] of people." Aristotle, *Secreta Secretorum* (1528; New York, 1970) sig. H3v. This book was also wrongly attributed to Aristotle throughout the medieval and early modern period.

13. Thomas Hill, *The Contemplation of Mankinde*, contayning a singuler discourse after the *Art of Phisiognomie* (1571). (The second quotation is taken from the Epistle to Thomas, Duke of Norfolk [sigs. 9 iii–v]; the pages of this section are out of order.) Hill's book is a translation of Bartolommeo della Rocca's (known as "Cocles") *Anastasis*, which enjoyed a "considerable vogue" in the sixteenth century, according to Thorndike, being both reprinted numerous times and translated into Italian, French, and English. See Thorndike, V, 63–65.

14. For examples of such symptoms of wickedness, see Hill, sigs. Ee4–v and Ee7, Arcandam, sigs. M8v, N1, and N3–N3v, Hill, sig. R7–R7v, and Arcandam, sig. P8.

15. A brave man, for example, is said to have "an erect carriage of body," broad shoulders, and "bones, sides and extremities of the body strong and large" (p. 99); a gentle man will have an upright figure (p. 103) and men "whose shoulders and shoulder-blades are well-articulated have strong characters" (p. 119). By contrast, the "marks of a shameless man" will include "shoulders raised high" and a figure "not erect but incline[d] to stoop forward" (p. 101); a "low-spirited man" will be "stooping in figure and feeble in his movements" (pp. 101–03); and "Ill-proportioned men are scoundrels" (p. 135). In addition to correlating virtues and vices with physiognomy, the *Physiognomics* also differentiates between genders, praising the male body and its assumed superiority while contrasting it to the weaker, poorly proportioned female body and the vices that it reveals; see pp. 109 ff. For a discussion of similar contrasts between male and female bodies, and the misogyny they express in Giovan Battista Della Porta's *Della fisionomia dell'uomo* (1610), see

Juliana Schiesari, "The Face of Domestication: Physiognomy, Gender Politics, and Humanism's Others," *Women, "Race," and Writing in the Early Modern Period*, ed. Margo Hendricks and Patricia Parker (New York, 1994), pp. 59–63.

16. He qualifies this assertion slightly when, just below, he states, "The back bone crooked, if the same be couered with soft fleshe, and slender in the gyrting place: doth denote such a person, to excell in naturall giftes, and to haue verie great pleasure in hunting. Yet some affirme, that the crookednesse of the backe, to declare the wickednesse of conditions" (sigs. Bb2v–Bb3). "Innuate" means "to intimate, hint," although the *OED* notes that it may also be a misprint for "insinuate."

17. "Retching" means "capable of stretching" (*OED* ppl. a [f. retch v. 1]); a "fetch" is "a contrivance, dodge, stratagem, trick" (*OED* sb. 1).

18. For similar statements, see Ferrand, sig. L5; Arcandam, sigs. N1–N1v; *Secreta*, sig. I1v; and *Physiognomics* 95. The *Physiognomics* considers at length the problems involved in determining which signs can be considered reliable data for analysis; not all facial expressions are reliable, for instance, nor are all comparisons with animals helpful, and though some signs may be permanent, others may "come and go." Consequently, a list of acceptable signs is offered in an attempt to limit physiognomical data to a manageable amount; see pp. 87–93. For an account of Della Porta's similar efforts to define what constitutes reliable data, see Schiesari, pp. 65–66.

19. See Ferrand, sigs. L4–L4v; and Hill, *Preface*, sig. 99iiii–iiii^v. They give different names to the physiognomer in question, but their stories are essentially the same.

20. Hill and the *Secreta* recount the same story about Hippocrates which provides an excuse for inaccurate judgments and thus illustrates this point. As Hill puts it, Hippocrates "by his face was iudged wicked, yet thorow Philosophic [was] knowne to be well conditioned" (sig. *iv), and later he describes the misjudgment of Hippocrates in more detail (Preface, sig. iii^v–iiii). The *Secreta*, however, includes a more elaborate narrative concerning the physiognomical incompetence that Hippocrates ("ypocras") inspired. It describes the misadventures of Physonomyas, who it claims was the founder of physiognomy, as follows:

> In the tyme of the sayde Physonomyas reygned the moost wyse physycye[n] ypocras. And because the fame of physonomyas and his wysdome was so gretely spreddde, the dyscyples and seruauntes of ypocras toke his fygure secretly, and bare it to Physonomyas to here how he woude Juge and say by [the] sayd fygure of ypocras. And bade hym say and tel the qualyte therof. Whan Physonomyas had well beholden it, he sayd, This man is a wrangler lecherous and rude. This herynge the dyscyples of ypocras, they woulde haue slayne Physonomyas, and sayd to him, Aa fole this is the fygure of the best man of the worlde. Wha[n] Physononomyas sawe them thus moeued, he appeased them the best waye that he coude with fayre wordes saynge, I knowe well that this is the fygure of the wyse ma[n] ypocras. And I haue shewed you by scyence as I knowe. Whan the dyscyples were come to ypocras they tolde hym what Physonomyas had sayd. And ypocras sayd, Truely Physonomyas hath tolde you the trouthe, and hath left nothynge of my complexyon in the whiche ben all my vyces. But reason that is in me ouercometh and ruleth the vyces of my complexyon. (sigs. H3v–H4)

Aside from offering a worst-case scenario of the occupational hazards of physiognomy, then, the *Secreta* explains how physiognomical judgments can be right, even when they are, as it were, absolutely wrong.

21. Similarly, although not a physiognomer, Thomas Wright claims that "it cannot be doubted of, but that the passions of our minder worke diuers effects in our faces" (p. 26), and that "wise men often, thorow the windowes of the face, behold the secrets of the heart" (p. 27). He also notes, however, that the process of analyzing bodily appearances is inevitably speculative. Everyone, he writes, "may discouer his fellowes naturall inclinations, not by philosophicall demonstrations, but onely by naturall coniectures and probabilities, because that wise men mortifie their passions, and craftie men dissemble: yet we may for the most part attaine vnto the knowledge of them, for that most men follow the instinct of Nature, and few, either the precepts of reason, or exquisite craftinesse, by which two meanes passions are concealed" (pp. 104–05). Wisdom and dissembling can complicate the assessment of others, and if more people were rational and wise, or if more were adept at dissembling, knowing their inclinations would be impossible. Since most people are governed by their inclinations, however—since most are of "the brutish sort"—their temperaments can be discerned, if only, as Wright then cautions, by "some effects and externall operations," by their words and deeds (p. 105). *The Passions of the Minde in Generall* (1604), ed. Thomas O. Sloan (Urbana, 1970.

For a recent discussion of physiognomy's ability to acknowledge discrepancies between the implications of appearance and the reality of character and conduct, see K. J. H. Berland, "The Marks of Character: Physiology and Physiognomy in Absalom and Achitophel, " *Philological Quarterly* 76.2 (1997), 193–218.

22. *The Complete Essays of Montaigne*, ed. Donald Frame (Stanford, 1957), p. 809.

23. For a discussion of how Socrates functions as the "pivot" of Montaigne's essay, his ugly form providing the "organizing figure and metaphor" of Montaigne's exploration of the uncertainties of physiognomy, see Raymond C. La Charité, "'Of Physiognomy': The Staging and Reading of Facial Narrative," in *Approaches to Teaching Montaigne's Essays*, ed. Patrick Henry (New York, 1994), pp. 166–67 and 170–71.

24. His uncertainty may derive, however, from his highly attuned sense of irony. Immediately after his metaphor of the "well-formed shoe," he writes, "So Socrates said of his ugliness that it betrayed what would have been just as much ugliness in his soul, if he had not corrected it by training. But in saying this I hold that he was jesting according to his wont. So excellent a soul was never self-made" (p. 810). Unlike the physiognomers, then, Montaigne does not accept at face value Socrates' claim to have disciplined his own vices, apparently because he assumes that the soul is divinely made rather than self-fashioned. But if he sees Socrates' response as an ironic joke, he also seems to see the irony of the physiognomers' penchant for attributing the fallibility of their judgments to the virtue of the person analyzed. The physiognomers did not realize, Montaigne implies, that Socrates was poking fun at them, and Socrates poked fun at them because they had no sense of irony, because in their programmatic attempts to read bodies they had no ability to discern that "Not every shoe of smooth leather but every well-formed shoe shows the form of the foot within." It is this irony—that some bodies may reveal much more than other bodies do—which Montaigne seems to discover as he ponders the problem of Socrates' ugliness, and this irony breeds the uncertainty

that Montaigne's essay, like the physiognomical texts but with far more self-consciousness, ultimately betrays.

25. As La Charité points out, "Of physiognomy" presents a whole series of faces to consider, a "gallery of portraits" which serves, among other things, as "a reminder that the 'art' of physical and moral portraiture is neither simple nor easy to pin down" and as "a way of blurring and ultimately jettisoning the beauty/ugliness pattern that the critical discourse has been deconstructing all along" (p. 169).

26. The extent to which Montaigne associates physiognomical analysis with danger and crisis can be seen in the two stories about himself which he recounts in the final section of his essay, just after the passage discussed above. In the first story a man who covets Montaigne's house concocts a scheme by which he and his soldiers can gain entry into it, in order to take it by force. Arriving in a series of groups, they claim to have been attacked on the road, and although Montaigne's suspicions are gradually aroused, he grants them entry, until a large force occupies the house and he is at their merry. At the moment when the ringleader can execute his plan, however, he refrains from doing so because, as Montaigne puts it, "my face and my frankness had disarmed him of his treachery" (pp. 812–13). In the second story Montaigne is taken prisoner by a large force of "masked gentlemen" after having ventured forth during a truce. These men initially take his possessions, scatter his servants, set his ransom at an exorbitant price, and begin to spirit him away. Suddenly their leader returns his money and belongings to him, sets him free, and tells him that he owes his liberty to his face and to the "freedom and firmness" of his speech (pp. 813–14). About these incidents, Montaigne then concludes, "If my face did not answer for me, if people did not read in my eyes and my voice the innocence of my intentions, I would not have lasted so long without quarrel and without harm, considering my indiscreet freedom in saying, right or wrong, whatever comes into my head, and in judging things rashly" (p. 814). His point in telling these stories is to show that "It has often happened that on the mere credit of my presence and manner, persons who had no knowledge of me have placed great trust in me, both for their own affairs and for mine" (pp. 811–12), and together the stories reassert, despite the shortcomings of physiognomy that he has pondered, the idea that at least *something* of the soul can be seen in the body, particularly (or if only) in moments of great pressure and risk. Beauty and ugliness may not ordinarily tell the observer what he needs to know, Montaigne seems to suggest, but in a crisis, the true spirit will shine through so that one can see in others—or others can see in one—the character that will determine one's choices. La Charité notes, however, that even in these two stories, hesitancy and uncertainty can be seen, both in the men who study Montaigne's face and in Montaigne's accounts of the incidents (pp. 171–72). Ambivalence thus remains an important element of Montaigne's physiognomical discourse, even in anecdotes designed to validate the legitimacy of at least some analyses of appearance.

27. Bacon, "Of Deformity," *The Essays*, ed. John Pitcher (New York, 1985), p. 191.

28. Interestingly, Thorndike notes that Michael Savonarola, in his *Mirror of Physiognomy*, similarly states that he "has found that many hunchbacks possess great intellectual ingenuity and astuteness" (IV, 197). For a discussion of Savonarola's text, see IV, 190–96.

29. In his study of French novelists influenced by Lavater and other physiognomists, Christopher Rivers states that "these authors seem to take as their most fundamental agenda the denial of the arbitrary nature of human existence" (p. 6). His comment, coupled with his later statement that in physiognomical thought "the body always serv[es] as an index to some fundamental, innate truth which orders and explains an individual" (p. 9), indicates how physiognomy attempts to impose a visible order on the chaotic variety of bodily forms. Christopher Rivers, *Face Value: Physiognomical Thought and the Legible Body in Marivaux, Lavater, Balzac, Gautier, and Zola* (Madison, 1994).

30. Katharine Eisaman Maus, *Inwardness and Theater in the English Renaissance* (Chicago, 1995), p. 8.

31. Shakespeare drew upon a variety of sources in writing *Richard III*, ranging from Ovid and Seneca to Marlowe and Spenser, as Antony Hammond discusses in his Arden introduction (pp. 73–97). In characterizing Richard, however, Shakespeare was more particularly influenced by the traditions that Tudor historians and chroniclers had produced, traditions which had, as modern historians have shown, a tenuous relationship to fact. Little evidence survives to suggest that Richard was actually deformed, and in *Shakespeare's English Kings: History, Chronicle, and Drama* (New York, 1977). Peter Saccio notes that "the fact that [Richard] permitted himself to be stripped to the waist for anointing at his own coronation suggests that his torso could bear public inspection" (p. 159). According to A. R. Myers, however, stories of Richard's deformity "appear almost as soon as Richard was dead," starting with John Rous' *Historia Regum Anglie* (1489–1491) ("Richard III and Historical Tradition," *History* 53 [1968], 183). For discussion of how accounts of his deformity often conflict, see Hugh M. Richmond, *King Richard III* (New York, 1989), and Marjorie Garber, pp. 31, 35. Regarding the development of the tradition concerning Richard, see Myers; Alison Hanham, *Richard III and his Early Historians 1483–1335* (Oxford, 1975); Charles Ross, "The Historical Reputation of Richard III: Fact and Fiction," *Richard III* (Berkeley and Los Angeles, 1981), pp. xix–liii; Hammond, Introduction, pp. 74–80; and Judith H. Anderson, *Biographical Truth: The Representation of Historical Persons in Tudor-Stuart Writing* (New Haven, 1984), pp. 110–23.

32. Richard's alleged penchant for dissembling appears to be a fabrication of Tudor historiography. According to Charles Ross, Polydore Vergil first described how Richard hid his malicious motives behind a fair facade (p. xxv), and this view of Richard was perpetuated by later Tudor chroniclers without any question of its factual authenticity. Just after the passage quoted above (n. 7), for instance, Holinshed writes: "He was close and secret, a deep dissembler, lowlie of countenance, arrogant of heart, outwardlie companionable where he inwardlie hated, not letting to kisse whome he thought to kill: despitous and cruel, not for evil will alway, but offer for ambition" (p. 712). Waldo F. McNeir points out that when Richard feigns loyalty to Prince Edward upon his arrival in London, Holinshed writes in the margin of his chronicle, "O dissimulation," "The Masks of Richard III," *Studies in English Literature* (Spring 1971), 178.

33. Approaching the play from a variety of perspectives, critics have demonstrated the different yet complementary elements of Richard's duplicity. His descent from the Vice of the morality plays, for instance, provides one way of understanding his deceit, as Bernard Spivack argues in *Shakespeare and the Allegory of Evil* (New York, 1958). Protean changeability and the tactical use of deceit are

also parts of the Machiavel's repertoire, and Richard's possession of these skills reflects the broader influence of *The Prince* upon the English stage. In addition, the Machiavel's relentless mendacity equally reproduces early modern anxieties about both the potential abuse of rhetoric and the moral status of the stage and its players, who trafficked in illusions. In stage Machiavels, then, and in Richard III, several strains of early modern thinking about the perils of deception are brought together. For a recent discussion of Richard's connection to stage Machiavels, see Maus, pp. 35–54; for an analysis of Shakespeare's history plays as "dramatic meditations" on the "Machiavellian challenge to providentialist views of history" see Phyllis Rackin, *Stages of History: Shakespeare's English Chronicles* (Ithaca, New York, 1990, p. 59); see also Tracy B. Strong, "Shakespeare: Elizabethan Statecraft and Machiavellianism," *The Artist and Political Vision*, ed. Benjamin R. Barber and Michael J. Gargas McGrath (New Brunswick, 1982), pp. 193–220.

For discussions of *Richard III* in relation to rhetoric, see Louis E. Dollarhide, "The Logic of Villainy: Shakespeare's Use of the Fallacies." *University of Mississippi Studies in English* 10 (1969), pp. 49–57; Dolores M. Burton, "Discourse and Decorum in the First Act of *Richard III*," *Shakespeare Studies* 14 (1981), 55–84; and Russ McDonald, "*Richard III* and the Tropes of Treachery," *Philological Quarterly* 68 (Fall 1989), 465–83. Finally, for accounts of the perception that the theater, and more particularly actors, were associated with deceit and wickedness, see Anne Righter, *Shakespeare and the Idea of the Play* (London, 1962), 89–96; Ann Wierum, "'Actors' and 'Play Acting' in the Morality Tradition," *Renaissance Drama* 3 (1970), 189–214; and Rackin, *Stages of History*, pp. 72–74, and "History into Tragedy: The Case of *Richard III*," in *Shakespearean Tragedy and Gender*, ed. Shirley Nelson Garner and Madelon Sprengnether (Bloomington and Indianapolis, 1996), pp. 40–43.

34. Plasse suggests that an early modern audience would have asked very similar questions about a stage representation of Richard. Noting the influence of More's account of Richard's deformity, she postulates that "many members of Shakespeare's audience would have been predisposed to pay particular attention to Richard's physical presence and to anticipate with interest the theatrical representation of his legendary deformity. What would this notorious monster look like? Sound like? What would he do?" (p. 12).

35. *OED* a and b.

36. Charnes associates Richard's manipulations of the significance of his appearance with the medieval idea of the King's Two Bodies, arguing that Richard attempts to replace his deformed body with the mystified, flawless monarch's body. She later adds, "Since Richard's experience of himself is inseparable from how he 'reads' the signs of his own body as a signifying text, his entire course of action can be seen as directed toward gaining control over the social construction, perception, and manipulation of bodily signifiers" (p. 32). He attempts to make others see him as he wants to see himself, rather than seeing himself as others initially see him, because of the significance customarily given to deformity in early modern thought. See pp. 31–33. In a slightly different vein, Robert N. Watson argues that Richard seeks to revise his own distorted birth and "deformed identity," and to generate his own rebirth as king, because "The perfect and immortal body politic, which resides in a monarch for the duration of his reign, would have been a tempting prize to a man so understandably unhappy with his body natural." See *Shakespeare and the Hazards of Ambition* (Cambridge, Mass., 1984), p. 21.

37. Her flirtatiousness comes across in exchanges at 1.2.2.01–06 and 2.26–28. Taking a critical view of Anne in *The Dramatist and the Received Idea: Studies in the Plays of Marlow and Shakespeare* (Cambridge, Eng., 1968), Wilber Sanders calls her actions at this point an exercise in "coquetry at the edge of a grave" (p. 87), but the point seems to be less that she is coquettish and more that Richard has fooled her. For discussions of gender roles and Richard's. manipulation of them in this scene, see Rackin, "History into Tragedy," pp. 39–40, and Charnes, pp. 42–43.

38. Bridget Gellert Lyons comments that Richard's seduction of Anne shows how he is "able to wield others to his will by controlling their sense of what they are seeing" (pp. 19–10). See "'King's Games': Stage Imagery and Political Symbolism in *Richard III*," *Criticism* 20 (1978), 17–30.

39. Charnes points out that Richard's success in altering Anne's perception of him is also linked to the presence of Henry's corpse, as Richard changes the significance of its wounds from signs of his villainy to signs of his desire and her seductiveness. As she wittily puts it, "The bleeding witness for the prosecution becomes a witness for the defense" (pp. 41). In his soliloquy at the end of the scene, she adds, Richard begins "to envision the possibility of eliding his monstrousness from public perception, demonstrating how rhetorical success reorganizes bodily subjectivity" (pp. 50–511). In addition, the fact that Shakespeare includes an invented scene of seduction so early in his play points to the connection between deformity and eroticism that was frequently made. As Moulton demonstrates, in broadside ballads of the time, as well as in Montaigne and Bacon, deformity is associated with sin, especially sexual sin, and is seen as a sign of perverse desire, with social rising serving as a displacement of erotic energy (pp. 262–65). For a very different reading of this scene, one which argues that Richard makes Anne let him see an undeformed image of himself and that the two are paradoxically dependent on each other to create the illusion of autonomy for themselves, see Marguerite Waller, "Usurpation, Seduction, and the Problematics of the Proper: A 'Deconstructive', 'Feminist' Rereading of the Seductions of Richard and Anne in Shakespeare's *Richard III*," *Reuniting the Renaissance: The Discourses of Sexual Difference in Early Modern Europe*, ed. Margaret W. Ferguson, Maureen Quilligan, and Nancy J. Vickers (Chicago and London, 1986), pp. 159–74.

40. Charnes notes that in claiming to be the victim of Elizabeth's and Mistress Shore's witchcraft, Richard uses "the misogynist tradition of blaming male infirmity on 'monstrous' female power," displacing the monstrousness of his arm onto women who allegedly have plotted against him. In setting the men in this scene against women, moreover, he uses his deformity to create solidarity among the men, thereby preventing any of them from objecting to his absurd claim to victimization through witchcraft (pp. 52–53).

41. Again, Charnes connects Richard's revision of his deformity's meaning to the misogynist tradition. Attempting to counteract the overdetermined meanings assigned to his deformity, she argues, Richard draws upon the (for him, conveniently available) contempt of women that his slanderous rumors about his mother represent. His misogyny, however, also suggests an identification with women, since both he and they have been marked by tradition as flawed, inferior bodies. None of the men in the play, as Charnes puts it, "are as aware of what bodies can be made to mean" as the women are, and Richard ultimately attempts to silence the women in the play because he must silence his own body's significance, which the women are most aware of (pp. 53–56).

42. The phrase is A. P. Rossiter's, in *Angel with Horns* (New York, 1961), p. 13. Ralph Berry goes so far as to say that Richard's humor borders on camp. *The Shakespearean Metaphor: Studies in Language and Form* (London and Basingstoke; Totowa, N.J., 1978), p. 10.

43. See, for example, 1.1.115, 2.2.109–11, and 3.1.111.

44. Lyons comments that in his falsely reluctant acceptance of the crown and his reference to his own back, Richard suggests that kingship will be a cross for him to bear and also transforms his deformity into an emblem of Hope, who is traditionally portrayed as being bent over by having to carry the Wheel of Fortune on her back (pp. 23–24).

45. As Garber puts it, Richard "generates and theorizes deformity as a form of power" (p. 42). She also points out that Richard does so, here and when he jokes that "Some tardy cripple" bore the countermand for Clarence's execution too late (2.1.87–91), by "projecting and displacing" the characteristic of deformity onto others, either "the hypothetical messenger or the diseased polity" (pp. 39–40).

46. St. Thomas More, *The History of King Richard III and Selections from* the *English and Latin Poems*, ed. Richard S. Sylvester (New Haven and London, 1976), pp. 48–49 (emphasis added).

47. Righter, p. 99; Greenblatt, *Renaissance Self-Fashioning* (Chicago, 1980), p. 13.

48. The multiplication of inscrutable bodies in this scene, the significance of which the audience must try to discern, is the result of a process similar to what Barkan describes in early modern analogies between the human body and the state. In the most sophisticated analogies, he argues, an "infinite regress of analogous bodies" can occur, because "if the individual's body contains the State, it must contain smaller bodies, which contain smaller bodies, etc." (p. 81). In the English Renaissance in particular, the depiction of the king "becomes that of a man containing his own society within himself," and "When we see a man as containing his whole society, we diversify and multiply that man. When we turn our gaze,back to society, which contains men who contain societies within them, we begin to see an infinite regress of bodies within bodies" (p. 89). The idea that the king's body is a microcosm of the state thus leads to a sense that there are many bodies within his body. Likewise, the sense in *Richard III* that Richard's deformed body must be seen as a microcosmic emblem of the condition of England during his rise and reign leads to a scene in which there is suddenly a multiplication of further bodies to be observed, scrutinized, and interpreted. When we "turn our gaze back to (Richard's) society," we see the beginning of a potentially infinite regress of bodies which invite—yet frustrate—interpretation, as the citizens' bodies displayed for contemplation fail to reveal those citizens' thoughts. This dynamic, strikingly similar to what Barkan identifies, reaffirms the more general notion that when one body is identified as having larger significance, other bodies will in turn become objects of interpretation, however inconclusive that interpretation may prove to be.

49. As Lacey Baldwin Smith has argued, in sixteenth-century England silence was often the only protection of the perceptive because the Tudor political structure made candor quite dangerous (pp. 58–77). On how the monarch determined the fortunes of courtiers, Smith later quotes Francis Bacon, who once referred to the "deep and unscrutable centre of the Court, which is her majesty's mind." See *Treason in Tudor England: Politics and Paranoia* (London, 1986), p. 198.

50. Devon L. Hodges, *Renaissance Fictions of Anatomy* (Amherst, 1985), p. 2.

—————————— —————————— ——————————

2005—Jeremy Lopez. "Time and Talk in Richard III I.iv," from *Studies in English Literature*

Jeremy Lopez has been an assistant professor of English literature at the University of Toronto and theater review editor of the *Shakespeare Bulletin*. He is the author of *Theatrical Convention and Audience Response in Early Modern Drama* (2003), "Imagining the Actor's Body on the Early Modern Stage" (2007), and "A Partial Theory of Original Practice" (2008).

Clarence's murder is more important in Shakespeare than in Raphael Holinshed. Holinshed, like other historians of the period, focuses only on the detail of the malmsey butt: "finallie the duke was cast into the Tower, and therewith adiuged for a traitor, and priuilie drowned in a butt of malmsie."[1] As is not uncommon in Shakespeare, the amount of time given to the episode is inversely proportional to the amount of time given to it in the source. While the first three scenes of the play show Richard's plotting his brother's "accidental" execution, St. Thomas More's *History of Richard the Third*, in a passage that appears verbatim in the *Chronicles*, says only (in More's typically half-insinuating, understated way) that "[s]ome wise men also ween that his drift covertly conveyed, lacked not in helping forth his brother of Clarence to his death."[2] Further, the amount of time and words given to Clarence and his anonymous murderers is truly remarkable. In this play, execution is repeatedly and almost exclusively represented by ellipsis. Rivers, Grey, and Vaughan are carried "to death at Pomfret" in III.iii, but we do not see them die; Hastings is led off to be executed at the end of III.iv, and his head is brought in at III.v.21; Richard consults with Tyrrel about the young princes in IV.ii, and IV.iii begins with Tyrrel saying, "The tyrannous and bloody act is done"; and Buckingham is led off to execution in V.i. Besides Clarence's, the only other onstage death is Richard's.[3]

The scene stands out in other ways. It is the first scene in the play not to include Richard. It is the only scene in Q or F to contain prose. And it is remarkably inefficient. In contrast to the rapid and precise (if not always logical) action that precedes and follows it, this scene dwells on itself and toys with the audience's perception of time and of temporal verisimilitude. The audience is made to wait for something it knows will happen—the murder of Clarence—and it must work to see how that waiting is meaningful. The murderers do not enter until line 83 (line 77 in Q), and they are preceded by Clarence's lengthy explanation of his difficult night to a minor character. In

F, Clarence is accompanied onstage by an anonymous Keeper. After Clarence falls asleep, Brakenbury enters to virtually no purpose—he makes a speech about sorrow and time—and leaves only twenty-two lines later when the murderers enter. Even in Q, which eliminates the Keeper and gives his lines to Brakenbury, the speech about sorrow and Brakenbury's exit seem abrupt.[4] Once the murderers have the stage to themselves with Clarence, they argue for fifty lines about whether or not they should wake their victim, and once he wakes up, they take another 105 lines to act. Even after the waiting is over, we do not get the outcome we expect. Historians of the period repeatedly say that Clarence was drowned in a butt of malmsey, but for all the effort Shakespeare puts into dramatizing the events around this detail, he has the drowning occur offstage *after* Clarence is stabbed.[5] The First Murderer drags his body offstage while the other stays and expresses feelings of guilt; the First Murderer must then return and upbraid his partner for being "slack" in helping him with the drowning—a drowning that is necessary in case the stabbing did not do the job (F, I.iv.259–60). Even the murderers' exit creates practical and interpretive difficulties: they must either exit separately, indicating that the Second Murderer is no longer involved, or together, in spite of the Second Murderer's indication that he is no longer involved.

The inefficiency of the scene's entrances, exits, and actions is similar and importantly related to the convoluted and inefficient way in which it represents time. The scene begins with Clarence's waking—"Oh, I have passed a miserable night"—but about only seventy lines later he is ready to sleep again (F, I.iv.2). Brakenbury's unexpected entrance and his musing that "Sorrow breaks seasons and reposing hours, / Makes the night morning and the noontide night" does not help to clarify matters (F, I.iv.76–7). Clarence's dream begins in the present ("Methoughts that I had broken from the Tower") but moves immediately to the past in an allusion to Clarence and Richard's boyhood journey to France ("And was embarked to cross to Burgundy") (F, I.iv.9, 10). A further temporal level opens up as Richard and Clarence are imagined reminiscing about "a thousand heavy times / During the wars of York and Lancaster / That had befall'n us" (F, I.iv.14–6). The going gets rougher still as Clarence describes the imagined time of his dream:

> Methought I had [time to gaze upon the secrets of the deep],
>   and often did I strive
> To yield the ghost; but still the envious flood
> Stopped in my soul and would not let it forth
> To find the empty, vast, and wandering air,
> But smothered it within my panting bulk,
> Who almost burst to belch it in the sea.
>   KEEPER. Awaked you not in this sore agony?

CLARENCE. No, no, my dream was lengthened after life.
Oh, then began the tempest to my soul.
I passed, methought, the melancholy flood,
With that sour ferryman which poets write of,
Unto the kingdom of perpetual night.

    (F, I.iv.36–47)

Clarence's "then began the tempest to my soul" is temporally difficult because of the way it blurs the literal and figurative signals of the word "tempest" (F, I.iv.44). "Tempest to my soul" sounds like, and is, figurative language, but "tempest" in the context of the "tumbling billows of the main," the "dreadful noise of water," and the "fearful wracks" of the preceding speech bring out the literal connotations of the word (F, I.iv.20, 22, 24). "Then began," then, is strange because as a temporal marker it makes us look ahead to an action that is on the verge of happening, but we have just seen Clarence go through what might be described as a "tempest to my soul." "Then began" suggests forward movement, but keeps us standing still. We stay still until the ambiguous "flood" of line 45—extra ambiguous because of its echo of the literal "flood" at line 37—is clarified to be the River Styx. Line 44 means (partially figuratively, but not entirely, as we are still talking about water) "*then* began the tempest to my *soul*." This spiritual torment is distinct from the (partially figurative) tempest that wracked his *body* in the previous lines. The levels of literal and figurative significance are still more difficult to sort out because what Clarence is recounting is a dream. The action of lines 36–47, and of the entire description of the dream, is similar to the action of the first half of the scene: in the speech, one event moves into another slowly, uncertainly, all the while retracing ground it has gone over, just as in the action, Clarence wakes from a dream, describes that dream and his waking from it, and goes to sleep again.

The Keeper wonders at lines 34–5, "Had you such leisure in the time of death / To gaze upon these secrets of the deep?" Here, the scene seems momentarily to concede the fact of its representational burden. The interpretive, theatrical significance of the events of the scene is largely unrelated to the temporal markers that order them. We understand Clarence's dream, Brakenbury's speech, and the argument between the murderers and Clarence as metaphors, as extratemporal encapsulations of certain meanings the play is concerned to convey: Clarence has a premonition of his fate and its appropriateness; Brakenbury, like the audience, is profoundly aware of the way in which natural, political, and temporal order are out of joint; the murderers are cowardly but perhaps no more cowardly than Clarence. Our understanding of these extratemporal meanings is characterized by the collision of each moment's obvious extratemporality with its explicit concern with literal temporality—the bygone years of Clarence's dream, the time of day or night, the need for haste in accomplishing the murder.

The disjuncture between theatrical significance and temporal verisimilitude that results from this collision is particularly important for this scene in this play because it is a history. Clarence begins the narrative of his dream with reference to a historical event—his trip to Burgundy—and the reference is dilated into a premonition of his own death. The reference to Burgundy creates the expectation of one kind of narrative time—the kind of time that we see in the play's first scenes, where significance is determined by sequence. The details that turn the dream into a premonition create the expectation of another kind of narrative time—the kind of time in which sequence ironically is or is not the result of signals that foreshadow it. History plays, because they represent known history, always involve both kinds of time. Tragedy tends to involve only the latter. Historical tragedies, such as *Richard III*, manipulate an audience's sense of the significance of "real time" by stretching out stage time to accommodate the ominous ironies characteristic of tragedy. *Richard III* I.iv does this particularly well because it is so insistent about the importance of the real time of the scene.

The anxiety an audience feels as the play violates the temporal verisimilitude it simultaneously insists upon is evident, and highly magnified, in editorial discussion of differences between the beginning of Clarence's narrative in the two early versions of the play. While F's version of Clarence's narrative of his dream begins "Methoughts that I had broken from the Tower, / And was embarked to cross to Burgundy" (I.iv.10–11), Q's version begins without a reference to the Tower: simply, "Methoughts I was embarked for Burgundy" (I.iv.9–10, 9). John Jowett's footnote says that "[t]he loss of narrative connection with Clarence's present situation in Q1 makes the dream more dream-like and removed from time" (Q, p. 194n9). Antony Hammond's note to the beginning of the dream speech in his Folio-based Arden edition says that "[t]he absence from Q of the information that Clarence, in his dream, was still aware of his incarceration is very hard to explain. His imprisonment clearly began Clarence's mind on its journey towards an awareness of his own guilt . . . These two lines seem crucial to the development of the scene and Clarence's state of mind: either an actor's or a copyist's oversight must be invoked to account for their omission from Q."[6] Both observations seem quite overstated in their desire to differentiate Q and F. But the fact of the overstatement in each case bespeaks an anxiety about the temporal status of the dream and of its relationship to the rest of the scene—an anxiety that manifests itself in the desire either to show how the speech is supposed to be out of place, unattached, and removed, or to show how it is absolutely not. Jowett wants an unsettling mimesis—the dream is an extratemporal mirror of the coming action and so should be experienced *as* extratemporal—while Hammond wants naturalism—a *development* of action and "state of mind." The scene does not allow for one *or* the other. Instead, the scene introduces two different ways of understanding time—stage time, historical time—and blurs them, just as it elides and blurs the distinctions between other crucial elements throughout: between sleeping and waking, pity and cruelty, human law and divine law, murderer and victim.

Things in this scene are constantly turning into other things. Before the murderers enter, we do not know whether this will be Clarence's death scene or merely a foreshadowing of it. Once the murderers enter we do not know whether they are cowardly clowns, clownish philosophers, or merciless killers who simply enjoy drawing out their task.[7] The lame Gloucester of Clarence's dream seems to stumble upon the "giddy footing of the hatches," but the dramatic irony makes the stumble just as easily interpretable as an attack. Clarence's act of rescue then seems to become an opportunity for Gloucester's violence (F, I.iv.16–20). The same dramatic irony merges with or perhaps creates what seems to be Clarence's, or Clarence's dream's, potential knowledge of things he cannot know. The "envious flood" of line 37 becomes the "melancholy flood" of line 45, and once Clarence awakes from his dream, he cannot "for a season" believe "but that I was in hell" (F, I.iv.61–2). In F Brakenbury enters, speaking lines that would be less unexpected from the Keeper, and lines that are concerned with the convergence of apparently separate things: night and day, "titles" and "low name" (I.iv.76–82).[8] When Clarence wakes, he calls immediately for a cup of wine. "You shall have wine enough, my lord, anon," the Second Murderer says, signaling to the audience that he is thinking of an altogether different kind of "cup of wine" (F, I.iv.152). More subtly, the First Murderer's line, "[Conscience is] even now at my elbow, persuading me not to / kill the duke," alludes to the proverb, "the devil is at one's elbow," but puts conscience in the place of the devil—a confusion which is partly clarified by the Second Murderer's "Take the devil in thy mind," and partly exacerbated by his ambiguous pronouns (F, I.iv.138–9, 140–1). Throughout the dialogue the murderers and Clarence go over and over again problems that involve important but often impossible-to-make distinctions: the problem of killing Clarence in his sleep and his "waking" at the "great judgment day" to say "we stabbed him sleeping"; of having a "warrant" to kill Clarence, but no "warrant" to "defend" them from being "damned for killing him"; of the difference between "men"—royal and common—and between loyalty and royalty; of the difference between earthly kings and the divine King, earthly and divine law and retribution, beggars and princes (F, I.iv.100–3, 108–10, 154–6, 183–9, 194–208, 247–57). The characters constantly repeat each other's words, each giving them his own nuance.

The murderers themselves are highly mutable, their separate and collective personalities merging into surprising new identities. With the fully alert Brakenbury, the murderers are brusque and confident, but once left alone with the sleeping Clarence they talk of cowardice and fear. Before Clarence wakes, the murderers repeatedly express imminent action—"Come, he dies," "Come, shall we fall to work?," "Strike!"—that is delayed by further discussion (F, I.iv.121, 144, 149). In F, Clarence finds that the First Murderer's "voice is thunder, but thy looks are humble," and that his "eyes do menace me," but he looks "pale" (F, I.iv.157, 160). In Q, however, "Thy voice is thunder, but thy looks are humble" is addressed to the Second Executioner, and the line about looking pale is absent (Q, I.iv.151). The reason Clarence addresses different murderers in the different texts is that the F lines,

> FIRST MURDERER. Soft, he wakes.
> SECOND MURDERER. Strike!
> FIRST MURDERER. No, we'll reason with him.
>
>   (F, I.iv.148–50)

are a separated version of what appears in Q as:

> FIRST EXECUTIONER. Hark, he stirs. Shall I strike?
> SECOND EXECUTIONER. No, first let's reason with him.
>
>   (Q, I.iv.145–6)

Here, Q presents perhaps a slightly more coherent picture of the murderers than F, in that the Second Murderer is the one who repents at the end of the scene in both texts. But at the same time, Q gives the stumbling hesitation "To, to, to—" in response to Clarence's "wherefore come you hither?" to *both* executioners, while F gives it to the Second Murderer alone (Q, I.iv.155, 154). Similar to the intertextual confusion of Brakenbury and the Keeper, the conflation and separation of the murderers' personalities within and between each text is symptomatic of the interpretive problems the texts themselves present. As we see perhaps most clearly when, at line 182 in F (line 174 in Q), the murderers begin to speak in vehement, rhetorical verse, there is very little hope of understanding the motivation or character of either or both murderers except from one moment to the next.

On the way through these moments to Clarence's death, an audience gropes for concretely meaningful signals, for indications of the kind of scene this is and how to interpret it, both theatrically and morally. Theatrically, the time scheme is a mess, and the terms that define the experience of the scene are extremely fluid. Morally, it is more and more difficult to separate the good guys from the bad. An audience's urge is to use the differences between the two murderers or between the murderers and Clarence to solve these interpretive problems. The latter helps explain how we should feel about what we are seeing—Clarence is worthy of pity, the murderers of terror—and the former helps explain our experience of the scene's weirdly amorphous dilation—one of the murderers, penitent or fearful or both, is stalling. As to the distinction between the two murderers, Hammond's footnote to the scene convincingly describes the way in which the scene refuses its audiences any interpretive comfort: "these minor figures have no 'character' in any consistent sense . . . [T]hey act according to the immediate dramatic needs of the moment."[9] Janis Lull and Jowett make evident in their notes the search for this comfort—the terrified groping for clarity of a perplexed audience. Lull's note on the loss of synchrony in the murderers' lines between Q and F, which begins at line 150, attempts to make an interpretive point about the difference between the two texts: "In F, the First Murderer appears to be the leader; he is tougher and pushier than his accomplice" (F, p. 92n150). This claim of course must almost immediately be revised: "Although the First Murderer seems to experience an attack of conscience at 138–44, he may just be testing the wavering resolve of his companion." Jowett too wants consistency and seems to worry that Q, which omits the Second Murderer's "Look behind you, my lord," is straying too far from the path it seemed to be on (F, I.iv.258). He adds a bracketed stage direction, "To Second Executioner," after the first line of Clarence's speech beginning, "Not to relent is beastly, savage, devilish" (Q, I.iv.239–42). This stage direction attempts to compensate for the fact that, with First Executioner's lines on either side of Clarence's speech, Clarence seems to be spying pity in the looks of the executioner we have come to know as pitiless. These notes and emendations overemphasize both the difference between the two murderers and the difference between the two texts. Both texts present a scene in which it is difficult to tell at any given moment what one or the other murderer is up to, or how we are to think of them in relation to one another. The tension created by this difficulty finds release in the scene's climactic violence. In their mirroring of one another, their parroting of one another's and of Clarence's words, their insistent repetition—to no purpose—of the word or idea of *conscience*, the two murderers resemble what Scott McMillin says of the identical masquers and second-masquers at the end of *The Revenger's Tragedy*: "the revenger proliferates . . . and becomes many selves who are all one self, a violent self."[10]

A good performance will never allow it to be entirely clear that one murderer is "pitiful" and the other "merciless": the Second Murderer's "Look behind you, my lord" might as well be a cruel joke as a warning. On a deeper and more unsettling level, the scene should go some way toward blurring the distinction on which it most importantly rests for its tragic effect: the distinction between Clarence and Richard. This happens first in the description of Clarence's fall from the ship in his dream, where it is unclear whether he is attacked or brings his fall on himself; next when the murderers remind Clarence that he helped to kill Prince Edward; and later when Richard III, on the verge of getting the justice (human or divine?) due him, is awakened by the ghosts of his past (F, I.iv.194–6). An audience's uncertainty over whether to like the murderers as clowns or fear them as assassins, or whether to pity Clarence as a victim or simply feel indifference toward him as another royal murderer, is vitally related to its uncertainty (shared by the Keeper in F) over whether to view Clarence's description of the dream as a theatrical necessity or mere theatricality. To the

extent that he is made to seem like Richard, Clarence, too, becomes implicated
in this violent self-proliferation. At the heart of the terror of the scene is the
way in which the inevitability of its final action allows incidents and characters
to be completely different in tone from one moment to the next. An audience
responds to this unevenness by interpreting based upon what it knows will
happen: Clarence will die. This knowledge provides the only secure position
from which events can be judged and understood. Imminent violence helps to
smooth the bumps raised by a dramaturgy that depends on dilation. Clarence's
death is theatrically effective because we enjoy it when it happens; it is what we
have been waiting for. Of course, violence is particularly imminent in this scene
because the play is a history as well as a tragedy. The inevitability of its closure
makes the freedom of the scene's form all the more harrowing. History is a
nightmare from which Clarence is trying to wake.

* * *

Theatrical time on the Elizabethan stage would have always been exaggeratedly swift or exaggeratedly slow. The nonnaturalistic mode of the early modern
theater is based on dilation and exposition: playwrights tend to fill the stage
with words before action. Simple actions represented in this mode always seem
to take a long time to occur. *Richard III* I.iv is a long scene and, because of the
proportion of dilation to action, seems yet longer than it is. Complex series of
actions, like the first three acts of *Richard III*, performed in this mode seem
to happen very fast because it is hard for the audience to keep up with all the
information being presented. One reason most of *Richard III* moves so quickly
is that we do not have to watch anyone be killed between I.iv and V.v: we have
to infer action from dialogue, and this keeps us feeling just half a step behind.
The tension between difficult-to-follow, rapidly presented action and elaborately dilated, almost extratemporal set-pieces is a habit of early modern drama:
think of the first three and a half acts of *Revenger's Tragedy* in contrast with the
scene where the Duke is killed; or the first three scenes of *3 Henry VI* in contrast
to the scene with York on the molehill. The tension inherent in sequences like
this erupts in *Richard III* in the shift between I.iii and I.iv. Wolfgang Clemen
called I.iv "almost a tragedy in miniature with a dramatic curve complete in
itself."[11] This observation gets at the scene's separateness from the rest of the
play, but the word "miniature" seems inaccurate. This scene presents tragedy,
as well as both the pleasures and difficulties of Elizabethan tragic dramaturgy,
close up and highly magnified. The scene builds tension around the audience's
simultaneous sense of urgency and of leisure; of artificiality and the awareness
of its impracticalities; of the construction of metaphors based in the action and
metaphors that seem to govern the action. The resolution of this tension is

sudden, inevitable, and absolute; the play harnesses the power of the audience's potential impatience and incredulity and uses this power to detonate the explosion that is Clarence's death.

The tensions of a scene such as *Richard III* I.iv do not always get resolved suddenly, absolutely, or violently. Inefficient scenes involving talkative murderers are in fact fairly common in Renaissance drama, though they never occur, as far as I can tell, in histories outside of *Richard III*.[12] Instead, they occur in tragedies. Like *Richard III* I.iv, these scenes rely on somewhat jarring dilation to create a sense of imminent violence. Unlike Shakespeare's scene, they generally do so in service of underscoring or clarifying the difference between victim and murderer. As with Shakespeare's scene, the strange temporality of talkative-murderer scenes in other plays is part of a shift in generic signals and expectations, but the shift is from tragic to comic rather than historic to tragic. An Elizabethan audience would have, I think, found *Richard III* I.iv a particularly gripping experience not only because of how the scene works in and of itself, but also because of the way in which it alludes to and thwarts the expectations created by other, similar scenes—scenes that almost always work themselves out in a comic, or at least a not-tragic, way.

The mysterious Messenger of *King Leir* is something of a cross between a traditional Ambidexter figure (such as Ambidexter in *Cambises*) and a Jacobean clown messenger (such as Dondolo in *The Revenger's Tragedy*), and his eerie comic manner is out of place in the sternly officious world of Ragan and Gonorill. He appears in scene xii to take a message from Gonorill to Ragan and disappears at the end of scene xix—apparently in the play for no other reason than to fail at the one task he is meant to perform.[13] Asked whether he will have the heart to kill Leir should Ragan order it, the Messenger tells Gonorill that "Few words are best in so small a matter . . . / . . . I will" (xii.112–3). But once he gets to Ragan's, even as he insists that he has a "heart compact of adamant," and that money "will make me do the deed," the play begins to stretch itself out somewhat in favor of talking over action (xv.53, 64).[14] Ragan tells the Messenger that he may be needed to "give a stab or two" in scene xv, but delays giving the order completely until scene xvii (xvii.52). When it comes time to do so, she "cannot utter it in words" because it is "such a thing as I do shame to speak" (xvii.16, 23). The Messenger must coax words from her:

> MESSENGER. I'll speak it for thee, queen; shall I kill thy father?
> I know 'tis that, and if it be so, say.
> RAGAN. Aye.
> MESSENGER. Why, that's enough.
> RAGAN. And yet that is not all.
> MESSENGER. What else?

RAGAN. Thou must kill that old man that came with him.
MESSENGER. Here are two hands; for each of them is one.

   (xvii.25–31)

Before the Messenger leaves, Ragan warns him not to relent should her father attempt to "speak fair" and plead for mercy (xix.51). Predictably, Leir and Perillus do attempt to speak fair, but their entreaties for mercy are not what deter the Messenger. What changes his mind is the clap of thunder that follows after he has sworn first by heaven and then hell to kill Leir, and Leir says, "Swear not by hell, for that stands gaping wide / To swallow thee and if thou do this deed" (xix.190–1). The Messenger begins to believe that the "old man is some strong magician," and while this is laughable, Leir must speak his lines with a kind of force—even if it is a comic force—that makes the thunder clap seem more than coincidental (xix.194).

   And of course, the thunderclap is more than coincidental: it is overtly theatrical. It is a signal that Leir's words somehow still carry power—a signal that makes it possible (in a way that it never is in *King Lear*, where "Blow wind and crack your cheeks" does not precede but merely vies with the storm)[15] for the play to end with Leir thanking the heavens for his restoration and dismissing his two evil daughters with a damning parenthesis: "daughters did I say?" (xxix.173). At the end of the scene, when a second clap of thunder causes the Messenger to quake and let fall his daggers once and for all, the Messenger enjoins his erstwhile victims, "If any ask you why the case so stands, / Say that your tongues were better than your hands" (xix.307–8). But this rings hollow: the Messenger has not even *not* killed Leir for the reasons he now puts forth. His delay in killing Leir upon seeing him asleep at the beginning of the scene, his ironic interpretations of Leir's fearful dream once Leir is awake, his flaunting the money Ragan gave him to do the deed all become interpretable as ways in which the Messenger is somehow always in awe of Leir's true majesty. The pressure his bizarre clowning exerts on the structure of the tragedy is dispersed into a more manageable energy once he leaves: the next time we see Leir, he and Perillus exchange clothes with some mariners, and in the following scene they meet Cordella while she is on a picnic with the King of Gallia, "disguised like country folk" (xxiv.17). The urgency of action characteristic of tragedies, which the Messenger and his employers have resisted in scenes xii through xvii, metamorphoses into a different kind of theatrical time altogether: the leisurely movement of pastoral comedy.

   Like Clarence in *Richard III*, Leir and Perillus are asleep when their would-be assassin comes; so is Marius when Favorinus and Pausanius come with a Frenchman they have hired to kill him in Thomas Lodge's *The Wounds of Civil War*, and Pertillo when the two murderers his uncle has hired to kill him stop to argue about doing so in Robert Yarington's *Two Lamentable Tragedies*.[16] When

Caratach and his young nephew Hengo are first attacked by the Roman soldiers in John Fletcher's *Bonduca*, it is by the ineffectual "hungry courtier" Judas.[17] The circumstances in each case serve to make the aggressors look cowardly and the victims noble, and only in Shakespeare's play is the murder carried out more or less as planned. Lodge's Frenchman, whose heavily accented speech will come at the turn of the century to signal a common foppish parody of the court intriguer,[18] seems to see a heavenly vision that prevents him from killing Marius.[19] This is similar to the Messenger and the thunder in *Leir*, but Pedro's accent makes him a purely comic figure and, like Judas in the later *Bonduca*, probably just a coward. What is central in Lodge's scene is the apparent humanity of Favorinus and Pausanius, who suddenly see in Marius what, when the Frenchman saw it, we could not consider seriously: "Marius in his infancy / Was born to greater fortunes than we deem" (III.ii.100–1). This happens too at the end of *Bonduca*, when the Romans freely grant Caratach for his courage the mercy that Judas could not choose but grant earlier (V.i.2570). The dilation of the comic-murderer scene creates an elaborately artificial or theatrical picture of cowardice that reveals a basic and real greatness that is then dramatically realized—even if this realization is, as in the case of Marius in *Wounds*, through a noble suicide.

The situation in *Two Lamentable Tragedies* is somewhat but not altogether different. The lengthy argument off to the side between the two murderers, the fact that they kill each other after the boy has been killed, and the fact that Murderer 1 (the evil one) uses his last bit of strength to stab Murderer 2 again work to make Pertillo seem all but incidental to the scene (E4v). The conflict between the two murderers takes on a structural significance that embodies the central idea of the play, and does so at the expense of the victim's humanity in a way that is characteristic of the play's overall project: the actor playing Pertillo in the Italian plot may also have played (and is in any case paralleled by) Beech's boy in the English plot, a character who spends most of the play half-alive with a hammer sticking in his head after Merry's botched murder attempt (C4v). Even more than Pertillo, Beech's boy is a silent emblem of violence and suffering, his horrible spectacle driving home the fact that some people never learn: just as Murderer 1 stabs Murderer 2 unnecessarily after his death, so Merry tries to silence Beech's boy after Beech's death, and will go on to cut Beech's body into pieces in an effort to get it safely hidden (E2v). While the dilation of the murder or postmurder scenes in Yarington's play is not exactly comic (though it is absurd), it ultimately rests, as in the other scenes, on a clear distinction between killer and victim. The silence of the victim characters—dead, alive, or asleep—gives the sense that the two Murderers, or Merry and his wife, in their constant arguing, plotting, and justifying, are simply trying to fill a void.

The dilation of talkative murderer scenes in Elizabethan drama tends to suggest a movement away from or beyond violence. The inefficiency of such scenes tends to be resolved by means of a generic shift—tragedy becomes farce or pastoral—or through grotesque parody of tragic action itself—the extremity of Merry's actions comes back to haunt him in the form of the reassembled pieces of Beech's body. *Richard III* I.iv, however, provides the audience with no such opportunity for perspective, and that is why this scene is so extraordinary. In *Richard III* I.iv Clarence does nothing *but* demonstrate his nobility and humanity. Shakespeare goes out of his way to make Clarence sympathetic. As Edmond Malone points out, Clarence in I.iv speaks as though he has been imprisoned without due process, but "the truth is, that he was tried and found guilty by his Peers, and a bill of attainder was afterwards passed against him."[20] The Clarence of the stage struggles against the Clarence of history. And the Clarence of the stage believes himself to be on the verge of a breakthrough just before he dies:

> My friend, I spy some pity in thy looks.
> Oh, if thine eye be not a flatterer,
> Come thou on my side and entreat for me;
> A begging prince, what beggar pities not?
>
>   (F, I.iv.254–7)

The murderers will have none of this talk of honesty, this comforting beggar-prince equivocation. For perhaps the first and only time in the scene, everything is perfectly clear: the murderers at last do the job they were sent to do. History, comedy, and tragedy converge on the point of a knife. The scene has appeared as though it is about to open up some comic space within which Clarence has room to maneuver—and then that space is sealed off abruptly, making the lengthy and sympathetic expostulations of Clarence the foolish and ineffectual dilation of the scene.

Jeremy Lopez is assistant professor of English literature at the College of William and Mary. He is the theater-review editor of *Shakespeare Bulletin* and the author of *Theatrical Convention and Audience Response in Early Modern Drama*.

NOTES

1. Raphael Holinshed, *Holinshed's Chronicles of England, Scotland, and Ireland*, ed. Henry Ellis, 6 vols. (London; 1587; rprt. J. Johnson, 1807–08), 3:712.

2. Thomas More, *The History of Richard the Third and Selections from the English and Latin Poems*, ed. Richard Sylvester, Yale Edition of the Works of St. Thomas More, ed. Sylvester (New Haven: Yale Univ. Press, 1976), p. 9.

3. Shakespeare, *King Richard III*, ed. Janis Lull, The New Cambridge Shakespeare, ed. Brian Gibbons (Cambridge: Cambridge Univ. Press, 1999), III.iii.1, III.iv.78, IV.ii.73–83, IV.iii.1, V.i.1. Subsequent references will be to this edition and will be cited parenthetically in the text by line number and denoted with an "F." Citations of Q will be taken from *The Tragedy of King Richard III*, ed. John

Jowett, Oxford Shakespeare (Oxford: Oxford Univ. Press, 2000). These references will also be cited parenthetically in the text by line number and will be denoted by a "Q."

4. This speech has tended to cause ripples in editions of the play. Antony Hammond's footnote in the Arden edition (London: Methuen, 1981) says that it is "odd . . . that this monologue should not be a soliloquy, and that Brakenbury should voice his suspicions with the Keeper for a witness" (p. 175n76). Brakenbury does not have an audience in Q. Jowett's edition, however, provides *three* footnotes on the speech—one on its resemblance to "the eight-line *strambottoe* form that Wyatt practised" (an observation he culls from Emrys Jones's *The Origins of Shakespeare* [Oxford: Clarendon Press, 1977], p. 194); one on the passage's echoes of Job 17:11–2; and one on the syntax of the first line (p. 198nn69–76, 69–70, 69). Lull notes that the speech is similar to Henry V's "ceremony" soliloquy in *Henry V* IV.i.209–12 (p. 89n78–83). Wolfgang Clemen found this speech to be "the weakest part of the scene, lacking any real relation to the action or to the character who speaks it" (*A Commentary on Shakespeare's "Richard III*," trans. Jean Bonheim [London: Methuen, 1968], p. 78). The eagerness of the three editors discussed here to place the speech within some kind of context would seem to indicate that audiences continue to feel what Clemen felt.

5. The detail of the malmsey butt also appears in More, *History of Richard the Third*, p. 8; in Robert Fabyan's *New Chronicles of England and France in Two Parts* (1516; rprt. London, 1811), fol. 4Qv; Edward Hall's *Vnion of the Two Noble and Illustre Famelies of Lancastre and York* (London, 1548), fol. 239v; and *Mirrour for Magistrates*, ed. Lily B. Campbell, Huntington Library Publications (1559; rprt. Cambridge: Cambridge Univ. Press, 1938), p. 219.

6. Shakespeare, *King Richard III*, ed. Antony Hammond, Arden Edition of the Works of William Shakespeare (London and New York: Methuen, 1981), p. 171n9–10.

7. A production will of course have to make some kind of decision in this matter. But since the texts suggest with equal conviction each of the different possibilities at different times, the tension in the very act of making a production decision and thus potentially suppressing—not eliminating—certain possibilities will inevitably carry over onto the stage.

8. Q does away with the Keeper and gives his lines to Brakenbury. Whatever the actual relationship is between these two texts, the slippage between Brakenbury and the Keeper is a good intertextual example of the conflation of separate things I am talking about.

9. Shakespeare, *King Richard III*, ed. Antony Hammond, p. 177nn110–1.

10. Scott McMillin, "Acting and Violence: *The Revenger's Tragedy* and Its Departures from *Hamlet*," *SEL* 24, 2 (Spring 1984): 275–91, 290.

11. Clemen, p. 64.

12. Thomas Heywood's *Edward IV*, for example, brings three quarreling, penitent murderers onstage *after* the murder of the young princes (T2) (*The First and Second Parts of King Edward IV. Histories by Thomas Heywood*, ed. Barron Field [London: Shakespeare Society, 1842], part 2, III.v).

13. *A Critical Edition of the True Chronicle History of King Leir and His Three Daughters, Gonorill, Ragan, and Cordella*, ed. Donald M. Michie, Renaissance Imagination: Important Literary and Theatrical Texts from the Late Middle Ages through the Seventeenth Century, ed. Stephen Orgel (1605; New York and

London: Garland Publishing, Inc., 1991), xii. 46. Subsequent references will be to this edition and will appear parenthetically by scene and line number.

14. One might make the case that it has already done this stretching to some degree, in that Gonorill decides to leave it up to her sister to order Leir's death.

15. Shakespeare, *The Tragedy of King Lear*, in *The Norton Shakespeare Based on the Oxford Edition*, ed. Stephen Greenblatt (New York and London: W. W. Norton and Co., 1997), pp. 2307–2553, III.ii.1.

16. Thomas Lodge, *The Wounds of Civil War*, ed. Joseph W. Houppert, Regents Renaissance Drama Series, ed. Cyrus Hoy (Lincoln: Univ. of Nebraska Press, 1969), III.ii.58; Robert Yarington, *Two Lamentable Tragedies* (London, 1601), E4v. Subsequent references to these works will appear parenthetically in the text, Lodge by line number and Yarington by folio.

17. John Fletcher, *Bonduca*, prepared by Walter Wilson Greg, vol. 85, Malone Society Reprints (Oxford: Oxford Univ. Press, 1951), I.ii.300. Subsequent references will be to this edition and will appear parenthetically in the text by act, scene, and line numbers.

18. Especially in such plays as Henry Chettle's *The Tragedy of Hoffman* or the anonymous *Wisdom of Doctor Dodypoll*.

19. "der be a great diable in ce eyes, qui dart de flame, and with de voice d'un bear, cries out, villain dare you kill Marius" (III.ii.86–8).

20. Edmond Malone, quoted in Paul Werstine, "'Is It upon Record?': The Reduction of the History Play to History," in *New Ways of Looking at Old Texts, II*, ed. W. Speed Hill, Papers of the Renaissance English Text Society, 1992–1996 (Tempe: Renaissance English Text Society, 1998), pp. 71–82, 75.

BIBLIOGRAPHY

❧

Alexander, Peter. *Shakespeare's Henry VI and Richard III*. Folcroft, PA: Folcroft Library Editions, 1973.

Arnold, Aerol. "The Recapitulation Dream in *Richard III* and *Macbeth*." *Shakespeare Quarterly*, vol. 6, no. 1 (Winter 1955): 51–62.

Becker, George J. *Shakespeare's Histories*. New York: Frederick Ungar, 1977.

Berry, Ralph. "Richard III: Bonding the Audience." In *Shakespeare and the Awareness of the Audience*. New York: St. Martin's Press (1985): 16–29.

Besnault, Marie-Hélène and Michael Bitot. "Historical legacy and fiction: the poetical reinvention of King Richard III." In *The Cambridge Companion to Shakespeare's History Plays*, edited by Michael Hattaway. Cambridge, UK: Cambridge University Press (2002): 106–25.

Blanpied, John W. *Time and the Artist in Shakespeare's English Histories*. Newark: University of Delaware Press; London: Associated University Presses, 1983.

Bonetto, Sandra. "Coward Conscience and Bad Conscience in Shakespeare and Nietzsche." *Philosophy and Literature*, vol. 30, no. 2 (October, 2006): 512–27.

Brooke, Nicholas. "Reflecting Gems and Dead Bones: Tragedy Versus History in *Richard III*." *Critical Quarterly* 7 (1965): 123–34.

Brooks, Harold F. "*Richard III*: Unhistorical Amplifications: The Women's Scenes and Seneca." *Modern Language Review*, vol. 75, no. 4 (October 1980): 721–37.

Campbell, Lily B. "The Tragical Doings of King Richard III." In *Shakespeare's "Histories": Mirrors of Elizabethan Policy*. San Marino, CA: The Huntington Library (1947): 306–34.

Carroll, William. "'The Form of Law': Ritual and Succession in Richard III." In Linda Woodbridge and Edward Berry, eds., *True and Maimed Rites: Ritual and Anti-Ritual in Shakespeare and His Age*. Urbana: University of Illinois Press (1992): 203–19.

Charlton, H.B. "Apprentice Pieces: *Titus Andronicus, Richard III & Richard II*." In *Shakespearean Tragedy*. London: Cambridge University Press (1948): 18–48.

Dubrow, Heather. "'The Infant of Your Care': Guardianship in Shakespeare's *Richard III* and Early Modern England." In McBride, Kari Boyd, ed.

Domestic Arrangements in Early Modern England. Pittsburgh, PA: Duquesne University Press (2002): 147–68.

Garber, Marjorie. "Descanting on Deformity: *Richard III* and the Shape of History." In *Shakespeare's Ghost Writers: Literature as Uncanny Causality*. New York and London: Methuen (1987): 28–51.

Gillingham, John. *Richard III: A Medieval Kingship*. New York: St. Martin's Press, 1993.

Goodland, Katharine. "'Obsequious Laments': Mourning and Communal Memory in Shakespeare's *Richard III*." *Religion and the Arts*, vol. 7, nos. 1–2 (2003): 31–64.

Hamel, Guy. "Time in Richard III." *Shakespeare Survey* 40 (1988): 41–50.

Hanham, Alison. *Richard III and his Early Historians: 1483–1535*. Oxford: Clarendon Press, 1975.

Hassel, Chris R. *Songs of Death : Performance, Interpretation, and the Text of Richard III*. Lincoln : University of Nebraska Press, 1987.

Heilman, Robert A. "Satiety and Conscience: Aspects of Richard III." *The Antioch Review*, vol. 24, no. 1 (Spring, 1964): 57–73.

Hicks, Michael A. *Richard III: The Man Behind the Myth*. London: Collins & Brown, 1991.

Hodgdon, Barbara. "'The Coming on of Time': *Richard III*." In *The End Crowns All: Closure and Contradictions in Shakespeare's History*. Princeton, NJ: Princeton University Press (1991): 100–26.

Horrox, Rosemary. *Richard III: A Study of Service*. New York: Cambridge University Press, 1989.

Hunt, Maurice. "Ordering Disorder in *Richard III*." *South Central Review*, vol. 6, no. 4 (1989): 11–29.

Kehler, Dorothea. "Canard and the Common Lot: The Making of Shakespeare's Margaret of Anjou." *Journal of Drama Studies*, vol. 1 (January, 2007): 4–19.

Krieger, Murray. "The Dark Generations of *Richard III*." *Criticism* 1 (1959): 32–48.

Lyons, Bridget Gellert. "'King's Games': Stage Imagery and Political Symbolism in *Richard III*." *Criticism*, vol. 20 (1978): 17–30.

McNeir, Waldo F. "The Masks of Richard the Third." *Studies in English Literature*, vol. 11 no. 2 (Spring 1971): 167–86.

Moore, James A. "The Grotesque Comedy of *Richard III*." *Studies in the Literary Imagination* 5, no. 1 (April, 1972): 51–64.

Morriss, Henry Partee. "Innocence and Evil in *Richard III*." *Childhood in Shakespeare's Plays*. New York: P. Lang, 2006.

Moulton, Ian. "'A Monster Great Deformed': The Unruly Masculinity of Richard III. *Shakespeare Quarterly*, vol. 47, no. 3 (1996): 251–68.

Neill, Michael. "Shakespeare's Halle of Mirrors: Plays, Politics, and Psychology in *Richard III*." *Shakespeare Studies* 8 (1975): 99–129.

Olson, Greta. "Richard III's Animalistic Criminal Body." *Philological Quarterly*, vol. 82, no. 3 (2003): 301–24.

Ornstein, Robert. "Richard III." *A Kingdom for a Stage: The Achievement of Shakespeare's History Plays*. Cambridge: Harvard University Press (1972): 62–82.

Paris, Bernard. "Richard III." In *Character as a Subversive Force in Shakespeare: The History and Roman Plays*. Rutherford, NJ: Fairleigh Dickinson University Press (1991): 31–52.

Pearlman, E. *"The Tragedy of King Richard III."* In *William Shakespeare: The History Plays*. New York: Twayne Publishers (1992): 48–64.

———. "The Invention of Richard of Gloucester." *Shakespeare Quarterly*, vol. 43, no. 4 (Winter, 1992): 410–29.

Pierce, Robert B. "Richard III." In *Shakespeare's History Plays: The Family and the State*. Columbus: Ohio State University Press (1971): 89–124.

Prescott, Paul. *Richard III*. Houndmills, Basingstoke, Hampshire; New York: Palgrave Macmillan, 2006.

Reese, M. M. *"Richard III."* In *The Cease of Majesty: A Study of Shakespeare's History Plays*. London: Edward Arnold Ltd. (1961): 207–25.

Ribner, Irving. *"Richard III* as an English History Play. From *The English History Play in the Age of Shakespeare*. Princeton, NJ: Princeton University Press (1957): 116–24.

Sanders, Wilbur. "Providence and Policy in *Richard III*." In *The Dramatist and the Received Idea*. Cambridge, England: Cambridge University Press (1968): 72–109.

Seward, Desmond. *Richard III: England's Black Legend*. New York: F. Watts, 1984.

Targoff, Ramie. "'Dirty Amens': Devotion, Applause, and Consent in *Richard III*." *Renaissance Drama*, vol. 31 (2002): 61–84.

Torey, Michael. *"'The plain devil and dissembling looks': Ambivalent Physiognomy and Shakespeare's* Richard III." *English Literary Renaissance*, vol. 30, no. 2 (Spring, 2000): 123–53.

Watson, Robert N. "Kinship and Kingship": Ambition in Shakespeare's Major Histories." In *Shakespeare and the Hazards of Ambition*. Cambridge, MA: Harvard University Press (1984): 14–82.

Webster, Richard. "Two Hells: Comparison and Contrast Between Dante and Shakespeare with Particular Reference to *Inferno*, X, and *Richard III*, I.iv." *Nottingham Medieval Studies* 18 (1974): 17–47.

Wheeler, Richard P. "History, Character and Conscience in *Richard III*." *Comparative Drama*, vol. 5 (1971): 301–21.

Weimann, Robert and Douglas Bruster. "Performance, Game, and Representation in *Richard III*." In *Shakespeare and the Power of Performance: Stage and Page in the Elizabethan Theatre*. Cambridge, England: Cambridge University Press (2008): 42–56.

ACKNOWLEDGMENTS

❧

Richard III in the Twentieth Century

E.M.W. Tillyard, "*Richard III*," from *Shakespeare's History Plays*, pp. 198–214. Published by Chatto & Windus, 1944, 1961. Copyright © the Literary Estate of E.M.W. Tillyard.

W. H. Auden, "*Richard III*," from *Lectures on Shakespeare*, edited by Arthur Kirsch, pp. 13–22, 366–68. Published by Princeton University Press. Copyright © 2000 by the Estate of W. H. Auden. Reprinted by permission of Curtis Brown, Ltd.

Wolfgang H. Clemen, "Tradition and Originality in Shakespeare's *Richard III*," *Shakespeare Quarterly*, vol. 5, no. 3, (Summer 1954): 247–57. © 1954 Folger Shakespeare Library. Reprinted with permission of the Johns Hopkins University Press.

Madonne M. Miner, "'Neither Mother, Wife, nor England's Queen': The Roles of Women in *Richard III*," from *The Woman's Part: Feminist Criticism of Shakespeare*, edited by Carolyn Ruth Swift Lenz, Gayle Greene, and Carol Thomas Neely, pp. 35–55. Copyright © 1980 by the Board of Trustees of the University of Illinois. Used with permission of the author and the University of Illinois Press.

Richard III in the Twenty-first Century

Michael Torrey, "'The plain devil and dissembling looks': Ambivalent Physiognomy and Shakespeare's *Richard III*," from *English Literary Renaissance*, vol. 30, no. 2 (Spring 2000): 123–53. Copyright © 2000 by *English Literary Renaissance*.

Jeremy Lopez, "Time and Talk in *Richard III*," from *Studies in English Literature, 1500–1900*, vol. 45, no. 2 (Spring 2005): 299–314. Copyright © 2005 and reprinted with permission of *SEL*.

INDEX

Characters in *Richard III* are indexed as shown in the List of Characters (e.g., Lady Anne). Characters in other literary works are indexed by first name followed by name of work in parentheses.